IN
DARKEST
SOUTH
CAROLINA

Also by Brian Hicks

Greetings from Charleston

The Mayor

Sea of Darkness

City of Ruin

Toward the Setting Sun

When the Dancing Stopped

Ghost Ship

Raising the Hunley (with Schuyler Kropf)

Into the Wind (with Tony Bartelme)

IN DARKEST SOUTH CAROLINA

J. Waties Waring and the secret plan that sparked a civil rights movement

BRIAN HICKS

EVENING POST
BOOKS

Published by
Evening Post Books
Charleston, South Carolina

Editors: Rick Nelson, Mitch Pugh and Bob Kinney
Designer: Gill Guerry
Cover Photo: Gill Guerry

First printing 2018
Printed in the United States of America

A CIP catalog record for this book has been applied
for from the Library of Congress.

ISBN: 978-1-929647-38-5

For Alan

CONTENTS

OCTOBER 9, 1950

The sound of gunfire echoed through the alleys south of Broad Street, hanging in the humid night air like Spanish moss from the live oaks.

It was a noise decidedly out of place in Charleston's finest neighborhood, at least since the war had ended nearly a century earlier. While the rest of the city endured more crime than was typical for its size, the area South of Broad – as locals called it – was largely immune from such unpleasantness. In many ways, the 20th century ended at the business district. On the narrow streets of the peninsula's tip, crowded with antebellum homes passed from one generation to the next, residents carried on as if it were still 1850.

Inside the relatively modest stucco house at 61 Meeting Street, Waties Waring was startled by the sound but not overly surprised. He had always assumed it would come to this. There had been too many threats, too many promises of violence. In fact, President Truman had received word of a planned attack against Waring just three days earlier. The White House ignored the warning – there were simply too many to take them all seriously, even those from the National Association for the Advancement of Colored People.

At first, Waring thought the noise was simply a car backfiring – he'd heard one outside just a moment before. He'd taken note of this because there was typically little traffic in the neighborhood past 9 p.m., and because it was impossible not to hear; his living room sat less than 20 feet from the street. He was still trying to determine whether the sound came from a tailpipe when he heard the crash.

Waring and his wife, Elizabeth, had been playing canasta in the living room. It was the newest fad in cards, ideally a game for two couples, but the Warings had little company these days. Their neighbors didn't visit, few friends called on them and they had been blackballed from all of Charleston's elite social clubs. On the street, most passersby ignored them – except, of course, the ones who hurled insults and epithets. The only people who spoke to the Warings regularly were anonymous callers who suggested in hushed tones that they leave town and never come back.

The threatening phone calls may have persuaded the Warings to stay in and play cards instead of walking up King Street to the Riviera Theater, where Humphrey Bogart's newest film noir, *In a Lonely Place*, was playing on the 50-foot screen. The judge at least could appreciate the sentiment. Months earlier, Collier's magazine had dispatched a reporter to chronicle his ostracism from Charleston's complex social strata. That article had carried the headline, "The Lonesomest Man in Town."

South Carolina had branded the Warings agitators, which was an impolite, euphemistic way of saying they were civil rights advocates. But unlike most crusaders, the Warings were in a position to promote their cause. They had become national figures, favorites of journalists around the country, their message covered breathlessly by national news outlets as far away as New York City and California. That made them dangerous. The birthplace of the Confederacy would not stand for such radical ideas; South Carolina's political leaders promised they would never submit to integration. So the Warings had to go.

From the living room, the Warings could not see what was happening outside. The windows of the former carriage house were set high in the wall, affording them no view of the street. They simply heard a car slow down, then a sharp crack, followed in quick succession by two more. Before they could react, a brick crashed through the window above the sofa, sailed over a framed photograph of Elizabeth and hit the opposite wall. Shattered glass rained down on the room.

Waring, still spry at 70, dove to the floor and pulled Elizabeth down with him. He landed on top of her, trying to protect her. Lying in broken glass and playing cards, disoriented from the fall, he heard something slam into the front door. Then more rocks, or something, began to pelt the front of the house, and he worried what might come next. He glanced at the door that opened into the house's other front room. That door led to the patio, and the garden gate wasn't locked. If the attackers came in from the back yard, he knew they were dead.

As the bombardment continued, the couple crawled through the debris and into the dining room. There, Waring pulled the telephone off its stand and made a call to report what was happening.

The home of a federal judge was under attack.

Once, Julius Waties Waring had been Charleston royalty – a political insider, scion of a respected family, the Lord of Broad Street. Although the Warings were never the city's most affluent family, they had been among its first settlers in the 17th century. In a town that revered its own history above all else, nothing mattered as much as lineage. The Warings were the local equivalent of *Mayflower* descendants, and although Waring personally held such trappings in low regard, he had traded on them most of his life.

Like many Charleston families, the Warings lost nearly everything in the Civil War, but the judge had restored their name to a measure of influence not seen in decades. He'd studied law independently as a young man, established a private practice, served as the local U.S. assistant attorney and the city's corporation counsel. He dabbled in politics, never running for office himself but guiding the careers of many prominent leaders. Waring even orchestrated a successful campaign that put one of his closest allies in the South Carolina governor's office.

Waring had no personal political aspirations, but harbored similarly ambitious goals. He had always coveted a federal judgeship, and thought the friends he'd helped over the years would eventually return the favor. His legal resume was impeccable, his social standing unparalleled. Charleston was a society town, and Waring belonged to all the right clubs. For most of his life, he had been a man of stature in a town of manners. In his younger years he'd had a reputation as a notorious bachelor, but eventually married a local woman of equal social standing. For most of his life, Waring had everything that mattered in Charleston.

In 1941, at the age of 61, Waring finally got what he wanted most. He was nominated to the bench by President Franklin D. Roosevelt on the recommendation of South Carolina's two senators – both of whom were, in fact, friends of his. For a while, he followed the expected path; his rulings were well-reasoned and unsurprising. Waring was a competent, unpretentious jurist with a reputation for harsh sentences and occasional bouts of empathy. But there were aberrations.

One of his earliest decisions equalized pay between black and white public school teachers. Most of his peers dismissed this as merely strict interpretation of federal law, but it was only a glimpse of all that would follow.

Within a few years, Waring upended both his personal and professional life. One evening in 1945 he abruptly told his wife that he no longer loved her. After 32 years of marriage, the judge sent her to live with his brother's family in Florida, where she could establish residency and file for divorce – such a thing was not even legal in South Carolina at the time. Humiliated, Annie Waring did as she was asked. Within a week of the final decree, Waring married Elizabeth Avery, a two-time divorcee from Detroit. Charleston was shocked by the scandal.

Such tawdry behavior was reason enough for Charleston to snub Waring. He was either ejected or resigned from the St. Cecilia Society, the St. George Society, the Charleston Light Dragoons and the Episcopal Church. His membership in most other organizations was simply not renewed, his name no longer spoken in their halls. Waring and his new wife spent a lot of time alone, and often passed the time driving around the nearby sea islands. There, he found many of South Carolina's poor, black residents living in slouching shacks on muddy roads. The disparity between their lives and his own made him ashamed. If not for the familiar palmetto trees scattered among these shanties, he could have believed it was a different world.

Waring had never completely adopted typical Charleston attitudes on race, but he began to see things in a vastly different light after his appointment to the bench. He was confronted with the injustice and cruelty black residents faced on a regular basis. These cases forced him to question the world from which he hailed. As a young man, he'd hardly given any thought to racial injustice or inequality. It never occurred to him that his nanny hadn't been family, that she had once – before he was born – *belonged* to his family. When this realization washed over him like the Lowcountry tide, everything changed.

The judge reorganized the courthouse, the only part of the world he truly controlled, in a manner that was in pronounced conflict with local standards. He integrated seating, forcing blacks and whites to sit together in the courtroom, and ordered his clerk to stop putting a "C" – for colored – next to the names of potential black jurors. He even hired an African-American bailiff, something no other Charleston judge had ever done.

Some locals claimed Waring adopted the cause of civil rights in retaliation for Charleston's refusal to accept his new bride, but this political awakening had shown signs of blossoming long before his divorce. When Waring ordered the city to pay black and white teachers the same salaries, NAACP attorney Thurgood Marshall later said it was the only case he ever tried "with my mouth hanging open half the time." Southern judges simply did not hand down such decisions.

More curious rulings followed, but they were largely ignored until Waring committed a sin for which there was no forgiveness. He ordered the state Democratic Party to open its rolls to black voters, a particularly controversial decision given his status as a former party officer. At the time, the South Carolina Democratic primary essentially *was* the election. Republicans never won the general election, and often didn't bother to field candidates. White politicians had devised this political system in the years after Reconstruction, and it was ruthlessly efficient. It also, as Waring ruled, violated the constitutional rights of thousands of black citizens.

When Waring declared that it was time for South Carolina to "rejoin the Union," the war began.

The state's power structure had fought back mercilessly.

Waring's associates denied any role in his appointment, congressmen called for his impeachment, and the South Carolina legislature offered to fund the hearings – and bus tickets for the couple to leave the state. The Charleston newspapers labeled the judge a traitor to his race and his party, and demanded his resignation. Capitalizing on this outrage, Gov. Strom Thurmond mounted a presidential campaign under the banner of the Dixiecrats, a party built on a near-religious devotion to preserving segregation.

These demagogues and their divisive rhetoric stirred a vicious onslaught of racism and resentment, eventually sparking a resurgence of the Ku Klux Klan. The group lamented the end of the white race, paraded through the streets of South Carolina towns and burned crosses in the judge's yard. One evening, a man showed up at 61 Meeting Street – oblivious to where he was – and tried to recruit Waring himself into the secret society. It was the first invitation to join a club he'd had in years.

Never one to ignore an offense, Waring antagonized his critics with condescending insults that attracted even more news coverage and inflamed more controversy. The sheer number of threatening calls he received on a nightly basis forced Waring to install a second, private telephone line. The postman delivered his hate mail by the sack. And after Elizabeth described Southerners as "weak and morally low" on national television, her mail rivaled the judge's. One anonymous letter asked her, "How would you like to go to bed with a nigger and have a little nigger baby calling you Mama?"

By the fall of 1950, many people couldn't decide if they were more offended by the judge's rulings, his public statements or the company he kept. The Warings had begun to entertain members of Charleston's most prominent and politically active black families at 61 Meeting Street. Well-known agitators including Felicia Goodwin, Ruby Cornwell and Septima Clark were frequent guests in their home. It was outrageous; in most Charleston homes, the only black people found around the dinner table were serving the food.

The Warings remained defiant through three years of incessant attacks, but quietly made concessions to the situation. They escaped the harassment by traveling frequently – vacationing out West, in New England and New York. Waring routinely volunteered to fill in for vacationing judges in states far from South Carolina. In fact, when the attack came, he and Elizabeth had just returned from a month in San Francisco.

Nothing the police said reassured the Warings.

The first officers to arrive at 61 Meeting Street questioned their account of the attack and chief detective Herman Berkman was openly dismissive. He doubted they'd actually heard gunfire, even ventured to guess it was just a prank. He picked up one of the rocks on the sidewalk and said, "See, it's really nothing but a brick. There's nothing to it."

They imagined Berkman smiled as he said it.

The judge had long suspected that the Charleston police were sympathetic to such harassment, if not complicit in covering up the crimes. Six months earlier, someone had burned a cross outside his house – the letters "KKK" carved into the wood. Berkman had called that a teenager's prank as well. He'd even told newspapers there was no proof of Klan involvement. Now, he wanted to downplay an all-out assault.

Something had happened this time, however, and the police could not deny it. They found rocks on the sidewalk and scattered throughout the living room, although the only serious damage was a broken window and a ripped screen door. The officers saw no bullet holes. When Berkman suggested this was simply vandalism, Elizabeth ordered him out of the house.

By then, two FBI agents were sifting through the broken glass, and the Charleston officers gratefully left the investigation to them. Waring wasn't sure he was in better hands. He feared J. Edgar Hoover's men weren't any more concerned about white supremacists than the locals, a low opinion of the bureau shared by the president's own Civil Rights Commission. But the agents quietly collected the rocks and dutifully looked for evidence that someone had shot at the house.

As the FBI agents examined the scene, the Warings kept busy. Elizabeth spent the evening on the phone, confessing to friends that she feared they'd be killed while the police stood idly by. The judge prepared a press statement, promising that the rest of the world would now recognize the "dying gasp of white supremacy" – an unusually naïve assessment. But he also cautiously backed off his initial account.

After a two-hour search turned up no proof of bullet holes or shell casings, Waring told a New York reporter, "I won't say they were bullets, but something certainly sounded like explosives." He told other reporters the attack would not dissuade him from his job. "My wife and I are staying right here. You can bet on that." But he no longer sounded so sure.

The New York City papers called for a national investigation and criticized the federal government for its lackadaisical protection of a district court judge. But locally, the attack garnered little sympathy. The News and Courier claimed the vandalism was a public relations coup for the Warings. "The Judge and his wife could not employ with money more effective publicity agents than the hoodlums who toss rocks at their house and give them the opportunity to sound off about persecution for their views to assume the role of martyrs."

Waring's suspicion had been correct; the FBI had little interest in investigating the incident. But President Truman, who'd once said he wanted a hundred more judges like Waring, ordered Attorney General J. Howard McGrath to intervene. Soon, the FBI was interviewing suspects and U.S. marshals were guarding the couple. An entire team was assigned to follow the judge to the courthouse and watch over Elizabeth by day. At night, marshals parked outside 61 Meeting Street.

Although Waring recognized the imminent danger, and knew what his neighbors were capable of doing, he protested such protection. He didn't want a security detail. It made him look weak, and he realized it would become more political fodder. Which, of course, it did. Soon, the politicians were calling Waring "the most expensive luxury on the federal payroll." It did little to help his image, or community relations, when the federal government set up a no-parking zone outside his house.

"These guards even accompany Waring when he goes to visit his Negro friends to play canasta," congressman Mendel Rivers told The News and Courier.

The publicity surrounding the attack spurred even more hate mail and threatening phone calls, and the security detail's assignment was extended into the spring. Waring finally toned down his attacks on the white supremacists, both because he was worried and, at that moment, he was busy plotting his next move. The judge believed he'd found a way to win this war.

For months, Waring had been studying a series of recent court cases that challenged *Plessy v. Ferguson*, the 1896 U.S. Supreme Court decision that provided the basis for "separate but equal" laws. He considered *Plessy* ludicrous, a contradiction of the United States Constitution, but one that had allowed South Carolina and other states to justify decades of segregation and Jim Crow laws. There could be no change in the country, he knew, unless *Plessy* was overturned.

Reversing that single court decision could usher in a true era of civil rights, Waring realized; all he needed was the right case and a brave lawyer. As it happened, he had both. Thurgood Marshall had filed a lawsuit against rural Clarendon County for not providing equitable schools to black children, and the state had foolishly rose to the district's defense. The case had merit, but Waring decided it didn't go far enough. He secretly urged Marshall to recast the lawsuit, to think bigger. Asking for equal, yet separate, schools only perpetuated segregation. The goal, Waring argued, was to abolish the entire system.

"Raise the issue for all time as to whether a state can segregate by race in its schools."

Marshall had listened politely, but feared it was a waste of time. *Plessy* had stood for more than half a century, and the courts had ruled against so many NAACP lawsuits that the group had considered quietly giving up. But Waring had a plan – one he would not fully share with Marshall or anyone else. The judge had discovered a way to force the U.S. Supreme Court to confront the unconstitutional notion of "separate but equal" once and for all. Waring knew his plan would work, even if he had to bend the rules of judicial ethics.

So, the racists could threaten him and South Carolina politicians could castigate him, but to stop him they'd have to kill him. Waring would not leave Charleston, or the bench, until he was finished. He had made up his mind, and he was determined.

He was going to end segregation in America.

PART I

THE IVORY CITY

OPEN TO THE WORLD

Nearly everyone in Charleston showed up for the parade.

They began trickling out of their homes at sunrise, children playing in the streets while their parents angled for the best vantage point to watch the troops assembling in Marion Square. The men all sported coats and ties, the women wore their most formal, frilly dresses – the last vestiges of Victorian-era fashion still on full display in 1901. Even though 20th-century apparel had yet to reach the city, the occasion was such that no one dared to underdress. After four decades of disaster and destitution, Charleston was ready to declare itself open to the world.

On this morning, even the weather cooperated briefly. After a long spell of dreary, wet days, the crisp air and sunshine brought a touch of spring to the proceedings. It buoyed the mood of the crowd, which clogged every street around Marion Square. By 8 a.m., there was scarcely a sliver of available sidewalk within blocks, and police officers busied themselves shooing spectators off the grass. Every inch of the park would be needed for the procession, which included five military divisions, Citadel cadets, carriages filled with VIPs and floats promoting the city's tradesmen. The newspapers later estimated the size of the crowd at 40,000 – in a city of only 55,000 residents.

The lucky people who lived along the parade route – west on Calhoun, north on Rutledge, then west again on Grove Street – waited on their porches, many of which were adorned with red, white and blue bunting. Their anxious chatter echoed to the corner of Calhoun and Rutledge, where one black man pushed his children down the street in a wheelbarrow, looking for an empty spot from which to watch the spectacle. The News and Courier proclaimed that Charleston's sizable black population made a strong and impressive showing, Jim Crow laws be damned. For one day at least, there would be no segregation on the streets of Charleston.

It was Dec. 2, 1901, and the South Carolina Inter-state and West Indian Exposition was about to begin.

The parade started promptly at 10 a.m., led by the First Artillery Band and several divisions of soldiers and Marines. The patriotic music and sound of boots striking the street in unison were followed by a carriage ferrying Mayor J. Adger Smyth, Gov. Miles B. McSweeney, New York Sen. Chauncey Depew and Frederick W. Wagener – the exposition's benefactor, landlord and president. The four men waved enthusiastically, relieved that the show was finally underway.

Succeeding carriages brought aldermen and other pols, followed in turn by Citadel cadets, local students from area high schools and the military academy. Including the floats, most of which displayed the wares of local artisans, more than a thousand people participated in the parade. The procession covered the width of Calhoun Street, nearly brushing against the people crammed onto the sidewalks. The spectators cheered gleefully as it passed, perhaps simply because it had been a long time since Charleston had anything to celebrate.

It took three hours for the entire parade to make its way from Marion Square to the gates of the exposition on Grove Street, and the cavalcade grew longer as it moved through the city. Many people abandoned their perches on the sidewalks and fell in line behind the floats, reaching for souvenir medallions thrown by the people onboard. When the last float made the turn from Calhoun onto Rutledge, the newspaper reported that a "mass of people fell in its wake like water at the stern of a moving ship."

Their destination was a 250-acre assemblage of buildings and gardens constructed in less than a year on the site of the old Washington Race Course – where former slaves first celebrated Memorial Day in 1865. The land had been donated by Wagener, a wealthy local grocer, in patriotic response to the calls of railroad executive J.H. Averill. He'd suggested this fair after recognizing how much the 1895 Cotton States Exposition had profited the city of Atlanta. It was no coincidence that the centerpiece of Charleston's exposition was dubbed the Cotton Palace – a 320-foot domed building that symbolized the importance of the state's most famous and important export.

The sunken garden and manmade lake at the exposition's center was surrounded by a series of similarly ornate buildings – the Palace of Agriculture, the Palace of Commerce and a grand auditorium. Each of these edifices had been painted a creamy off-white hue, which inspired local papers to dub the fairgrounds the "Ivory City." At night, the buildings were illuminated with more light bulbs than Charleston had ever seen in one place. The entire city glowed, a gleaming jewel in a tarnished crown.

The buildings orbiting the center of the exposition were notably less ornate. The outer rings of the fair were dedicated to secondary concerns – women, fine arts, mines and forestry, as well as the contributions of black South Carolinians. The famous activist and author Booker T. Washington was ostensibly in charge of the Negro Building exhibits, which highlighted the craftsmanship and size of the state's black workforce. It had been a stretch to get the expo ready for opening day, and many of the exhibits were not finished – including the Negro Building. But even the Midway, which would feature games and rides on elephants and camels, was still under construction. It would not open for another three weeks.

The parade dispersed as it reached the grounds of the exposition. The soldiers and sailors were left to gawk at the enormous buildings and meander around the garden with the first ticketholders through the gate. The crowd was impressive. So many people had shown up that thousands would be turned away from the opening ceremonies inside the packed auditorium. There, the mayor and governor would speak while awaiting an electronic signal from President Theodore Roosevelt that officially opened the fair. Mayor Smyth used the occasion – and the captive audience – to stir local optimism and civic pride.

"I congratulate every citizen of Charleston upon the admirable success of this magnificent exposition, the results of which we feel already, and will continue to feel in the impetus given to our efforts in behalf of Charleston and the state of South Carolina, and the confidence thus awakened in every breast as to what this so-called 'dead old city' can accomplish when even a few of her citizens get together."

It was a telling remark. Although the mood was jubilant, and the newspapers bragged that the 22,000 paid admissions easily topped the opening day of Buffalo's Pan-American Exposition, there was desperation in the air as palpable as the coming rain. Charleston had been decimated by the Civil War and had yet to recover. In the 10 years leading up to the exposition, the value of trade at the port – still ostensibly the largest south of Baltimore – had declined by almost 75 percent. Disease was so rampant that the city had been named one of the 10 most dangerous places in the world. Charleston was literally dying. The exposition, and its largely symbolic attempt to expand trade with Latin American countries, was just about the Holy City's last hope.

The signal came at 2:45 p.m.

President Roosevelt was hosting a small party at the White House in honor of the exposition's grand opening. He'd invited South Carolina's entire congressional delegation, including senators John McLaurin and Ben Tillman. Charleston officials were no doubt annoyed by Tillman's opportunistic appearance; he certainly deserved no credit for the fair.

Tillman had failed, or hadn't even tried, to get federal funding for the exposition. In recent years, every other world's fair had been financed at least in part with federal money – but not Charleston's. As a result, locals had struggled with construction costs that threatened to derail the exposition before it even began. They blamed these setbacks on the senator's undisguised contempt for the city.

Tillman personified the perpetual rift between South Carolina's Upstate and Lowcountry. As governor, his reapportionment plan diluted Charleston's influence by moving four legislative seats to other counties, and he'd once suggested transforming The Citadel into a school for women. In turn, the city had flouted some of Tillman's most onerous Jim Crow laws – not out of progressive spirit so much as spite. Those efforts complicated an already complex racial caste system in Charleston. And on this day, the simmering resistance threatened to ruin the White House party.

The president's staff had set up an electric key in the telegraph and cipher room to signal exposition officials in Charleston. Everything had been choreographed carefully, timed to the minute. The operator would prompt the president, and he'd tap the key three times – the agreed-upon code. In the exposition auditorium, Wagener would receive the signal and then read a personal message from Roosevelt. At precisely 2:45, with only minor fanfare, the president pressed the button.

The exposition crowd erupted as the tinny signal echoed through the auditorium, but it generated only polite applause at the White House. Roosevelt made just a few brief remarks. "I wish the exposition every success and you will see in my message to Congress tomorrow that I have made earnest request for an appropriation to cover the expenses attending the display of the government exhibits at the exposition."

It was a discreet acknowledgment of the fair's tenuous financial condition, and perhaps an unsubtle insult aimed at Tillman – who, as everyone in the room realized, hadn't done his job.

"I regret exceedingly that I could not be present at the opening, but I certainly intend to visit the exposition before it closes," the president said.

Tillman took his cue and slyly asked if Roosevelt had ever visited Charleston. When the president admitted that he hadn't, the senator proceeded to insult the city in front of the state congressional delegation. He said Charleston was a city "rich in history, but poor in making it." When Roosevelt offered a mild defense of the city, mentioning the oratorical skills of its advocates, Tillman abruptly cut him off.

"Oh, yes. We have a few windbags down in South Carolina, who are occasionally letting off some hot air under the impression that they are helping to make history."

It was clear that most of the White House guests thought the true windbag was the senator. But the president ignored the insult, politely said his goodbyes, then invited Sen. McLaurin to join him for a private meeting. He pointedly did not extend the offer to Tillman.

In Charleston, the celebration ended just as anticlimactically. The steady drizzle of recent weeks resumed during the opening ceremonies, and the rain persisted into the afternoon. The expo gardens were soon flooded, and most of the crowd scurried for the gates with their fine clothing thoroughly soaked.

They abandoned the exposition grounds by streetcars or ferries docked along the Ashley River. The first day of the exposition, which began with a 46-gun salute – one for each of the 45 states and another for the other territories – went out with a whimper.

The fireworks show for that evening would have to be postponed.

RICE AND RECOLLECTIONS

Waties Waring was one of the few Charleston residents who didn't attend the opening ceremonies of the South Carolina Inter-state and West Indian Exposition. Although he was never one to miss a good party – and scarcely would for the next 30 years – on that day Waring had more pressing priorities.

He had to study.

Waring was scheduled to take the Bar exam in Columbia the following week, and already had a job lined up at the Broad Street law firm of J.P. Kennedy Bryan. For most young men, that might have seemed presumptuous; after all, Waring was just 21 and had never attended law school. But he was not a typical young man, and nothing if not confident. Still, he rarely left anything to chance. So he studied.

The idea of pursuing a career in law came to Waring while he was a student at the College of Charleston, but the seed had been planted much earlier. In some ways he'd been groomed for it, nudged in that direction all his life. When he was a child, his mother talked incessantly of her youngest son one day becoming an attorney. His father, a genial man with a gentle wit, often played along. He'd ask his son, "How's the judge today?"

Perhaps his mother's great expectations had something to do with family history, as most things did in Charleston. Waring's maternal great-grandfather, Thomas Waties, had been a chancellor in the state court of equity and a delegate to the state convention that ratified the U.S. Constitution in 1788. His son, Waring's grandfather, was also an attorney. But in truth that branch of the family tree had no direct influence on Waring. He never met any of his Waties relatives, and had very little in the way of extended family. By the time he was born, all but one of his grandparents were dead.

The law may have been in his blood, but Waring did not follow the traditional path to a lofty Broad Street practice. The day after he graduated from college in the spring of 1900 – with honors, second in his class – Waring left Charleston to vacation with his parents at their North Carolina cabin. That summer, he regularly trekked into Asheville to attend court proceedings. He would learn to be an attorney on his own. This wasn't hubris; his family simply couldn't afford law school.

When he returned to Charleston in the fall, Waring sat through hours of state and federal court, read law in Bryan's office library and sometimes helped with cases. By the end of 1901, after just a year and a half of study and apprenticeship, he declared himself ready for the Bar exam. As Charleston attempted to revive its reputation, Waring was trying to launch his career.

By all outward appearances, Waring would make a fine attorney. He was a tall man with sharp features and a booming Lowcountry drawl, and carried himself with an unmistakable air of self-confidence. Already, he was a man of high ideals, strong opinions and great personal ambition. He was smart but, despite his overtly social nature, often came off as aloof. Some even said his attitude bordered on insolence. Certainly he never suffered from a lack of will or absence of self-sufficiency. The times, and his childhood, had demanded no less.

Julius Waties Waring was born on July 27, 1880, the fourth and final child of Edward P. Waring and the former Anna Thomasine Waties. They believed his name alone was a gift that would serve him well – it announced he was the scion of two grand old Charleston families. At least in theory, that made him twice as respectable in a city that worshipped genealogy above all else. Both families had been a part of Charleston since nearly the beginning.

The Warings arrived from England in 1683, the year Charleston was officially founded, and just 13 years after the first settlers landed at Albemarle Point. The Waties family, which hailed from Wales, followed little more than a decade later. As Charleston became one of the country's most important ports – due in large part to its most lucrative import, slaves – generations of both families entrenched themselves into every facet of the city's legal, business and social communities. A few even held elected office. Neither was the most affluent or influential family in Charleston, but both were decidedly among the upper crust.

By the time Waring was born, most of his ancestors were long gone – in fact, his mother was the sole survivor of the Waties bloodline. The Warings were dwindling in numbers as well, and those who remained were struggling. Once a family prosperous enough to own slaves, the Civil War left them destitute. Four years of the Confederacy wiped out all the affluence they had accumulated in two centuries.

Edward Waring was not bitter; he'd believed in the Southern cause. Several of his brothers fought for the Confederate States Army, and one of them was even killed in battle. Young Edward was called into service at 17, when he was a cadet at a Columbia military academy. In fact, he was there when Sherman burned the city. His role in the War Between the States was small, but Edward never forgot it. He became one of Charleston's most dedicated organizers of Confederate veteran reunions, of which there were many.

Not long after the war ended, Edward Waring married Anna Waties, a young woman whose fortunes were even worse than his. She'd been orphaned as a child, her only family a single brother who'd relocated to Texas. The young couple had nothing left save their good names, but in Charleston that counted for something. Edward got a job with the South Carolina Railway, and over two decades worked himself into a position of modest prominence in the company. But his ascension was slow. At the time of his youngest son's birth, Edward barely made enough money to keep his family fed.

The Waring family's plight was hopelessly common. All of Charleston struggled during Reconstruction and the decades that followed. Federal money was trickling into the city – engineers built massive jetties in the harbor channel, laborers finished the grand waterfront Custom House – but Charleston seemed incapable of economic viability. Nature did not help.

In 1885, a hurricane with 125-mph winds traumatized the city with little advance warning. Almost 90 percent of the buildings in Charleston suffered some damage; about a quarter of the homes lost their roofs. The next year, on Aug. 31, an earthquake damaged 2,000 buildings and killed 27 people in an instant. The city suffered $6 million in damages at a time when the total value of all its property was only $24 million.

Before the city dug itself out of the rubble, another 83 deaths were attributed to the quake and its aftermath. But then, death was commonplace in late 19th-century Charleston. Most of the city's drinking water was contaminated by leaking privy vaults, which officials blamed for the diphtheria and scarlet fever epidemics that claimed dozens – sometimes hundreds – of lives every year. Charleston was one of the most disease-ridden cities in the country. It sometimes seemed as if a plague had descended on the city, divine punishment for setting the country on the path to war.

Although it was a traumatic period in Charleston history, Waties Waring came out of it without scars. Death and destruction were common during his childhood, and he knew nothing else. Compared to most of the city's residents, he had a good life. The Warings always had food, and no one in the family got seriously ill. His father was an attentive man who enjoyed playing with his children, often taking them on picnics or sightseeing trips around Charleston. His mother was quiet, a devoted reader, but she always had time for her youngest boy.

Waring was close to both his parents, although he wasn't very much like either of them. They were faithful Episcopalians, but even as a child Waring only tolerated the church. He had almost no interest in family history, which his mother and father seemed to discuss daily. Waring would never warm to Charleston's most peculiar customs, particularly its obsession with the past. Later, he derisively claimed that he'd been raised on "rice and recollections."

As the youngest child in the family, Waring had it easier than his siblings. Margaret, 10 years his senior, Thomas, nine, and Edward Jr., four, had suffered the hardships and poverty of Reconstruction that young Waties would never know. As their father rose through the ranks of the railroad, the family's circumstances improved immeasurably – they even took vacations. One of the most valuable fringe benefits of Edward's job was a nearly unlimited supply of rail passes. The family used them to visit the mountains of Virginia, and once even ventured across the country to California. Waring got a glimpse of the barren whistle stops and frontier towns of the old West, places that only reminded him how much his hometown differed from most of the country.

By the time Waring came along, his parents were in a position to afford more of the extravagances expected of proper Charleston families. They sent their children to private academies and even hired a former family slave to serve as Waring's nanny. He would always have fond yet indistinct memories of Hannah, but lamented that he couldn't remember her last name – or whether she even had one. He simply called her Dah.

"She was an ex-slave and her husband was an ex-slave," Waring later recalled. "Most of the Negroes I knew were ex-slaves and you loved them, were good to them. We didn't give them any rights, but they never asked for any rights, and I didn't question it. I was raised in the atmosphere that we ought to take care of these people."

That was the prevailing patriarchal attitude toward race in 1880s Charleston, although no one spoke openly of such matters. Waring, like most children, did not realize that the civil rights black citizens had gained during Reconstruction had been abolished after federal oversight of the state ended in 1877. There was no longer slavery, but there was indentured servitude and there was nothing very equal about it. Many former slaves simply ended up working for the families that had once owned them.

Race relations in the city were more nuanced than in other places, due in part to history – or perhaps because black residents outnumbered the white population by a substantial margin. Conditions were far from ideal for black citizens, but Charleston was not as hostile as some places in the South. In fact, Waring and his parents considered Hannah and her husband – a longshoreman named James – part of their family. On more than one occasion, Waring watched his father rush out of the house to rescue Hannah's husband from the police.

"Oh, my heavens. I've got to go get James," Edward would say. "Why does he always go off and get into trouble?"

The bail was usually $5 or $10, money the Warings scarcely had to spare. But that was simply what they did. In Charleston, the peculiar institution of slavery had morphed into a series of peculiar relationships. Edward Waring never reconciled his nostalgia for the Confederacy, which had been created to perpetuate slavery, with his affection for Hannah and James. That was not surprising; the Southerners who set the conflict into motion had cast it as a nebulous quest for "states' rights," rarely detailing exactly which rights they wanted to defend. It would have been difficult to recruit dirt-poor farmers to fight for an economic system that only enriched the ruling class. So Charleston was complicated, and kind men such as Edward Waring either ignored the situation or dealt with it in their own ways. As Waring later noted, the patriarchal model worked just fine – so long as you were on the paternal side. But he wouldn't have that revelation for years.

Charleston families of a certain lineage did not attend public schools, no matter how burdensome the private-school tuition. It just wasn't *proper*. When Waring came of age, he was enrolled in a small, private institution on Meeting Street. For a few years, his sister and brothers had endured classes operated out of the church, which was the most economical choice available at the time. But by the mid-1880s, Edward Waring could afford more secular options for his children.

The University School operated out of the back of the new Charleston Gas Light Company building, which sat a few blocks north of Broad Street. It wasn't the most prestigious school in town, or the largest; the enrollment never strayed beyond 80 students. But it was an ideal setting for a serious young man, and he was inspired by the school's headmaster, Walter McKenney. He would become the most important figure in Waring's early life.

The University School was in session between the second week of October and early June. Classes began at 9 a.m. and ran until 3 p.m. Waring took all the usual courses, including Latin, but eschewed Greek in favor of French. The lessons that made the greatest impression on him, however, were not in the textbooks. McKenney, a lean Virginian with a fashionably thick mustache, demanded honesty from his students. He taught them character, ethics and fairness; he instilled in them a sense of morality – all valuable traits for a future judge.

He enjoyed the University School more than anything else in his childhood; even the daily, two-mile journey to class was an adventure. Left to make his own way downtown, Waring rode horse carriages and streetcars through the cluttered urban center of Charleston every morning. It became a game to jump off the carriage without alerting the driver. For a tall, lanky boy who didn't particularly enjoy playing ball, that was the height of fun.

Waring took to his studies well, never complaining about the considerable workload. Good grades came naturally. His name appeared on the honor roll every year he attended University School, and he was usually ranked in the top five for his class. At 12, he won the prize for best scholarship in the lower school. The year he graduated, he was runner-up for the high school.

McKenney introduced Waring to the classics, but his brother, Thomas, fueled his love of reading. Thomas encouraged Waring's scholarship by constantly giving him books, and the two remained close well into adulthood, long after Margaret and Edward had moved out of the state. When Thomas later became editor of The Evening Post, he sometimes allowed his younger brother to ghostwrite editorials – although not about politics. In Charleston, some subjects were far too complicated to leave in the hands of an amateur.

In the fall of 1896, Waring began classes at the College of Charleston. The choice was largely one of economics; its location spared him the cost of a dormitory. The college was little more than a half-mile from his family's new home at 42 Rutledge Avenue, across the street from Colonial Lake. It wasn't the tony South of Broad neighborhood where most of Charleston's best families lived, but it was within a few blocks.

The independence of college life suited Waring. For his entire childhood, Waring had been left largely to his own devices and interests. He played sports with the neighborhood kids on occasion, but had never showed great interest. Even as a boy he was more of a thinker, a reader, an observer of his small station in life. As a young man, Waring developed a disdain for the trappings of Charleston society. But even if he sometimes voiced such aberrant opinions, he played the expected role.

Later, Waring claimed that the College of Charleston fraternities were too aristocratic for his tastes, but he joined Alpha Tau Omega readily – and excluded his friends who lacked the class to measure up. It was practically tradition. "Boys that graduated and lived in Charleston and had full access to the highest social circles, if we didn't like them, they didn't come in our fraternity. That is cruel. We liked it. The governing group always likes it. The stricter the rules the better."

The fraternity was good training for life in Charleston society, but Waring's primary preoccupation throughout college was the literary society. He participated in weekly debates – readings and "orations," as he called them – and eventually became an officer in the literary club. He remained a mentor to the group long after he graduated. "It was a rather small college with small classes, and almost everybody took some part," he said. He would serve on the college's alumni association and its board of trustees for decades.

College expanded Waring's already burgeoning independence, and encouraged his restless thoughts on the nature of society. "A student ought to be a little bit in revolt against things, feel that the college administrator, the city fathers, are all wrong. That's a good thing." Waring may have debated such lofty ideals as theory, but in practice he was not above using his station as a Charleston blueblood to forge a career path.

He'd decided to go into law during his senior year, just as his mother had always suggested, but Waring couldn't afford law school tuition, and neither could his parents. Edward had lost his job when the railroad was sold, and was once again perilously close to poverty. But he was a man with connections, and J.P. Kennedy Bryan was such a good friend that he agreed to forego custom and allow Waring to use his library without charge.

From the start, Waring had high-minded ideas about the law. He believed it should be easy for laymen to understand, even though he did not look at it simplistically. Sitting in a tiny office in Bryan's Broad Street firm, he devoured stacks of dense tomes. He began with *Commentaries on the Laws of England* by William Blackstone, which taught him legal theory. Then he studied statutes and analyses of them, including Kent's Commentaries, Parsons on Contracts, Greenleaf on Evidence. On many afternoons, Bryan was exasperated to find Waring with his nose in a book.

"What are you doing here? You ought to be in court," Bryan advised him. "Go over there, sit down and listen. You'll learn more law there than you will in books."

Bryan was an invaluable mentor. Books may have taught Waring the principles and particulars of the law, but Bryan taught him how to practice. Sometimes Waring helped with cases, questioning witnesses and writing summaries. He learned the tricks of legal strategy – which facts to use, which to ignore. When Waring brought Bryan a deposition from one potential witness, the old man skimmed it and tossed it aside.

"We won't call him," Bryan said. "He isn't so good for us."

Working for the veteran Charleston attorney provided Waring the practical education he needed to round out his intense study of theories. He followed Bryan's advice faithfully, and alternated between the courtroom and the library for 18 months. Finally, Waring decided, he was ready to practice law on his own.

On Thursday, Dec. 12, 1901, Waring arrived in Columbia to take the Bar exam. The test included no oral arguments – it was entirely written – but still consumed most of the day. Afterward, he nervously loitered in the lobby with all the others who'd been through the ordeal. It was early evening before officials emerged and posted the results, and Waring quickly found his name on the sheet along with 11 others who'd passed. The new barristers celebrated together that evening in a Columbia bar.

He first heard his name called in a courtroom the next morning. Before gaveling the South Carolina Supreme Court into session, Chief Justice Henry McIver – an aging Confederate veteran who'd been on the bench nearly a quarter-century – read the list of new attorneys who'd just passed the Bar. McIver swore them in as officers of the court, pontificated for a moment, then quickly dismissed them.

Satisfied, Waring left Columbia on the afternoon train bound for a new job and his old room at the family's house. In Charleston, the South Carolina Interstate and West Indian Exposition was finishing its second week. Now, Waring had time to attend the festivities. And he could walk through the gardens of the Ivory City proudly.

After all, he was a Broad Street lawyer.

SABOTAGE AT THE EXPOSITION

Poor weather plagued Charleston throughout December. For most of the month, attendance at the exposition fell well below daily projections, despite constant and hyperbolic promotion from the local newspapers. On some days rain discouraged the crowds; on others, unseasonably cold temperatures kept people away. Every week fair officials tried to concoct new schemes to lure in more customers.

Just after Christmas, Dec. 28 was declared "children's day" at the exposition. The papers helpfully predicted "it will be a great day and all of the children in the city and adjoining towns will be out in full force." The Evening Post suggested adults would no doubt want to take advantage of the low admission that day – 25 cents, or 15 cents for children – as if that were a discounted rate, and not simply the regular ticket price.

A respectable crowd of 6,000 turned out on New Year's Day, which Booker T. Washington had declared "Negro Day" in honor of his exhibit's debut. The next week, 10,000 showed up when the Liberty Bell arrived from Philadelphia. The News and Courier said if the expo did nothing more than bring the country's most sacred relic to the city, it had accomplished a great deal. The grand old bell would remain on the grounds through June – one of the few times it had ever been transported out of sight of Independence Hall – and was easily the exposition's most popular draw.

In mid-February, South Carolina and Georgia troops re-created the opening-day parade by marching from Marion Square to the exposition grounds. These troops spent the afternoon on the midway, playing games and admiring the stoic indifference of the camels and elephants on display. The papers declared it a record-setting day for attendance, save for the opening, of course. All this hoopla and tireless promotion belied a growing concern. Ticket sales had been less than stellar. And the president had repeatedly postponed his much-publicized and anticipated appearance. Soon, Sen. Ben Tillman began conspiring to keep him away altogether.

President Roosevelt planned to visit Charleston in February, but his son was declared too sick to travel. Theodore Jr. had been diagnosed with pneumonia and was bedridden for weeks, forcing the First Family to delay or cancel several trips. Some people saw this as an inconvenience or disappointment, but for exposition organizers it was an unmitigated disaster. They'd counted on an appearance by the president to drum up business, at least for one day, and had promoted his arrival since before December. A cancellation would be horrible publicity – and they could scarcely afford that.

As city and exposition officials fretted about Roosevelt's schedule, Lt. Gov. James Tillman – nephew of the senator – attempted to cancel the visit outright. On Feb. 28, while traveling through Charleston, the lieutenant governor told reporters the exposition board planned to withdraw its invitation to the president. Tillman said Roosevelt had insulted his uncle by excluding him from a White House banquet in honor of Prince Henry of Prussia. Exposition officials, the lieutenant governor claimed, were highly offended.

The White House, in fact, had rescinded Tillman's invitation to the banquet – but only because it was unclear whether he still *was* a member of the Senate. He'd been suspended from office the prior week for physically attacking South Carolina's other senator, John McLaurin, on the Senate floor. It was an embarrassing spectacle. A Wisconsin senator had been droning on about the Paris Treaty when Tillman stood up and suggested the votes for its ratification had been bought through federal patronage. He claimed McLaurin had been given the right to name every federal officeholder in South Carolina since the treaty vote. When McLaurin stood and denounced the claim as a despicable lie, Tillman leaped across the aisle and punched his colleague in the forehead. He'd been aiming for his eye.

McLaurin recovered quickly and fought back, hitting Tillman squarely on the nose. Soon, the two bloody men were wrestling in the aisle as their colleagues and Senate staff tried to separate them. When Tillman attempted to punch

McLaurin again, he instead hit the sergeant-at-arms. It was an insufferable breach of protocol. With little hesitation, the Senate voted to expel both men and send them back to South Carolina. By the time the chamber cooled off and decided mere censure was a more appropriate punishment – especially for McLaurin – the White House had un-invited Tillman.

Privately, Roosevelt likely relished the opportunity to exclude Tillman. Just five months into his presidency, he'd already heard enough from the South Carolina demagogue. In October, the First Family had dined with Booker T. Washington – whose recent book, *Up From Slavery*, was a national bestseller – in the executive mansion. It was the first time a black man had been invited to dinner at the White House, and unsurprisingly it sparked a monumental controversy. But no one was more bombastic or inflammatory in their condemnation than Tillman – the former governor, instigator and lynch-mob leader. He practically delighted in the chance to shock.

"The action of President Roosevelt in entertaining that nigger will necessitate our killing a thousand niggers in the South before they will learn their place again," Tillman said.

The senator's statement was so incendiary it provoked outrage even in the South. But it particularly upset Charleston officials planning the exposition's opening. They worried not only about the bad publicity, since Washington was on the board, but also feared the president might shun South Carolina in response. The exposition managed to weather that firestorm without losing either Washington or Roosevelt, but now Tillman was threatening to stir up more trouble.

Most people saw through the ruse immediately. Between the senator's failure to secure federal money for the exposition, and his ongoing feud with Charleston and the president, it was unlikely any city official cared about a perceived slight to Tillman – and they said so publicly. The local papers even questioned the veracity of the lieutenant governor's claim, but had to acknowledge the damage it could cause.

"Of course, in those places where the second officer of South Carolina is known thoroughly no serious account is taken of what he says or does, and silent contempt for his latest exhibition is sufficient," The Evening Post opined, "but in Washington he is known as the Lieutenant Governor of South Carolina and his expressions may be taken as having some weight."

Tillman wasn't finished, however. Two days later, The New York Times reported that the president had been advised to stay away from Charleston. The story said Tillman had asked New York Sen. Thomas Platt to warn Roosevelt that it would be dangerous for him to appear at the exposition. Platt later claimed the message came through a third party, and Tillman denied sending it.

In the press, Gov. McSweeney questioned the accuracy of the Times account. He conceded the Booker T. Washington "incident" had aggrieved many residents, but claimed no one in South Carolina would dare threaten the president of the United States. The perceived snub to Tillman was so inconsequential the governor didn't bother mentioning it. Most people understood the true motive behind the warning.

Still, the White House could not afford to ignore any threat. Roosevelt had ascended to the presidency only six months earlier, following the assassination of President William McKinley at the Pan-American Exposition in Buffalo. Three American presidents had been killed in the 40 years since the end of the Civil War. Hinting that another assassination attempt was possible – particularly at another exposition, and in the city where the war began – was insidious even by Tillman's standards.

The Evening Post accused Tillman of "trying to scare the president," but optimistically predicted his efforts would fail. Charleston could not afford to take that chance, however. As soon as the news reached the city, Mayor Smyth, two aldermen and a handful of exposition officials rushed to Washington on the next train. They had to reassure the president that he was welcome in Charleston and try to secure a new date for his visit.

The success of the exposition depended on it.

The president saw them immediately.

Mayor Smyth reported that, upon their arrival in Washington, Roosevelt met the group in the red room of the White House – and assured them he would attend the exposition as soon as was practical. The president promised "he had never for a moment thought of canceling his contemplated visit to Charleston, and that he was looking forward to the trip with much pleasure."

The Charleston delegation received royal treatment that day. The mayor and exposition officials were invited to lunch at the White House, where Mrs. Roosevelt and the president entertained them for nearly two hours. Smyth said it was an informal meal, Roosevelt joking and in good spirits the entire time. They made plans for a presidential visit later in the month, which would include not only the First Family but several members of the Cabinet.

Afterward, Smyth and his party dropped by the Capitol, as he euphemistically put it, to "pay their respects" to South Carolina's senators. Staff informed the mayor that McLaurin and Tillman were out of town, a convenient excuse to avoid the embarrassment that *they* had not been invited to dine at the White House. The mayor declared the quick trip a great success, but the city would have to wait more than a month for the payoff. It was April before Roosevelt arrived in Charleston.

By the spring, it seemed the exposition's fortunes had changed. Attendance figures were trending upward and expected to go even higher with the president's appearance on April 9. More people were visiting from out of state and, on Saturday, April 5, the fairgrounds welcomed its most famous guest yet. Samuel Clemens – better known as the world-famous author and orator Mark Twain – arrived in Charleston aboard a yacht owned by Standard Oil President H.H. Rogers.

The *Huckleberry Finn* author, Rogers and former speaker of the U.S. House Tom Reed had decided to drop in while traveling up the coast following a trip to Cuba. Rogers no doubt wanted to see the Standard Oil exhibit in the exposition's mining and forestry building. Twain, with his trademark thick, white moustache, was perhaps simply looking for a new audience.

Reporters followed Twain for hours as he toured the various buildings, a mint julep in one hand and cigar in his mouth. Playing to the locals, he called the exposition "the greatest the world had ever seen." Twain joked that he was on his way home, where he would have to quit having so much fun and be good.

The local press devoured every word. It was a perfect build-up to the coming appearance of another very famous man.

When the Roosevelts finally arrived in the Lowcountry, they stayed for three days. On the afternoon of April 8, the president and first lady were treated to a harbor tour by boat, where they had hoped to see the Navy training vessel *Hornet*. But the ship, en route from Wilmington, had been delayed. That evening, the Roosevelts dined in a private home before their carriage delivered them to the Queen Street entrance of the St. John Hotel. The sidewalks along Queen and Meeting streets were thick with people trying to get a glimpse of the president. But he didn't reach the hotel until late that night, and only waved briefly on his way inside.

Most of the crowd stayed outside the hotel all night, awaiting the parade that would carry Roosevelt to the exposition. Some hoped to see him at breakfast, but the president carefully avoided the lobby on his way to the dining room. Still, at least one person slipped past security. The newspapers reported that a local "Negro politician" ducked into the hotel and tried to shake hands with Roosevelt. He was quickly ejected.

The procession that led President Roosevelt to the exposition was even larger than the parade on opening day. A full military escort, including Citadel cadets, marched alongside the carriage up Meeting Street that morning, and exposition officials were ecstatic to see the president ham it up along the route. As he passed Marion Square, Roosevelt even gave a slight nod to the statue of John C. Calhoun – South Carolina's most prominent statesman, and another former vice president.

Charleston quickly dispelled any notion that the Republican president would not be welcome in such a Democratic stronghold, even if he had slighted Tillman. There were thousands of people along the sidewalks – a crowd that dwarfed the turnout for the opening ceremony – and they never stopped cheering. Most simply seemed eager for any interaction with the president; one girl managed to throw a bouquet into Roosevelt's carriage. He picked up the flowers and read the attached card as the procession rolled up Rutledge Avenue.

When his carriage reached the exposition auditorium, Roosevelt was stationed on a temporary podium constructed over the steps – a wooden platform skirted with American flags. From there, he reviewed the troops for half an hour, tipping his top hat and saluting intermittently. The sight of President Roosevelt waving, chatting and laughing with his wife, Edith, would be the exposition's finest hour. More than 25,000 paying customers showed up.

Unwilling to compete with such fanfare, every business in Charleston had closed. The News and Courier called it nothing less than "the greatest day Charleston had known in half a century."

Roosevelt knew his audience, and played to it shamelessly. When he spoke inside the auditorium that afternoon, he began by bragging about the patriotism of all the former Confederate soldiers who fought alongside him in the Spanish-American War. The crowd cheered. He then complimented Charleston's foresight in recognizing the importance of trade with the West Indies and Latin America, a personal interest of his. Another cheer.

Then, a slight pivot away from platitudes. The president had decided he could not speak in South Carolina, the home of "Pitchfork" Ben Tillman, without at least some tacit acknowledgement of the need for American civil rights. Since the end of Reconstruction, black citizens had seen their rights stripped away, replaced by Jim Crow laws that limited their freedom and put targets on their backs. Thousands of African Americans had been lynched in the preceding two decades, most of them in the South – some of them for no offense greater than looking troublesome in the eyes of a white person.

Such a message, the president knew, would not go over well in the city where the Civil War began. The outrage over his dinner with Booker T. Washington had been enough to convince him that some subjects were simply too sensitive for 1901 America. But, even without a single mention of racial politics, he could at the very least nudge his audience. So Roosevelt noted that the exposition should remind everyone of the social and economic complexities that make the country's industrial system work. For that reason, he proclaimed, laws should be fair, based on common sense and designed for neither the poor nor the rich.

"They are simply to be administered justly," the president said.

Roosevelt's subliminal plea for civil rights was largely lost in his speech, which purposely focused largely on Charleston's unique history and deep ties to Cuba. There was enough sweet praise for the city to dilute the bitter medicine hidden in the president's remarks. It seemed to work; the crowd, and the newspapers, were satisfied. No one criticized Roosevelt that day.

The president toured nearly every building on the exposition grounds before boarding a train to Summerville that afternoon. The town hosted a dinner in his honor at the Pine Forest Inn that evening, and the Roosevelts spent the night in the hotel before returning to Washington the next day.

By the time the South Carolina Inter-state and West Indian Exposition closed on May 31, 1902, more than a half-million people had toured the Ivory City. The president's appearance boosted final attendance figures significantly, but not enough to declare the fair a success. The crowds were not as large as exposition officials had hoped, but they boasted that it pumped millions of dollars into the local economy.

City officials announced no new trade deals with Latin America, however, because there were none. In the end, Charleston had hosted a six-month party – the highlight of which was a presidential address that merely implied a need for civil rights laws.

In some ways, the exposition amplified the city's myriad problems. Not even the sheen of the Ivory City could gloss over Charleston's chronic economic stagnation, and the fair seemed to only increase its burgeoning crime rate. On the day of the president's visit, for instance, pickpockets had clandestinely robbed dozens of people.

Such troubles did not bode well for the city, but it was good business for Charleston's newest lawyer.

HIS PLACE IN CHARLESTON

Waties Waring's early days as a Broad Street attorney were busy, but not particularly glamorous.

Bryan gave him an unused office in the back of the firm, and Waring repaid him in part by running down title work and taking depositions. Like most young lawyers, he relied on the charity of veteran attorneys to toss him cases, usually jobs they didn't want – tax filings, real estate closings and the like. In turn-of-the-century Charleston, attorneys didn't specialize; they took whatever came along. Some days, Bryan would stick his head in Waring's office and give him a casual, albeit involuntary, referral. It was simply the price of rent.

"I wish you'd take this fellow," Bryan said. "Handle it your own way and charge him what you want."

Waring was Broad Street's rookie attorney, and that meant he often had to take the picayune criminal cases – public drunkenness, fighting and other misdemeanors. These cases usually resulted in little, if any, money, but he rarely had a choice. Even when Bryan didn't foist undesirable assignments on him, the court often appointed young attorneys to represent indigent clients, of which there were many in Charleston.

Because the city police focused their efforts primarily on the black community, Waring often ended up with African-American clients. Although this did not seem significant to him at the time, and seemingly left little impression on him even in later years, Waring did not relax his standards for poor or black defendants. He fought for those clients as he would any others. He did his job.

"Often in the criminal courts judges would send for lawyers, and usually they'd send for the youngsters, who were assigned to represent people who had no lawyers," Waring said. "I did my part in that – not a great deal, but some. Usually two or three would work together, and you'd represent those poor devils who were generally guilty and had very little chance. We lawyers would do what we could for them, which usually wasn't very much. It helped them sometimes and gave us practice – sort of like interns practicing on patients in a hospital. Patients sometimes get a bad deal but the doctors get a lot of experience."

But Waring often did surprisingly well, even in his first months of practice. In the waning days of the exposition he represented Nathan Brown, one of 13 Charleston residents arrested over the weekend of May 17. The Evening Post had noted that "(t)he defendants were all Negroes; the Caucasians were evidently on their good behavior yesterday and the day before." Brown was charged with disorderly conduct and possession of a weapon, and he pleaded guilty. But when he was sentenced to 60 days on a chain gang, Brown thought it was outrageous and asked for an attorney. Waring was assigned to his case.

A lawyer for just five months, Waring already showed an innate understanding of the court system; he quickly got Brown a new trial. The prosecution argued that Brown received a harsh sentence because he'd assaulted an officer. But under questioning from Waring, the prosecutor conceded Brown actually had not struck anyone. He merely laid his hands on the officer who searched him – and, in 1902, a black man could not touch a white person. Hence, the assault charge.

Waring argued for two hours. Brown was only standing on the street, with a razor in his pocket, when the officer rousted him for dubious cause. His client, Waring claimed, was the victim in this incident. He'd committed no crime. The Evening Post proclaimed the hearing the biggest waste of time in the court's history, but when Waring finished, Brown's sentence was reduced to 20 days or $35. Given the circumstances, and the defendant, it was a resounding victory.

The local newspapers wouldn't normally devote so much ink to a minor crime. Perhaps the coverage suggested that instances of a black defendant winning a reduced sentence was an anomaly; or maybe there was simply nothing else in Charleston worth reporting at the time. Even in its final weeks, the South Carolina Inter-state and West Indian Exposition seemed to consume the entire city.

Waring missed most of the festivities. His only memory of the exposition was Wagener, its president and benefactor. He reminded Waring of his childhood.

The East Bay grocer had advertised in the newspapers regularly in the late 19th century. The ads for his store often featured a train car, noting that a load of flour was coming to Charleston – and Wagener's store was the only place to get any. That's how it was in the city of Waring's youth; limited opportunities abounded. In some ways, Wagener's Victorian advertisements reminded him of his young law practice.

Those limited opportunities for Waring continued throughout the year. On the final weekend of the exposition, a local black man named Richard Brown was arrested for fighting and Waring defended him. He talked the judge into releasing Brown with time served and a $5 fee – the same fine his father often paid for the release of James, his nanny's husband. Waring was familiar with the system.

A month later, Waring tried his first case as co-counsel with Bryan, and its unchivalrous nature attracted much attention in a city suffering post-exposition doldrums. A local woman claimed she was unjustly attacked by a local tour boat operator, and she demanded damages. Charleston was consumed by the lurid tale for days.

Julia Jenkins said Albert Washington had hit her in the chest as she tried to board the steamer *Washington*. The tour boat had been chartered by a local black church, Calvary Baptist, to take congregants on a picnic that afternoon. But Jenkins was stopped at the gangplank. Washington told the court she bought a ticket only to sell liquor on the cruise – a common Charleston practice in those days, even on church excursions. Waring and Bryan lost, but filed a civil suit months later.

Most of Waring's cases held far less entertainment value, and even fewer made him significant money. Business was slow in the city, opportunity scarce. To save on rent, Waring still lived with his family on Rutledge Avenue. And when his parents left to vacation at their North Carolina cabin for a few weeks in September 1902, Waring went with them. His absence didn't hurt the practice, because in truth he had little to do. But that would soon change.

In the first decade of the 20th century, Charleston's moribund economy was finally revived. This had little to do with the celebrated exposition or foreign trade, however. It was almost entirely, and ironically, the work of the federal government.

Just before the fair's opening ceremony, the Navy had agreed to locate a new base upstream of Charleston on the Cooper River. The decision had everything to do with geography – and the new harbor jetties that allowed ships easy access to the Atlantic Ocean. Locals cheered the news, and welcomed the U.S. Navy into the city for the first time in decades, simply because it would be good for business. The Navy's arrival would change Charleston immeasurably. Suddenly, the dying old port town was a military hub, surviving off the largesse of a federal government it had once tried to disown.

With this influx of federal dollars and supporting businesses, the city embarked on a series of expensive, labor-intensive public works projects, including a sewage system that would cut down on the disease that had plagued Charleston for decades. That meant more work for laborers and, of course, lawyers. Broad Street was frenzied by the opportunities, and the accompanying politics. An Irish-Catholic politician named John P. Grace – who'd once run for the state Senate against future Waring law partner George F. Von Kolnitz Jr. – was laying the groundwork to become the next mayor. It would stir turmoil on Broad Street for years.

Waring thrived in this environment. Everything he'd learned – from his colleagues, from the boring family history recited to him as a child – taught him that relationships led to business. So Waring insinuated himself into the community. Given his bloodline, and his upbringing, he could move gracefully from one crowd to the next. He joined the Charleston Light Dragoons, the local Masonic Lodge, and was elected secretary of the College of Charleston alumni association. Soon, Waring had no shortage of clients.

Within a few years he was an officer in a half-dozen of the city's most elite organizations. Often, these positions were little more than thin excuses to attend parties such as the alumni association banquet on the Isle of Palms, or the Light Dragoons' annual minstrel show. Waring became a constant presence at nearly every function of Charleston society, whether it was a debutante ball or a dance at the St. Cecilia Society.

Of all these groups, the St. Cecilia Society was by far the most important. Named for the patron saint of music, the society dated back to Charleston's first century, when it was founded as a subscription concert series. Over the years it had transformed itself into the city's most exclusive social institution, the very personification of Charleston's insular society. Waring's name, which predated even the society, won his admittance. But then, he was accepted graciously everywhere he went.

These respectable functions allowed Waring to mingle with "his crowd," as he called them. He was one of Charleston's bluebloods, a man who could dramatically recount the exploits of his ancestors going back to the days when the city rose out of the unforgiving Lowcountry saltmarsh. Among some of his peers, however, there were whispers that Waring had the chameleon-like ability to blend into any scene – including Charleston's less proper establishments.

The Lutherans and the Baptists had complained for years that city officials did little to police the proliferation of seedy bars operating outside of state law – blind tigers, they were called. These churches also fretted over the prostitutes who walked the streets in neighborhoods perilously close to the Holy City's many houses of worships. It was practically an epidemic. The Navy base, and the thousands of sailors it brought to town, had been a boon for such business.

Later, long after Waring had been excommunicated from Charleston society, some of his friends suggested he had more than a passing acquaintance with the city's unseemly underworld. They claimed he'd held credit accounts with Charleston's finest madams, and that his fellow attorneys once jokingly called him "king of the tenderloin district." But there was no proof of these rumors, which may have been a bit of revisionist history in a city famous for it.

Waring's life fell into a pattern: He passed his days on Broad Street and his nights bounding from one social function to the next, fumbling home seemingly later each night. But he was still devoted to his family. In September 1903, he again vacationed with his parents in North Carolina, and it would be his last with his mother. Anna Thomasine Waring died on Dec. 23, 1903, four days before her 54th birthday.

Her death turned the Rutledge Avenue house into an empty bachelor pad, and changed both her son and husband. Waring spent even more time at work and out on the party circuit, and his father took a job as Charleston schools superintendent, a position he would hold until his death a dozen years later. Edward had dubious qualifications for the position, but – like his son – he still had his name.

In January 1904, just weeks after his mother passed away, Waring was appointed United States commissioner – sort of a magistrate or justice of the peace for the federal government. The position had been created decades earlier, at a time when Southern states, reeling from the oversight of Reconstruction, often ignored federal law. The part-time job provided Waring with extra income, but its true value was opportunity.

For the most part, Waring dealt with minor issues not worth the U.S. attorney's time. He sent people to jail and scheduled trials for defendants accused of perjury or the surprisingly common offense of robbing post offices. Waring had a prosecutor's zeal, and sentenced people so harshly the courts occasionally reversed his decisions. But as a result of this work, Waring gained a deeper understanding of federal statutes and discovered a world of connections beyond Broad Street.

Waring's apprenticeship was over. After a year as commissioner, he politely resigned from Bryan's law firm and opened his own practice with George F. Von Kolnitz at 11 Broad Street. It was a career move that would change his life. Von Kolnitz was a state senator, and he drew Waring deeper into the byzantine world of local politics, where a good lawyer's career path often flourished or died.

This was a natural progression for Waring. Most of the Broad Street ring – as Charleston's attorneys were called – dabbled in politics. It was a good way to meet people, both clients and local residents who might end up on juries. Waring looked at this as just one more social function. Before long, he even lent his support to the campaign of Julien Jervey. It was an unsurprising choice; Jervey was the Broad Street ring's candidate for 9th Circuit solicitor.

Waring had become exactly what was expected of a young man from an established Charleston family. He had a business, social connections and quickly made himself an integral and respected member of the community. His name appeared in the newspapers regularly, whether he was serving as a groomsman, pallbearer or a member of the social committee for one of the city's countless galas.

At 24, Waring was every bit as much a part of Charleston as any of his ancestors had been. He was particularly active in College of Charleston affairs. He served on the alumni association, mentored students in the writing society and lobbied to secure athletic fields for the college on the site of the old exposition, which had been dismantled shortly after the fair ended. Waring also curiously remained silent when his colleagues opposed admitting female students into his alma mater.

That was a decision completely in line with Charleston opinion of the day, although ironic given Waring's future as a crusader for equal rights. But then, Waring never claimed he was born with a preternatural sense of right and wrong; he always said his passion for justice only awakened late in life. As a young man, Waring was simply going along with his crowd. And for two years, he was going constantly.

Between 1904 and 1906, Waring became a ranking officer in the Charleston Light Dragoons, sat on the events committee for the Masons and the executive committee of the Carolina Yacht Club. He even accepted special research assignments as a member of the Chamber of Commerce. Waring was pulled in so many directions that it was a relief when he took off with his father each summer to vacation at the North Carolina cabin – which in itself was a mark of status. All the best Charleston families summered in the mountains.

His growing list of commitments increasingly conspired to distract Waring from his law practice, however, and that was a problem. So in April 1906, he resigned his federal post and recommended that Arthur B. Young succeed him as U.S. commissioner. He said the job too often kept him away from Charleston; as commissioner, he routinely had to hold court in North Carolina. Of course, his schedule did not prevent him from accepting the presidency of Alpha Tau

Omega's alumni association. That was simply good business.

Waring's connections eventually paid dividends. He was hired to represent the Citizens' Light and Power Company in its bid to win a Charleston utilities franchise. This brought him into direct contact – and conflict – with city aldermen for the first time, and his time wandering the corridors of City Hall further stoked his interest in local politics.

He'd decided early on that he had no desire to run for public office – he saw the headaches Von Kolnitz dealt with on a daily basis – but Waring enjoyed the gamesmanship of politics. He was no doubt attracted to the intellectual exercise of developing policy, but also relished the idea of being an influential, behind-the-scenes power broker. Ultimately, he volunteered to be a precinct officer for the county Democratic Party. Waring likely considered it just another social obligation.

His increasing awareness of political machinations led Waring to reclaim his job as a U.S. commissioner. In 1911, Arthur Young – the man who'd replaced him – was appointed assistant U.S. attorney in Charleston. Waring had come to covet such a position, and now he knew how to get it. So he accepted his old part-time duties and was soon on the road again, traveling to Greenville or North Carolina every month. It was a calculated political move that would lead him deeper into the federal justice system – and politics – in the coming year. But the payoff would be worth the trouble. Waring had become almost obsessed with the idea of being a prosecutor or, better still, a federal judge.

A WEDDING, A RECOUNT, A SHOOTING

W aring passed his days in the company of bootleggers, kidnappers and scam artists. He spent his evenings with socialites, politicians and the volunteer militia. The venues changed, the faces blurred.

Crime – petty and otherwise – was rampant across the South in 1912, and the young U.S. commissioner constantly traveled the Carolinas to preside over the resulting preliminary hearings. When he was home, Waring's schedule was filled with board meetings, mixers and his law partner's congressional campaign. There was no respite in his schedule, day or night. Still, he somehow found the time to begin courting a proper Charleston woman.

He'd known Annie Gammell most of his life. They saw each other at various social functions – two people of the same age and station could hardly avoid one another in a town so small – and their mothers had known each other and often visited. Annie was blond, kind and reserved to the point of shyness, a gentle member of Charleston's gentility. It's unclear what sparked their romance, but it was unlike anything else in Waring's life. Annie was completely undemanding.

Their relationship was, in some ways, simply convenient. They were both over 30, their prospects dwindling, and it was time to settle down. Each had attractive qualities: He was a successful professional with a promising future; she was cultured, charming and pliable. But there was more to it. By the spring of 1912, Annie was deeply in love. When she traveled overseas, which was often, she sent him playful, risqué letters.

"Yesterday the sea was milder and so I thought of you and what you want me to do – by night," she wrote to him aboard the SS *Ryndam* on a voyage to Rotterdam. "If you had been there I think I should have said something that would have made you very happy – I loved you so much."

Annie's letters to Waring – sent to his office, not the house he shared with his father – were mostly rambling travelogues with frequent asides about her feelings for him. Although she professed her love, Annie seemed willing to accept life as a spinster if he didn't care strongly enough about her. There was nothing coquettish about this; given Waring's inherently cold demeanor, it was a reasonable position. But Annie made it clear she wanted a future as his wife, standing beside him at every one of his many Charleston obligations.

It was what she was born to do.

Annie was the youngest daughter of William and Marie Gammell, a surname that belied her place in local society. Her father was a Savannah native, but her mother was a Charleston Ancrum – a family that traced its lineage back to Revolution-era politicians and wealthy indigo planters. That gave her more than sufficient standing among the South of Broad set, even though her life had not been as charmed as that heritage might have suggested.

Her father died when she was 9, and at 14 Annie was shipped off to Miss Peck's finishing school in Philadelphia. That was not an uncommon route for Charleston girls, but Annie may have felt somewhat isolated and awkward. Even though friends bragged about her striking features, others maintained there was something slightly plain about young Annie. Some society types whispered that she'd never even had a coming-out party, a troublesome sign for a Charleston lady. But then, the Gammells were otherwise preoccupied. They traveled often after her father died, and Annie's mother died in Toronto when she was barely an adult, leaving two sisters as her only family.

Perhaps the most striking thing about Annie was her friendship with the famous French stage actress Sarah Bernhardt. She'd written her first fan letter to Bernhardt when she was just 16 and studying drama in New York. The actress was appearing on Broadway at the time, and Annie was in the audience for every matinee and evening performance. She sent flowers backstage after each show, and finally persuaded her French teacher to help her compose the letter. Annie was astonished to get a reply. The actress, charmed by the note, invited Annie to lunch.

"Do you ever come to Paris?" Bernhardt had asked her that day.

A friendship began. Back in Charleston for the summer, Annie studied French and made plans to travel that fall. When she reached France in October, she contacted Bernhardt and found the actress hadn't forgotten her. Soon, they were having lunch together again – this time in Paris. Eventually, Annie was granted backstage privileges at Bernhardt's shows and crossed the ocean five times to visit her. When the actress became ill, Annie insisted on serving as her nurse. She became a regular guest in Bernhardt's house.

One of Annie's most cherished possessions was a copy of the actress' memoir signed, "To Annie Gammell, the most adorable child that I know. A souvenir of the great affection of Sarah Bernhardt." Annie remained close to Bernhardt long past her childhood. In fact, she was still visiting the actress regularly when Waring began courting her. In the spring of 1913, he met Annie briefly at a stopover in Savannah during one trip, and he stayed overnight. It earned him another gushing love letter.

By the time she was 31, Annie was a world traveler accustomed to standing just outside the spotlight. She was comfortable and accepted at the endless parties of her hometown, but also adaptable. Annie didn't really need anyone. She was exactly the sort of person a notorious bachelor like Waring was supposed to marry.

After two years of courtship, they were wed at the Christ Church in Bronxville, New York, on Oct. 30, 1913. It was a very Charleston thing to do, getting married elsewhere – Waring routinely traveled out-of-state for his local friends' weddings. Perhaps they didn't want to choose between the numerous Holy City churches, or they just wanted to cut down on their costs, and their guest list. But it appeared Waring and Annie simply didn't want to make a fuss. The wedding notice ran all of one sentence in The Evening Post.

Waring's friends considered Annie charming and sweet, but nowhere near her husband's intellectual equal. They privately called her a frivolous woman, devoted only to Waring and a handful of social clubs. But that was typical Charleston snobbery, and hypocrisy. Annie did no less than any woman of her standing. And like Waring, she was a joiner. She served on the women's auxiliary at the Hibernian Hall, chaperoned dances at the St. Cecilia Society and started a study club for women to read and indulge in their own creative writing. Not long after their marriage, the Warings began to appear regularly in the local society columns, and Annie's faith in her husband's potential was soon vindicated.

In August 1914, Waring's decision to resume his job as a federal commissioner finally paid off. Francis Weston, South Carolina's U.S. attorney, appointed him to succeed Arthur Young as assistant U.S. attorney for Charleston. President Woodrow Wilson's election had shaken up the Justice Department, and Weston suddenly needed a new assistant. Weston's first choice was deemed incompetent and, at Young's urging, Waring applied for the job.

It was an ideal situation for Waring. Weston worked out of Columbia and, after years on the job, was admittedly just going through the motions. He happily gave Waring the authority to run the Charleston office as he wanted – and to pick his own cases. Waring quickly built a prosecutorial record by taking on high-profile murders and bank robberies. The job led him to federal courthouses around the South, sometimes wandering as far north as Richmond. In between all those miles, he learned the intricacies of the federal justice system.

"It gave me a great opportunity to learn federal practice, and I think that I became somewhat of an expert," he later recalled.

Weston was impressed with his work, and gave Waring so much latitude that many South Carolina lawyers came to consider him the de facto U.S. attorney. When someone complained to Weston about one of Waring's decisions, the old man always deferred to his protégé. Even when he disagreed with his assistant, he did nothing to undermine him. Waring recognized his luck, and tried to avoid anything that might reflect poorly on the boss. He also realized the position came with great access to the state's most powerful politicians, including U.S. Sen. Ellison DuRant "Cotton Ed" Smith – a good friend of Weston's.

The most significant case in Waring's tenure as assistant U.S. attorney was one of his first. A German ship, the *Liebenfels*, sailed into Charleston Harbor in August 1914 – just as the Great War was beginning. The British Navy had German ships on the run, and the *Liebenfels* sought refuge in South Carolina after delivering a load of fertilizer to Charleston. When the British consulate came for the East Indian crew, the officers stayed with the ship. They soon became regulars on the streets of Charleston, a city with a large German population – many of whom still spoke in their native tongue.

Just as the war escalated, the *Liebenfels* suddenly sank in shallow water near the western bank of the Cooper River – and that threatened an international incident. It appeared the Germans had scuttled their own ship to keep it out of American hands, assuming the United States would soon join the fight as British allies. Waring and other federal officials inspected the abandoned ship and found the engine room full of water. Every clue suggested sabotage.

Waring studied the situation for months before finally filing charges. He decided to prosecute based on a statute that outlawed abandoning a ship that was a hazard to navigation, and he had the crew detained for illegally entering the country. It was delicate work, and the Justice Department constantly warned him not to do anything the Germans could protest. Waring dragged out the case until investigators found enough evidence of sabotage to bring more charges against the sailors.

The case consumed nearly half of Waring's time as assistant U.S. attorney, and gained considerable notoriety after America got into the war. The crewmen were ultimately convicted of sinking the ship intentionally, but acquitted of conspiracy. By then, the *Liebenfels* case had lingered for three years. For a while it was Waring's claim to fame, and he kept a souvenir from the ship in his office, even after he was appointed to the bench.

Waring settled into a comfortable life – a high-profile job, a little money and a city full of influential friends. He and Annie moved into a house at 61 Meeting Street, which her sister, Bessie, had bought and renovated a few months before their wedding. The house sat in the perfect location: one block south of Broad Street, the federal courthouse and St. Michael's Church, which the couple attended – her religiously, him dutifully.

The Meeting Street house had been a stable – and later, slave quarters – for the Branford-Horry mansion, which was one of the city's finest examples of colonial architecture. Before Bessie's renovations, the building for several years had housed the Hyde Drug Co. The Warings made the place their own, adding a brick patio in the small garden. It wasn't the grandest home South of Broad, but it was sturdy and comfortable.

Charleston was not doing nearly as well as the Warings, or much better than it had been 20 years earlier. The Navy and the two railroads provided a sizable portion of the jobs in the area, but the port had yet to rebound. The Warings' new neighborhood reflected the city's depressing predicament. Many of the people South of Broad, the descendants of Charleston's founders, were – as they derisively joked – "too poor to paint, too proud to whitewash."

For most, times were desperate. As Charleston limped along under the threat of another war, local gallows humor held that at least this one might bring in some business.

The city was on its own, more or less. Charleston had feuded intermittently with the rest of the state throughout history, and once again relationships were strained. The new governor, Richard Manning, took over the police department after Mayor Grace refused to shut down the local bars that operated outside of state law. Fed up, Manning recruited Tristram T. Hyde to run against Grace in the 1915 election. Hyde had come within 200 votes of beating Grace four years earlier, and was eager to try again. The Broad Street ring preferred Hyde, but no one had any idea how the election might go. Most predicted a riot – no matter who won.

Campaign tension consumed Charleston most of the summer. Old friends quit speaking, South of Broad parties were marred by partisan bickering, and there were even rumors that the St. Cecilia Society would bar all Grace supporters from its annual ball. As the election approached, the hostility was so rampant that the governor sent the state militia to maintain order in the city. But on Oct. 12, ballots were cast without any serious incidents. Hyde won by 14 votes. Grace demanded a recount.

Then the trouble began.

The recount was scheduled three days after the election, at the county Democratic Executive Committee headquarters on the corner of King and George streets. That day, the small committee room was packed with partisans from both sides, a crowd that spilled out into the anteroom. Waring was there, ostensibly to represent clients whose ballots were being challenged, but in truth he was just another gawker. He arrived too late to get into the committee room, which turned out to be fortunate.

Joseph Black, chairman of the executive committee, asked police to clear the committee room just before the recount was set to begin. That raised eyebrows and started the murmurs – it was subterfuge, they were going to rig the count. The rumbling quickly reached a crescendo, the whispers turning to shouts, and then a shot rang out. Someone promptly returned fire, and all hell broke loose.

People in the committee room ran for the exit, and the men in the anteroom tried to get inside to see the spectacle. The result was complete gridlock. A few tried climbing out the windows to avoid the crossfire, including a reporter from The News and Courier. He was halfway out when he was hit by a stray bullet and fell to the sidewalk. The reporter would die on the way to the hospital.

Several others were injured before police took control of the scene, and it was a wonder more weren't killed. At least 12 shots had been fired in the crowded room. And in the confusion, someone tossed a few of the sequestered ballot boxes out the window, their contents scattering in the street.

Waring had no desire to witness the melee. He ducked out of the anteroom the second the shooting started. Later, he told a police officer, "I went out of the outer door while the fusillade of shots were going on. It was after I got outside there was a pause, and then one or two more shots – I can't say how many – were fired in the committee room."

The scene on the street was nearly as chaotic: Fire engines barreled down King Street and the Washington Light Infantry marched in to help the state militia and police keep order. The central business district hadn't seen so much traffic in years. It took the troops the rest of the day to clear out the rubbernecking crowd.

Both candidates tried to turn the disaster to electoral advantage. Hyde spoke out first, slyly insinuating that the incumbent administration had allowed this to happen. He called the incident "one of the most frightful things in the political history of the city and in itself a complete indictment of the conditions which exist in Charleston today. I solemnly pledge to the people of Charleston that nothing of the kind shall happen during my administration as mayor."

Forced to play defense, Mayor Grace mildly proclaimed, "I have done everything I can to preserve peace and order. In the midst of the profound peace, we find ourselves face to face with innocent blood. It is not for me to fix the guilt at this time. Nor will I further aggravate the tension by expressing an opinion."

The next day, the Democratic executive committee again declared Hyde the winner, this time by 28 votes. No one ever said whether the lost ballots were recovered, or counted. The controversy would linger for weeks.

The Evening Post reported rumors that claimed the police had not only failed to stop the violence, but participated in the shootout. Eventually, three men were arrested for carrying concealed weapons into the meeting, and Henry J. Brown and Edward R. McDonald were charged in the shooting. The police were exonerated.

Edward Waring died in March of 1916, and his youngest son was named executor of the estate. It was about the only private legal work Waring did that year. He'd set up a new office at 13 Broad Street, but his job as assistant U.S. attorney kept him too busy to use it. He prosecuted bootleggers and thieves who stole government supplies from the Navy base, and when the war began he tried a few people accused of aiding "alien Germans."

The war brought out the activist in Waring. He sold Liberty Bonds, helped with Red Cross food drives and delivered patriotic messages around the Lowcountry: In Walterboro he told people how to spot German spies; on James Island he stressed the importance of conserving food. He and Annie served as chaperones at a dance for submariners. He considered all this his modest contribution to the war effort. By then, he was too old to enlist.

His other nights were no less busy. Waring had been named president of the College of Charleston alumni association, a title that came with numerous social obligations. Other evenings, he and Annie mingled with their friends and neighbors at the city's most important parties. And when Sarah Bernhardt arrived in Charleston to perform a series of scenes from her plays in January 1917, the Warings watched from box seats near the stage. Later, they hosted a dinner for the actress at 61 Meeting Street.

Bernhardt would remain close to Annie the rest of her life. When the Warings' only child, Anne, was born in October 1918, the actress agreed to be her godmother.

After the war, Waring slowly drifted back into private practice. He formed a new law partnership with state legislator D.A. Brockinton and helped establish the Carolina Coastal Oil Development Company, serving as its president. All of that soon attracted other corporate clients. It was either fortuitous timing, or Waring had sensed what was coming. In 1920, Republican Warren G. Harding won the presidential election, and Francis Weston was out of a job.

Waring stayed on as assistant U.S. attorney for a while, but finally resigned in September 1921. He didn't particularly like the new attorney general, and was sick of trying Volstead Act cases. Unsurprisingly, he hated Prohibition.

At 41, Waring was not worried about losing his steady paycheck. He expected his considerable experience as a prosecutor would profit him in private practice. Besides, he fully considered this mid-career shift little more than an intermission.

He wasn't finished with the federal justice system – he was only beginning.

TWO CITIES

As Waring's life drifted into middle age, prosperity and comfort, other quarters of Charleston were growing more unsettled and contentious each day.

Most of his crowd – as Waring called his peers – wouldn't notice for a while, but there was a new generation of black Charlestonians desperate to improve their lives. They questioned the social order and stood up for their rights. White Charleston had no interest in change, particularly the kind championed by black people, but they could not ignore the coming movement for long.

By 1918, more than two generations had passed since the end of Reconstruction. That period was only a faint recollection for most black Charlestonians, perhaps even more alien than the horrors of slavery – simply because it had been their only glimpse of civil rights. The federal occupation had afforded African Americans the right to vote and, since they comprised the majority of Charleston's population, hold office. For more than a decade, blacks had served on city council and in the state legislature; a few were even elected to Congress. Once, half the city's police force had been black, including its chief of detectives.

Since that time, however, Charleston had reverted to its old ways. Black politicians were slowly removed from office in the decade after Reconstruction ended. As the city's economy eroded in the 1880s, black police officers and firefighters were the first to lose their jobs. Work was scarce for everyone, but it was even more pronounced in the black community. The most prosperous black men were often longshoremen, who had established a union during Reconstruction and still held sway at the port. Black women rarely had little choice but to work in hotels or private homes as cooks and domestic servants, jobs that were often a reminder of how things had once been in Charleston.

Peter Porcher Poinsette remembered all too well. He'd been born into slavery on a Wando River Plantation. As a boy he carried the books of his white owner's children to school; as a teenager he was pressed into service for the Confederate Army. Like most South Carolinians, he'd struggled ever since. He scrambled to earn a living, taking work as a custodian or waiter, often catering parties at the St. Cecilia Society or in private homes. His wife, Victoria, did laundry and ironing for white families. The money they made was barely enough to get by, especially with seven children.

Poinsette was a kind man who, his daughter later said, loved all people. But he was also wary, old times not forgotten. He kept a watchful eye on how Charleston changed – and how it didn't. He'd decided early on that he didn't want his children to fall into domestic work, either in a home or a hotel, as locals expected from people of their station. He recognized the dangers there for a young black girl in Charleston.

On Henrietta Street, where the Poinsettes lived, four of their neighbors were single women raising mixed-race children. They were the mistresses of white men, and their children – called mulattoes by Charleston society – grew up within two miles of half-siblings they would never meet. Poinsette did not want that life for his own children. When one of his daughters, Septima, showed an interest in becoming a schoolteacher, he encouraged her dreams as much as he could. Anything to avoid seeing her caught between the two Charlestons.

For most of Waring's life, the city had operated on delicate customs. White residents coexisted with Charleston's sizable black population, separated by the Jim Crow laws of the 1890s. As governor, Ben Tillman not only segregated South Carolina, he rewrote the state's constitution to prevent any chance of blacks attaining political power. The Democratic Party refused black men (or women of any color) the right to vote. White men had lost their power once, and Tillman was determined it would not happen again.

Tillman had any number of sympathetic accomplices. A year after the governor overhauled the South Carolina Constitution with the cooperation of state lawmakers, the United States Supreme Court validated segregation laws nationally in a decision that spawned the inherently contradictory phrase "separate but equal." Charleston had limped along ever since. The first monuments to Tillman were the "whites" and "colored" signs plastered across the city.

In some ways, Charleston was two distinct cities that overlapped only at very precise, and limited, junctures. The white families that employed black housekeepers or nannies, like the Warings, were kind in a patriarchal way, but avoided developing relationships that were considered socially inappropriate. Some black businesses catered to a white clientele – seamstresses who made dresses for the South of Broad women, barbershops that serviced white men. But that was largely the extent of interaction.

Blacks and whites worshipped at their own churches, rode on separate street-cars and did not see each other socially. Their children, naturally, attended different schools. This is how the vast majority of white people wanted it, and blacks had no say in such matters. But by the time the United States entered the Great War, some had begun to take limited, calculated stands. The Navy base was expanding rapidly as a result of the fighting, and soon opened 1,000 new positions for civilian women. Black community leaders persuaded the federal government to give 300 of those jobs to black women.

By then, the National Association for the Advancement of Colored People had opened a Charleston office, joining an expanding chorus of civil rights activists in the city. The YWCA was already the hub of the black community, and the Jenkins Orphanage was established to help African-American children succeed. The orphanage had strong support in the white community, but for the most part people of different races ignored one another. They occupied two distinct Charlestons, living together on a narrow peninsula, but worlds apart. And by 1918, their uneasy détente showed signs of crumbling.

Thomas E. Miller started it all with a relatively mild proposal.

A former legislator and congressman in the days of Reconstruction, he had retired to Charleston a few years before the war. Miller had been the first president of the State Colored Agricultural and Mechanical College in Orangeburg, but was dismissed after a turnover in the governor's office. He passed his days quietly for several years, but had decided to resume his life's mission: Miller wanted black educators teaching in South Carolina's black schools.

Charleston, like every other city in the state, maintained separate schools for black and white students, and both systems exclusively employed white faculties. With the support of the local NAACP office, Miller began to promote his idea in a series of public speeches. At first, few people outside the black community listened. But when he asked the legislature to hire black teachers for public schools, whites were promptly outraged. They claimed only mulattoes would accept black teachers; the cooks and laundresses of Charleston – the only black residents they knew – preferred white teachers.

Miller eventually took his plan to Benjamin Cox, principal of Avery Normal Institute. The school had been founded by Northern missionaries in the late 19th century and, according to the newspapers, catered to the "higher-class Negroes." In truth, the school was open to any black student whose parents could afford the modest tuition. Miller saw a kindred spirit in Cox, who had replaced Avery's white principal a few years earlier and immediately began to hire black teachers.

Other private African-American schools had black faculty, but locals took exception to mixed-race hiring practices at Avery. The News and Courier even published a story quoting locals that claimed "(c)olored people prefer white teachers at Avery." Local ministers disputed the contention, and Avery's alumni association passed a resolution in support of Cox and his policies. The newspaper quietly dropped the issue.

Charleston had little control over a private institution, but used Jim Crow laws to hinder Cox's efforts. City Council banned the co-mingling of races in Avery's faculty dormitories, and soon white teachers began to quit because they couldn't afford to live off campus. Avery students were sad, and many whites in Charleston were elated. Avery's teachers had a reputation in some circles as defiant agitators. They often took students on field trips to public historical sights, flaunting segregation laws, and some took this as an overt political statement. As a result, many white Avery teachers – missionaries that they were – had been unwelcome in Charleston churches.

The controversy was largely forgotten by the time Miller recruited Cox's faculty for a petition drive. His goal was to collect 10,000 signatures from peninsular residents asking the General Assembly to hire black teachers for black schools. Miller believed the Avery teachers would make good ambassadors for this campaign, and Cox agreed. One of the teachers who volunteered was an Avery alumnus named Septima Poinsette – Peter's daughter. For weeks, she carried petitions up and down Calhoun Street, targeting houses between Rutledge Avenue and King Street. It was an area she knew well. After all, she'd grown up in the neighborhood.

Septima Poinsette, who was in her first year of teaching at Avery, had been drawn to Miller's crusade from the beginning. She knew the value of black teachers, because she'd had several growing up. In some ways, they shaped her entire life.

In 1903, when she was just 5, her mother, Victoria, enrolled her in a private school that operated out of a two-room house in downtown Charleston. The family could barely afford the tuition, which was $1.50 per month, but the Poinsettes valued education and instilled that attitude in their children. It may have led young Septima to her career path.

Throughout her childhood, Septima changed schools constantly. Her parents reluctantly sent her to public schools when they couldn't pay their bills, and re-enrolled her in private classes as soon as they saved enough money. Septima was a good student – smart enough to skip grades if she'd wanted – but she decided to quit after seventh grade. With her family constantly in financial straits, Septima believed she should get a teaching certificate and start contributing to the family income. But Victoria would not allow it.

"You must get some more education," her mother said. "You'll go to Avery next year."

So, Septima went. She later called Avery a "paradise" – she loved the teachers, the students and the campus. She was a junior when Cox took over as principal and began to integrate the faculty. When the city ordered Avery's dorms segregated, forcing several white members of the staff to quit, Septima lost some of her favorite teachers. It was her first brush with the backlash to civil rights. The politics eluded her at the time, but they wouldn't for long. She was a fast learner.

After she graduated from Avery in 1916, the family pastor helped Septima get her first teaching job. It was a private school on Johns Island, which at the time was a long boat ride from downtown Charleston. Her mother took her to the dock near the peninsula's tip for her first trip away from home. Both of them cried that day on The Battery; it felt like Septima was shipping off to a different world.

She enjoyed her work on the island. Septima was one of the school's two teachers, and also its principal – a position that paid her $30 per month. She sent some of that money home to her parents, but soon realized her salary was a pittance. White teachers who were her age made $85 per month. And the workload was just as unfair as the economics. She had 132 students; most white teachers were responsible for no more than 18.

After two years on Johns Island, Cox had recruited Septima to teach sixth grade at Avery. She moved back into her parents' house, which was fortunate. Peter and Victoria needed her help to pay the bills; they'd nearly lost the Henrietta Street house on more than one occasion. In those years before America joined the Great War, many people in Charleston struggled, particularly the Poinsettes.

The petition drive sparked an activist's heart. Not long after her long days of collecting signatures along Calhoun Street, Septima joined the local NAACP. Later, she volunteered for the USO, entertaining sailors who came into port. At one dance, she met a young man named Nerie David Clark. A brief court-ship ensued.

Many locals, black and white, supported the USO. It was important to the Navy, and the base was vital to Charleston. In some ways, the Navy had resurrected the city. The military had brought thousands of jobs and ancillary businesses, which kept the economy – such as it was – afloat. But the transition to a military town was not always smooth, and it soon threatened Charleston's delicate racial balance.

One Saturday evening in May 1919, a group of bluejackets on night passes from the Navy base were cruising the Market Street bars – the city's most popular draw for sailors. A black man passed the group on the sidewalk and one of the sailors, Roscoe Coleman, who was white, was pushed into the street.

It was never clear whether the man intentionally shoved Coleman or simply brushed against the group on the crowded sidewalk, setting off a chain reaction. It didn't matter to the sailors; they took off in pursuit, screaming for him to stop. He ran.

They chased the man down Market Street, and the action attracted the attention of several barflies. Soon, a dozen others had fallen in with the sailors. They tracked the man to a house in Ansonborough, and pelted the home with bottles and bricks. The mob demanded the man come outside. Finally, another black man stepped out of the house – and he had a gun, which he fired into the air. A warning shot.

The riot started within minutes.

Years of frustration erupted that night. Black residents poured out of their homes to take on the drunken mob. At first, they fought with their fists or anything lying around – sticks, broken bottles. The violence escalated when the sailors who'd started the melee broke into armories on King and Market streets. They stole 18 rifles and more than a half-dozen revolvers, and quickly put them to use.

By the time the police arrived, the city was in chaos. The sailors were shooting into the crowd and white rioters were looting black-owned businesses. Gunfire echoed across the peninsula for the rest of the night. There was no stopping the fight.

By morning, two black men were dead and 27 were wounded – including seven sailors and one police officer. Nearly 50 people were arrested, 15 for carrying concealed weapons, two for assaulting officers and three for public intoxication; another 27 were held without charges. Two men were charged with the murder of Isaac Doctor, one of the black men killed in the rioting. The Navy canceled all liberty for its sailors, and Charleston put every police officer it had on the streets to prevent further bloodshed.

The city was on edge all summer. Less than a week after the riot, the newspapers reported rumors that a truckload of sailors had fired shots at someone while driving down Meeting Street. After Navy officials demanded a retraction, the paper claimed a backfiring car led to the confusion and that no sailors had been involved. But the Navy could not deny the larger blame. It was sailors from the base, and not local residents, who'd sparked the violence.

The incident put Mayor Hyde in the unusual position of demanding justice for the city's black residents. He promised increased police protection in African-American neighborhoods, and suggested the city reimburse black-owned businesses damaged in the rioting.

"There will be an investigation into the cause of the riot and steps will be taken to guard against future occurrences of the same order. I will ask W.G. Fridie, whose barbershop on King Street was demolished by the sailors, to draw up a bill of damages to be presented to the city government," the mayor said. "This might set a precedent, but the Negroes of Charleston must be protected. We are hoping that this morning saw the end of the disturbances, but if any action is taken by the Negroes against the whites, or vice versa, I will ask that martial law be established."

Ultimately, the Navy filed charges against the sailors who started the riot. Two of them spent a year in military prison, but the city – despite Mayor Hyde's assurances – never prosecuted any civilians. It was just another incident that Charleston thought best to let lie.

That summer the Avery teachers collected more than 10,000 signatures, and Miller presented them to the state legislature in January 1920. Within months, the General Assembly reluctantly, and surprisingly, approved a plan that would allow Charleston to employ black teachers in its black public schools. This unprecedented policy change passed with little fanfare. It appeared no one in Charleston wanted another fight, not at that moment.

One of the first black teachers hired by Charleston County was assigned to a school in McClellanville, a small fishing village 30 miles up the coast. Septima Poinsette would be one of three teachers in the rural school, and she was responsible for all the fourth-, fifth- and sixth-grade classes. A minister took one of the other teaching positions, and on the days he traveled for church business, Septima taught his classes as well.

She found McClellanville similar to Johns Island; it was quiet, isolated and time moved slowly. The preacher tried to court her, but she rebuffed him. Septima had no interest in becoming a minister's wife. Near the end of the school year, the sailor she'd met at the USO dance showed up in McClellanville. He'd caught a ride with the mailman, and ridden more than an hour out of Charleston, just so he could propose.

They were married on a Friday and, on Saturday, Nerie David Clark shipped out for Holland. Septima would stay behind to finish out her teaching contract. It was her third job in four years and, for a while, it would be her last. She was destined for a change even more dramatic than the one awaiting Waring. But like the future judge, Septima Clark was confident that she knew what she was doing.

THE LIVIN' IS EASY

O nce again, Charleston was too poor to paint.

The city's short-lived, war-fueled renaissance had all but dissipated by the early 1920s. The cotton market bottomed out, the port fell into disrepair and, shortly after the armistice, the Navy cut 2,000 civilian jobs. So many people left town to find work that by 1922 Charleston's population had declined by 4,000. There was no way to whitewash it.

Mayor John P. Grace, who reclaimed the office in 1919, tried to resuscitate the local economy with a lavish spending spree. He'd always fancied infrastructure – paving streets throughout his first term – so he turned his attention to the city's dilapidated docks. The mayor bought the waterfront land from the railroads and turned it over to a commission that eventually would become the State Ports Authority. When the $1.5 million check cleared, the city's debt, already perilously high, grew exponentially.

Grace was frustrated. His limited tax base couldn't handle the debt, yet nothing he did lured new investments to Charleston. It seemed everyone in the country was carrying their money to Florida, which wasn't fair. South Carolina had the same sun, the same beaches and the same ocean – but Florida had all the tourists. Of course, this gave the mayor an idea.

The city donated land on The Battery for a waterfront inn, which would open in 1924 as the Fort Sumter Hotel. At the same time, the grand Francis Marion Hotel was under construction across from Marion Square. Both would be ready by the time the city gained some fame, and tourists, for "The Charleston" dance craze.

Before either hotel opened, however, Grace would lose his job again. Thomas Porcher Stoney won the 1923 mayor's race. But Grace wasn't finished building things in Charleston just yet.

Waring fared better than his hometown throughout the 1920s. It was a glorious – and lucrative – time for him, his longest sustained period as an attorney exclusively in private practice. Much of his work unsurprisingly came in federal court, where he represented former mayor Tristram Hyde when he was charged with violating national bank laws. Waring even defended bootleggers in Prohibition cases, his preferred side of the Volstead Act. And he benefitted from the emerging tourism market when he represented a man who sued the Francis Marion builders for fraud.

His oddest case came out of Columbia and consumed nearly three years. A woman was accused of sending poison pen letters to a young couple, which was an abuse of the U.S. mail. Allegedly she had unrequited fantasies about the man and was jealous. Waring trudged to Florence and Columbia through two mistrials before the woman was convicted. If Waring was displeased by the outcome, he at least appreciated the free advertising. The state's newspapers ran countless, and breathless, stories about the case – nothing sold rack copies as well as headlines that included the words "poison pen."

Not that Waring needed much publicity. At 42, he was as connected as anyone in Charleston. He was part of the Broad Street ring, an officer in the Democratic Party and served on the College of Charleston board of trustees. His brother was editor of the local paper, his law partner was in the legislature and, in May 1922, his brother-in-law became governor.

Waring's sister, Margaret, had married widower Wilson Godfrey Harvey not long after his first wife died. A Charleston native, Harvey was a businessman and had been a city alderman before his election as lieutenant governor in 1920. Waring liked him a good deal and respected his opinion. In fact, Harvey had suggested his law partnership with D.A. Brockinton – who was also, conveniently, his son-in-law. The firm got a nice retainer handling all the legal business for Harvey's bank.

When Gov. Robert Cooper resigned to take a position on the Federal Farm Loan Board, Harvey took his place. He became the first governor from Charleston since before the Civil War, which said more about South Carolina attitudes toward the Holy City than anything else. Waring's connection to the governor brought him even more business, but it didn't last long. There was less than a year left in Cooper's term, and Harvey opted not to run. He wanted to get back to his business.

That executive decision may have come, in part, from Margaret. She was no more pleased to be the state's first lady than her husband was to be governor. The Charleston papers noted that Mrs. Harvey was forced to spend most of the summer entertaining at the governor's mansion in Columbia, as was expected. This cut into her annual vacation in the mountains of North Carolina.

Like most Charlestonians of the day, Waring lamented what little change had come to his hometown. He groused about the 10-cent stores and chain retailers – Sears and Roebuck, A&P supermarkets and S.H. Kress & Co. – that increasingly dominated the peninsula, most of them on King Street. Charleston was on the verge of becoming another generic Southern city, and the idea did not appeal to him.

He wouldn't let this wariness cut into his profits, of course. Kress eventually hired Waring & Brockinton to handle all its local legal matters. That included buying several buildings and setting up a grand new store – complete with soda fountain – on King Street.

Waring made more money than his family had seen in generations by mingling with these newcomers, but his social life was still grounded in old Charleston society. He remained active, if slightly less involved, in most of the groups that had dominated his calendar a decade earlier. Even with a young daughter at home, Waring didn't miss the St. Cecilia Society ball. But more often, he was distracted by work and, like Margaret, had to forego his annual mountain vacations.

Downtown residents had abandoned the peninsula every summer for two centuries, initially to avoid disease spurred by the volatile mixture of heat and urban life. Over time, summering in the North Carolina mountains became just another Charleston custom – one that had grown to include nearby beaches as an acceptable alternative. Waring finally had enough money to honor that tradition: He bought a beach house on Sullivan's Island.

It was the perfect time to relax. He and Annie were in their 40s, little Anne was 4, and they wanted for nothing. So the family would close up 61 Meeting Street, usually in July, and retreat to their cozy cabin at Station 26 – just a few blocks from the swanky Atlantic Beach Hotel. They usually stayed two months.

At the time, Sullivan's Island still belonged to the federal government and there were strict development rules. Anyone could lease at least a half-acre and build a house, with the understanding that the government could reclaim the property at its whim. The gamble, however, was worth the payoff.

It was quiet on the island. The sea breeze kept the temperature down, the beaches were calm and the water shallow. Most mornings, Waring left his wife and daughter to roam the sandy shore while he took the trolley to Mount Pleasant, where he caught the downtown ferry. Broad Street called, no matter what the temperature.

The living was easy for Waring. He could sit on the beach house porch at night and drink to a soundtrack of rustling palm fronds and gull calls. But he could never completely relax – he had to be involved. By the end of 1923, he was secretary and treasurer of the Sullivan's Island Improvement Society. Two years later, around the time the Atlantic Beach Hotel burned down, he was appointed the society's president.

Waring helped draft a limited development plan for the island, one that prohibited future hotels. Sullivan's, he declared, would not become a Florida-style tourist mecca. By then, the Florida land boom had run its course. Old Charlestonians, who'd never bought in to the tourism idea, felt vindicated.

As Waring plotted a future for Sullivan's Island, his downtown neighbors were pursuing similar measures to protect the historic district. And one of them, a former Sullivan's Island resident, was about to make Charleston famous for something other than the Civil War.

Many of Waring's peers feared modern development would destroy Charleston's historic façade and unique character. In response to this threat, Susan Frost Pringle led efforts to establish the Society for Preservation of Old Dwellings. The group, which would eventually become the Preservation Society of Charleston, formed during an afternoon tea at 20 South Battery to save the Joseph Manigault House. The mansion, which dated to at least 1803, was slated for demolition. Developers wanted to replace it with, of all things, a gas station.

Rescuing the Manigault House emboldened the society to take on even more ambitious projects. The group raised money to buy and restore property around the peninsula, and lobbied the city to protect historic buildings with new zoning laws. The Warings were early contributors, particularly Annie. One of the society's first investments was a handful of houses along East Bay Street that would come to be called Rainbow Row. This pastel-colored collection of narrow homes would launch a thousand postcards and become a famous tourist attraction. For years, however, many tourists mistook Rainbow Row for nearby Cabbage Row, which held a far different claim to fame.

DuBose Heyward was an insurance salesman by trade, and an artist at heart. A published poet, he attempted to revive the local arts scene with his own poetry society. He soon had an idea for his first novel, based on a newspaper story about a local man – a cripple and a beggar, he was called – who'd been charged with shooting a woman. Heyward put these characters into an atmospheric world that blended Church Street's Cabbage Row with the waterfront wharves. *Porgy* was an instant success.

It seemed absurd – a South of Broad white man writing about Charleston culture. Like Waring, Heyward could trace his lineage to the city's earliest days, and his name represented two prestigious local families. But Heyward had a greater perspective than most of his peers. His father died when Heyward was just a boy, and his grieving mother had turned her attention to the Lowcountry's Gullah culture. She learned the language, recorded the legends of the people in unpublished stories – and passed all this down to her son.

As a young man, Heyward worked alongside African Americans on a cotton plantation and on the city's docks. He kept up with the people he met while selling burial insurance in black tenements such as Cabbage Row. He came to know people his neighbors barely acknowledged, and it opened his eyes to a different world. *Porgy* reflected years of observation, and was the first novel written by a white man to portray black characters as anything other than stereotypes.

Heyward hadn't intended to make a political statement – those would come later – but his novel's humanity and empathy was hailed nationally. If The New York Times' attention provoked skepticism among locals, The Evening Post allayed their suspicions. The local paper called *Porgy* a "remarkable analysis of the Negro's psychology." But The Post also claimed the book was not a statement on race relations, it merely studied black lifestyles.

Heyward did little to dissuade that opinion locally. In talks around the city, he spoke more about art than the struggle of black Charlestonians. He realized that wasn't a conversation his hometown was ready to have. But he would keep steering it in that direction.

The poetry society was one of the few local clubs Waring never joined. His brother, Thomas, was a member and, of course, Waring knew Heyward. But his appreciation of the poet's work, and message, would not come until later.

Views on race notwithstanding, Charleston was slowly becoming a less insular place.

In 1926, a bridge opened that connected the peninsula to the western mainland, and former Mayor Grace was working on a span to link the city to Mount Pleasant. Both opened downtown to rural families, many of them black, who had rarely ventured into Charleston. At the Cooper River bridge dedication in August 1929, Grace was hailed as a champion of the poor. No one was impolite enough to mention the bridge was actually designed to connect Charleston to an Isle of Palms resort.

By the time the Grace toll bridge opened, however, the Seashore Hotel had burned down in a fire similar to the one that claimed the Atlantic Hotel on Sullivan's. Soon, the loss of those resorts wouldn't matter. Charleston's flirtation with tourism ended, at least temporarily, when the stock market crashed a few months later.

Most Charleston residents didn't even notice the Great Depression for a while; they'd been living in similarly hardscrabble conditions for years. The city's debt had reached the point of crisis, and unemployment was so rampant that many people couldn't pay their property taxes. Mayor Stoney didn't bother to seek re-election, a decision that changed Waring's life.

After years of turmoil, and a mayoral election with a death toll, the city had no appetite for another fight. Charleston's most prominent leaders decided they wanted a consensus candidate for mayor, and spent months debating their options in smoke-filled rooms at the Francis Marion Hotel. Eventually, they agreed the next mayor should be first-term city alderman Burnet Rhett Maybank.

He was the prototypical Charlestonian. Maybank's family dated back to the city's earliest days, and even included a couple of former governors. He belonged to all of Charleston's most exclusive clubs, including the Episcopal Church, and even made his money the old-fashioned way – exporting cotton. Maybank was a savvy businessman, just the sort of person needed to stop the city's economic death spiral.

Maybank agreed to run, and persuaded Waring to serve as his legal adviser. The two men knew each other socially, but weren't particularly close; at 32, Maybank was nearly 20 years younger. Perhaps Maybank recruited Waring because they had similar backgrounds, but it was more likely that he simply wanted a smart lawyer with ties to the Democratic Party. Because, in truth, there really was no consensus in Charleston.

The city power brokers asked former Mayor Grace for an endorsement, hoping to avoid a contentious – or contested – election. He agreed at first, but Grace soon quarreled with Maybank and, in retaliation, recruited city alderman Lawrence M. Pinckney to run. In truth, Grace relished the chance to take on the Broad Street ring, which had never shown him much support.

The two sides dug in for a long summer, and the campaign was a study in contrasts. Maybank was the young newcomer businessman and Pinckney, 26 years his senior, was a local insurance agent and veteran politician. Waring called it "a pretty bitter" campaign, but in the end, it was no contest. Maybank won the Democratic primary by 4,600 votes, sweeping every ward. No Republican bothered to file, so Maybank was anointed in the December election.

Waring became one of the new mayor's advisers, a part of the inner circle. One of Maybank's first acts was to appoint him corporation counsel, which was basically the city's attorney. Waring realized this wasn't simply another retainer, but had no idea how much municipal government would consume his life.

Shortly after the election, the People's Bank of South Carolina failed – another victim of the Great Depression. This was a delicate problem on many levels, but primarily because that's where all the city's funds were on deposit. Charleston was in effect bankrupt, too – no cash, no way to pay its employees. Waring's job was to remedy the situation.

Because bankruptcy court was part of the federal judicial system, Waring went into court confident. He argued that government funds were protected by law, but the judge quickly told him to get in line with the other creditors. It took months to reclaim the money. To keep Charleston operating, Maybank persuaded city workers to accept scrips – IOUs, basically – instead of their salaries. City workers would get their pay, with four percent interest, when property taxes were collected in November.

It was Waring's job to make sure people actually paid their taxes, which wasn't easy.

"Friends of the former administration hadn't been bothered, and a lot of them owed an awful lot of money. They thought it was a great hardship that they had to pay," Waring recalled. "Well, the little people had been paying. The big ones hadn't. We put the squeeze on them, gave them time when they showed that they needed time, provided that they started doing something."

That sense of fairness guided Waring, but it wasn't consistent during his time as corporation counsel. Years later, when the city leased part of Stoney Field to the Army, Waring insisted only white soldiers could use the park. He was only doing what his client, the city of Charleston, had asked of him. At the time, it likely didn't even occur to Waring that this was discriminatory.

He'd lived his entire life in a segregated society.

Every New Year's Day, the Warings hosted a drop-in party at 61 Meeting Street. They opened the door at 1 p.m. and, for a few hours, people casually stopped by to chat, have a drink or eat collard greens and Hoppin' John. Most of Charleston's influential and elite made an appearance, at least for a minute. It had become an annual tradition that always warranted mention in the social columns.

Waring's life became a pattern, a series of regular events as reliable as any calendar. He attended every formal at the St. Cecilia Society and, on St. Patrick's Day, he was always at Hibernian Hall. The whole family followed a life established by their ancestors. Waring worked on Broad Street, Annie stayed busy with her clubs and Anne went to Ashley Hall, because it was the only acceptable school for South of Broad girls. Then they summered on Sullivan's Island. That's just the way it was.

The summers at the beach house became one long party with a revolving cast of guests. Their friends wandered out for the weekend, and Waring's brother, Thomas, stopped by occasionally. In 1932, Margaret came in from Tampa and stayed a week. The next year, Waring's brother, Edward, drove up from his home in Jacksonville and reminisced for a few days.

In September 1933, the Warings closed the beach house early and set out on a cross-country road trip. They took Anne, soon to be 15, and one of her friends to the Century of Progress Exposition in Chicago. The family spent a week touring endless exhibits that promised a glimpse of the future, and watching performances by future stars such as Judy Garland and the Andrews Sisters.

Soon after the Warings returned home, Charleston had its own brush with celebrity. The famed composer George Gershwin was in town doing research for a new opera with a local connection. DuBose Heyward and his wife, Dorothy, had written a play based on *Porgy*, and Gershwin decided to set it to music. By summer, Gershwin had rented a piano on King Street and a cabin on Folly Beach, where he would write his libretto.

Gershwin spent a month immersed in Gullah culture, attending church services and trying to pick up the local dialect. Frank Gilbreth, a young reporter from The News and Courier, found the composer tanned and bare-chested on Folly. Depending on his mood, he passed his days roaming the beach or banging out "I Got Rhythm" for his housekeeper. He claimed the island was so relaxing he could barely work, but he did. The Heywards, who had their own cabin nearby, supplied most of the lyrics – a job normally reserved for Gershwin's brother, Ira.

Porgy and Bess would become an instant Broadway classic and, within two years, Billie Holiday would be singing its most famous aria, "Summertime," on the radio. But Gershwin and the Heywards would be dead before the opera was performed in Charleston – the city where it was set, and where it was written. Local ordinances, and the tenets of segregation, prohibited black actors from performing onstage in public facilities.

In Charleston of the 1930s, that's also just the way it was.

THE CAMPAIGN

T he first hint that Waring was destined for the bench came in 1934, and it surprised absolutely no one who knew him.

Waring had quietly coveted a federal judgeship for at least two decades. He believed U.S. District judges were among the most influential people in the country, public officials with the unilateral power to set all things right. He rarely spoke of this ambition – that would have been unseemly – but everyone knew. It was the reason he'd briefly campaigned for an appointment as U.S. attorney in 1930. He thought a strong prosecutorial record would help him get the job he really wanted, a means to an end.

The Justice Department had passed on him for the U.S. attorney post, in part because of his outspoken opposition to Prohibition. By 1934, however, there was a new administration, Prohibition had been repealed and Waring became a leading contender for the judgeship he'd wanted for so long. But it came at a price.

U.S. District Judge Ernest F. Cochran was nearing the end of his tenure. The former district attorney had been on the bench since 1923, and most people expected him to retire within a year – if he made it even that long. Cochran had taken an extended leave of absence the previous summer, and rumors were that he'd had a nervous breakdown and spent weeks in an out-of-state hospital.

Waring admired Cochran, even if he was a Republican, and felt he always got a fair shake in his courtroom. He was encouraged to hear the old man was getting better, although he had not yet returned from his absence. And he never would.

On Saturday night, March 3, 1934, the judge played cards with some friends at his Tradd Street home. When the game broke up, Cochran retired to his bedroom. His wife decided to let him sleep in the next morning, but when he didn't appear by 10 a.m. she went to check on him. She found the judge dead – a silk scarf around his neck, the other end tied to the bedpost.

The tragedy, including details of Cochran's extended stay in a mental institution, filled the Monday newspapers. His friends did their best to bury the scandal, and the judge. The coroner ruled his death a suicide on Sunday, before anyone knew what had happened, and the family held a hasty funeral service in his home the next day. Waring was one of the pallbearers.

The jockeying to replace Cochran began before the services ended.

Waring later said he had nothing to do with the campaign, and certainly never asked for any endorsements. But his friends bombarded the Justice Department with letters recommending him for Cochran's seat. Lawyers and former clients were Waring's greatest advocates but, although tireless in their efforts, they carried little weight. Politics reigned in judicial nominations. South Carolina's two U.S. senators would have the final say. Everything else was just noise.

The state's senior senator was Ellison DuRant Smith, or "Cotton Ed" as most people knew him. He'd earned that nickname for his vast knowledge of farming issues, which was famously his only field of expertise – other than demagoguery. Smith had held his seat for 25 years by playing the populist foe of the Washington establishment. He was slowly expanding his repertoire to include race-baiting, a trick he'd learned serving nine years alongside Ben Tillman.

Waring had known Smith for years, even liked him. They met through his old boss, Francis Weston, who managed several of Cotton Ed's campaigns. In elections past, Waring had organized events for the senator and once served as his Charleston campaign chairman. He thought the old man was charming and funny – even if he often found his politics ridiculous.

"His racial talks were to get the boys in the backwoods to vote for him, and they did," Waring later recalled. "He was a nice old chap in a great many ways and very amusing and could make a wonderful speech to a half-literate group of voters."

Within days of Cochran's death, Smith leaked the names of his preferences for a replacement – and Waring was unsurprisingly second on the shortlist. Most people assumed he had the inside track, given his close ties to Cotton Ed. But it wasn't that simple. South Carolina's other senator, Jimmy Byrnes, soon got involved. And it appeared he'd promised the judgeship to someone else.

Byrnes would have seemed like a natural advocate for Waring. He was also from an old Charleston family, belonged to the same clubs and had gone into law as a young man. But Byrnes had been more interested in making law than practicing it. He got elected to Congress in 1910 and served 14 years before losing his first bid for the U.S. Senate. He finally won the seat in 1930. Waring wasn't close to Byrnes, but knew him well enough to realize that as soon as Frank Myers was mentioned as a candidate, he'd lost the judgeship.

Myers was a state master-in-equity and local attorney, although nowhere near Waring's equal; he'd never even been admitted to practice in federal court. He was a nice man – and completely unqualified for the job. But years earlier, Myers had been law partners with a young Charlestonian named James Byrnes.

When Myers' name surfaced, a story – probably apocryphal – began circulating in Charleston. As young lawyers, Byrnes and Myers once talked about their respective ambitions. Byrnes had confessed he wanted to be a United States senator, and Myers said he dreamed of becoming a federal judge. So, the story went, Byrnes had told him, "When I become United States senator, I'll appoint you United States judge." Waring was skeptical of the story, but knew its veracity mattered little. The fix was in.

The parlor game dragged on long enough to give Waring a glimmer of hope. There were rumors the Justice Department had serious concerns about Myers: He knew little about federal practice and had no experience in bankruptcy or criminal law. Among the Broad Street ring, the conventional wisdom was that Byrnes would be laughed out of Washington if he tried to appoint his former partner. Beside, most attorneys noted, Smith was the senior senator and held more sway.

But the politics were slightly more complicated. Byrnes was close to President Franklin Delano Roosevelt, and Smith's support for the administration, always tepid, was noticeably slipping. Myers also had other Roosevelt allies in his corner. His daughter was married to a vocal FDR supporter, who also happened to be the mayor of Charleston … and Waring's boss. Burnet Maybank assured his friend that he was probably a lock for the job, but made no secret of his loyalties.

"You know, I've talked to you about federal judge sometime, and I'm for you unless my father-in-law is appointed, and I don't think there's any chance of that," Maybank told Waring.

Three months after Cochran's death, Roosevelt nominated Myers for U.S. district judge in the Eastern District of South Carolina. He was confirmed by the Senate and sworn into office in less than two weeks.

He'd been so close.

Waring was disappointed to lose the judgeship, but he understood the politics better than most. He wasn't one to whine, so he simply went about his business – and there was no shortage of it in the Charleston corporation counsel's office.

He prosecuted the former treasurer of the city waterworks for embezzling $48,000. Then he wrote new rules for city taxis. And when the city courted a paper mill, Waring double-dipped and represented both sides. He spent more than a year working out the details of a tunnel to carry water from the Edisto River to Goose Creek for the plant.

Maybank's ties to the Roosevelt administration, including the head of the new Works Progress Administration, kept Waring in Washington regularly. The mayor secured a series of grants that slowly pulled Charleston out of debt. The city invested this money in public works projects, and hired locals to do the work – even if it was just repairing old buildings or sweeping streets. Some of it was sheer largesse, but Maybank also won $350,000 to renovate the Dock Street Theatre.

When it was finally finished in late 1937, Life Magazine showed up to chronicle the celebration – "First U.S. Theatre Restored: Charleston blue bloods give it gala opening." Annie appeared in one of the magazine's photographs, sitting in one of the elegant theatre's private boxes.

The South of Broad crowd scoffed at the unsustainability of accepting these federal handouts, but Waring credited Maybank with saving the city – and most residents agreed. In 1935, he was re-elected without opposition. Charleston hadn't seen such a calm election in years.

No one welcomed the reprieve from another campaign more than Waring; he had more pressing duties at the time. For several weeks that summer, he toured northeastern college campuses with Anne. They visited Bryn Mawr in Pennsylvania before moving on to Massachusetts and New Hampshire. Finally, Anne decided on Goucher College, just outside of Baltimore. She promised to come home for the holidays.

Life was changing for Waring, and not for the better. His brother, Thomas, died in June, leaving him the only remaining member of the immediate family in Charleston. In little more than a year, his other brother, Edward, would pass as well. Waring felt more alone than ever. When Annie took an extended trip to New York City to visit her sister, stopping in Baltimore to see Anne, Waring was left to rattle around 61 Meeting Street by himself for weeks. It did little to help his increasing feelings of isolation.

Anne was home enough in 1937 to keep Waring somewhat happy. She showed up at the Sullivan's Island beach house late that summer, following a trip to Paris, and returned in December for her coming-out party. It began with a fete at the Yacht Club and, a week later, she was formally presented to society with a dance at Hibernian Hall. By the time Waring and Annie opened 61 Meeting Street for the New Year's Day drop-in, they were exhausted.

He wouldn't have long to recuperate. In early 1938, Maybank announced his candidacy for governor and asked Waring to serve as one of the campaign's advisers. He was reluctant to take on a statewide operation, but he dutifully agreed.

Maybank had considered running for the Senate against Cotton Ed, but abandoned the idea when Gov. Olin Johnston jumped into the race. Governor was simply the next logical move. Even though Charleston candidates rarely did well in statewide contests, Democratic Party officials could hardly grouse about Maybank. In two terms as Charleston's mayor he'd completely turned around a city that had been crippled by debt and, to be honest, had never recovered from the Civil War. He was a strong candidate.

Maybank ran on his mayoral record and the usual statewide political niceties, including fiscal responsibility and a bright future for children. At the state convention that May, Waring stood and made the nomination himself. But when the meeting ended, there were eight candidates – two of whom posed a serious threat.

Coleman Blease was almost a caricature of the typical South Carolina politician, which made him wildly popular in the hinterlands. He'd been a U.S. senator and governor, and a loyal disciple of Ben Tillman. Blease was a staunch proponent of segregation and lynching and, as senator, once proposed an anti-miscegenation amendment to the U.S. Constitution. He'd resigned as governor five days before his term expired to avoid the inauguration of Richard Manning III – who won on an anti-Blease progressive platform. When his name appeared on the 1938 ballot, it marked Blease's fourth try to reclaim the governor's office.

His perennial campaign was interesting only because one of the other candidates was Wyndham Manning, son of the former governor that Blease so despised. Manning had ridden his family name to two terms in the state House of Representatives, and unsuccessfully ran for governor against Johnston in 1934. Between these two retreads, Maybank believed his fresh face would carry him. But no Charlestonian had ever won a statewide popular vote for governor.

It was another long summer. The candidates roamed the state, pandering to whatever region they happened to visit that day – the Upstate, Midlands or Pee Dee. They accused one another of corruption, called their opponents party hacks and FDR loyalists. In other words, it was a typical South Carolina campaign. Buoyed by a strong turnout in the Lowcountry, Maybank carried 35 percent of the vote in the Aug. 30 primary. Manning came in second with 22 percent, setting up a Sept. 13 runoff.

Then things turned even nastier.

Manning worried about low turnout for the runoff, and the Charleston machine's ability to take advantage of it, so he asked the state to dispatch National Guardsmen as poll watchers. Gov. Johnston helpfully obliged, which most people read as a tacit endorsement. And on election night, it appeared Manning's concerns had been justified.

With most of the state's precincts reporting, Manning had a comfortable 7,000-vote lead. Then Charleston delivered its ballots. There were only 1,365 recorded votes for Manning – and 21,532 for Maybank. Although the mayor could be expected to win his home county, he had miraculously taken 94 percent of the vote, a suspiciously lopsided victory.

Of course, Manning supporters cried foul. They called the Charleston vote a "riotous orgy of partisanship" and filed a challenge with the state Democratic executive committee. They had no shortage of outlandish stories to back up their tawdry accusations.

Manning claimed the Charleston ballot boxes had not been padlocked and a large number of dead people appeared on the voter rolls. His campaign supplied the executive committee with 18 affidavits from poll watchers, some of whom claimed the tally sheets in many precincts were filled out before the voting. Others said various precincts closed while voters were still in line. And, most audaciously, one witness claimed that he'd watched men drop handfuls of ballots into several boxes.

The Democratic executive committee agreed to hear the case the following week. The job of defending Maybank, and Charleston's entire political machine, fell to Waring.

The South Carolina Democratic Party executive committee met in the old Columbia city hall on Tuesday, Sept. 20. Manning campaign staffers filled half the room, and more than 50 people from Charleston had driven up to attend. Some packed the benches behind Maybank and his wife, the rest spilled out into the hall. The crowd was restless and loud, the governor's office and regional pride at stake.

Most of the people in the room had known Waring for decades, but few had ever watched him perform. That afternoon, he put on a show none of them would ever forget. He played the outraged, offended victim perfectly, with three decades of courtroom experience behind him. His melodrama was masterful.

The charges by Manning, Waring said, were "false and slanderous," and he denied them "in toto" – throwing in his best legalese for effect. He said there was no question why so many Charleston County residents had come out to vote. During the primary they had been "singled out and defamed from one end of South Carolina to the other" by the Manning campaign. It would have been more surprising, he argued, had the turnout been weaker.

"The astonishing thing was not that Maybank received over 20,000 votes," Waring said, "but that Manning received more than 1,300."

Waring conceded there were irregularities – as he put it – with one ballot box. But he argued that even if the results from every precinct Manning had challenged were thrown out, Maybank would still win the county by 11,000 votes; this, when all he needed was 6,000 to prevail statewide. Waring even provided tally sheets to prove his point.

It was one of the greatest defenses Waring had ever presented, and it hadn't come in a courtroom. Most importantly, it convinced the only person who mattered. When Waring finished, state Sen. Edgar Brown, an influential member of the executive committee, announced that he didn't think the statements of 18 people should disenfranchise more than 20,000 voters. That was all it took. The committee voted 41-0 – with six members abstaining – to dismiss Manning's protest. The vote handed Maybank the nomination.

That night, thousands of cheering supporters met Maybank at the county line. After a few handshakes, three police cars escorted him to Marion Square, where even more people turned out to celebrate the first Charlestonian elected governor by popular vote. Although the general election was more than a month away, everyone knew it was merely a formality. In November, fewer than 50,000 people statewide bothered to vote. The Republican nominee, Joseph Augustis Tolbert, failed to win even 300 votes.

South Carolina remained the definition of a one-party state.

Waring could have had his pick of jobs in the new administration, but he turned down every overture from Maybank. He made feeble excuses – he wanted to stay in Charleston, his law practice needed attention, incoming Mayor Henry Lockwood had asked him to remain corporation counsel. Of course, there was more to it than that.

Over the course of the gubernatorial campaign, Waring had cooled to Maybank. He never said exactly why. It didn't take much to set off Waring; friends said he wouldn't forget the smallest slight. But something had happened, and Waring held a grudge. He would visit Maybank in Columbia on occasion, and they remained outwardly friendly – but privately Waring became critical of the governor.

And soon, Maybank would give him good reason to feel that way.

Waring had claimed he didn't want to upend his life, but following the 1938 governor's campaign, that is exactly what he did. He resigned as vice president of the College of Charleston's board of trustees after 20 years. He stopped volunteering to organize events and chair committees. He remained the city's attorney, but did little of note. Annie's name appeared in the newspaper more regularly than his.

By 1940, Waring seemed very much like a man who was clearing the decks, waiting for something. Perhaps it had something to do with the recent gossip in Charleston. According to some, U.S. District Judge Frank Myers was gravely ill.

Waring had passed on a federal judgeship in 1939. South Carolina had three district judges – one for the Eastern District, another for the Western and a "roving" judge that filled in for the others. The roving judge had died, and most people assumed Waring would replace him. But he'd quashed that speculation by publicly announcing he wasn't interested. That judgeship, he said, should go to someone outside Charleston. He was so dismissive that "Cotton Ed" didn't bother to put him up for the job.

It appeared Waring had simply lost his ambition, given up the dream. He was 60, only a few years younger than his brothers had been when they died, and some people assumed he was contemplating his own mortality. Or perhaps he was just ready to retire. But then a series of political dominoes fell that he could not ignore. All his plans, whatever they were, changed.

Judge Myers died of cancer in August 1940. A few months later, President Roosevelt appointed Byrnes to the United States Supreme Court, and his Senate seat went to South Carolina's new roving U.S. District judge. Suddenly, two of the state's three federal judgeships were open – including the Eastern District seat based in Charleston.

When Gov. Maybank announced his plans to campaign for Byrnes' Senate seat in a special election, the Broad Street ring quickly did the calculus: Maybank would win, and Waring would have two senators in his corner. Everything had fallen into place. But whenever Waring was asked about such a scenario, he simply said "I don't know." It was at least an honest answer. Waring didn't know, because he was too stubborn to ask.

He had every right to expect a favor and, by any measure, Maybank owed him – but Waring wouldn't make the call. According to the Broad Street grapevine, Maybank had promised Myers' seat to a number of people, and it only confirmed Waring's growing opinion. The governor would say anything to the person standing in front of him, he believed, then promptly forget it. Waring's internal hostility lingered, and grew, for months.

Waring refused to beg. Maybank knew he wanted the Charleston judgeship, and he shouldn't have to ask for it – or stand in line behind party hacks. He was still seething about this on the day Maybank unexpectedly walked into his Broad Street law office.

"I want to talk to you about the campaign," the governor said.

Maybank asked Waring to run his Senate race, at least in Charleston County, maybe statewide. It made perfect sense to the governor. Waring had been a key part of every major campaign he'd won, and he saw no reason to change the formula. Perhaps Maybank expected his old friend to be flattered, but Waring was furious – and he did a poor job of hiding it.

"I don't know if I can do that or not," Waring said.

Managing the campaign, Waring said, would put him in an awkward position. He reminded Maybank of his past offers to help him secure a judgeship and said he'd prefer to avoid any conflicts of interest. Waring explained that he didn't want any "future appointment" to look like patronage or payback – although he wouldn't hold the governor to any past promises. Of course, that's exactly what he was doing.

It was not an unreasonable position for Waring to take, but Maybank wouldn't bite, or even acknowledge his past assurances. The governor said he'd only come to talk about the Senate campaign; he couldn't discuss the judgeship or make any commitments.

"Neither can I," Waring replied. "I'll vote for you but that's all."

As Waring remembered it later, Maybank left the office "pretty disgruntled."

From their exchange, Waring assumed the rumors on Broad Street were true, and that he'd just thrown away any chance of a federal judgeship.

Maybank won the U.S. Senate race without Waring's help.

The two men never spoke during the campaign, and hadn't seen each other since their testy meeting at Waring's law office. But they couldn't avoid each other forever. Myers had fallen behind on his caseload long before his death, and the roving judgeship had been vacant for most of a year. South Carolina's docket was backed up, and the Justice Department wanted nominees as soon as Maybank was sworn in.

Sen. Smith already had submitted a list of potential candidates, including Waring's name near the top of his list. Maybank agreed he'd make a good nominee, and suggested the Justice Department consider him for the Eastern District seat – which is exactly what Waring wanted. But again, the politics were more complicated than that.

Later, Waring learned that Maybank was under pressure to appoint Midlands attorney and former state lawmaker George Bell Timmerman to the bench. The only problem was, Cotton Ed hated Timmerman. At a stalemate, the two senators cut a deal: Smith wouldn't oppose Timmerman's nomination for the roving judgeship, which was perfect for a man who lived in the middle of the state. In return, Maybank would support Waring for the Eastern District.

One evening in November 1941, the phone rang at 61 Meeting Street. It was late, an odd time for a call. But when Waring answered, he heard Maybank's unmistakable, nearly indecipherable drawl on the line. He was calling long distance from Washington, ready to make amends with his old friend.

"I just wanted to tell you that the president is going to send in two names for the judgeships, and you are the one from Charleston," Maybank said.

Years later, Waring claimed he almost fainted. At 61, he'd given up nearly all hope. Now, a voice from the past, a man he'd practically run out of his office a few months earlier, was offering him the one thing he'd always wanted. He could do little more than stammer and ask inane questions.

"What?" he asked. "Who else?"

Maybank patiently explained the deal and told him about Timmerman, obviously pleased with his political horse-trading abilities. He said the arrangement was perfect, and pointed out that Waring would be working out of the Charleston courthouse, just a block from his home.

"This is highly confidential. Don't mention it to anyone," Maybank said. "It will go over. The Department of Justice has arranged it. It's just a matter of the president signing the designation. It may go to the Senate tomorrow."

It wasn't quite that easy. The Justice Department was leery of appointing a man so old to the bench, and initially balked at Waring, but the court was too backlogged to argue for long. Then Waring's friends worried about his confirmation hearing, and urged him to avoid his disdainful views on religion and his typical contrarian opinions of federal law. But Waring knew what to do. He'd prepared for this his entire life.

The world was about to change, even more than Waring realized. Within a few weeks, the Japanese would attack Pearl Harbor, drawing the United States into another worldwide conflict. By the time it ended, everything would be different – Charleston, the country and Waring.

Twelve days after Pearl Harbor, The News and Courier reported that President Roosevelt had nominated J. Waties Waring as the next U.S. District judge for the Eastern District of South Carolina. It had been 40 years and one week since he'd left the Ivory City to take the Bar exam and begin his legal career, but he'd finally fulfilled his parents' prediction.

He was a federal court judge.

PART II

THE SEEDS OF JUSTICE

A SERVANT OF THE PUBLIC

On Jan. 26, 1942, Waties Waring walked the single block from 61 Meeting Street to the courthouse with Annie and his sister, Margaret. It was a comfortable, sunny morning, the temperature on its way to 67 degrees – far above normal for the month.

They chatted as they strolled past the twin staircases of the neoclassical South Carolina Society Hall and the brick walls that hid South of Broad gardens. Ahead, they could just see the familiar white spire of St. Michael's Church peeking over a moss-laden live oak. A postcard, a perfect Charleston scene.

The federal courthouse he knew so well looked different that morning. Its granite exterior, weathered by nearly a half-century in the Lowcountry sun, seemed to glow on this day. For years, he had practiced inside the building's second-floor courtroom – an elegant, Victorian chamber with polished dark paneling. Now, that would be his office.

This was the walk he'd waited decades to make and, save for one thing, it was idyllic. The war overshadowed Waring's ascension to the bench.

On this day, Charleston was preoccupied with reports that the U.S. fleet had retaliated for Pearl Harbor over the weekend, sinking at least seven Japanese ships in the Makassar Strait. Five of those ships were troop transports carrying nearly 35,000 Japanese soldiers to invade Borneo. Military officials called it the first large-scale naval engagement of the new war, and noted that no U.S. warships were lost in the battle. It was timely, and much-needed, good news.

In the weeks following President Roosevelt's declaration of war, the city had been unable to focus on anything other than the fighting in the Pacific. The prospects of another world war – Germany and Italy also had aligned against the United States – were terrifying, but some locals couldn't help but wonder how the conflict might benefit the local economy. After all, the Great War had saved Charleston from bankruptcy. World War II would bail it out again.

Over the next two years, the Navy base would hire 25,000 civilians to build, outfit and service U.S. warships. The Coast Guard would open a new station on the harbor and the Army would establish an air base near the county airport. Few cities in the country could claim such a sizable, diverse military presence. And that presented opportunity. Developers would build hundreds of new houses between the Army Air Base and the Navy base in an area locals called north Charleston. Within a year, military spending would raise the per-capita income in Charleston County to triple the state average. War was big business for the city.

As a result, almost all other local news – a new Santee Cooper power station at Pinopolis, the state's plan to establish a South Carolina department of educa-tion, the shooting of a black teenager at a peninsula pool hall – was relegated to the back pages of the newspapers. The announcement that a new judge would take his oath of office at noon barely warranted a mention.

Waring had waited decades to don the black robe, but now his anticipation was tempered by his concerns about the war. Although his unbridled cynicism knew almost no bounds, Waring was also deeply patriotic. As an assistant U.S. attorney, he'd handled most cases with detached professionalism, rarely show-ing emotion. It was just his job. But during the war, he'd prosecuted accused war criminals, even those only caught stealing rations, with a cold vengeance. Such things offended him.

The new war dominated his thoughts as his family and friends shuffled into the second-floor courtroom. Mayor Lockwood brought his police chief, and the County Bar Association and Broad Street ring were out in full force. The local district attorney and a few state lawmakers lingered near Waring's law partner, D.A. Brockinton. Charles Waring would take his uncle's place in the practice. His other nephew, Tom, was there as family – not as city editor of The News and Courier. The only person of color at the ceremony was Corine Chisolm, who'd worked in Waring's home for two decades.

U.S. District Judge C.C. Wyche from Spartanburg administered the oath of office promptly at noon and, afterward, a marshal draped the black robe over Waring's shoulders and escorted him to the bench. Waring spoke only a few minutes. He recalled the judges he'd worked with as a federal prosecutor, promised cooperation with the local Bar Association and declared himself "a servant of the public." He finished with a sober, patriotic message.

"This court is one of the things that we are fighting for now," Waring said. "This court and all the other courts, because a free court is a court where a judge is at liberty to express his views and exercise his own discretion, a court where a jury of citizens hears the evidence and decides issues according to the facts presented to them, without any coercion or pressure from anyone. That is liberty, and that is what America stands for, and that is why America is at war now, to preserve the way of American living, of which the judicial system is an integral and important part."

When he finished, Waring stepped down into the swell of people waiting to congratulate him. As he hugged Annie, he spotted his daughter in the crowd. Anne had flown in from New York for the ceremony and would leave before the day's end. When Waring saw her, he called out "My daughter!" and pulled her in for a kiss. It was the most overt public display of joy anyone had ever seen from Waring.

Before he left chambers, Waring announced that court would convene the next morning at 10. He was eager to begin, and never forgot that he was fortunate to have the opportunity. His appointment had not been nearly as easy as Maybank predicted.

After the White House announcement in December, a News and Courier editorial predicted Waring would be received "with satisfaction by the people of South Carolina, especially the people of Charleston." The paper called him an industrious lawyer and a man of excellent character. "Mr. Waring's appointment is a happy ending to what, for inexplicable reasons, has been too long delayed." But that sentiment was not universal, at least not in Washington.

"Cotton Ed" Smith was livid. Although he supported Waring, he was enraged by George Timmerman's appointment – which suggested Maybank's deal was not as ironclad as he'd claimed. Smith had been outfoxed. Even though he still held great sway in the Senate, the junior senator had much more pull with Roosevelt. When his supporters complained about Timmerman, "Cotton Ed" either feigned regret or groused that Maybank had snuck one past him. Either way, he would get revenge.

During the Senate confirmation hearings, Smith endorsed Waring – but not before mentioning that he'd assumed the Charleston lawyer was too old for the bench. It was a sly echo of the Justice Department's own concerns. The previous two judges for South Carolina's Eastern District, both elderly and ill, had allowed a monumental backlog of cases to accumulate. Justice officials worried that Waring would be no better, but eventually gave in to Maybank. In truth, they just needed someone to clear the docket.

Waring found this out on his own. That first week, he discovered the court's calendar was "encrusted with barnacles." Some of the cases dated back 14 years, into Judge Cochran's tenure. Waring had the clerk compile a list of the moldy cases and began calling lawyers, telling them to get ready for trial. The attorneys who complained, and many did, were given two months to prepare. The judge was amazed by the pushback; it was as if they didn't want to work – an attitude that Waring, once a hungry young lawyer, could not comprehend.

"I thought they owed me a debt of gratitude," he later said. "I suppose that they sent bills for their fees."

But Waring didn't upset anyone too much. Within months, the Bar Associations in Charleston and Columbia hosted banquets in honor of the new judge.

It didn't take long for Waring to settle in and put his own mark on the job. He found the federal court system slow and burdensome, and constantly looked for ways to streamline it. To clear the docket, he dismissed cases that weren't ready for trial, telling attorneys to re-file when they were prepared. In his first few weeks he sentenced 10 men who pleaded guilty to moonshining, and convicted another of attempting to impersonate an Army officer. Before long, the court was caught up and running smoothly.

In his first year on the bench, Waring traveled constantly. He held court in Florence and Spartanburg, and sat on a three-judge panel for the Fourth Circuit Court of Appeals in Richmond. The trips were exhausting, the hours long, but

Annie often went along to help him maintain some semblance of normalcy. She would soon be otherwise occupied, however. In June, during Waring's second court session in Charleston, Anne called her parents. She was getting married.

They spent most of the summer planning a proper Charleston wedding. Anne was engaged to Francis Edgar Stanley Warren, a Harvard graduate and theater publicist more than 10 years her senior. But Warren was a friendly enough fellow, the judge thought, and he approved of the marriage. The couple wed in a midweek ceremony at the Unitarian Church on Nov. 4.

The local papers featured the wedding on their society pages, but it was hardly a traditional Charleston affair. For one thing, Anne refused to wear a white gown. When Waring walked his daughter down the aisle, she wore a gold velveteen frock. Her mother made her own fashion statement. Annie watched from the front row in a wine-colored wool frock, in front of a crowd dominated by South of Broad regulars and Warren's Massachusetts family. Afterward, the Warings hosted what they considered a small reception at 61 Meeting Street.

The wedding was only a brief respite from his judicial schedule.

A few days after Anne and Stanley left town, Waring cleared the docket in Orangeburg – a town that didn't warrant a separate district but saw its share of federal cases. Although Timmerman had been appointed the state's roving judge, Waring also regularly filled in for other judges. In April 1943, he spent a week presiding at the Greenville courthouse, Annie waiting for him in the hotel every afternoon.

That spring, Waring briefly found himself on the other side of the bench. The government had decided to revoke the citizenship of Albert Orth, a native of Germany. Orth had lived in the United States for decades, but Justice Department officials were leery of a German roaming the countryside during a war – particularly one who'd been overheard bragging about Nazi victories and kept a framed picture of Adolf Hitler on his mantel. Waring was pulled into the case when he recused himself from the trial.

As assistant U.S. attorney, Waring had prosecuted Orth for harboring the crew of the *Liebenfels*, the ship that sank in Charleston during World War I.

Prosecutors recognized the potential for conflict and simply moved the case to Timmerman's court. But the German's attorney called Waring as a witness. He claimed Orth and Waring were friends, and produced a witness who said the judge had once called him a fine American citizen.

Waring was not intimidated by the witness stand, but he was outraged to have his patriotism questioned. When he appeared in Timmerman's court-room, Waring called the claims of his friendship with Orth "fantastical" and testified that he'd recommended revoking his citizenship two decades earlier. The Justice Department had sat on the request, he said, and quietly dropped it after the armistice. Timmerman took Waring at his word, revoked Orth's citizenship, and called in immigration authorities. The United States was no place for Nazi sympathizers.

In less than two years, Waring built a reputation as a capable, efficient jurist.

He was everywhere – attending the annual federal judges' conference in Asheville, substituting on the Fourth Circuit Court of Appeals in Baltimore – and senior judges took notice of his expedient courtroom style. Soon, he was invited to sit for vacationing judges around the country. During one session in Newark, Waring conducted 15 trials in 29 days. His no-nonsense approach prompted the local paper to write a story about his short tenure under the headline "Assembly-line justice."

"The visiting judge proved a stickler for opening court on the tick of the hour scheduled," the article said. It noted that he hustled one jury into the courtroom as quickly as the last one left, and courthouse regulars claimed they could set their watch to Waring's arrival. He later said his performance stood out only because the Newark courthouse was a little lax on discipline.

When he asked what time court began, the clerk had said, "Oh, sometime after 10 'o clock, 10:30 or 11, judge, whenever it's convenient." Unperturbed, Waring said that court would start at 10 a.m., and that did not mean 10:15. Such antics made quite an impression with the local reporters.

"Judge Waring kept the attorneys who argued before him in rein by cushioned suggestions rather than sharp rebukes," the paper reported. "He seldom upheld an objection to a question based on its materiality. Instead of ruling the query out, he would say to the objector: 'Oh, I agree with you. It's perfectly immaterial – but I'll let him ask it.' It was an unwise examiner who failed to take the hint."

Waring enjoyed his command of the courtroom. He liked listening to cases – and handing down sentences. The judge never forgot any of his trials, and could recall even the most arcane trivia. For years, he recounted an intricate con he'd once heard from a gang trying to steal American Express travelers' checks. He thought it was hilarious.

The criminal trials were the most entertaining, but he didn't mind admiralty cases or even bankruptcies. As a prosecutor, he'd once said, "I don't know anything about running a bank – but I know everything about how not to." Now he was paid to hear such cases all day, and render his own verdicts. Waring was even free to ask questions he believed the attorneys missed.

He often extolled the virtues of the jury trial, claiming it was what made the American court system so fair, but secretly Waring preferred to make his own rulings. And he was good at it. In his first two years on the bench, nearly every decision he issued was upheld on appeal. It wasn't a bad record for a man who'd never attended law school.

If that had been his legacy, Waring could've retired happy. He was a judge, and a good one – respected by his peers, attorneys who appeared before him and the Justice Department. It was all he'd ever wanted. But just before his second anniversary on the bench, a lawsuit landed on his docket that changed everything. The case would make him work harder, and study the law more closely, than he ever had before.

A black schoolteacher in Charleston sued the state, claiming she was paid less than white teachers with similar experience – and that was unfair. More than two decades after Septima Clark first lamented this pay disparity, South Carolina still maintained a system that was chronically discriminatory. The NAACP had been fighting the same battle around the country for years, and now it was South Carolina's turn.

He didn't recognize it at the time, but the case was Waring's first step into a broader world. There would be other, more significant, lawsuits that challenged

– and changed – his views. But one poor teacher from Burke High School, and the attorney who represented her, would stir something in Waring. In the ensuing years, he often referred to it as his "passion for justice."

That passion would change his life, and the country.

PRISONERS AT THE BAR

Viola Louise Duvall did not particularly consider herself an activist. She was just a science teacher.

In the fall of 1943, she was 24 and beginning her third year teaching at Burke Industrial, Charleston's only public black high school. Although Duvall was born and raised in the city, she hadn't attended Burke; her mother sent her to Immaculate Conception High on Coming Street, a private Catholic school for African Americans founded by the Sisters of Our Lady of Mercy. Duvall did well in her studies, graduating as salutatorian in 1937. She went on to Howard University in Washington, chose science as her major and earned a bachelor's degree in four years.

Duvall returned home after graduation and was immediately hired to teach at Burke. The year she was born, the state legislature had passed a law allowing black public schools to hire black teachers, so Duvall never knew a world where she wasn't permitted to hold such a job. But there was still inherent discrimination, which she soon recognized.

Black teachers in Charleston were paid roughly 60 percent as much as their white counterparts. It appeared the school district considered black teachers worth 3/5ths as much as whites, ironically the same value given to slaves during the 1787 constitutional convention. Duvall made only $12 a week, but she did not complain – not out loud, anyway. Most teachers didn't, for fear of losing their jobs.

Her only foray into social activism had come when she complained about the textbooks provided by the school district. Duvall's students were forced to learn science from outdated tomes handed down from white schools, and she didn't think that was fair. So she launched a fundraising drive to buy new books. Duvall collected money from parents and the community, determined to give her classes the most modern education possible. The campaign was a modest success; it also indirectly led the NAACP to her doorstep.

By the time Harold Boulware met Duvall in October 1943, he was getting desperate. The young Columbia attorney – the NAACP's legal point man in South Carolina – had been tasked with finding a teacher willing to serve as lead plaintiff in a teacher-pay lawsuit. The civil rights group had been challenging unfair wages across the country for years, but had yet to file a single suit in the birthplace of the Confederacy. Part of the problem, as Boulware learned, was that nobody wanted to get involved. Most potential plaintiffs begged off, fearing they would lose their jobs.

Boulware initially recruited Melissa Smith, another Burke teacher. At his direction, she'd petitioned the Charleston school board for equal pay back in June – and quickly felt the predicted backlash. Her bosses complained and colleagues begged her to quit stirring up trouble. The pressure became unbearable, and may have led Smith to sabotage her own case. In September, just after the school year began, she called in sick and took off two days to get married. The district used her unexcused absence as grounds to fire her, ridding itself of her complaint.

Eugene Hinton, also a teacher at Burke, agreed to lend his name to the lawsuit, but Boulware was reluctant to use him. The draft board recently had classified Hinton 1-A, and the NAACP feared he might be conveniently shipped overseas in the middle of the case. He suggested Boulware approach Duvall, perhaps because he remembered her textbook drive. Duvall once had fearlessly challenged the status quo. Perhaps she would again.

Duvall was not oblivious to the struggle for equal rights, and understood the underlying politics as well as anyone. At Howard, she'd taken a couple of political science classes from Ralph Bunche – a man who would eventually help establish the United Nations and become the first black American to win a Nobel Prize. It was impossible to avoid civil rights in his classroom. And Duvall realized black teachers weren't being treated fairly.

Boulware believed Duvall was a perfect candidate for his lawsuit: She was a native of Charleston, a salutatorian and an attractive woman. She would make a good, credible witness. For weeks, he pressed her, buttered her up with shared memories of Howard University – where he'd graduated from law school. Finally, Duvall agreed. The suit, which named members of the Charleston District 20 school board and its superintendent as defendants, was filed in U.S. District Court by early November.

The fallout was immediate. Duvall's bosses chided her, neighbors dodged her and co-workers snubbed her. Most of the faculty wanted to avoid any appearance of guilt by association – including Duvall's best friend, who ignored her when they shared recess duty. Burke teachers realized they were being cheated, but believed a job that paid poorly was better than none at all. It was practically a mantra among black educators. The president of the teachers' union had warned them not to complain about anything, especially their salaries.

"You know these white people aren't going to pay you the same money they make," John P. Burgess had said.

In 1943, few had the appetite to stir simmering racial tensions.

Charleston officials asked the court to dismiss Duvall's lawsuit just days after it was filed. School attorneys argued that she had signed a contract and couldn't legally dispute her salary. It was a common tactic. School districts around the country had successfully fended off NAACP lawsuits by insisting they couldn't renegotiate legal agreements. Then, litigious teachers simply weren't offered new contracts, taking away their jobs – and their standing for a lawsuit.

The Charleston school district offered an even more clever excuse. The state provided most of the funding for teachers, its lawyers argued, so the district was helpless to intervene. Equalizing salaries would cost $80,000 a year, and the district just didn't have the money. The local newspapers accepted that logic but, curiously enough, the federal court did not. Every one of the district's motions to dismiss was rejected, and a hearing was scheduled for February.

Thurgood Marshall had heard it all before, more times than he could count.

In eight years as the NAACP's roving legal counsel, much of his time had been dominated by teacher-pay cases. He won some, lost others, and trudged along in pursuit of African-American civil rights. The job kept him train-hopping constantly. One day, he'd file a voting-rights lawsuit in one state; the next, he was defending a man accused of dubious crimes in another. Marshall's work was often a blur, but teacher-pay-disparity lawsuits were of particular significance to him. His mother had been a schoolteacher.

Just 35 years old, Marshall was already a legend. He was one of the few black attorneys to argue – and win – a case before the United States Supreme Court. In 1940, he'd successfully petitioned the court to overturn the convictions of four black men accused of murdering a white man in Pompano Beach, Florida. He argued that their confessions had been coerced and were inadmissible. Although Florida courts upheld the death sentences, the Supreme Court unanimously sided with Marshall.

That was the first of 32 civil rights cases Marshall would take to the nation's highest court over two decades. He won 29 of them. In fact, just before traveling to South Carolina to argue Duvall's case, Marshall had appeared in the Supreme Court and was awaiting a verdict. He'd win.

Marshall was born in Baltimore in 1908, the son of a railroad porter descended from a long line of free blacks. Only one of his grandparents had been held in slavery, but that was one too many for Marshall. He later claimed his father instilled in him a love of the law, but he'd originally considered becoming a dentist. He was only a fair student as a child, but became more committed to his education when he followed his brother to Lincoln University, a black college in Pennsylvania.

In 1930, he applied to the University of Maryland Law School, which rejected him solely because of his skin color. So Marshall got his law degree from Howard, then sued the University of Maryland. He won. That early victory caught the attention of the NAACP, which hired him as its chief legal counsel. He had been fighting ever since.

Marshall juggled cases in Oklahoma, Connecticut, Florida, New York and Virginia – anywhere the NAACP saw injustice for people of color. He suffered the indignities of racism in both small Southern towns and New England hamlets. Marshall had learned there was no Mason-Dixon Line for prejudice in early 20th-century America. But he'd never tried a case in South Carolina, the birthplace of secession. He was understandably leery.

The news that Duvall's case would be heard in the court of U.S. District Judge Waties Waring did little to ease his concerns. Waring was an appointee of Sens. Burnet Maybank and "Cotton Ed" Smith, and Marshall could only imagine the sort of jurist a racist demagogue like Cotton Ed might support. He didn't have a great record with Southern judges anyway. Marshall expected that, as usual, he would lose the case and then try to win on appeal. In those days, it was NAACP standard operating procedure.

Marshall had an audience that morning.

On Feb. 10, 1944, Charleston's most influential black leaders – ministers, doctors and principals among them – greeted him at the federal courthouse, eager to see the famous attorney at work. They followed him into the courtroom, where they most likely had trouble finding seats. Teachers packed the pews, most of them black, although The Evening Post reported "a small scattering of white people" also attended. Most of those were teachers, too.

Locals predicted that the hearing, no matter the outcome, should prove entertaining, but Marshall wasn't so sure. Waring had a reputation as a tough judge who doled out harsh sentences to everyone. He'd shown little mercy, or empathy, in his two years on the bench. But there was some room for measured optimism. Without elaboration, Waring had thus far refused every one of the school district's motions to dismiss. Marshall was still trying to decide what that meant when the judge gaveled the session to order.

This wouldn't take long.

J. Arthur Johnson, the business manager and clerk of the school board, was the only witness called. He testified that teacher salaries were paid through state funding, with some federal aid, and as a result the school board – with no taxing authority – had to take what it was given. Even if the district wanted to equalize salaries, Johnson said, it would cost $80,000 that the schools didn't have to spare.

For that reason, school district attorney H.L. Erckmann argued, the lawsuit should be dismissed. He said the school board had passed a resolution that dictated teachers would be graded and classified by experience, preparation and ability without regard to race or color. In other words, the board didn't discriminate, it just had no additional funds to pay its black teachers better. Marshall unsurprisingly objected.

"The mere fact that you say you are going to do something is no grounds to dismiss the suit," Marshall argued.

Erckmann was not finished, however. He regurgitated the usual litany of excuses school districts used in teacher-pay lawsuits: Duvall was under contract, the federal government had no jurisdiction in a state issue. The judge allowed Erckmann to ramble on for minutes, but when he attempted to read a local newspaper article into the record, Waring stopped him.

"Newspaper evidence is the worst sort of hearsay," he said, a pleasant smirk on his face.

When the audience stopped laughing, Waring turned to face the defense table. How long had it been, he asked, since the *Alston* ruling? He was referring to *Alston v. School Board of the City of Norfolk*, a Virginia lawsuit identical to Duvall's case. As Erckmann shuffled through his paper, searching for the answer, Marshall stood to speak. Waring told him to sit down.

"I did not ask you, Mr. Marshall."

The Fourth Circuit Court of Appeals, Erckmann read from one of his files, issued its opinion on *Alston* in June 1940. Waring nodded and asked about a similar case out of Montgomery County, Maryland. Again, Erckmann scrambled and Marshall rose to answer. Waring once more told him to sit down. The audience took note.

"They don't even let her lawyer talk. Dear Jesus," one woman in the crowd said.

It looked bad for the plaintiff. Duvall sat between Marshall and Boulware, trying to hold back tears. She was scared. The judge was stern and hostile, and wouldn't even listen to her attorney. Her career, she feared, was over. Marshall was scarcely more optimistic. He was already planning his argument for appeals court. At least, he thought, this hadn't taken much time.

Erckmann finally found the Montgomery County ruling, which dated back to 1937, six-and-a-half years earlier. Waring said nothing, he simply swiveled his chair around to face the silent plaintiff's table. If he paused, it was only for dramatic effect; the judge knew he had the room's attention.

"Mr. Marshall, I don't want you to think I was being rude in not permitting you to answer those questions," Waring said. "I knew you knew the answers. You were the attorney of record in most of them. I was trying to determine how long it has been that the school board of Charleston has known that it must pay equal salaries to all of its teachers. This is a simple case and there is no need to take up the court's time. I have a question for you. What kind of order do you want entered? Do you want salaries equalized immediately? Do you want to give the board some time to equalize?"

For perhaps the first time in his life, Thurgood Marshall was speechless.

He had pegged Waring as a typical Southern judge, Marshall later recalled, who would give him a "legal head-whipping" and send him limping off to appeals court. Instead, Waring had studied the NAACP's past cases and knew the law. He dismissed the school district's states' rights argument, pointing out the 14th Amendment of the U.S. Constitution gave him the jurisdiction to intervene. It was the same argument Marshall had made a dozen times in his career.

After he recovered from the shock, Marshall asked the judge for a moment to confer with his co-counsel. Waring said that was fine, he'd give him three days to file paperwork outlining the plaintiff's demands. Then he adjourned the court. The hearing had lasted 15 minutes.

Waring's order followed four days later. He ruled that the Charleston school district had violated the equal protection clause of the 14th Amendment and was permanently restrained from "discriminating in the payment of salaries against plaintiffs and any other Negro teachers and/or principals in the public school system." Black teachers and principals, Waring declared, could not be paid less than white teachers and principals with the same qualifications, experience and job performance.

The judge said the district must equalize teacher salaries by the beginning of the 1946 school year, so long as the board made up half the pay gap between black and white teachers immediately. It was a resounding defeat for the district. School officials told the newspapers that, to comply with the order, they would have to ask for a tax increase.

Although he recognized the racial implications of the case, Waring believed his ruling was simply an interpretation of well-established law. School districts had challenged the Fourth Circuit Court of Appeals' rulings time and again, always failing. The U.S. Supreme Court had refused to hear any of the cases, always allowing the appeals court decisions to stand. Waring was confident he would not be overturned.

Years later, Waring could not recall any backlash to his decision in *Duvall v. Seignious*. It was true, no state or federal official ever questioned the order, and it was upheld on appeal. But the newspapers took note. The day after Waring issued his decree, The News and Courier published an editorial with the ominous headline "The Submissive South."

The editors found no fault in Waring's ruling and couldn't blame "the Negro teachers for demanding and getting what they can," but suggested the decision would prompt the state to close public schools. The newspaper argued that the South was impoverished because it had been forced to carry the burden of black people since emancipation, and the notion that "Southern white people have exploited Negro labor is nonsense."

The only solution, the editors opined, was to set up private schools for whites and abandon public education – an argument that would resurface with increasing frequency in coming years. Otherwise, it predicted, "The white people of South Carolina will stagger along under the load of high schools and colleges for 814,000 Negroes, 45 percent of the population. … The white South is a prisoner at the bar."

The newspaper reflected the prevailing attitude in 1944 Charleston, but neither Waring nor Duvall faced any repercussions. The community largely ignored the lawsuit and its ramifications. Duvall's colleagues apologized for shunning her. Most told her they'd feared for their jobs, and never imagined a local judge would side with a black teacher. It was at least an honest excuse.

Duvall was relieved it was over and grateful she was no longer a pariah. But she would not teach at Burke for long. A year later, Duvall had a blind date with Nathaniel Stewart, a second lieutenant with the Tuskegee Airmen stationed in Walterboro. The couple hit it off, married in August 1945 and moved to Philadelphia. She briefly became a pharmacist, but spent 20 years raising their two sons. She took up teaching again in the 1960s, but never went back to Charleston. Duvall would miss all that her lawsuit sparked.

Thurgood Marshall, however, would spend a lot of time in South Carolina over the next decade. Part of the reason for that was Duvall's lawsuit. He later said it was "the only case I ever tried with my mouth hanging open half of the time. Judge Waring was so fair that I found my apprehension totally unwarranted."

Waring made an impression on Marshall. He believed he'd found a sympathetic, or at least fair, judge in the South – and that was exceedingly rare. Perhaps, Marshall thought, this was the beginning of a beautiful friendship.

THE FIRES OF COLUMBIA

Charleston was too distracted by the war to ponder the gravity of Judge Waring's unexpected ruling. News from the Pacific and the European front filled the local papers every day; the war was all-consuming. Food and gas rationing were rampant, the society types led unending paper and rubber drives. Even the streets were torn up to help the war effort.

The military had excavated Charleston's abandoned trolley tracks for the steel, eventually netting 1,800 tons of the increasingly rare alloy. Digging up those tracks, which hadn't been used since Charleston switched to buses in 1938, forced the city and state to undertake a massive repaving project. By summer, crews would finally reach the streets of the northwestern peninsula, where the Ivory City once stood. But that was two generations – and one war – ago.

The national steel shortage was most apparent at the Charleston Naval Shipyard, where civilians worked three shifts daily building the replacements for lost fleets. The military hired so many people the Census Bureau reported the county had grown by 38 percent in four years – to 167,000 residents. Mayor Henry Lockwood said the estimate missed at least 35,000; but then, he felt the growth more acutely than most. There were upward of 70,000 people living on the Charleston peninsula.

The war, and all those new residents, led to a resurgence of Charleston's nightlife and its red-light district. This illicit activity inflated the city's crime rate, and kept the courts busy. Over the course of the year, Waring imposed 362 sentences – an average of more than one every business day. There were bankruptcies and admiralty cases, and no small amount of war-related offenses. The judge sentenced one teenager to five years' probation after he was caught wearing the uniform of a U.S. Army officer.

In April, Waring committed a 16-year-old boy to a mental institution for killing an 8-year-old girl on Parris Island. When a black man from Orangeburg was found guilty of selling illegal whiskey, the judge gave him five months but suspended the sentence and put him on probation. Four months later, the man was arrested for selling moonshine outside a local church – during children's day festivities. Waring revoked the probation and sent him to jail.

Time passed. Mayor Lockwood died of a heart attack on the eve of D-Day, and the colossal Normandy landing overshadowed his obituary. Waring issued a sad statement lamenting Lockwood's passing just before he and Annie left for the annual federal judges' conference in Asheville. Two months later, the couple took the train to New York City and checked into the Essex House for a week of vacation before Waring began a four-week stint on the bench in Newark.

Shortly after the Warings returned to Charleston that fall, Sen. Ellison D. Smith died – also of a heart attack. The judge offered a kind eulogy to his old friend "Cotton Ed," but he didn't gush. Waring rarely did.

Charleston may have missed the implications of the Duvall case, but the state legislature didn't.

Within a month of Waring's ruling, South Carolina lawmakers established a grievance process for teachers who had complaints about their salaries. Legislative leaders claimed the intention was to give teachers a voice, but the real purpose was to prevent any more class-action lawsuits such as *Duvall v. Seignious*. The NAACP noted that the legislation was worth little, that federal law trumped state statutes. The grievance bill passed anyway.

At the same time, state Sen. Edgar Brown – one of South Carolina's most powerful politicians – was shopping a new system to set teacher pay. Devised by the state Board of Education, this recertification plan would test teachers to assess their abilities and determine their pay grade. Teachers complained, but Brown said if the state didn't enact this new policy, taxpayers would be gouged out of $3.25 million "by federal court orders making pay for whites and Negroes equal." At least in this instance, the legislature's purpose was abundantly clear.

Lawmakers left Columbia in late March, satisfied they'd put an end to the nuisance of teacher-pay lawsuits. But they were soon called back into emergency session to clean up what they considered another potential mess, also caused by Thurgood Marshall and the NAACP.

A month before the Charleston teacher lawsuit, Marshall represented a black Houston dentist in the U.S. Supreme Court case *Smith v. Allwright*. Lonnie E. Smith, a resident of Harris County, Texas, had been barred from voting in the Democratic primary – just as the state intended. Twenty years earlier, the Texas General Assembly had passed a law that allowed political parties to set their own rules. Of course, the Democrats opted to exclude any non-whites from voting in their primaries.

Marshall argued that the Texas law violated the 14th Amendment, allowing a third party to discriminate against citizens in public elections. At the time, the Democratic Party dominated Texas – and most of the South. Its nominees were assured of victory, which meant anyone banned from voting in the primary essentially had no voice in elections. The Supreme Court ruled in April 1944 that Texas had denied Smith equal protection under the law.

Marshall considered *Smith v. Allwright* his most important court victory to date. He believed it was a landmark decision that established the basis for civil rights. This case, he thought, would change everything.

To be sure, it led to change in South Carolina. Within days of the Supreme Court decision, Gov. Olin Johnston called the General Assembly into special session to excise any mention of the Democratic Party from state law. South Carolina, the governor declared, would not fall victim to the same court order as Texas.

"White supremacy will be maintained in our primaries," Johnston promised.

By-mid April, the legislature was back at work. The governor urged lawmakers to rewrite all election laws, reminding them of the Reconstruction era when blacks held considerable power – and a number of seats – in the General Assembly. Because African Americans constituted about one-third of South Carolina's voting-age population, he said, the Democratic Party primary must not be opened to them.

"Where you now sit, there sat a majority of Negroes," Johnston said. "What kind of government did they give South Carolina when they were in power? The records will bear me out that fraud, corruption, immorality and graft existed during that regime that has never been paralleled in the history of our state. They left a stench in the nostrils of the people of South Carolina that will exist for generations to come. … History has taught us that we must keep our white Democratic primaries pure."

Within weeks, lawmakers stripped more than 200 references to the primary election process from South Carolina statutes – editing the code so thoroughly there were no longer any laws governing elections. The presidents of the state's black colleges and universities released a joint statement that said the General Assembly was fanning the flames of racial tension, and the NAACP announced plans for a primary to accommodate black voters. It was all-out war.

On its editorial page, The News and Courier suggested these protests were a confession that black people could not hold successful primaries, and needed white people to vote properly. If that were the case, the editors said, did such statements imply that African Americans conceded whites were the "superior race?"

"The News and Courier is saying nothing about superior races, but why are colored people incessantly knocking at the doors of white societies?"

A week later, the editors argued that "of course" black people could vote – in general elections, and if they paid a poll tax. "The amazing ignorance abroad in the land that in South Carolina and other Southern states Negroes cannot vote probably cannot be removed from the minds of the weak-minded."

Of course, that argument ignored one small detail: In South Carolina, like Texas, the Democratic primary *was* the election.

As state officials struggled to preserve South Carolina's "purity," the NAACP was preparing another teacher-pay lawsuit.

The group planned to file suit against Columbia's Richland County school district but, as they learned in Charleston, it was difficult to find a lead plaintiff. At one community meeting, a black principal called their efforts "foolish" – Columbia teachers, like those in Charleston, feared losing their jobs. When Thurgood Marshall returned to South Carolina, he was astounded by the reluctance among black educators. But one local teacher was trying to persuade her colleagues to cooperate, because she knew a little about unfair pay.

Septima Clark had been teaching in Columbia for 15 years, after a long, painful journey through western North Carolina. She'd followed Nerie David Clark to his hometown in part because his family was there, and because her parents were infuriated by their marriage. A change of scenery seemed a good way to avoid the consternation. She found a teaching job near Hickory and it was fine, although she didn't like the mountains nearly as much as the Lowcountry.

Clark might have stayed in those mountains forever, but a series of tragedies altered the course of her life. The Clarks' first child, a daughter, died just three weeks after she was born in 1921. Four years later, Clark had their second child, a boy she named after his father. And then Nerie David Clark died of kidney failure shortly after his son's birth.

Widowed with an infant, Clark considered becoming a foreign missionary. Instead, she returned to Charleston and teaching on Johns Island. A Columbia school recruited her a short time later, and she'd been there ever since. The pay wasn't great; it never was. When the Great Depression reached South Carolina, Clark could no longer afford to support her son. So she sent young Nerie to live with his grandparents in Hickory – a common practice during the Depression. It was not ideal, but Clark had little choice.

The years passed, and Clark kept busy. She taught at Booker T. Washington High School and finished her bachelor's degree at Benedict College. Columbia's social order proved far less rigid than Charleston society, which suited Clark just fine. She made friends, learned to play bridge and attended meetings where both whites and blacks were welcome. It was like a different world.

Clark hadn't forgotten her activist beginnings in Charleston, however, and that came in handy when the legislature passed its teacher recertification plan. She helped her colleagues prepare for their tests, but it wasn't easy. Some told her they'd rather quit than face recertification. At one meeting, she was forced to deliver a motivational speech that was – by her standards – fairly harsh.

"If you say that you are not going to take that examination in the morning,

I will be with you," Clark said. "But if some of you say tonight that you are on the fence on this proposition … I will let you know right now that I am going. I'm not afraid to take that examination."

Clark not only passed the state's test, she recorded the highest possible score. Her salary was immediately tripled, she later claimed. But not everyone, neither black nor white, fared as well.

After the stress of those tests, Clark found that most teachers wanted nothing to do with the NAACP lawsuit. But she believed their fears were unfounded. In fact, she suspected the superintendent privately agreed teacher pay should be equal – but, like everyone else, he was afraid to take the first step. So she did it.

Recalling her days at Avery, Clark suggested Columbia teachers canvass Columbia neighborhoods and poll residents about teacher pay. Later, she would call it her first job as a radical, "the first time I had worked against people directing a system for which I was working."

Slowly, Clark was becoming an influential leader.

By June, the NAACP found its plaintiff.

Albert Thompson had been teaching at Booker Washington Heights Elementary School for two years at an annual salary of $950. A white teacher with similar experience in the Richland County school district was routinely paid $1,300. So on June 7, 1944, while the world was consumed by news of the Normandy invasion, Thompson – with the help of NAACP state secretary James Hinton – submitted a petition asking the school board for equal pay. On Marshall's advice, they opted to skip a grievance hearing.

Months passed before the lawsuit was filed. Marshall was busy with other cases, and Harold Boulware, the NAACP's best South Carolina attorney, had enlisted and gone off to war. The group had trouble finding another lawyer to put the case together. Eventually, Clark stepped in to help gather the needed affidavits and, in early 1945, *Thompson v. Gibbes* landed in Columbia's federal court.

The lawsuit was assigned to George Bell Timmerman's docket, but in March the federal court clerk announced Judge Waring would hear *Thompson*. The excuse was that Timmerman has been scheduled to fill in for a vacationing judge in Newark and didn't want to delay the case. In truth, Judge Timmerman wanted no part of a teacher-pay dispute. Too controversial. Later, Waring admitted the judge specifically asked him to hear the case.

"I got all those cases," Waring said. But he didn't mind, and set the hearing for early May.

The lawsuit, and the crowd it attracted, was reminiscent of the Charleston case from the year before. Columbia's federal courthouse was filled to capacity on May 9, the benches in the courtroom packed with local teachers and community activists. Marshall had been delighted to learn that Waring would hear the case, but he had a conflict, so the NAACP sent New York attorney Edward Dudley in his stead.

Dudley's orders were simple: repeat Marshall's arguments from *Duvall*. Everyone assumed Waring would once again take the teacher's side. But from the start, the *Thompson* case was less clear than *Duvall*.

Richland County did not accept the premise of the NAACP's argument. Officials claimed school district salaries were based on merit, experience – and what a teacher was willing to accept. On the stand, school board Chairman J. Heyward Gibbes said he wholeheartedly believed black and white teachers should be paid the same ... unless they agreed to work for less. And that, he said, was usually what happened. Gibbes said every new teacher was offered a starting annual salary of $900.

"White teachers refuse it, and we have to go higher," the chairman said. "Negro teachers accept it, so that's what they're hired for."

Gibbes claimed that salary discrepancies were being eliminated through re-certification, although "there will still be a distinction on basis of merit." As a result of these policies, he said, the pay gap between black and white teachers was not nearly as wide as it once had been. For the current school year, the average pay for white teachers was $1,420, and $1,206 for black teachers.

Next, superintendent A.C. Flora testified that race did not figure into salaries in his school district. He noted that Thompson had been hired for $700, and his pay had increased to $950 in three years. The raises were based on merit, the superintendent said.

Listening to him on the stand, Waring decided he liked Flora. Later, the judge said he detected something decent and frank about the man – which was similar to Clark's opinion. Since Waring was hearing the case without a jury, he was able to ask more questions. And that day, he kept Flora on the stand more than an hour, grilling him every bit as meticulously as Dudley did.

Waring dug through the district's paperwork and pulled out detailed personnel sheets for two high schools that Flora agreed used the same curriculum and had a similar number of students. The superintendent said the teachers in both schools were capable, so Waring began comparing salaries.

"Now, here is a teacher who seems to be teaching English 3 or 4 or 5," Waring said. "He's been approximately 10 years a teacher, with an M.A. degree. He has a class of 40 or something like that – large class there. There's that school. Now, here is a teacher over here – he's got a different name, but he's been a teacher about 10 years, got an M.A. degree, has a class of approximately the same number – instead of 40, he's got 47 – and he's teaching the same English course. Do you know these teachers?"

Flora said yes, calling them both "top-notch" men.

"One man here gets $35 a month more than the other man," Waring said. "What's the reason for it?"

"One's a white school and the other's a Negro school," Flora said.

"Well," Waring said, "Mr. Flora, do you mean to say that the teachers – you say those teachers are exactly the same, so far as two human beings can be?"

Flora agreed both teachers were "capable and satisfactory." And when Waring asked why one was paid more than the other, he was blunt: "I told you. One is a white school, the other is a Negro school."

The superintendent explained that he set all salaries according to the school board's instructions. It was a telling statement. In effect, Flora was admitting pay was decided by the school board – and there was nothing he could do, like it or not. When Waring asked if salary standards might be changed by the beginning of the next school year, he was even less subtle.

"I'll be very glad, judge, if it is," Flora said.

Waring rushed through the rest of the witnesses and concluded the hearing that afternoon, with the promise of a decision within the week.

In many ways, his *Thompson* ruling would be identical to *Duvall* – based on the premise that the 14th Amendment protected black teachers from discriminatory pay practices. But there was one substantial difference. Waring said it was also appropriate for the state teacher recertification system to factor into actual salaries.

"I maintain that the act is supposed to be a benefit to the pupils and not for the support of indigent, ignorant, helpless and inadequately prepared teachers," he wrote in his decision.

Waring realized the NAACP wouldn't consider *Thompson* an unqualified victory, but neither would the Richland County school district. "Some of the teachers were going to have a bad time under it, because they were so inadequately prepared," he later said. "And it happened." But the decision also cost the school district a lot of money, because those tests revealed that hundreds of teachers were underpaid.

Still, the judge heard no complaints from either side. In fact, Sen. Edgar Brown wrote him a letter praising the decision, and Waring responded with a note complimenting the recertification plan. "It is likely that at first the Negro teachers are going to suffer more in teachers' raises because of inadequacy of preparation and, frankly, because most of them haven't an equal ability, Waring wrote.

"However, those few who have the qualifications are going to and should be equally paid."

From those remarks, Waring seemed only slightly more progressive than the average South Carolina resident of the time. He comes off as patriarchal and slightly condescending to African-American teachers. Perhaps he felt that way, but he may have been playing to his audience. Because there was a subtle message to the senator in that note: People of equal ability must be treated the same, no matter the color of their skin.

Brown likely didn't notice the subtext.

The judge was more open in a series of letters he later exchanged with J. Heyward Gibbes, the Richland school board chairman. Waring considered the Columbia officials more enlightened than their Charleston counterparts, and at least somewhat sympathetic to the plight of black teachers. To Gibbes, he lamented that "the people of our state are going to be hard to educate along these lines."

"It is fortunate for Columbia to have you in charge of its school system," Waring wrote to Gibbes. "I really believe that we liberal minded Southerners may be able to eventually cure this situation, not by the radical methods of the Eleanor Roosevelt-Wendell Wilkie school, nor by the reactionary methods of the old slave holders, but by moderate, gradual and understanding action."

Waring found himself pondering race, history and issues of fairness often in the months following the teacher-pay cases. They challenged his preconceived notions and, he later claimed, laid the groundwork for everything that followed. Neither lawsuit made much difference, at least not in Waring's world – it would take something far more barbaric to spur his nagging conscience into action. But his "passion for justice," as he later called it, was beginning to simmer.

"It made me begin to think an awful lot, because every time you looked into one of these things, the less reason you can see for resistance to what we commonly call the American creed of equality of all citizens in this country," he later said. "Every time a case came up, or discussion came up politically or otherwise of these situations, you saw the old sophistry of trying to keep within the law, but declaring two classes of citizens, and that Negroes or people of partial Negro descent were not treated as ordinary American human beings, but were put in a separate classification – whether on pay or jobs or association or anything else. The whole thing worried me a great deal, and I knew the thing was coming to a showdown someday, and probably was coming in my state. The question arose as to whether I should dodge it or meet it."

It was the question that would define Waring's career, and entire life. He just didn't know it yet.

EXILE ON MEETING STREET

T he College of Charleston's commencement was still held in the Cistern Yard, a grand expanse of grass shaded by live oaks dripping with Spanish moss. The female graduates still wore white dresses and carried red roses when they marched in to the strains of "Pomp and Circumstance;" the four men in the class donned white suits adorned with red carnations. The traditions had not changed.

Waring had probably attended more than a dozen of these ceremonies since his own graduation in 1900, either as a member of the board of trustees or the alumni association. But on this day – Tuesday, May 29, 1945 – he was once again dressed as a graduate, right down to his white shoes. Even at 64, his Southern fashion sense remained impeccable.

This commencement, which came two days after he issued his decision in the Columbia teacher-pay case, was special and no doubt nostalgic for Waring. The judge had been awarded an honorary law degree from his alma mater – one of three dignitaries recognized by the college as "men of peace." It was a sly reference to the ongoing war, which had worn thin on everyone and was directly responsible for the stark gender gap among the 32 graduates – a gap that would persist at the college for decades.

The occasion afforded the judge a chance to visit with some of his old colleagues, including Harrison Randolph, who'd recently retired after 45 years as college president. On this day, Waring was jovial, sociable – carrying on like the scion of Charleston he had been all his life. If anyone noticed that he showed up alone, they were too polite to mention it. But his wife's absence only served as further confirmation of the rumors circulating around town. Everyone suspected the judge was having marital troubles.

No one had seen Mrs. Waring in months – not at church, the St. Cecilia

Society or any South of Broad socials. She'd even missed several regular meetings of her own literary club. Normally, she was by her husband's side whenever he went out in public, but Annie Gammell Waring had not been spotted anywhere around Charleston since the previous winter. Few people could say with any certainty what was going on, although the judge's extended family knew: The couple had been separated since February.

Waring acted as if nothing was wrong. He walked the single block from 61 Meeting Street to the courthouse every morning, his routine unchanged. The judge was by turns wry or aloof, as usual, and his demeanor on the bench was steady as ever. The day before commencement he'd opened a new term of court and disposed of 20 criminal cases in two hours. He even took time to lecture the courtroom on the history of jury trials, his Lowcountry drawl thick as molasses. If he was under undue stress, it didn't show.

By the time he received his honorary degree, the judge had been living as a bachelor for nearly three months. He'd come home one evening and surprised his wife with the blunt announcement that he no longer loved her. He wanted a divorce. Annie, already fragile from various ailments, was shocked. She begged him to reconsider, but his mind was made up.

Later, Waring offered various nebulous excuses for their split. He said they'd been moderately happy for most of their marriage, but "there was a good deal of change, and things became pretty routine. Not difficult, but routine." His vague reasons only danced around the truth. The simple fact was, he'd fallen in love with another woman.

For years, Charleston gossip held that Waring was not immune to the charms of women. His former law partners said he was notorious for flirting with legal secretaries and, at most social functions, he invariably could be found talking to the prettiest woman in the room. Most people around Charleston believed Annie was either oblivious to this, or didn't care. If he flirted on occasion, well, who didn't? She was still hopelessly devoted to Waring.

Some of the judge's friends had always thought Annie was a poor match for Waring. They said although she enjoyed living in his orbit, and doted on him shamelessly, they had little in common. Annie Gammell Waring, some of the judge's associates claimed, was too frivolous to hold his interest. Despite his extensive travels on the party circuit, such arguments went, Waring was an intellectual and loner. The bench had only fueled his interest in lofty issues – and raised his sense of self-importance. She could not keep up.

Some of that was no doubt typical Charleston snobbery and chauvinism, but there was no question Waring was changing. He increasingly believed he had a higher calling. And mistress or not, perhaps he didn't believe Annie fit into those plans.

The *Duvall* and *Thompson* cases forced Waring to reconsider any number of things. He was not yet an outright civil rights crusader, but the judge re-evaluated the way he conducted his own business. He represented America, Waring reasoned, and his court had to be "a court of all the people, and we couldn't differentiate according to race or caste or color or creed or anything of that kind." Waring was under no illusion that he could change the country – not at that point, anyway – but he'd become conscious of the subtle segregation in his own courtroom. He could change that.

These changes came slowly – often triggered when he detected something out of place. First, he noticed that court employees regularly scanned the list of potential jurors and put a "c" – for colored – next to any black person's name. Although it was mostly a courtesy for the attorneys, Waring ordered his clerks to stop. Race should not matter to justice, he said.

The judge also directed his clerks to assign jurors to specific seats so they didn't consciously or unconsciously segregate themselves. At first, courthouse staff didn't even recognize these seating charts as a means to racial socialization; from their point of view it simply helped keep jurors' names straight.

Finally, Waring told bailiffs to quit directing spectators to seats. In state court, the audience was forcibly segregated, and it had become an unwritten practice in federal court. But the judge said he no longer wanted to see black people sitting on one side of his courtroom while whites sat on the other. The bailiffs followed his orders without question – and without doubt when he eventually hired a black bailiff.

One incident left an indelible impression on Waring. The marshal took a jury out for lunch one day during a routine trial. Later, the judge learned there'd been trouble at the restaurant. The manager demanded the two black jurors eat in the kitchen – he wouldn't seat them in the main dining room; some customers had complained. One of the two men refused, and he was eventually allowed to eat with the other jurors – but only after he invoked Waring's name.

The judge was livid when he learned what had happened, accused the restaurant of breaking the law. Such segregation was morally and constitutionally wrong, he proclaimed, and if the restaurant had a problem with that, it would get no more of the federal court's business. The marshal promised to find a new restaurant.

If the lawyers who practiced in Waring's court noticed, most assumed the judge had decided he should practice what he'd preached in the teacher-pay cases, lest he look like a hypocrite. Some of those same people suggested Annie probably didn't show enough interest in her husband's emerging politics. But that was a mass rationalization that obscured the simple truth.

Waring wanted a divorce because he had become completely obsessed with Elizabeth Avery Hoffman.

No one really knew when Waring met Elizabeth. One of his law partners claimed they could've met in New York, because the judge knew her son-in-law's family. But it's more likely they crossed paths at one of Charleston's countless soirees shortly after she and her second husband started spending their winters in the city. Henry Hoffman, a wealthy Connecticut businessman, was fond of antiques, and that interest eventually drew him to Charleston.

Elizabeth was unlike any woman Waring knew. Born and raised in a wealthy Detroit family, she was liberal, outspoken and opinionated – and didn't much care who liked it. At 20, she'd married a man of similar social status. Wilson Mills was a banker and a lawyer, and he maintained the lifestyle to which Elizabeth had become accustomed. For two decades, she taught music, played tennis and volunteered for various charitable causes. The couple had two sons and one daughter.

Just when it seemed her life was set, Elizabeth met Hoffman while wintering in Ormond Beach, Fla., near Daytona. He was older, but seemed to share her interests. In 1933, she flew to Reno for a quickie divorce from Mills – a betrayal that left her estranged from her children. Cut off from her old life, Elizabeth darted around the country with Hoffman and, in 1943, they bought a house South of Broad to pass their winters.

Later, Charleston legend held that the Hoffmans were frequent guests at 61 Meeting Street, where they sometimes played couples bridge. But that may have been a story invented to set up punchlines about exactly what sort of "player" Elizabeth actually had been. At some point, however, Waring secretly started seeing Elizabeth, and it quickly turned into more than illicit sex. His friends understood the physical attraction – Elizabeth was a striking woman – but few in Charleston cared for her Yankee attitude. They thought even less of Waring for jilting his wife of 31 years. But Waring didn't care what anyone thought. He was in love.

In 1945, divorce was not only taboo in South Carolina – it was illegal. To get around this technicality, Waring had asked Annie to move in with his widowed sister-in-law in Jacksonville, Fla. He instructed her to declare residency and, after 90 days, file for divorce. Annie tried to talk him out of it, even after he admitted his adultery. She offered to continue as they were. There was too much shame in divorce and, in truth, she still loved him.

Waring knew he'd treated Annie terribly, and later conceded to interviewers that it was all his fault. Even in contemporary letters to his sister-in-law, Rowena Taylor Waring, the judge took the blame and admitted Annie had done nothing wrong. But he didn't feel guilty enough to change anything. His decision was final.

"You probably think I have acted brutally and cruelly to her," he wrote to his sister-in-law. "In your eyes I assume, I have acted badly. I cannot enter any denial … I have chosen to be frank."

But there was no use denying that he loved another woman, Waring said, or ignoring his "desire to be free." The judge was at least as forthright in his personal life as he was in the courtroom, even if it only confirmed his family's suspicions that he was a callous and cold man.

The terms of their divorce only made Waring look worse, although that was not entirely his fault. He offered to move out of 61 Meeting Street – it was Annie's house, after all – but she told him to keep it. She'd decided to move to New York, where she would be close to Anne. So Waring kept the house, gave Annie $20,000 in cash, a life insurance policy on himself and promised Anne would inherit his entire estate.

It only made the judge seem more of a villain in the eyes of Charleston when Annie later moved back to town and was forced to live modestly within sight of her old home.

Waring would not even show up for his own divorce. On June 6, little more than a week after the judge received his honorary degree, Annie appeared alone in a Duval County courtroom. Haggard and heartbroken, she testified that they had once been the "most completely happy couple in Charleston." Annie claimed she'd been ill for months, and the idea of her husband seeing Elizabeth Hoffman behind her back was unbearable. She'd lost 25 pounds since moving to Florida, and remained inconsolable. The judge granted her a divorce immediately.

As Annie Gammell Waring cried in a Jacksonville courtroom, Elizabeth Avery Hoffman was on a plane to Reno, returning to Nevada for her second divorce in 12 years.

After the divorce papers were filed, Waring summoned his nephew to the federal courthouse. Tom Waring had followed his father – Waring's brother, Thomas – into the newspaper business and was an editor at The News and Courier. He was on fairly good terms with his uncle. They saw each other around town, usually at parties, and served together on a board or two. They weren't particularly close, however; he'd only heard of the judge's marital troubles from his mother.

Waring asked his nephew to publish a short notice that reported his divorce had been finalized. Tom briefly tried to talk him out of it. He explained that, even though the separation had become common knowledge, any official notice was liable to "rock Charleston." But the judge had ulterior motives, and said he didn't care about the fallout.

"Let her rock," the judge said.

The News and Courier carried the notice on June 9. It simply said, "Mrs. Annie Gammell Waring has been granted a divorce from Federal Judge J. Waties Waring in an uncontested suit. ... Mrs. Waring will reside in New York." The Evening Post ran the exact same blurb in that afternoon's editions. The timing was likely intentional. On that day, the judge was conveniently out of town.

Waring had left Charleston for a judicial conference in Hot Springs, Virginia. He stopped in Columbia to pick up Judge Timmerman and together they collected Judge C.C. Wyche. They stayed for the entire conference, but Waring didn't return to South Carolina with the other judges. He took a train to New York City, where he met Elizabeth. And on June 15, less than two weeks after his divorce was final, Waring married Elizabeth Avery Hoffman in the chambers of a Greenwich, Connecticut, municipal court judge.

When they returned to Charleston, Waring resigned from the St. Cecilia Society before he could be expelled. The group did not extend membership to divorcees, and he wanted to spare them the trouble of kicking him out. The judge knew his quickie marriage to a twice-divorced woman – especially one from the North – would not be accepted in his hometown. But he seriously underestimated just how reviled he would become among his friends and neighbors.

Even his family took Annie's side, although none of them quit speaking to him immediately, and his sister, Margaret, remained loyal. Waring knew it looked unseemly, moving a new woman into Annie's house, and her bed. But eventually he grew angry and returned their scorn because they wouldn't get over it, and would not accept Elizabeth.

Some locals claimed the city's later hostility toward Waring was a direct response to his treatment of Annie. No doubt many found it distasteful to see this old man jilt his wife and take up with a woman 15 years his junior. And, in truth, Elizabeth did little to endear herself to anyone. But the notion that everyone abandoned Waring entirely because of his divorce was just another bit of Charleston's revisionist history.

In the year following their marriage, Waring and Elizabeth were invited to numerous public functions – although not many private parties. The judge was even asked to join a committee organizing a meet-and-greet with the cast of a new play at the Dock Street Theatre. Waring's social obligations may have declined, but they had not yet evaporated. That happened only after he committed sins that were, from Charleston's perspective, much greater.

Still, Waring took every opportunity to avoid the sidelong glances and disapproving glares on the streets of Charleston. In August 1945, Waring and Elizabeth took the train to New York, where he was scheduled to spend a month presiding over court for the state's Southern District. They arrived just a few days too late to see the V-J Day celebration in Times Square. When the couple returned in September, the newspapers dutifully carried notices that the judge and his wife were back in town.

From the start, the two were inseparable – Elizabeth not only traveled with Waring, she even sat in court some days, which caused some grumbling among the lawyers. They claimed the judge lost focus when his new bride was present. But they said nothing to him; instead, they mercilessly mocked him behind his back.

For the next year, Waring volunteered to fill in for judges in New York any time one of them took a vacation. Elizabeth, of course, always came along. She jumped at the chance to see Broadway shows and eat in fine restaurants. But in truth, she simply welcomed any excuse to be away from Charleston. As much as she loved the judge, she didn't care for his hometown. In fact, she detested the entire South.

Her opinion – of the South in general, and Charleston in particular – would not improve in the coming years.

EXCESSIVE FORCE

The 1946 winter docket was crowded, and Waring welcomed the work. Between his personal drama and the war's end, the past year had been tumultuous and distracting. The courtroom was almost a respite.

He heard cases of sawmill owners stealing gasoline, McClellanville constables defrauding the Internal Revenue Service and the lurid tale of a taxi driver accused of violating the Mann Act – he'd allegedly taken a young woman to Florida and held her in a hotel for a week. It was all scandalous, but Waring handed out sentences without any emotion. Just doing his job.

The most interesting case on his docket involved Jacob Gethers, a 33-year-old black man indicted for assault with a deadly weapon and intimidating a game warden. The defense, perhaps playing to the judge's emerging reputation as a social moderate, tried to claim racial discrimination. John Eadie, the game warden, had found Gethers and his half-brother carrying shotguns on a dike in the Santee National Wildlife Reserve, 60 miles north of Charleston. Eadie asked to see their hunting licenses.

"What the hell do you want it for?" Gethers had asked, and pointed his shotgun at the warden.

Eadie climbed out of his truck holding his own shotgun, and their standoff devolved into a fight. Gethers ultimately took both guns, pulled a knife and then took off running, warning the warden not to follow him. "I've got my hunting license in my gun," Gethers said. When Eadie chased him, Gethers fired. One of the pellets bounced off a tree and lodged itself in the warden's scalp.

Following the testimony, Gethers' lawyer asked the jury – 11 whites and one African American – how they'd feel if everyone involved in the scuffle had been white. The attorney answered his own question.

"There wouldn't be any case," he claimed. "Eadie's feelings had been hurt because he, an officer for the United States government, didn't get the kind of response he wanted from Gethers."

It was the wrong case, wrong defendant, to try a civil rights defense. Gethers had a long record of violent criminal offenses. The case wasn't even his first indictment for assault with a deadly weapon – he'd once tried to shoot a constable. The jury took only 30 minutes to deliver a guilty verdict, and Waring sent Gethers to prison for two years. The newspapers noted it was one of the heaviest sentences the judge had imposed all winter.

Waring increasingly believed justice must be color blind, but he also recognized crime when he saw it. He was a strict judge with little tolerance for anyone who violated the simplest law – no matter what their color. But as he trudged through his winter docket, an incident on the other side of the state would challenge all his preconceptions.

On Tuesday, Feb. 12, 1946, Sgt. Isaac Woodard Jr. was honorably discharged from the U.S. Army. He mustered out at Camp Gordon near Augusta, Georgia, after serving nearly 3½ years during the war. Because he was black, Woodard never actually fought. He spent most of his time as a longshoreman for the Pacific fleet in the Philippines, and earned a good-conduct award as well as a battle star for unloading ships during a firefight in New Guinea. Now, finally, he was going home.

Woodard rushed to the bus station around 5:30 that afternoon to buy his ticket. His wife was waiting for him in Winnsboro, a small farm town in Fairfield County, South Carolina, just north of Columbia. He'd been born there and, although his family moved to North Carolina when he was 15, Woodard returned after high school, took work at a local sawmill and married his childhood sweetheart. Now, she was just 100 miles and a few hours away.

He would never make it.

Woodard met some other soldiers at the station, and they celebrated their freedom with a few drinks. When the Greyhound showed up at 8:30, they piled into seats near the back. Passengers recalled the group laughing and joking around during the trip, and it was hard to blame them. They had been through a bloody war and lived to tell about it. Later, Woodard insisted he was not drinking on the bus – he was just happy.

After an hour, the bus stopped at a drug store near Aiken. Woodard, 27, tall and lanky, made his way up to the front and asked if he had time to use the restroom. The driver, A.C. Blackwell, told him to sit down. But their accounts of the exchange differed dramatically. Woodard claimed the driver cursed at him. Blackwell later testified that he only told Woodard to be quiet.

Either way, Woodard – still in his dress uniform – was insulted. And although his memory of what he said next would be inconsistent over the years, the gist of it was, "Talk to me like I'm talking to you. I'm a man just like you."

Fuming, Blackwell relented, but told him to hurry. And soon they were underway. But a half-hour later the bus stopped again, this time in Batesburg, South Carolina, and the driver stepped outside. When he returned, Blackwell walked to the back of the bus and tapped Woodard on the shoulder. Someone wanted to see him in the parking lot.

Batesburg Police Chief Lynwood Shull and another officer were waiting outside the bus. When Woodard emerged, he heard the driver complaining that he was causing a disturbance on the bus. Blackwell claimed he was drunk, Woodard later testified, and had bothered other passengers – even frightened one woman. And, he said, Woodard even cussed at him. Out of all these various infractions, Blackwell seemed most offended that a black man had dared to talk back to him.

Woodard denied he was drinking, told his side of the story and argued that he'd done nothing wrong – and certainly nothing that warranted a call to the police. Before he could finish, Shull told him to shut up and hit him on the head with a blackjack.

At first, the chief seemed content to make Woodard wait for the next bus. But he contradicted himself within minutes and decided to arrest Woodard. He grabbed his arm, twisted it behind his back and started leading him to the police station down a dark Batesburg street. Woodard later said the chief twisted his arm so hard it was like he wanted a reaction, anything that would give him the excuse to charge him with resisting arrest – or to beat him. So Woodard kept still and kept walking.

Shull tried talking to Woodard, first asking if he'd been discharged. Woodard claimed when he said "yes," the chief hit him again with the blackjack and demanded that he be addressed as "sir." It was the final insult.

Woodard couldn't help himself; he refused to take this beating. He grabbed the blackjack out of Shull's hand, both to stop the assault and protect himself. The chief lunged at him and they struggled until the second officer showed up – with his gun drawn. Woodard let go of Shull, and the blackjack. Slowly, he raised his hands.

They didn't beat him anymore, not then. Shull and the other officer simply marched Woodard toward the jail, the chief casually swatting him with the blackjack as they walked. But at the door to the station, Shull smacked Woodard hard enough to knock him out. He woke to the sound of the chief screaming for him to get up. But when he tried, the two men pummeled him. And finally, Shull gouged him in both eyes with the end of the blackjack. Then they dragged him inside and threw him in a cell.

The next morning, Woodard couldn't see.

He was taken to municipal court. Mayor H.E. Quarles was presiding, and he listened to Shull recount how Woodard has resisted arrest. He was quickly found guilty, sentenced to 30 days and fined $50. They searched his pockets for the money, but only found $44 and a check from the Army for nearly $700. It was his mustering out pay. The mayor asked Woodard to sign over the check, but he couldn't see to sign his name. Eventually, the fine was reduced to $44 and he was taken back to jail.

For the rest of the day, Shull half-heartedly tried to patch up his prisoner – even offered him whiskey. Finally, the chief rid himself of the problem by driving Woodard to a Columbia hospital, where he told staff the soldier had been injured while resisting arrest. When a doctor asked if he'd been drunk at the time, Woodard later claimed he heard Shull say "No."

It took Woodard's family three weeks to find him in that Columbia hospital, blind and suffering from partial amnesia. They moved him to a veteran's hospital in Spartanburg, where military doctors said his corneas had been ruptured.

The damage was beyond repair. Woodard spent two months recovering in the hospital, but he would never see again.

Woodard's entire life was ruined.

Blind, he had no way to make a living. And soon after he was released from the hospital, his wife left him. She saw no future for them, had no desire to spend her life taking care of him and filed for a separation in May. Woodard's parents took him to their home in the Bronx and called the NAACP. Walter White, the organization's executive secretary, would make Woodard famous – the symbol of mistreated black veterans returning from the war.

The Army could do nothing. His story was too vague to press charges, and the secretary of war told White he couldn't intervene because Woodard had been a civilian at the time of the attack. He suggested the sergeant apply for a pension through the Veterans Administration, which brought in $50 a month – the early 21st-century equivalent of about $675. But Woodard and White didn't want money, they wanted justice.

Because Woodard still suffered from bouts of amnesia, he couldn't remember who attacked him or where he'd been jailed. He first suggested it might have been Aiken, South Carolina, and the NAACP asked Gov. Ransome Williams to help solve the crime. But Aiken police denied arresting Woodard, and the state refused to investigate. Finally, White turned to James Hinton in the South Carolina NAACP office.

Somebody had to know something.

New York newspapers ran the first accounts of Woodard's story in July, but the case rose to national prominence when Orson Welles highlighted it on his weekly ABC radio show. The *Citizen Kane* director and star was outraged by Woodard's blinding. Spurred on by White, Welles challenged the "officer X" who blinded Woodard to come forward.

"He was just another white man with a stick who wanted to teach a Negro boy a lesson, to show a Negro boy where he belonged – in the darkness," Welles said on the air, his resonant voice filled with rage.

Welles took Woodard's faulty memory as fact and blamed the Aiken police for the atrocity. The city responded by banning Welles' films from local theaters.

The next month, a handful of African-American entertainers and celebrities – including the boxer Joe Louis – organized a benefit for Woodard in New York. The fundraiser brought in some money for the family, and folk singer Woody Guthrie composed a song for the event titled "The Blinding of Isaac Woodard." For a while, it seemed a movement was stirring. But there were more atrocities, other injustices, and soon the blind man from South Carolina was largely forgotten.

Then, unexpectedly, the mystery was solved.

Although military police decided the case was outside their jurisdiction, the Army had looked into Woodard's story – and someone was offended enough by his treatment to leak the results of the investigation to The Associated Press. Cornered by a reporter, Batesburg Police Chief Lynwood Shull admitted he'd arrested Woodard in February. But he told a story that was vastly different from the tragedy recounted by the NAACP and Orson Welles.

Basically, the chief said, Woodard was injured while resisting arrest. "I hit him across the front of the head after he attempted to take away my blackjack." Shull conceded that single blow "may have" landed in Woodard's eyes, but said he'd reported it immediately to the Federal Bureau of Investigation. He would have spoken up sooner, Shull claimed, but the feds told him not to talk about the incident.

To many people, it appeared no one cared about Woodard's plight. The state had ignored the NAACP's pleas to investigate and, if Shull was telling the truth, the feds had covered it up. President Truman was livid.

On Sept. 19, Walter White met with Truman in the Oval Office and recounted Woodard's story. In some ways, it was just another tale of strife between civilians and black soldiers returning from war, many of them set in the South. But few incidents were as barbaric, and Truman was offended on several levels. *How could the country ask a man to risk his life in war and then treat him this way?*

The president immediately ordered Attorney General Tom Clark to investigate, and the case was assigned to the U.S. attorney in Columbia. But no one wanted to make trouble with South Carolina officials, so a week passed without any movement. Fed up, Truman told the Justice Department to launch its own inquiry – and to get results. Shull was indicted almost immediately.

In late September, FBI agents arrested Shull and charged him with violating Woodard's constitutional rights. The indictment accused the chief of beating and torturing the war veteran, but Shull told reporters he would plead self-defense. He was out of jail almost immediately, his bail paid by the town of Batesburg.

The warrant for Shull's arrest was signed by U.S. District Judge George Timmerman, but he wouldn't hear the case. Timmerman actively avoided controversy, particularly involving state officials and issues of race, but this time he had a legitimate – if convenient – excuse. He was a native of Batesburg, had known the chief for years. Even if Timmerman had wanted to hear the case, which he didn't, judicial ethics required his recusal. Timmerman asked Waring to take over.

The case troubled Waring from the start. It appeared the U.S. attorney's office was either indifferent, or incompetent. U.S. Attorney Claud Sapp asked the judge to schedule the trial for early November, but confessed he knew little about it yet. The Justice Department had sent him only a thin file, and it seemed the entire prosecution was built solely on Woodard's testimony. The feds hadn't even bothered to take it to a grand jury.

Without a grand jury indictment, Shull could not be sentenced to more than a year in prison; the federal government was prosecuting charges that amounted to nothing more than a misdemeanor. Incensed, Waring pointed this out to the U.S. attorney. Sapp was sympathetic, but claimed he'd been ordered to hurry and had no time to prepare for a grand jury. Besides, he said, it was unlikely any South Carolina grand jury would agree to indict the chief. Which was a fair point.

Nothing Waring saw in the month before the trial suggested his initial concerns were unfounded. NAACP attorneys reported that prosecutors didn't know even the most basic details of the case, and Sapp conceded his office wasn't ready. Finally, he asked for a continuance. Waring denied the request. He suspected the Justice Department was using Woodard's case as a campaign ploy.

The Democrats were in danger of losing control of Congress, and the judge suspected this was a White House stunt to turn out the black vote. He feared that if the case was delayed until after the election, it would be quietly dropped.

"I do not believe that this poor blinded creature should be a football in a contest between box office and ballot box," Waring told Sapp.

The trial of Lynwood Shull began on election day, Nov. 5, 1946.

Waring heard the case in Timmerman's Columbia courtroom, and Elizabeth made the trip with him. The judge had to use his pull with the bailiffs to get her a seat – the courtroom benches were filled with national reporters, gawking attorneys and an unusually large contingent of black and white spectators. It seemed the trial was a bigger draw than the day's congressional elections.

Isaac Woodard Jr. was the first witness called. He recounted the story of his short bus trip, the argument with the driver and the beating he suffered at the hands of Shull. Woodard admitted he'd had a drink or two earlier in the day, but swore he had no alcohol on the bus. He detailed every blow, ending with Shull gouging out his eyes with the blackjack.

The prosecutors called three doctors to testify – two from the veterans' hospital and a third who said he examined Woodard in the Batesburg jail. The military's physicians simply described the nature of the injuries. The Batesburg doctor, however, contradicted Woodard's statement that he'd received no treatment while in jail, and backed up Shull's claim that the injuries could have come from a single blow. His testimony considerably weakened the government's case.

Sapp had witnesses from the bus willing to testify that Woodard hadn't been drunk, but rested his case after the doctors spoke. He'd chosen to save them for his rebuttal, and Waring was outraged by the misstep. By the time the defense finished its presentation, the judge knew, it would be too late. He realized the government's entire case was a sham.

"The bus was pretty well filled with passengers," Waring later said. "That, to my mind, was quite a shocking instance of whether the government was really prosecuting the case under pressure or sincerely."

As the trial drifted into the afternoon, Shull's defense team put the bus driver on the stand. Blackwell claimed Woodard had been riotous during the trip, using such vulgar language that one passenger complained that his wife was offended by the profanity. Woodard had asked to "take a piss," the driver said. He had no choice, Blackwell said, but to call the police and have the soldier removed from the bus.

On the stand, Shull was reserved and repentant. He hadn't planned to arrest Woodard, the chief said, but he'd become argumentative and abusive in the parking lot. Shull said he hit Woodard only once, in self-defense – although he conceded on cross-examination that he might have "bumped" him lightly in the bus station parking lot.

"I did not mean to hit him in the eyes," Shull said. "I'm sorry I blinded him ... if I blinded him."

In more than an hour of testimony, the chief disputed nearly every point in Woodard's story. But Elliott Long, the other officer on the scene, contradicted some minor points he'd made in his statement to the FBI – although Sapp didn't capitalize on the mistakes. The defense repaired Long's misstep with a series of character witnesses who praised Shull, including a black Batesburg minister who called the chief an "extra good" peace officer.

The entire defense rested on Woodard resisting arrest, which justified the use of force. By focusing on his actions in the parking lot, the defense made any testimony from the bus passengers irrelevant. In the end, it was simply the chief's word against Woodard's. There was little doubt whose side an all-white jury would take.

But Shull's attorney wanted insurance, so he shamelessly stoked the fires of prejudice in his closing remarks, referring to Woodard as a member of an "inferior race" and claiming that if the chief was convicted, no police officer in South Carolina would be able to protect good – in other words, white – families. Finally, the attorney called Woodard "uppity" and suggested his conduct was "not the talk of a sober nigger from South Carolina."

Waring told the lawyer to shut up, but the damage had been done.

"I attempted to instruct the jury very carefully as to the fact that color had nothing to do with the matter and it was purely a question as to whether this man's civil rights had been violated by an officer using undue force and attacking him physically," Waring later said.

But he knew that argument fell on deaf ears. The defense had reinforced everything the jurors were predisposed to believe, and wanted to hear.

Waring knew Shull would be acquitted.

After he charged the jury, Waring retreated to Timmerman's chambers to stew. The trial was a farce, and there was no way he'd allow that jury to acquit the chief in two minutes. It would be disrespectful to the court, and another blow to Woodard. So the judge put on his hat, walked out of the office and told the deputy marshal, "I'm going for a walk, and I will be back in 20 minutes' time."

"But judge," the marshal said, "that jury ain't going to stay out for 20 minutes."

"They're going to stay out 20 minutes, because they can't come in until I come back," Waring said, "and I'm not going to be back here for 20 minutes."

Walking the streets of Columbia that crisp, fall afternoon, Waring could not shake his anger. What he'd just seen was not justice. Woodard hadn't gotten a fair trial – it was close to a lynching. The teacher-pay lawsuits exposed Waring to the inherent inequities of the country, but this case laid bare the injustice that black Americans faced every day, and he would never forget it.

As promised, the judge was back at the courthouse in 20 minutes. The marshal met him at the door and reported that the jury was antsy to deliver its verdict. Waring stalled some more before returning to the courtroom, then sent the marshal to fetch the jurors.

It went even worse than Waring had feared. When the foreman, a man from Charleston, read the words "not guilty," the white people in the courtroom cheered. Woodard didn't need to see the audience's reaction, it echoed in his ears. The judge tried to cut them off, thanking the jurors for their service before excusing them. He wanted to say more, but didn't.

"I made no comment," Waring recalled later. "I have no comment or criticism of them now. I couldn't ask them to find guilty on the slimness of that case, but I was shocked by the hypocrisy of my government … in submitting that disgraceful case before a jury. I was also hurt that I had been made party to it, however unwilling I was."

A year later, NAACP attorneys filed a lawsuit on Woodard's behalf against Greyhound, claiming its driver had discriminated against him. Shull and Blackwell returned for the trial, and the bus company's lawyers submitted a deposition from a woman who claimed she was offended by Woodard's behavior. He lost that case too. Soon, Woodard was forgotten and lived the rest of his life in New York, and in obscurity. But his case spurred President Truman into action on civil rights, which would have dramatic repercussions in the coming years.

Waring wouldn't forget Isaac Woodard Jr., either. He left the courthouse that afternoon and found Elizabeth crying in their hotel room. She'd sat through the entire trial and was horrified by all that she'd heard. On her walk back to the hotel, Mrs. Waring had bumped into a woman she knew casually. As she recounted the awful treatment of Woodard, the woman just nodded her head sympathetically.

"Mrs. Waring, that sort of thing happens all the time," the woman said. "It's dreadful, but what are we going to do about it?"

Waring later said the Woodard case was Elizabeth's "baptism in racial prejudice." In some ways, it was also his own. The judge had never been an overt racist. He hadn't sympathized with the Ku Klux Klan during its 1920s resurgence, never talked in racial code about "us" and "them." Waring didn't wax poetic about antebellum South Carolina and the Confederacy's glorious Lost Cause. For his entire life, he'd at least been more kind and respectful to black people than most of his generation.

But he'd also lived in a world that systemically discriminated against black Americans and, for most of his life, largely ignored it. Now, that time had passed. Waring realized racial prejudice, inequality and injustice permeated the entire country, and too many people – including Elizabeth's friend on the street – simply shrugged and said, "What are we going to do about it?" He was haunted by that sympathetic, yet callous, remark.

What are we going to do about it? That sort of statement telegraphed subtle compliance. And Waties Waring was anything but compliant. He was a federal judge; it was his job to make things right.

And, Waring thought, there *were* some things he could do about it.

A CALCULATED CALL

Two weeks after the Woodard trial, Waring addressed a group of newly naturalized citizens in his Charleston courtroom. He enjoyed these ceremonies, swearing in new Americans, and often used the opportunity – and the captive audience – to launch into long spiels about history, one of his favorite subjects.

Waring urged them to not only enjoy their rights and privileges as American citizens, but to participate in the political process. He said freedom was the country's founding principle, and that freedom included religion, speech, assembly and – perhaps most importantly – the right to vote. Waring spoke for more than 10 minutes about the inherent greatness of a country built on tolerance. Tolerance, he said, must be displayed even in the face of intolerance.

"We have the right, and it is our duty, to treat people fairly, irrespective of their race or their religion or their beliefs or their actions," he said.

By that point, Waring was talking to himself as much as anyone.

The Woodard trial had changed Waring. Two weeks later, he still couldn't get the case off his mind. He remained shocked at the government's ineptitude; as U.S. attorney he would not have failed to win a conviction, no matter the jury. How, he wondered, could the Justice Department recognize the importance of filing federal charges and then do such a shoddy job? It made no sense, and now a war veteran's life was ruined simply because he was black. That turned his stomach.

The trial had no less effect on Elizabeth. Upon their return to Charleston, she began to read about Southern culture and politics incessantly. When the judge would lie down at night to rest his eyes, she read aloud to him – often excerpts from W.J. Cash's *The Mind of the South*. The book was a study of the region's attitudes toward race, religion and romanticism. Cash, a South Carolina native, had spent more than a decade writing his treatise on the culture of the region in the decades after the Civil War. He chronicled and lamented a culture filled with people who were at once friendly and generous, yet at the same time close-minded, prejudiced and incapable of any deep analysis of their beliefs.

It would have been in character for the Warings to contact Cash, to engage in the lofty intellectual discussions they both enjoyed. But by the time they read his book, Cash was dead. He'd been found hanged by his necktie in a Mexico City hotel room shortly after the book's publication. Authorities called it a suicide, but a whiff of conspiracy surrounded his odd death. For years, people would whisper that Cash had been pursued by Nazis.

The Mind of the South was a detailed study of the problems most evident in South Carolina, but it barely scratched the surface compared to Gunnar Myrdal's *An American Dilemma: The Negro Problem and Modern Democracy.* In 1,500 pages, the Swedish economist boiled down this dilemma to an unending cycle: whites oppressed blacks, which led to their poor performance in school, work and society. This, Myrdal argued, was used to justify white supremacy and the continued oppression of an entire race of people. His solution was to simply wipe out prejudice, which Waring no doubt found preposterous. It would be easier to rid the Lowcountry of salt marshes.

Waring listened carefully as Elizabeth read Myrdal's views on inequity in the legal system. To retain power, he wrote, politicians had to appease the majority – and the majority believed blacks were inferior and didn't deserve equal rights. At first, Waring thought Myrdal was at the very least guilty of egregious over-simplification. But he was too cerebral to dismiss such a serious hypothesis out of hand. He applied the theory to the Woodard case, and had to admit that it fit. He thought about this American dilemma in court, at home and even on the couple's regular Sunday drives.

Waring and Elizabeth still cruised the sea islands west of Charleston on the weekends, following dirt roads past dilapidated wooden shacks that looked as if they'd been standing – albeit barely – since the Civil War. Some of these homes didn't have electricity or running water, and many others barely offered shelter from the rain. It upset them, and reinforced their growing awareness of inequality gleaned from academic tomes and the injustice they saw in the courtroom.

After one of those drives, Elizabeth persuaded the judge to visit a local black family they knew. It would be a polite gesture, she argued, and it wasn't as if their social calendar was overwhelmed. Later, she recalled how uncomfortable her husband, and the families, had been during those visits. Waring had interacted with African Americans all his life, but in Charleston there had always been boundaries – and he was not accustomed to crossing them. Although he had newfound empathy for the plight of black Americans, he didn't know what to say to them.

"It was so strange for both of them," Elizabeth said. "All their lives stood in the way."

That awkwardness soon dissipated, and the Warings began to visit their black neighbors regularly. For Elizabeth, it was a wonderful solution to several problems. They were integrating society and making new friends – which was fortuitous, since the judge lost most of his old ones in the divorce. And within a year, he would alienate just about everyone else.

Still, the couple spent most of their time alone. They talked about current events, travel and their differing perspectives. Sometimes they simply re-read Cash or Myrdal. When Waring filled in for a judge in Richmond that winter, Elizabeth went with him. On their return, they stopped in Florence so the judge could clear the district docket.

By then, in the spring of 1947, Waring had an almost entirely new outlook on his duties as a federal judge. That new philosophy was about to be tested and, in the eyes of most of his friends and relatives, he would fail.

In August 1946, a man named George Elmore unsuccessfully tried to vote in the South Carolina Democratic primary. Elmore, a 41-year-old Columbia businessman, cab driver and member of the Richland County Progressive Democrats, knew exactly what he was doing. He was African American, after all, and barely two years had passed since Gov. Johnston called the legislature into special session to ensure no black person would vote in the party's primary.

Elmore's father had been Jewish and, as a result, his skin was so light he'd been permitted to vote in earlier primaries. This time he was stopped. Perhaps he was recognized – he owned a five-and-dime store on Gervais Street, as well as a couple of liquor stores that did business with white vendors. He was a popular, well-respected member of the community. But no matter what anyone thought of him personally, poll workers would not give him a ballot. Within days, he reported his treatment to the state branch of the NAACP.

Elmore volunteered to become the lead plaintiff in an NAACP lawsuit against the Richland County Democratic Party. The group had been looking for another Southern voting-rights case after the success of *Smith v. Allwright*, and South Carolina was a perfect venue to test that Supreme Court decision. Harold Boulware, home from the war, told Elmore that Thurgood Marshall himself would serve as lead counsel.

The lawsuit, filed on Feb. 21, 1947, argued that the General Assembly's repeal of all primary election laws actually changed nothing. The Democratic Party continued to perform the "same governmental function in conducting and supervising primary elections." Excluding black citizens from the primaries, the suit argued, violated their constitutional rights. The NAACP asked the federal court for an injunction to stop this practice.

The peril for South Carolina did not go unnoticed. On its front page, The Evening Post warned that the NAACP hoped to build on a series of court cases, most recently in Texas and Georgia, to stop the Democratic Party's "practice of excluding Negroes from its primary elections." If there was any doubt of the paper's sympathies, the story said lead plaintiff George Elmore "claimed he was denied the 'right' to ballot in the August 13, 1946, primary."

The Post's story also noted that Thurgood Marshall, general counsel for the NAACP, was listed as Elmore's principal attorney. That was more than simply journalistic thoroughness; the mention of Marshall was a signal the civil rights organization considered this a case of national significance. By 1947, most everyone had heard of the famous black attorney who routinely prevailed in the United States Supreme Court.

Richland County Democratic Party Chairman John Rice and state party

Chairman Tom Pearce were conspicuously unavailable for comment in all initial reports about the lawsuit. The Democrats would say nothing publicly for weeks; but it was all they talked about privately. The NAACP had been methodically undermining white primaries across the South, and the state's most powerful lawmakers had to wonder whether they'd done enough to insulate South Carolina from a similar fate.

This came at a particularly inconvenient time for the Democrats, and they suspected that was the intent. State lawmakers first learned of *Elmore v. Rice* while quietly amending the state budget to fend off yet another NAACP lawsuit. Somehow, they had to find enough money to build some semblance of a black law school in Orangeburg.

In January, the NAACP had filed suit on behalf of a man denied admission to the University of South Carolina's law school. John Wrighten, a Charleston resident, S.C. State graduate and civil rights activist, claimed the university violated his constitutional rights by failing to offer him the same educational opportunities given to white students. This was cause for significant concern among South Carolina legislators. Already, the NAACP had forced several other states – Oklahoma, Arkansas and Delaware among them – to make law school available to black students.

South Carolina officials had followed those cases closely, and for two years planned to build a black law school at S.C. State as insurance against similar challenges. But lawmakers had procrastinated. They saw no demand for the school and, frankly, were unwilling to part with the money. Shortly after Wrighten filed suit, however, the legislature appropriated a modest sum for the proposed law school – hopefully enough to fend off any court order.

The Elmore and Wrighten lawsuits were filed in Columbia's U.S. District Court, and both had been automatically assigned to Judge Timmerman – which worried him immensely. He didn't like controversial racial cases, particularly when state officials were the defendants. Timmerman considered this dilemma for several days, and finally concluded that he couldn't avoid hearing *Elmore v. Rice* – it was practically in his back yard. But he had a good excuse to beg off

Wrighten v. Board of Trustees of the University of South Carolina.

Timmerman had once served on the University of South Carolina's board of trustees and, although he'd quit years earlier, felt justified claiming a potential conflict of interest. He explained this in a letter to Judge Waring, who was in Virginia presiding over a complicated check-kiting trial. Timmerman realized Waring rarely shied away from such cases, so he didn't consider it impolite to pass on *Wrighten.*

Of course, Waring already knew about *Wrighten* – he'd trained his court clerks well. He was only surprised it had taken the NAACP so long to file it. Marshall had a similar case underway in Oklahoma, which Waring had been monitoring for months. The judge considered it such a simple issue that he could hardly believe the number of appeals. Waring didn't mind taking *Wrighten*, but he was much more interested in the *Elmore* case – which Timmerman hadn't mentioned.

Waring realized *Elmore v. Rice* had the potential to remake South Carolina's political landscape, and he wanted the case badly. It wasn't just ego; he feared Timmerman would be reluctant to cross the Democratic Party, regardless of the lawsuit's merits. But he also knew asking for it outright would look bad, and likely wasn't ethical. So he gave Timmerman the choice.

"I wrote him or called him up and said of course I'd be glad to do it, but that it had occurred to me that there were two cases that were very closely interlocked and would be in great part dependent on each other and would probably be heard one after another," Waring later recalled. "I thought the same judge that heard one case ought to hear the other, and if he wished me to take on the Elmore case, I would take that too."

Waring purposely overstated the significance of the Wrighten lawsuit to scare Timmerman and get what he wanted. In fact, he didn't consider *Wrighten* an attack on segregation at all – he believed it only perpetuated "separate but equal," and that sort of case didn't interest him in the least. It wasn't hard to imagine how this would play out: Faced with the prospects of admitting black students at the University of South Carolina, the legislature would set up some slipshod law school at S.C. State and that would be the end of it.

Elmore, on the other hand, was a lawsuit that could have significant consequences. It was nothing less than "an attack on the white primary," Waring said. And a lawsuit of such magnitude interested him greatly.

Waring had studied voting-rights lawsuits since South Carolina's hysterical reaction to *Smith v. Allwright*. At the time, then-Gov. Johnston admitted his intentions to preserve a whites-only Democratic primary. Lawmakers were even brazen enough to say their action had inoculated the party from federal meddling. But Waring disagreed with that assessment. Based on every case he'd read, the judge knew South Carolina was on very shaky legal ground.

"I felt that my state was backward, that it had been blind to decency and right, and that somebody had to … face the issue," Waring said.

Social change was coming, Waring believed, if not in the next year, certainly within the next decade. He saw *Elmore v. Rice* as a unique opportunity to make a difference in the lives of millions of people – as only a federal judge could. But Waring realized the lives most likely to be affected, at least at first, would be his and Elizabeth's. So they talked about the case, and what it would mean for them.

Tackling such a controversial and sensitive issue would have repercussions. Although their social calendar in Charleston was slim, the Warings were still regulars at cocktail parties and dinners in Columbia and Florence. And even though people suspected his growing liberalism – the judge said people often looked at him "queer" and wrote off his views as "you can't expect everybody to think with us" – this would be different. None of his other decisions had any real impact on the lives of most white people.

"There's a terrible feeling in this state about the racial matter, and this Elmore case is going to bring it to a head. … We may have to pay a heavy penalty. I don't know what'll happen," Waring told Elizabeth. "I haven't got to take this case, it isn't mandatory. I think it's my duty to take it. Somebody else might not present the issue clearly. The case can be decided the other way if you conceal some of the facts and don't have a complete picture."

From the start, Waring believed there was only one correct ruling in *Elmore* – and it would destroy a power structure in place since the days of Ben Tillman. If people wanted to shun him for that, he could live with it. But the judge was no fool. He knew what was at stake, and the people he'd known his entire life would never accept an all-out assault on white supremacy. To preserve their inherent advantage, and dominance of the state, they might even resort to violence.

Elizabeth had lived in South Carolina only a short time, but she understood. She'd watched the courtroom erupt in cheers when the police chief who maimed Woodard was acquitted. But she had grown just as disgusted by prejudice as Waring, and supported him completely. They were in it together.

"I think you ought to do it and I think you ought to do it right," she said. "I'm with you, start to finish. I think you ought to take it; we don't know what's going to happen if you don't."

So Waring made the call and offered his deal to Timmerman, who – as the judge expected – was more than happy to hand off *Elmore*. A few weeks later, Judge Waring announced that he would hear both NAACP cases in the late spring.

DECLARATION OF WAR

S outh Carolina officials were troubled by the news out of Georgia.

In 1946, the U.S. Supreme Court had ruled it unconstitutional for the state to exclude black voters from its Democratic primary. The decision was unsurprising; the court had reached the same conclusion in a Texas case two years earlier. Georgia lawmakers attempted to evade the order by stripping all primary election laws from state code and calling the Democratic Party a private club – an idea shamelessly stolen from South Carolina. It didn't work.

Gov. Melvin Thompson vetoed Georgia's "white primary" legislation in late March 1947, just as South Carolina Democrats were preparing their defense of the same ploy. Legal experts in Georgia concluded the ruse wouldn't work, that the state could not get around the Supreme Court's mandate. The governor apparently saw no need to waste money on another lawsuit and endless appeals.

The fall of another whites-only primary – and the Supreme Court's stubborn insistence on open elections – worried South Carolina's political establishment. The *Elmore v. Rice* case was on the same track, and Democrats saw no way to derail it. Even if they won the first round, they were certain to lose on appeal.

The pending lawsuits worried state leaders throughout the spring. The News and Courier characterized *Elmore* and *Wrighten* as attacks on the state's "institutions" – a term that South Carolinians had once used regularly to describe slavery. This was no coincidence. William Watts Ball, the paper's editor, was the son of a slave-owning Confederate officer, and a notorious traditionalist. A native of Laurens – in the state's "Upcountry," as he called it – Ball didn't believe blacks should compete with whites for jobs. And they certainly shouldn't influence Democratic Party politics.

Ball was given to fits of melodrama in his editorials. One of his News and Courier headlines declared the "White primary in danger," although the piece actually predicted the Democrats would prevail. Ball said that, unlike Texas, South Carolina had no laws governing primaries. He conceded the state had jettisoned such statutes only in reaction to *Smith v. Allwright*, but considered that a shrewd move against a federal government many Southerners still didn't trust.

"By doing so, they removed the party from the jurisdiction of federal and state laws in so far as the conduct of party business is concerned," Ball wrote.

The Democratic Party used almost the exact same argument when its attorneys filed a response to *Elmore* in April. Party officials declared themselves immune from federal oversight, the same as any private club. Despite their public displays of confidence, party leaders were not optimistic. And the judge had done little to ease their concerns.

The Democrats should have been relieved to have Waring on the case. He'd been a party officer most of his adult life, a confidant of two U.S. senators, brother-in-law of a former governor and the law partner of a state legislator. Waring was part of the power structure. Still, no one knew what the mercurial judge might do. After all, he'd been more than fair to the NAACP in two teacher-pay lawsuits. And since he'd taken *Elmore*, his public comments had been less than comforting.

In May, Waring announced he would hear *Elmore* and *Wrighten* back-to-back in Columbia the following month. He told The Associated Press neither case should take more than a few days; they weren't complex lawsuits. "If the Democratic Party can prove it is a private organization with no statutes regulating it, then it is outside the jurisdiction of this court or any other court," Waring said.

"If, however, it is proved that the Democratic Party is a state-controlled organization, then the Negroes win the case."

That was a telling qualification, and perhaps a warning shot, because everyone knew nothing had changed in South Carolina. But party officials were even more concerned about Waring's refusal to assign a jury in either case. If *Elmore* went to a jury, party officials knew they would win. Waring had denied them an easy victory, and they had to wonder why.

The judge explained that he would allow a jury to decide monetary awards, if warranted, but wanted to hear the lawsuits himself because they both turned on technical points of law. It was a valid point, but Waring also likely based his decision on the very reasoning party officials feared. The Woodard trial still fresh in his mind, the judge suspected no South Carolina jury could fairly decide any case outside the lens of race – and both *Elmore* and *Wrighten* were entirely about race.

The News and Courier telegraphed the misgivings of party officials in a story published the Sunday before the hearings were scheduled to begin. The paper noted that both lawsuits "were practically certain of eventually reaching the Supreme Court of the United States, whatever the initial outcome."

It seemed everyone was braced for an unfavorable ruling from Judge Waring.

The temperature inside the courtroom was stifling.

On Tuesday, June 3, arguments in *Elmore v. Rice* began at Columbia's federal courthouse on Laurel Street. The white stone edifice, barely 10 years old, could not repel the blistering Midlands heat – which was even more unbearable because of the standing-room-only crowd crammed into the courtroom. The few white people in attendance squeezed onto benches filled with more than 100 black residents.

Thurgood Marshall undoubtedly drew some of the public interest, but the NAACP's lead counsel deferred to Harold Boulware for the opening statement. Boulware laid out the case succinctly and, with no jury to win over, little in the way of dramatics. He and Marshall expected a fair hearing from Waring, so the argument was simple and blunt.

"The only opportunity the elector has to cast a meaningful ballot in South Carolina is in the primary," Boulware said. He described the legislature's decision to repeal primary election laws in 1944 as a deliberate effort to "evade and circumvent a Supreme Court decision in a Texas case that year, which opened that state's primaries to Negroes."

Marshall addressed the technical points of law. He said although the state had repealed all enabling statutes for primaries, it made no difference because the Democratic Party still served a government function. Citing an earlier U.S. Supreme Court decision – *United States v. Classic* – Marshall argued that the

General Assembly's actions were illegal and unconstitutional.

"The state of South Carolina cannot release its duty to hold elections, unless it wants to say its congressmen are not properly elected," Marshall said. "The situation down here is like the state repealing all its police laws and letting the Elks enforce the laws."

Marshall was at his oratorical best that day, his message stirring the crowd and the courtroom's still, humid air. He pointed out that no other political party even bothered to hold a primary in South Carolina because the Democratic nominee always won the general election. Voting for a Republican in South Carolina, he said, was "as nugatory as voting for a Democrat in the state of Maine." Denying black voters the right to cast ballots in the primary, Marshall argued, silenced their voices.

"No right in the world is as basic as the right to vote, and no one can deny the right of a Negro to vote in South Carolina if the only way a Negro can exercise the franchise is in the Democratic primary," he said. "The action of the Democratic Party is state action."

When Marshall finished, the party's attorneys made the obligatory motion to dismiss. Irvine Belser and Charles Elliott, a member of the university's law school faculty, noted that all of Marshall's legal citations referred to states in which primaries were regulated by law. That no longer applied in South Carolina, which pre-empted any federal court jurisdiction.

"No state action is involved in this case," Belser said.

The Democrats were sticking to their script. They maintained that the primary was only "party activity," and nothing prevented Elmore from voting – he was free to cast a ballot in the government-operated general election. Elliott warned the court that the NAACP lawsuit, if successful, would emasculate the U.S. Constitution's 10th Amendment, "which reserves to the people of the states all rights not specifically delegated to the federal government."

Waring remained silent, but he had to recognize the irony. The Democrats' attorneys fretted over the sanctity of the 10th Amendment while attempting to shred the 14th Amendment.

The judge listened to the two sides bicker for nearly four hours. He interrupted only occasionally, because he felt it was important to include every fact and argument in the court record. He allowed the NAACP to admit into evidence the state Democratic Party's rule book, as well as newspaper articles in which Johnston admitted the legislature had repealed election laws to save the "white primary."

And Waring allowed the Democratic Party to hang itself.

"The argument on behalf of the party state organization was that they were not in any way bound by law and nobody had anything to do with them," Waring later recalled. "(T)hey were a private club, and just as the federal court had no say-so as to who should be president of a social organization or a ladies' sewing circle or vacation picnic, so the federal court had nothing to do with the Democrats getting together and having a primary of their own under their own officials."

But a ladies' sewing circle didn't elect the president of the United States or the governor of South Carolina. No Republican had been elected sheriff – or even coroner – in nearly a half-century, and no one knew that better than Waring. "The general election amounted to nothing. It was simply a validation of the primary."

On the second day of the hearing, *Elmore v. Rice* became monotonous. Both sides simply found new ways to repeat the same arguments, with varying degrees of success. Although the lawsuit named only the Richland County Democratic Party as a defendant, Waring found it odd that neither side had called William Baskin to the stand. After all, he was sitting in the courtroom.

Baskin, a state senator from Lee County, was chairman of the state Democratic executive committee. He'd been elected to the post in April, following the death of longtime party head Thomas Butler Pearce. If anyone could explain the party's inner workings, the judge figured, it was the chairman. So Waring, tired of listening to the attorneys drone on, called Baskin as a witness for the court. Belser objected, but the judge quickly shut him down.

"Gentlemen, this is a case that I have to decide and I have to get all the facts, and I think Mr. Baskin could help me a good deal," Waring said, "so I'm going to call him as a witness for the court, and them I'm going to allow both sides to cross-examine him if they desire."

Belser had good reason to object. He knew the chairman well enough to realize his unrehearsed testimony could sink the case. Which it did.

Waring later described Baskin as comically short and self-important, and took great joy in grilling him. The judge asked if the Democratic Party was the same organization it had been prior to 1944, and Baskin protested. Of course not: The repeal left the party with "no statutory support," and members who violated the rules could no longer be fined or jailed, only expelled. He admitted the party still had most of the same rules and officers, but insisted it was now an entirely different organization. After all, they no longer used the word "election" when referring to their primary.

Both sides cross-examined Baskin, but uncovered no new revelations. There wasn't much left to say. In his summation, Marshall could do little more than repeat the arguments he'd made for two days. "The people who are running South Carolina are the same people who are running the Democratic Party. They have a vested interest in this primary."

Belser not only rehashed tired arguments in his closing statement, he spewed race-baiting vitriol. He claimed "Negroes slept on their rights" by not voting in the general election and complained that the NAACP "seems to think theirs is the only right involved here. One of our most precious rights … is to belong to a private club."

When Waring adjourned the hearing, he granted both sides another 10 days to file additional briefs, although he couldn't imagine there was anything more to say. He also knew his decision would prompt protests. William Watts Ball promised as much on The News and Courier editorial page.

"The white man's primary in South Carolina is nothing more or less than a voting to nominate candidates by a statewide collection of white-skinned clubs, and white-skinned or dark-skinned clubs are lawful," Ball opined the day after the hearing. "A primary election in South Carolina is an all-day meeting of a club, of 1,500 clubs."

As the state awaited Waring's ruling, the editorials continued – Ball growing more pessimistic each week. Finally, he warned that if the NAACP won the lawsuit, "the white people can and will return to the convention plan by which they nominated Wade Hampton in 1876. This is better than primaries anyway."

It was nearly an admission of defeat – and a sign the paper had lost all confidence in Waring.

The *Wrighten* lawsuit didn't generate quite as much public animosity as *Elmore*, but the newspapers considered it just as insidious. In fact, Ball speculated it was all a plot.

On The News and Courier editorial page, Ball warned that whites would be forced to attend classes with blacks if the NAACP won. But in truth, the parties to the lawsuit had agreed beforehand not to contest the issue of segregation. Waring found the agreement ludicrous; it made the lawsuit, in his eyes, a waste of time. Still, he had every intention of at least forcing the state to live up to the "equal" in "separate but equal" – and the judge knew the law was on his side.

A case out of Missouri set the precedent. In 1936, Lloyd Gaines applied to the University of Missouri law school, but the registrar refused to admit him because he was black. In the resulting lawsuit, *Gaines v. Canada*, the state argued that it wasn't worthwhile to build a black law school, as there was so little demand. State attorneys offered to pay Gaines' tuition to a Kansas school, but Gaines refused – he wanted to study law in his home state.

The U.S. Supreme Court eventually ordered Missouri to either build a separate law school for black students or admit Gaines to the university. Some considered the case one of the first cracks in *Plessy v. Ferguson*, the Supreme Court decision that created the separate but equal doctrine a half-century earlier. And it gave Waring a template for *Wrighten*.

Arguments in the case began the day after *Elmore* ended, and the hearing was held in the same Columbia courtroom. Marshall was again stationed at the plaintiff's table, but David Robinson – representing the University of South Carolina – now sat opposite him. The audience was not nearly as large as it had been for the other case, many of the seats filled with officials from USC and S.C. State A&M College in Orangeburg.

Marshall recounted Wrighten's efforts to attend law school and the university's refusal to admit him. This was an issue of equity, he said, and the state must provide equal educational opportunities to everyone, regardless of skin color. Robinson argued that the lawsuit was unnecessary, that Wrighten could get a law degree at S.C. State. He called the executive secretary of the college's board of trustees to testify that the new law school would be open in three months — just in time for the fall semester.

Waring interrupted Robinson's questioning to ask the witness, W.C. Bethea, if S.C. State's law school would be comparable to the University of South Carolina's. The board secretary boldly claimed, "We expect to make it better."

The judge had cut to the crux of the case, and Marshall realized he'd already lost. If S.C. State offered a comparable law school, Wrighten had no lawsuit. Marshall regrouped and surprised the defense by calling S.C. State President M.F. Whittaker to the stand. The president was sitting in the audience, but hadn't expected to be a witness. Robinson objected. Whittaker wasn't party to the suit, he said, and there was no reason for him to testify. But Waring allowed it.

He only hurt the case more. Whittaker claimed S.C. State would've opened its own law school sooner, but no one had ever applied. Which Waring considered curious. *Who would apply to a school that didn't exist?* But then, Whittaker claimed he'd offered Wrighten a spot in the proposed law school, and was turned down. It implied that Wrighten knew he had options, and had filed suit only as a nuisance.

Marshall pointed out the illogic of Whittaker's testimony and asked to have it struck from the record. Waring denied the request, and the direct examination continued. Finally, Marshall discovered a crack in the state's case. He simply asked Whittaker the same question the judge had asked Bethea, and their answers were in direct conflict.

"I don't think we can get set up by September a law school that would be the full and complete equal" of USC's, Whittaker admitted.

Robinson retaliated with the president of USC. Norman Smith testified that he was bound by state law not to admit black students and, besides, the law school faculty reported there weren't enough classrooms to accommodate all the freshmen they had. The message was clear: Even if segregation wasn't the law of the land, there was no place for Wrighten.

Each side violated their pre-trial agreement on the second day of testimony, and Waring had to rein in angry outbursts from both sides of a hostile courtroom.

T.C. Callison, the state's assistant attorney general, said it was "ridiculous" for South Carolina to spend money on a black law school when there was so little demand. Citing *Plessy*, Callison also claimed the state was within its legal rights to deny Wrighten's admission.

That provoked Robert Carter, an attorney assisting Marshall, to launch into a diatribe against the state's segregationist policies. There can be "no equality of educational facilities where there is segregation," Carter said. He argued that Wrighten's constitutional rights could be protected fully only if he was admitted to the USC School of Law.

James Price, another state lawyer, reminded the court that both sides had stipulated such a remedy was not on the table. The NAACP, Price said haughtily, "had agreed themselves out of court."

The case ended there. Marshall realized Waring couldn't rule in favor of Wrighten if the state built a law school at S.C. State. In his closing remarks, he simply tried to mend the damage done by his co-counsel. Marshall noted "the people of South Carolina brought this case on themselves" by not providing a black law school.

He was right, both about the state's culpability and Waring's position. If the state was foolish enough to spend hundreds of thousands of dollars on a second law school simply to separate black and white students, the judge knew, federal law allowed it. And he had no doubt the General Assembly would do it. In South Carolina, prejudice had no price tag.

"It would have been a lot cheaper for the state of South Carolina to buy three more chairs and put them in the room in the law school at Columbia than to build a $200,000 building and put an initial appropriation of $30,000 for a law library, and hire seven professors for these three would-be lawyers," he said.

Everyone realized the NAACP lawsuit was doomed – except Ball. He ranted about the case for weeks in The News and Courier. He breathlessly wrote that, if Wrighten won admission to USC, the people of South Carolina "would insist upon the closing of the institution to white students (and) withdrawing public support from it." The state must do everything, he wrote, "to save white youth from racial admixture."

Ball provided a telling glimpse of the underlying fear that drove some white supremacists. Just beneath the surface of every argument for segregation lay the implied threat of miscegenation.

More than a month passed before Waring issued a ruling in either *Elmore* or *Wrighten*. The judge normally worked faster, but his procrastination didn't reflect doubt. Waring knew both orders had to be crafted carefully to ensure they wouldn't be overturned on appeal, and that was the excuse he gave for the delay. But, in truth, he spent most of the time worried about the tone his decisions should take.

These were sensitive issues, and both had stirred resentment and prejudice in the state. During the *Wrighten* hearing, someone in the courtroom had the audacity to complain aloud that his alma mater was "threatened by this dark cloud." But the judge knew *Elmore* was even more contentious, as it "went to the very heart of South Carolina politics." He couldn't decide whether such emotions demanded a measured response or a vicious repudiation.

One evening, Waring told Elizabeth that no matter what he wrote, the rednecks and racists might come after him. "The Klan still rides in South Carolina," he said. Ultimately, he knew the correct legal decisions would prompt a tremendous public outcry, no matter how gently he worded them. The judge simply had to decide how badly he wanted to condemn state officials.

As Waring struggled with this dilemma, President Truman addressed the closing session of the NAACP's annual conference in June. Standing in front of the Lincoln Memorial, Truman spoke of civil rights with more empathy than perhaps any president in history. He said the United States had reached a turning point in its efforts to "guarantee freedom to all our citizens."

"Our immediate task is to remove the last remnants of the barriers which stand between millions of our citizens and their birthright. There is no justifiable reason for discrimination because of ancestry, or religion, or race, or color," the president said. "Every man should have the right to a decent home, the right to an education, the right to adequate medical care, the right to a worthwhile job, the right to an equal share in making the public decisions through the ballot, and the right to a fair trial in a fair court."

Waring felt Truman had given voice to his very thoughts. Inspired, the judge realized he had the opportunity to do something historic and right, and couldn't be timid. He even included excerpts of the president's speech in his *Elmore* order: "We can no longer afford the luxury of a leisurely attack upon prejudice and discrimination. There is much that state and local governments can do in providing positive safeguards for civil rights. But we cannot, any longer, await the growth of a will to action in the slowest state or the most backward community."

"I determined that it had to be done and it had to be done with a punch," Waring said years later. "Either you were going to be entirely governed by the white supremacy doctrine and just shut your eyes and bowl this thing through or you were going to be a federal judge and decide the law."

On July 12, 1947, Waring simultaneously released both opinions. In *Elmore*, he ruled that black residents had an undeniable right to vote in the Democratic primary. For *Wrighten*, he ordered the state to set up a law school at S.C. State by September – or else admit black students to the University of South Carolina's School of Law. Although that was technically a victory for the state, the judge earned no credit for the split decision. That was evident from The Evening Post headline that afternoon: "Right of Negroes to Vote in Democratic Primaries Upheld by Waring's Decision."

In some ways, Waring's ruling in *Elmore* only stated the obvious: The state repealed its primary election laws following the *Allwright* decision, yet allowed the system to continue exactly as it had before. He noted that the U.S. Supreme Court had ruled repeatedly that black citizens had a right to vote in other states' primary elections. "I cannot see where the skies will fall if South Carolina is put in the same class with these and other states," Waring wrote.

The judge decided there was no way to deliver the order without enraging the entire state's power structure, so he didn't even try. In his ruling, he said the governor, legislature and Democratic Party had tried to circumvent the laws and Constitution of the United States. And if there was any doubt Waring meant to sting the Democrats, it evaporated by the final page of the order. There, he had the audacity to cast aspersions on the state's revered Confederate past.

"It is time for South Carolina to rejoin the Union," Waring wrote.

The judge had not only issued a rebuke to the state's ruling class, he had declared war.

IN THE COURT OF APPEALS

T he orders in *Elmore* and *Wrighten* were released on a Saturday morning. As the brother of a longtime newspaper editor, Waring no doubt realized it was the perfect time to deliver bad news. The Evening Post reporters on duty had difficulty finding anyone to comment on the bombshell decision in *Elmore v. Rice*, but conveniently received statements well before deadline from the NAACP and the Progressive Democrats – a sign that the judge may have tipped off the groups in advance.

John McCray, chairman of the South Carolina Progressive Party, said Waring's decision "proves once again that ours is a great country and state and in itself has extended to South Carolina Negroes the privilege of selecting their rulers." James Hinton, chairman of the state chapter of the NAACP, said his group "will have Negroes prepare for the next Democratic primary and if they face any difficulty we will call upon the U.S. Department of Justice for full protection."

McCray's effusive praise of Waring was one of the last positive comments the judge would see printed in Charleston. Although most elected officials declined to discuss either decision before The Post went to press, a number of them offered anonymous warnings.

"This is the end of the Democratic Party as we have known it," one politician lawyer said. Another unidentified official claimed no fraternal, civic or religious club would have the right to exclude members for racial reasons if the order stood. "They can't be excluded from anything, anymore, if this decision holds." To some people, it seemed Waring had gaveled an entire world out of existence.

The only local dignitary who would attach his name to such criticism that morning was former Charleston Mayor Thomas Stoney. He condemned the *Elmore* ruling and promised a protracted fight, flamboyantly recalling the Civil War, Reconstruction and Jim Crow.

"I feel certain that South Carolina still has men of the stamp of Wade Hampton, Benjamin Ryan Tillman … and hundreds and thousands of others who will meet the test," Stoney said.

Democratic Party officials issued only a brief, unemotional statement in which they promised to appeal the decision. But by Saturday evening, Burnet Maybank was publicly castigating his old friend and associate. The senator said he was confident Waring had erred and his decision would be reversed by the United States Supreme Court. "To date we have kept the white Democratic Party of South Carolina safe and sound," Maybank said, "and I am absolutely certain that it shall survive this new effort to overturn it."

Although Maybank's comments were mild compared to the anonymous doomsday predictions, he drew the ire of the state's black leaders. McCray criticized the senator's "denunciation of our judicial system," and Hinton told The News and Courier that Maybank's idea of democracy "is contrary to the Constitution of the United States." But the senator's sentiments were nuanced and measured compared to what would follow.

In Sunday's News and Courier, William Watts Ball was apoplectic. He repeated his warning that USC's law school might have to be shut down, but said the more immediate threat was the demise of the white primary and all other efforts to "maintain the separation of white and colored people." If *Elmore* is upheld on appeal, Ball predicted, "there is nothing left for South Carolinians but to abandon completely the name of the Democratic Party, divorcing themselves from national party affiliation and re-establishing an exclusive white man's club under a new title."

The Evening Post was even more bombastic, lamenting in a headline that the "rights of citizens again invaded." The Post's editors feared the *Elmore* decision would never be overturned because the Supreme Court was stacked with Roosevelt New Deal appointees, men who forced upon the South "a social and political system repugnant and harmful to this section." As expected, Waring's remark about rejoining the Union touched a nerve. The newspapers would repeat the line for weeks.

"It would have been edifying to citizens of his state had Judge Waring informed them how long South Carolina has been out of the Union," according to one editorial in The Post. "Has it been since 1876, when the Democrats, led by Wade Hampton, crushed the carpetbaggers and scalawags and ended the Reconstruction orgy of corruption, oppression and plunder? The white Democratic party of today stemmed from the State's redemption in 1876."

Waring later claimed *Elmore v. Rice* was the first step in his estrangement from Charleston – the moment when the politicians, South of Broad society and even lifelong friends turned their backs on him. But other than taking exception to his remark about rejoining the Union, neither paper attacked him personally. They complained about Roosevelt's judges and the federal court, but rarely mentioned his name in these indictments. On some occasions, the newspapers even defended Waring – conceding he'd only followed federal law established by the Supreme Court.

Still, the judge quickly made his share of enemies. Hate mail poured in to the courthouse from around the state, some of which he saved. One of the first letters was sent by a woman from Columbia, who suggested Waring had diminished himself in the estimation of all good people. She said South Carolina would never stand for "Negro rule" and decried the possibility that "black apes" might sit in classrooms alongside white students. Before signing off with "white supremacy forevermore," the woman suggested all blacks should leave the country – and take Waring with them.

"I am sure it will be all right with South Carolina if you will go with them to Africa."

Most of the letters Waring received that summer alluded to the white supremacists' greatest fear – the prospect of mixing the races. No doubt their terror was stirred by Ball's editorials, which predicted that integration would spell the end of the white race. "Any white man not bereft of his senses well knows that when little boys and girls of the two races shall go to the same schools (from the kindergarten through all the common schools) there will in time cease to be two races in the South.

"The white Southerners will not stand for it," Ball wrote. "The South Carolinians would not stand for it though all the world were against them."

Thurgood Marshall was apparently the impetus for that particular tirade. A report out of New York, printed in the Charleston papers, quoted the NAACP attorney as saying there could be no true equality so long as there was segregation – a sentiment Waring later recited to Marshall using almost the exact same words. But Ball did not see Marshall's statement as a call for equality; he read it as a threat.

"To break down race segregation is to effect race amalgamation. The proposal, not said in those words, is that there be one race neither white nor Negro." It never occurred to Ball, or many others, that whites and blacks could coexist equally.

Waring might have grown discouraged and given up, but he soon found an entirely new constituency. Hundreds of black residents sent cards and letters thanking him for giving them the right to vote, and black ministers praised his name on Sunday mornings. The Lighthouse and Informer, an influential black-owned newspaper in Columbia, even called the *Elmore v. Rice* decision "the most eventful act in our history since Lincoln signed the Emancipation Proclamation."

But the most moving compliment Waring received in the summer of 1947 came from Walter Manigault, a member of the Negro Businessmen's League of Georgetown, South Carolina. Manigault said the judge had given him and every black person he knew an infinite amount of hope.

"For the first time in my life," Manigault wrote, "I feel like a citizen of South Carolina and would not be ashamed to admit its being my home state."

On the day Waring issued his order in *Wrighten*, South Carolina State A&M College announced that its new law school would open in the fall. W.C. Bethea, secretary of the board of trustees, said the college had been planning the school since the trial and already had interviewed a number of candidates for dean. The pool was down to seven men, Bethea said, and one of them would be hired within 10 days.

The law school would be housed in an existing building on campus initially and employ one law professor, in addition to the dean. Bethea said the school wouldn't need more faculty because the school expected no more than a dozen or so students in its first year. A separate law school building and library would follow as enrollment grew. Bethea said it would be comparable to the University of South Carolina's law school, eventually.

The governor's office had pressured S.C. State to get a law school open quickly – and to make it look good. Although USC prevailed in the lawsuit, attorneys wanted to appeal part of Waring's language as insurance. They feared S.C. State's modest law school wouldn't meet the judge's standards by the Sept. 15 deadline, and they would be forced to admit black students at the university. From Bethea's description of the forthcoming law school, NAACP officials were certain it wouldn't meet any interpretation of the "separate but equal" standard.

Wrighten would never apply to the law school his lawsuit created.

The state Democratic Party executive committee met on July 17 and voted to appeal Waring's decision. Members of the committee and Sen. Olin Johnston, the former governor, were unmoved by an NAACP telegraph read aloud by Baskin. Hinton asked the party – in the spirit of cooperation – to voluntarily end this court battle and allow black residents to vote in the primary. But they would not give up so easily.

Baskin told reporters the vote was unanimous, but rumors of discord leaked almost immediately. Some committee members argued that the party's position was untenable, the case unwinnable. They objected to the appeal and suggested the party simply acquiesce to Waring's order. Their pleas went ignored, but nearly a month passed before the Democrats actually filed the motion to appeal. It took another week to get a hearing before Judge Timmerman.

Party attorneys had asked Timmerman for a temporary stay to suspend Waring's order while the case worked its way through the Fourth Circuit Court of Appeals. At the hearing, Irvine Belser complained that Waring's ruling was too general and confusing. The lawsuit was a simple dispute between George Elmore and the Richland County executive committee, yet the judge had applied his order to the entire Democratic Party. The next primary was a year away so, Belser argued, there was no harm in a temporary injunction.

Harold Boulware noted several South Carolina municipal elections were scheduled for the coming months, and said black voters would be irreparably harmed if not allowed to participate in the primaries. Already, Anderson County had canceled a primary to fill a vacant seat in the state House of Representatives. Democratic officials said they wouldn't hold a primary if blacks were allowed to vote. Instead, the party would put the names of all qualified candidates on the general election ballot.

Timmerman ignored the NAACP attorney's warning, and the amount he asked Democrats to put up as a bond against damages, and granted the party its reprieve. Waring's order was suspended pending a verdict from the Fourth Circuit Court of Appeals. The entire hearing lasted 20 minutes.

Waring didn't criticize Timmerman's injunction; it was just procedure, he knew, and the only opinion that mattered was the Fourth Circuit's. It was out of his hands. The judge kept a low profile through the summer and into the fall. He and Elizabeth vacationed in California and New York before stopping in Richmond to open the court's fall docket. No sooner than he arrived, Waring once again found himself on the witness stand.

In the spring, Waring had presided over the Richmond trial of several people accused of misappropriating funds from a Fredericksburg bank. The jury found all defendants guilty, but the men now wanted a new trial – and used the judge as an excuse. Attorneys for the convicted embezzlers claimed one of the jurors had been asked to throw the verdict, and the judge knew about it. Waring admitted no wrongdoing, but conceded he'd heard – well after the case ended – that a juror had been approached. Rather than argue, Waring simply disqualified himself from the case. He received no reprimand, a clear sign the judiciary saw nothing unethical in his conduct.

The Warings returned to Charleston at the end of September. The evening after he opened the fall term of court, the judge and Elizabeth attended the Knights of Columbus annual banquet at the Francis Marion Hotel. It was no St. Cecilia Society ball, but Mayor Ed Wehman and incoming Mayor William McG. Morrison attended, along with state Sen. Oliver Wallace and several College of Charleston officials. The Warings were even mentioned on The News and Courier society page.

The judge may have been estranged from his family and the South of Broad crowd, but he hadn't been ostracized from Charleston. Not yet. But he would never be invited to another Columbus Day banquet, at least not in his hometown.

In October, the NAACP filed another lawsuit on behalf of John Wrighten, this time claiming the S.C. State law school was inferior in every way to the one at the University of South Carolina. James Hinton told reporters it was getting ridiculous to fight for the "equal" in separate but equal, hinting at future lawsuits along those lines.

The university responded by asking the Fourth Circuit Court of Appeals to amend Waring's original decision. Instead of requiring "equal facilities," the state's attorney said, they preferred the order to accept "reasonably similar facilities." It was practically an admission that the NAACP was right.

The two sides met at the Fourth Circuit Court of Appeals in Baltimore on Nov. 21, and it didn't go well for the University of South Carolina. Thurgood Marshall told the court he never believed the state could establish two equal law schools, and now he'd been proven correct. USC attorney David Robinson, ignoring the equity issue, insisted that Wrighten should have applied to S.C. State's law school instead of filing a frivolous lawsuit against the state.

"What sense could there be in applying to a school that doesn't exist?" asked Judge Morris Soper. "That's absurd. He doesn't have to wait until you (the state) make up your mind to build a law school."

Robinson told the judges that South Carolina's position was that it didn't need to set up a law school for black students until there was a demand for one. Judge Armistead Dobie stopped the attorney.

"True," Judge Dobie said. "But until that is done, they have got to admit him to the university."

Ultimately, the Court of Appeals announced it would not overturn or amend Waring's decision. Any further action was premature, the court said, until Judge Waring ruled on whether the law school in Orangeburg met the definition in his original order. The message was clear: S.C. State's law school had to meet

Waring's standards, or USC would be forced to admit black students.

The decision didn't surprise Waring – he knew his order was on firm legal ground – but the court's comments did. The appeals court judges' remarks could have come from him. It seemed the federal justice system was changing. Conservatives in South Carolina attributed that to more than a decade of Roosevelt court appointments, but Waring believed there was a simpler explanation: Times were changing. The separate but equal tenets of *Plessy v. Ferguson* were faltering, albeit too slowly for his tastes. Still, President Truman's Justice Department surprised Waring again in December, when federal prosecutors brought him a Darlington County case that involved debt-slavery.

John Ellis Wilhelm had recruited James DeWitt to work on his Hartsville farm and, as was common practice at the time, asked the black teenager to sign an "agricultural contract."

The contract simply said DeWitt would serve as a laborer on the farm, with some of his salary paid in advance. DeWitt took the money and worked for a while, but eventually quit. He didn't like the job. Wilhelm considered this breach of contract and persuaded a magistrate to sign a warrant that said DeWitt would be jailed if he didn't return to the farm.

DeWitt eluded deputies for a while, but one night Wilhelm caught him coming out of a Florence movie theater. He forced the teenager into his car, took him to the farm and locked him in a cabin overnight. Wilhelm's father was visiting at the time, and he offered to take DeWitt to his farm in Georgia.

Later, the elder Wilhelm explained that he was only trying to help. He realized his son and the teen did not get along, and wanted to mitigate the situation. But when James Fred Wilhelm drove DeWitt across the state line, the federal government had jurisdiction. And the Justice Department considered it kidnapping.

The U.S. Attorney's office arrested John Wilhelm on federal charges of peonage and kidnapping, and that worried him a great deal. State courts recognized agricultural contracts as legal documents – but federal law considered it slavery. Wilhelm agreed to plead guilty to peonage if prosecutors would drop the more serious kidnapping charge. Waring was asked to sentence Wilhelm, once he got over the shock that debt-slavery still existed.

"The statutes on the books of South Carolina, still there, make it a criminal offense to break an agricultural contract, for a laborer to leave his job," Waring said. "I knew the thing was there, and I knew it had been used many years ago, but I really thought it was one of those dead laws that you find on the statute books of almost all the states."

Waring summoned DeWitt, Wilhelm and his attorney to the Florence courthouse to question them before the sentencing. The teenager told his story without emotion, recounting the night Wilhelm found him in town and asked him to "get in the automobile." The attorney for Wilhelm conceded DeWitt had been locked in a cabin overnight, but argued that state statutes allowed it. And those statutes, the attorney said, had been ruled constitutional by other courts. The judge found that defense ridiculous.

"You're one of the best lawyers in South Carolina," Waring said, "and you know it's utter nonsense to say that statute is constitutional."

"Well, the South Carolina courts have held it so," the lawyer said.

"Yes, but I won't."

Waring called DeWitt back to the stand and asked why he hadn't mentioned being locked in a cabin, or forced to go to Georgia against his will. At first, the teenager made excuses – he actually liked it better in Georgia; the elder Wilhelm was much nicer than his son. Finally, DeWitt admitted he was scared to get his captors in trouble.

Waring fined John Ellis Wilhelm $500 and sentenced him to a year and a day in prison. That decision upended the entire Pee Dee economy, a local attorney later told the judge. After Wilhelm was sentenced, the Florence County sheriff refused all requests to arrest workers who violated their agricultural contracts. The sheriff was afraid he'd get indicted.

"You have upset the agricultural situation here," the attorney related with some amusement. "Farmers can no longer make laborers work under stress of law."

For a few days, agricultural contracts were the talk of the courthouse. On Friday, a Charlestonian in town for jury duty mentioned it when he stopped by Waring's chambers to say goodbye. He said all the jurors believed it was outrageous, and agreed with the judge's sentence. "But," the man said, "we also agreed that if we had had to pass upon it, we would not have found him guilty."

That was the pathetic political reality of racial politics in South Carolina, Waring thought. He'd hoped the Wilhelm case signaled that the world was changing and decency would prevail – even if the federal government had to help it along. In reality, he realized the law might change but too many people still had perceptions rooted in the 19th century.

"There was a man – and he was a first-class citizen – who knew the difference between right and wrong, but would not have been willing to do the right thing because of community pressure," Waring said of the Charleston juror. "The community pressure is so enormous that it's very hard to break it."

While Waring was in Florence, the Fourth Circuit Court of Appeals debated *Elmore v. Rice*. Attorneys for the Democrats and the NAACP had appeared before the panel in mid-November, and their arguments hadn't changed. Neither did the decision. It took six weeks, but on Dec. 30, the Court of Appeals upheld Waring's ruling in language that was no less incendiary than his own.

"For half a century or more, the Democratic Party has absolutely controlled the choice of elective officers in the state of South Carolina," wrote Judge John Parker of Charlotte, North Carolina. "The real elections in that state have been contests within the Democratic Party, the general elections serving only to ratify and give legal validity to the party choice.

"No election machinery can be upheld if its purpose or effect is to deny the Negro, on account of his race or color, an effective voice in the government of his country or the state or the community wherein he lives," Parker wrote.

The Democrats were stunned. Party Chairman William Baskin and Gov. Strom Thurmond both refused to comment on the decision; eventually party lawyer Irvine Belser was forced to confirm that the Democrats would appeal to the United States Supreme Court. But there was no guarantee the court would accept the case – in fact, most legal experts predicted it wouldn't. And Baskin and Thurmond didn't want to admit defeat.

The state Democratic primary was little more than seven months away, and party officials quietly began to search for other ways they might circumvent Waring's order. As 1947 ended, the Democrats were certain of only one thing: No matter what the judge said, there was no way black people would vote in their primary.

RISE OF THE DIXIECRATS

President Truman gave his State of the Union address to Congress on Jan. 7, 1948, and it only confirmed what most of Washington had already concluded: He would run for re-election.

The president laid out a wildly liberal agenda for the coming year, including increases in the minimum wage and corporate taxes to make up for $3.2 billion in lost federal revenue. He proposed a tax cut of $40 per person, a national health insurance program and additional support for the country's farmers. It was time, Truman said, to admit Alaska and Hawaii into the union. And he called on Congress to quickly approve the Marshall Plan – a "vital measure" and a "decisive contribution to world peace."

The president looked vigorous and ridiculously fit in his blue, double-breasted suit. He considered the speech a barn-burner, but it earned scant applause outside of Bess and Margaret, his wife and daughter. Most Democrats were no more pleased with the speech than Republicans; both sides of the aisle assumed he was shoring up his defenses against both a GOP challenger and former Vice President Henry Wallace – who planned to run as a progressive independent. But South Carolina officials were most alarmed by Truman's goals for racial equality.

"Our first goal is to secure fully the essential human rights of our citizens," the president said.

Almost to a man, South Carolina's congressional delegation "took sharp exception" to Truman's civil rights plan. They told The News and Courier the president sounded too much like Judge Waring in the *Elmore v. Rice* opinion. Congressman William Jennings Bryan Dorn said he was fed up with both parties legislating for the rights of radical minorities; the state's senators promised to oppose any recommendations from the president's Civil Rights Commission. Sen. Olin Johnston said Truman had gone farther than "was practical or workable." But Burnet Maybank took the harshest tone.

"You can tell the people of South Carolina that I will fight until I'm blue in the face to keep the federal government from meddling in affairs concerning voting matters and other matters that do not concern the federal government," Maybank said.

When Truman delivered his civil rights plan to Congress less than a month later, it was even less palatable than Maybank predicted. The president proposed federal laws against lynching, poll taxes and discrimination in voting or employment. He had a 10-point program to correct "flagrant" offenses against the American faith that "all men are created equal and that they have the right to equal justice." Realizing this would be unpopular in the South, Truman tried to rebut his critics before they could open their mouths.

"The federal government has a clear duty to see that constitutional guarantees of individual liberties and of equal protection under the law are not denied or abridged anywhere in our union," the president said.

Again, South Carolina officials were united in outrage. Maybank said poll taxes were a state issue and lynching a thing of the past, so there was no need for such a law. Dorn accused Truman of stirring up prejudice and said it was time for the Southern Democrats to take the party back from the radicals. And Charleston congressman Mendel Rivers accused the president of trying to drag South Carolina back into Reconstruction.

"Even the Republicans in the balmiest days of their prosperity never proposed to do to the South what President Truman proposes," Rivers said. "Mr. Truman is showing his true colors. He is hell-bent for election. … He is willing to obliterate states' rights and state lines, and make Southern states mere territories, subservient to federal jurisdiction. I, for one, do not intend to take this thing lying down."

It was always good politics to allude to the Civil War in South Carolina, but reaction to the president's plan was uniform across the South. Mississippi legislators said Southern Democrats must hold their own convention, independent of the national party meeting in Philadelphia that summer. They proposed nominating their own candidate for president – even if it meant throwing the election to the U.S. House of Representatives. One South Carolina politician was particularly inspired by this idea, and saw a possible path into the national spotlight.

Waring spent the first week of 1948 clearing up old cases before opening the January court term, which held the promise of a light docket.

He ruled against an insurance company seeking $3,000 in Social Security money from the government, and dropped charges against two Berkeley County men accused of interfering with Internal Revenue agents. The judge also dismissed a $50,000 lawsuit against the U.S. Army brought by three North Carolina teachers. The women had been injured in the wreck of an Army Jeep carrying them, and several soldiers, to a dance in Myrtle Beach. Waring said because the accident was the result of a blown-out tire, the government could not be faulted.

On the day before Truman delivered his civil rights message to Congress, Waring turned down a request from John Ellis Wilhelm to reduce his sentence in the peonage case to 60 days. His attorney argued that Wilhelm "was only following the custom of the country with his labor contracts." The judge disagreed, calling the farmer's crime "a wholesome expose of an unwholesome situation which should be cured, preferably by a change of sentiment in the community, but if that doesn't occur, then by force of law."

Waring admired Truman's plan for civil rights. It seemed the administration, like the courts, was coming around on issues of race – and he could certainly use the support. Since the Elmore case, he felt even more estranged from his friends and neighbors. The ostracism, he later said, wasn't complete by then. But it was coming.

On Feb. 7, the state Democrats announced their plan to appeal *Elmore v. Rice* to the United States Supreme Court. Waring said nothing; it was the party's legal right. But he suspected their efforts would be useless. Truman proved the climate in Washington was changing, even though it clearly hadn't in the South. In fact, the party's appeal was not even the most notable attack on civil rights that week.

The day after South Carolina Democrats filed their plea with the Supreme Court, the Southern Governors' Conference demanded concessions on "white supremacy" from President Truman. Meeting in Wakulla Springs, Florida, the governors insisted Truman had gone too far with his civil rights plan – and made the unforgivable mistake of not consulting them first. The governors said they would form their own political action committee and take these concerns to Washington. South Carolina Gov. J. Strom Thurmond was appointed chairman of the committee.

Thurmond seemed an unlikely choice to lead what The News and Courier openly called a white supremacy group. Until that point, in fact, the state's new governor had been considered a progressive. He had noticeably refused to criticize Waring's decision in *Elmore v. Rice* and, a year earlier, had been praised by the NAACP for his efforts to prosecute more than two-dozen men accused of lynching a black man in Greenville.

Shortly after Thurmond took office, a cab driver was robbed and stabbed to death in Pickens County. Based on circumstantial evidence, 24-year-old Willie Earle was dragged out of his mother's home and arrested the next day. That night, a mob led by local taxi drivers stormed the jail and took Earle into the woods – where they beat and stabbed him, then shot him in the head.

Thurmond was horrified, and asked the FBI to work alongside state police to find the culprits. Eventually 31 men were arrested and put on trial. A jury of 12 white men acquitted them in hours – seven months before Sen. Maybank claimed lynching was no longer a problem in South Carolina.

Strom Thurmond was an intriguing politician. The son of an Edgefield lawyer, he'd been a farmer, teacher and superintendent of education. His political career took off shortly after he passed the Bar exam. He was elected to the state Senate in 1932, and five years later was appointed to a judgeship. He resigned the bench to join the Army during World War II, eventually landing on the beach at Normandy. His war heroics, and folksy charisma, won him the governorship. Soon, his extensive resume would include anti-civil-rights crusader.

"The South demands and expects to receive greater participation in fixing policies of the Democratic Party, in writing its platform, and in selecting its candidates," Thurmond said, dismissing calls to form a new party. "The Democratic Party should settle its differences within the party and present a united front during the campaign."

The backlash to *Elmore v. Rice* and other NAACP victories had stirred a political movement, and Thurmond decided to take full advantage of it. It was a particularly cynical ploy because his own feelings on race were complicated, to say the least. Although he'd been a notorious bachelor before marrying his 21-year-old secretary a few months earlier, the 44-year-old Thurmond already had a child in college – and she was black.

Essie Mae was the daughter of the Thurmond family housekeeper, born when her mother was 16 and Strom was in his early 20s. Nothing had ever come of the relationship, of course, and the child was raised by her aunt and uncle. Thurmond met her for the first time when she was in high school, but had been supporting her ever since – even paying her tuition to S.C. State College. Sometimes, the governor visited her at the Orangeburg campus. Most whites knew nothing of the scandal, but it was common knowledge in the black community. And that only made Thurmond look even more hypocritical to African Americans in the months to come, when his talk of protecting a united Democratic Party was quietly dropped.

In April, the Supreme Court announced it would not review *Elmore v. Rice*. The appeals court ruling, affirming Waring's order, would stand. That meant black South Carolinians could vote in upcoming primaries, including the Columbia municipal election that week. Years later, U.S. Supreme Court Chief Justice Fred Vinson told Waring that decision had been a mistake. It allowed the Democrats to claim they were defeated only by a technicality. Vinson said one of the other justices felt that had been the wrong move.

"He thought we ought to have heard it and written an opinion on it. It would have been better," Vinson said.

The Democrats, of course, did portray the loss as a technicality, and that encouraged them to find other ways around Waring's order. The day after their appeal was dismissed, party officials announced they might limit participation in upcoming primaries to people already registered to vote in general elections. The list of qualifications grew more onerous as the spring wore on, with state officials encouraged by the increasingly divisive rhetoric from Southern delegates to the National Democratic Convention.

Those delegates met in Jackson, Mississippi, in early May to plan their strategy for the upcoming national convention. They decided to withhold support for Truman unless every civil rights measure in the party platform was dropped, and agreed to reconvene in Birmingham afterward to decide what, if any, further action was necessary. Thurmond was one of the ring leaders.

Thurmond promised the assembled crowd that Southern Democrats wouldn't support any nominee who advocated a national civil rights program, and the region would unite its electoral votes to block the nomination of any candidate who did – including the president. To reinforce that message, he ended his speech by singing an anti-Truman song and outlining the position of the delegates in the bluntest terms possible.

"All the laws of Washington, and all the bayonets of the army, cannot force the Negro into … the homes … schools … churches … and places of recreation and amusement of the Southern people," Thurmond said.

The delegates called themselves the States' Rights Democrats, but a Charlotte newspaper reporter coined a simpler, and catchier, name. He dubbed this splinter group the Dixiecrats.

They were, at least initially, a disjointed lot. The Dixiecrats' own members couldn't even stick to the program. When South Carolina Democrats met for their state convention a week later, they immediately scrapped the wait-and-see plan. Caught up in the moment, the state delegates nominated Thurmond as their choice for president of the United States. The banner headline in The News and Courier declared, "Truman is denied state's electoral votes."

With all the attention focused on the Democrats' rebellion, a small committee of party executives plotted ways to evade Waring's order. The group wrote new bylaws that said only whites could be members of the party, but blacks would be allowed to vote in primaries if they were registered to vote in general elections – and if they signed a party oath.

The four-paragraph oath said, in part, "I ... solemnly swear that I understand, believe in and will support the principles of the Democratic Party of South Carolina, and that I believe in and support the social, religious and educational separation of races." The group assumed no self-respecting black person would dare sign such a statement.

The oath also required primary voters to oppose civil rights laws, or any other federal statute relating to employment. Basically, the Democrats hoped African Americans would refuse to sign the oath, which would give the party legal standing to deny them a ballot. But the Democrats had clumsily overreached. Within a week, religious leaders were in revolt.

Catholic and Jewish Democrats balked at the mention of religion, predicting it would cost the party as many as 4,000 votes in Charleston County alone. The Evening Post called the oath a bad idea, and speculated it wouldn't fool the federal courts. After a few days of outrage and derision, party officials revised the oath to remove the word "religious" and – to Waring's amusement – the word "understand." Apparently, the Democrats didn't care if anyone even understood what they were signing. For a while, the ploy appeared to work. Most black voters refused to sign the oath.

But it would not dissuade everyone.

In June, Thurgood Marshall was back in South Carolina with a briefcase full of lawsuits – all of which he filed in Waring's district court. Most people around the courthouse had noticed the NAACP attorney spent a lot of time with the judge – he was often spotted going into Waring's chambers, sometimes staying for hours at a time. Clearly, they had become friends. So lawyers and editorial writers were stunned when Marshall's first lawsuit of the session was summarily dismissed by Waring.

The NAACP had asked for an injunction to force a Clarendon County school district to provide buses for its black schools. It was an open-and-shut case, adhering strictly to the separate-but-equal tenets of *Plessy v. Ferguson*. After all, Clarendon County supplied more than two dozen buses to carry white students – and none for black children. Most people suspected it would be an easy win for Marshall, but at the last minute he sheepishly asked Waring to dismiss the case. More than a year would pass before anyone realized Marshall was following private instructions from the judge.

Waring had bigger plans for that particular case, but the time wasn't right.

Marshall's suit against the University of South Carolina did not go over well either. He argued that the state hadn't complied with the judge's earlier ruling, that the black law school at S.C. State had serious "inadequacies." S.J. Prince, dean of the USC law school, insisted students at Orangeburg had "better opportunities to get a law education than do those at the university." He attributed this to the pupil-teacher ratio. At USC, Prince said there were 340 students and a faculty of 14. In comparison, S.C. State had three instructors – but only eight students.

"For effectiveness, the faculties are equal," Prince said.

Waring conceded the college had done an adequate job meeting his demands, although he couldn't resist repeating his joke about a state foolish enough to spend $200,000 on a school for a handful of black students. He dismissed the NAACP complaint. Strike two. But Marshall's third case, a complaint from Beaufort County, would fare better.

Beaufort County was a South Carolina anomaly. Captured early in the Civil War, the area had lived under Union rule longer than any other part of the state – and maintained some semblance of Northern politics. The county's sizable black population managed to hold political power for years following the end of Reconstruction. After all, it was the home of Robert Smalls – the daring former slave who'd stolen a ship from the Charleston docks during the war and delivered it to the U.S. Navy. Smalls had gone on to serve as a legislator, a congressman and an inspiration to many African Americans.

David Brown was one of those people. He wasn't a community leader or activist, as Waring later said; Brown simply ran a gas station and made a decent living. But he also kept up with current events. After *Elmore v. Rice*, Brown went to the Beaufort County Democratic Party headquarters and registered to vote. But county party officials decided Brown was not qualified and, on July

2, struck him from the rolls – along with 33 other black residents.

Four days later, James Hinton announced the NAACP's plans to ask Judge Waring for an injunction against the Beaufort County Democratic Party. In fact, he said, Marshall was preparing a lawsuit against party officials in 41 of South Carolina's 46 counties. Richland, Laurens, Spartanburg, Greenville and Pickens counties would be excluded because they had defied party orders to sabotage black voting; Richland because it lost the *Elmore* lawsuit, the rest because they didn't have enough black voters to bother with the subterfuge.

David Brown would serve as lead plaintiff for the lawsuit, which asked the court to grant black residents full enrollment and membership rights in the state Democratic Party – without being forced to sign any oath.

Beaufort County Democratic Chairman J.B. Cope told reporters that Brown and several other black residents had been disqualified on a peculiar technicality: They signed up without his knowledge or consent. They were stricken from the rolls, Cope claimed, in compliance with state party rules adopted at the May convention. The NAACP listed William Baskin, state party chairman, as the lead defendant, and Marshall asked Waring for an emergency hearing.

Two days later, the judge issued a temporary restraining order against the party and demanded that Democratic officials open their enrollment books to black voters until July 16. That day, Waring said, he would hear arguments in the case known as *Brown v. Baskin*, which had become a direct sequel to *Elmore v. Rice*. Waring knew any ruling against the party ran the risk of immediate, and high-profile, backlash: the day after the hearing, the Dixiecrats were scheduled to convene their national convention in Birmingham.

The 1948 South Carolina Democratic primary was little more than a month away.

'CAMPAIGN OF VILIFICATION'

The Democratic National Convention was even more inhospitable than Strom Thurmond had feared.

When the governor arrived in Philadelphia with the rest of the South Carolina delegation, the party was largely in disarray. After losing control of Congress in 1946, Democrats assumed President Truman would be defeated in the fall – and, as a result, showed little enthusiasm for the ticket. They were more excited to see the famous journalist Edward R. Murrow on the concourse than the endless parade of speakers filing on and off the stage. Still, the Southerners could not leverage that apathy to force a states' rights plank into the party platform.

The national Democrats seemed more hostile to Southern concerns than ever before. Delegates insisted the platform include civil rights language that promised continuing efforts to "eradicate all racial, religious and economic discrimination." Minneapolis Mayor Hubert Humphrey, a candidate for the United States Senate, even made civil rights the highlight of his address – and used the opportunity to berate the aspirant Dixiecrats.

"The time is now arrived in America for the Democratic Party to get out of the shadow of states' rights and walk forthrightly into the bright sunshine of human rights," Humphrey proclaimed.

The Democratic Party was changing, and leaving the South behind.

Eventually, the party's intransigence on civil rights – if not Humphrey's insult – led most of the Mississippi and Alabama delegates to walk out. Thurmond persuaded the South Carolina delegation to stay, although the only thing remotely Southern about this gathering was the humidity in the convention center. Between the TV lights, the lack of air conditioning and 12,000 people crammed into a single room, the hall felt like the Carolina Lowcountry in August.

Gov. Thurmond still had slim hopes of denying Truman the nomination, but he couldn't even keep his own people in line. One state delegate wanted to cast his ballot for the president, others begged off to prepare for Friday's court hearing on the party oath – Judge Waring had denied their request for a continuance. When state Sen. Edgar Brown announced he and Baskin had to return home "to protect whatever vestige of civil rights remain in South Carolina," the irony was lost on everyone.

Thurmond ultimately used the convention to boost his own image as a Southern power broker. He released his delegates from their commitment to nominate him for the presidency and threw his support behind Arkansas Gov. Ben Laney, prompting the Texas delegation to follow suit. Gov. Thurmond had painted himself as a selfless defender of states' rights, and ultimately lectured the convention on the folly of a half-hearted civil rights stance.

"We do not intend that our constitutional rights be sacrificed for the sordid purpose of gaining minority votes in doubtful states," he said. When pro-Truman delegates booed him, Thurmond was defiant. "It's medicine you don't want to hear."

Laney's candidacy was quickly abandoned in favor of Georgia Sen. Richard Russell, a staunch opponent of civil rights. By the time Thurmond seconded Russell's nomination, most of his own delegates were ready to follow Alabama and Mississippi out the door. The governor urged them to stay long enough to cast ballots for Russell. South Carolina, he said, should have a voice at the convention. But the South's voice had been effectively drowned out. Russell won 21 percent of the delegates and Truman took the rest – and the nomination.

The next morning, Thurmond left Philadelphia a pariah in the national party, but a hero among anti-civil rights Southerners. After demurring when his train arrived in Columbia, the governor soon announced he would leave that evening to attend the States' Rights Democrats' convention in Birmingham. It was the only way for the South to play a role in the election, he said. Once again, Thurmond would miss the state party's day in Judge Waring's court.

Thurmond didn't expect the Democrats to prevail in *Brown v. Baskin*; no one did. The Evening Post had bemoaned the futility in an editorial days earlier.

As a result of Roosevelt's New Deal-engineered revolution, the editorial said, the party "may just as well make up its mind that it will not by any subterfuge be able to evade federal court rulings that grant Negroes participation in its affairs on an equality with white members." The editors said the federal justice system's position became clear after the Supreme Court refused to hear arguments in *Elmore v. Rice*.

"It ought to be obvious that the Negroes will win the right to enroll on the same basis as whites," The Post opined. "The Democratic Party is now no more a white man's party than is the Republican Party."

On July 16, the Charleston federal courthouse was filled with people anticipating that outcome. The courtroom overflowed into the corridors, dozens – perhaps hundreds – of people denied seats. The wooden benches inside Waring's court were packed with local activists and black residents; most of the white people in attendance were defendants. When the judge took the bench at 10 a.m., it was clear he wanted the case over as quickly as possible.

Without fanfare, Waring launched into the business of the day. He first dismissed Greenville, Pickens and Laurens counties from the lawsuit. These three counties, he announced, had ignored the state party's directive and allowed black voters to register for the primary. He didn't mention they had few, if any, black voters to turn away – a telling technicality. Still, they got credit for following the original court order.

"I feel quite ashamed," Waring said, "that there are only three counties in the state who recognize my authority. I am glad to see that these three counties have men who have sense enough, who have nerve enough, who have patriotism enough to carry on despite pressure and coercion."

The hearing lasted barely two hours. Marshall and Harold Boulware recognized Waring's mood, and their position of strength. Because they had the upper hand, they kept it simple. The NAACP attorneys first put Brown on the stand to tell his story: How he'd registered to vote in Beaufort County, only to learn later that he and more than two dozen other black residents had been deemed unqualified electors and stricken from the rolls.

Attorneys for the Democrats stipulated Brown's account was factual, but argued that the federal court had no authority over a private club. It was virtually the same argument the party used in *Elmore v. Rice*, and Waring was offended they hadn't bothered to concoct a better excuse. He denied their motion to dismiss the case and allowed the NAACP to call William Baskin to the stand. At times, the judge helped Boulware question the chairman.

Even the newspapers later conceded Baskin offered confused and often contradictory testimony. At first, the state Democratic chairman claimed he had no authority to change party rules, but then admitted he'd amended the loyalty oath to eliminate the words "religious" and "understand." In other words, Waring asked, "a man must swear to something he doesn't understand?"

As Baskin fumbled to respond, party attorney Sidney Tyson stood and objected. The judge, he said, was badgering the witness. Waring seemed both amused and annoyed. "I am going to ask anything I want," he told Tyson. "Now sit down."

Baskin denied he'd written the oath, and haplessly claimed he didn't recall its origins. To the best of his recollection, he said, the oath simply came up for a vote at the state convention and was adopted by the delegates. Waring couldn't decide whether the Democrats were comically inept, or didn't take the lawsuit – or the court – seriously. He later recalled, "The position of the defendants was so hopelessly weak that it seemed to me almost ludicrous."

Baskin was the second and last witness called to the stand. There was nothing else to say; both sides had simple arguments. As soon as the chairman stepped down, Waring wrapped up the hearing. Because the Democratic primary was less than a month away, the judge said he would issue a ruling from the bench with a written order to follow on Monday.

In short, the plaintiffs won.

The Democratic Party, Waring said, had clearly and intentionally violated the law as set out in *Elmore v. Rice* and affirmed by the Fourth Circuit Court of Appeals. Any black resident who met age and residency requirements could vote in the Aug. 10 primary, as well as all future elections. The judge asked Marshall to draft the order so the plaintiffs got everything they wanted. And Waring dictated exactly what he wanted it to say.

"The order will provide that the books be open to all parties irrespective of race, color, creed or condition. I am going to say to the people of South Carolina that the time has come when racial discrimination in political affairs has got to stop," Waring said. "It's a disgrace and a shame that you've got to come into court and ask a judge to tell you that you are an American citizen and are going to obey the law."

The judge even threatened the Democrats with jail. He said anyone who tried to skirt the order – whether it was a county chairman or a poll worker – would be arrested for contempt. And he would be watching. Waring promised to clear his schedule on election day, and wait in his chambers for any crisis that might arise. Finally, he scolded the Democrats for putting him in such a position.

"Now, gentlemen, you've put that burden on me, and I'm going to do it. It isn't a popular thing to do," Waring conceded. "I don't care about popularity; I'm going to do my duty. The law of the land is going to be obeyed."

Before Waring could adjourn the hearing, a man stood up demanding to be heard. Alan Johnstone, a candidate for the U.S. Senate, had asked to speak before the hearing but the judge told him, "This is not the place to make political speeches." Now, Johnstone claimed he had papers to file with the court. Waring tried to gavel him quiet, but the man just kept talking.

Finally, the judge turned to court deputies and said, "Put him out." Johnstone was still screaming "But your honor" as he was dragged backward out of the courtroom.

It was only the first of many protests to come.

Full of fire and vinegar, Southern Democrats convened in Birmingham the next day.

They planned a coup against President Truman. They formed a committee to outline their principles – the first of which was "the racial integrity of each race." They supported segregation and opposed all efforts to "invade or destroy" individual rights (of white people, it went without saying), as well as the president's civil rights program. Former Alabama Gov. Frank Dixon even accused Truman of plotting a social revolution that would "reduce us to the status of mongrels, mixed in blood."

The Dixiecrats were serving a healthy helping of red meat to their constituents.

Thurmond got two separate, and distinctly different, greetings upon his arrival in Birmingham. The first was a raucous crowd singing "Dixie" and waving Confederate flags; the second was a whispered proposition. The group had offered Dixon and Arkansas Gov. Ben Laney their nomination for the presidency, but both declined. Thurmond was the next choice to lead the Dixiecrat ticket. And he had an hour to decide.

It's not clear whether Thurmond actually thought he could win. He dreamed of a Southern sweep that would throw the election into the U.S. House, but that was admittedly a longshot. Still, he had little to lose. His term as governor would expire in two years, and then what? He'd considered running for Senate against Olin Johnston, but knew the old man would be tough to beat. It might be easier, he reasoned, if he claimed the mantle of states' rights – since South Carolina was in an uproar over Waring's order to let blacks vote. So he accepted.

The Dixiecrats officially nominated Thurmond for president on Monday, the third day of the convention. Afterward, the governor told reporters he planned to win all the Southern states in November and defeat Truman. But the true goal of this insurgency, he said, was to give states the right to manage their own affairs without federal interference – echoing the glorious propaganda of the Lost Cause. He claimed this movement "was not based on racial hate or racial prejudice."

Thurmond sounded much less benevolent on the campaign trail. He barnstormed the South after the convention, telling his exclusively white audiences exactly what they wanted to hear. Any progress blacks had made since Reconstruction, he claimed, was completely a product of good-hearted Southern people giving them a hand up. All of that was fine, Thurmond said, but black people could not overreach; they had to know their place in society.

"I want to tell you, ladies and gentlemen, there's not enough troops in the Army to force the Southern people to break down segregation and admit the nigra race into our theaters, into our swimming pools, into our homes and into our churches," Thurmond proclaimed in one newsreel.

He did not mention voting booths in his stump speeches because the South had already lost that fight.

Thurmond held the same prejudices and patriarchal attitudes toward race as most entitled Southern white men, but he cynically ratcheted up his rhetoric for the crowds. His personal feelings were obviously more conflicted. Between campaign stops, he secretly visited his black daughter, showing her at least a measure of affection – even though he realized that, if she was discovered, he would be ruined politically.

Some of Essie Mae's classmates – including her boyfriend, who was enrolled in S.C. State's new law school – urged her to ask the governor why he made such racist statements during his campaign. They couldn't understand how a man could harbor such prejudice, yet treat his black daughter so kindly. It was the only time Essie Mae ever discussed race with her father, and he had little to say. Thurmond told her that his politics had nothing to do with their relationship.

"I have to represent the views of the voters," he explained.

It was a testament to the barriers of segregation that Thurmond's illegitimate daughter never came to light during the 1948 presidential campaign. Black activists in Columbia knew about Essie Mae and one, Modjeska Simkins, suggested NAACP officials expose the governor's repugnant hypocrisy. But nothing ever came of such talk, perhaps because South Carolina was too distracted by the other big story of the election – Judge Waring.

The day Thurmond formally accepted the Dixiecrat nomination for president, Waring issued his written order in *Brown v. Baskin*. The ruling was exactly what he'd dictated from the bench, with one surprise – he slyly accused the party of not acting "American." With the party's loyalty oath officially outlawed, more than two dozen Democrats threatened to drop out of the primary. Only five actually followed through; the rest made Waring the dominant, and only, issue of the campaign.

For three weeks, the judge would be lambasted, vilified and blamed for the ruin of the Democratic Party. Nearly every candidate in every race denounced Waring at some point, if not every day. These men claimed the judge was a traitor to his party and his race. He had committed an unpardonable sin against the people and must be removed from the bench. The only person these candidates despised nearly as much as Waring was Sen. Burnet Maybank.

At a campaign rally in Newberry, local attorney and U.S. Senate candidate Alan Johnstone – the man thrown out of Waring's courtroom – accused the judge of "government by injunction" and claimed he'd "stirred up race and religious prejudice" across the state. And Johnstone blamed Maybank for Waring's ascension to the federal bench. It was the attack the senator had feared most.

Maybank had called the *Brown v. Baskin* ruling "deplorable" the day after it was filed, and issued a statement in which he claimed the judge had "reached beyond the authority of his court." But he also attempted to pre-empt any criticism – or blame – for Waring's appointment by pinning it on "Cotton Ed" Smith, who was conveniently dead.

"Long before I went to the United States Senate he had been recommended by the late Sen. E.D. Smith along with others for a federal judgeship," Maybank said. "As a matter of fact, Waring was a strong supporter of the late senator when Smith was campaigning on a platform of white supremacy after having walked out of the Philadelphia convention in 1936. In 1941, I joined Sen. Smith in recommending the appointment of Judge Waring, who at that time was conceded to be a loyal Democrat of the Jeffersonian school. I am not responsible for his conduct on or off the bench.

"Remember," the statement ended, "Burnet Maybank was the first South Carolinian in public office to publicly state his opposition to the actions of Judge Waring."

Maybank's clumsy attempt at revisionist history backfired immediately. The Charleston newspapers reminded readers that he'd orchestrated the dual appointments of judges Timmerman and Waring without Smith's knowledge – and that Cotton Ed had questioned whether Waring was too old to serve. It was not exactly the sort of campaign coverage Maybank relished. Johnstone would read those reports in stump speeches for the rest of the campaign, repeatedly calling on Maybank and congressman William Jennings Bryan Dorn – another candidate for the Senate seat – to have Waring impeached.

Even Farley Smith, the late senator's son, called out Maybank for his sub-terfuge. He said it was widely known that Cotton Ed was persona non grata with the Roosevelt administration, and "anyone who had my father's stamp of approval would have been marked for defeat from the start." The younger Smith had several reasons to clarify the record, the most important of which was not Cotton Ed's reputation. Farley Smith was running for a seat in the state House of Representatives, and didn't want to be accused of any association – however tenuous – with Waring.

Even though the Charleston newspapers criticized Maybank's duplicity, they wouldn't side with any outsider over the former mayor. The Evening Post finally demanded that Johnstone cease his attacks. "It is as ridiculous as it is unjust to hold Senator Maybank in any way responsible for Judge Waring's interpretation of the Constitution or for his condemnation of South Carolinians who were upholding an institution from which Judge Waring's public career stemmed."

But Maybank and Dorn feared the hapless Johnstone had stumbled onto an issue that resonated with voters, and neither wanted to appear soft on Waring. On July 27, two weeks before the primary, Dorn called for a congressional investigation into Waring's conduct. He claimed to have evidence Waring had "usurped the rights of the free citizens of South Carolina by attempting to force down their throats his own ideas of governmental matters." The congressman said he wanted the judge impeached.

Dorn, who hailed from Greenwood, didn't hesitate to drag Charleston society into the campaign. While grandstanding on the floor of the U.S. House, he said, "The people would like to know how Judge Waring can obtain a separation from a lady to whom he had been married for approximately 30 years, remarry and serve on the federal bench in that great state." South Carolina, he noted, had no divorce law.

Waring's dirty laundry was soon broadcast across South Carolina. Dorn took his campaign to radio stations in every corner of the state, repeatedly calling the judge an immoral man. He perpetuated the myth that Judge Waring ruled in favor of blacks only to get revenge on his friends and neighbors, who "because of his ungentlemanly conduct in the past, have refused to associate with him, and even now treat him with silent contempt."

Maybank had been upstaged. He was forced to respond weakly, through an aide, that he'd planned to file a similar impeachment resolution in the Senate.

William Baskin had announced the Democrats would obey Judge Waring's ruling in the upcoming primary, but apparently he didn't speak for everyone in the party.

As the campaign season dragged on, many local Democratic chairmen portrayed themselves as soldiers in an ongoing legal battle, and swore they would not surrender. After all, it wasn't over – the lawyers were still filing briefs. Of course, all those appeals simply repeated the same claim, that the Democratic Party was a private club. It didn't matter that the Fourth Circuit had dismissed that argument once. It was the only one they had.

Waring didn't help matters when he issued a clarifying order that actually muddied the water. It said the party could ask voters to sign papers certifying they lived in the district where they were voting and would support the party's nominee in the general election. Even though the order specifically said pledges or statements of beliefs were barred, some local party figures believed it gave them the opening to simply ignore the whole lawsuit.

Just before the primary, members of the Charleston County Democratic Party executive committee grumbled that no judge would tell them how to run their elections. They vowed to ignore the order, and several committeemen suggested they simply force black voters to sign the original oath. Self-righteous indignation, testosterone and bigotry stirred the committee into a frenzy before the county chairman shut them down.

"It's all right for you to say you're not going to obey the order because your name is not in that injunction," the chairman said, "but my name's in that injunction and that judge said he was going to send a man to jail that disobeyed it. You don't have to go to jail if it's disobeyed and we aren't going to disobey it."

The failed insurrection gave Waring a much-needed laugh. He and Elizabeth were lying low at the Sullivan's Island beach cottage, but couldn't escape the campaign stories in the Charleston newspapers. The attacks on his character

– and on his wife – bothered him more than he'd expected, and he was still upset when one of his neighbors, a member of the county party, dropped by to tell him about the near-coup.

He was the sort of fellow, Waring later said, who tried to ingratiate himself to everyone. If he harbored any ill will about the *Brown* ruling, he was too polite to mention it. He simply saw the judge on the porch and stopped by to relate, matter-of-factly, how the committee had cussed his name. Waring had no doubt it was true, and it gave him hope that party officials had finally realized he was serious.

Tales of party infighting spread across Charleston, finally prompting The Evening Post to mock Democrats in a snarky editorial headlined "The Master Minds." The editors said it should've been evident from Waring's first ruling that the whites-only primary was over. The paper said the party should have found other ways to limit participation in primaries. Instead, the Democrats' feeble defense had failed – and they only had themselves to blame.

The attacks on Waring tapered off in the week before the primary, and congressman Mendel Rivers took advantage of the opportunity to earn some free publicity. He predicted that, unless the judge was impeached, there would be bloodshed in South Carolina.

To that point in the campaign, Rivers had been uncharacteristically quiet. Perhaps he feared saying too much, given the racial makeup of his district. The NAACP predicted 100,000 black South Carolinians would vote in the primary, and even if that was hopelessly optimistic, 5,000 had registered in Charleston County alone. Rivers needed to fire up white supporters without alienating potential black voters. By Aug. 4, he believed he'd found the appropriately indignant, yet oddly progressive, tone.

In a speech on the U.S. House floor, Rivers said black citizens had every right to vote in primaries, and should have been allowed to do so years earlier. Only illiterates of both races, he declared, should be barred from the polls. But, Rivers said, the law had to be interpreted with dignity so people would respect it. And Waring's "clumsy handling of a delicate situation has hurt the case of the Negro in South Carolina."

Rivers repeated Dorn's claim that the judge wanted to "extract a pound of flesh from the white people of South Carolina because through his own actions he has been ostracized from their society." He also speculated that Waring was attempting to curry favor with President Truman, in hopes of securing an appointment to the Court of Appeals. Rivers couldn't have made Satan sound much worse.

"He is as cold as a dead Eskimo in an abandoned igloo. Lemon juice flows in his rigid and calculating veins," Rivers said. "Every lawyer in South Carolina lives in mortal fear of this monster. And everyone who reads this statement will thank God I made it, because I am speaking for the vast majority of the Bar in South Carolina. Vast numbers of lawyers have abandoned practice in the federal courts because of this individual."

Finally, Rivers introduced what he called a "resolution precedent to impeachment" and asked the House Judiciary Committee to investigate Waring's conduct in office. At the very least, he said, Waring lacked the necessary judicial temperament to remain on the bench. But Rivers inexplicably backed off the next day. Congress was about to adjourn, he explained, so he'd renew his request at a later time.

Perhaps the congressman rethought his position after James Hinton, president of the state NAACP, rushed to Waring's defense, and told the newspapers that Rivers didn't speak for the black residents of South Carolina. Rivers knew nothing good could come from stirring up his constituents – especially since they now had the right to vote. But more likely, the congressman dropped his crusade because U.S. Supreme Court Chief Justice Fred Vinson announced that he would not investigate Waring.

Rivers did accomplish one thing, however. He provoked the only response from Waring during the 1948 campaign. Reached by one reporter, the judge had only a single comment about impeachment, igloos and congressmen.

"It should be unnecessary to comment on these silly, childish ravings."

Waring made that snide remark about Mendel Rivers on Thursday, Aug.

5 – a day he otherwise spent waiting for his daughter.

Anne and her husband, Stanley, had been upset by the slanderous attacks on the judge and decided it was important to show their support. So they'd planned a trip, and were due in from New York at any time. In a letter to Judge John Parker, Waring said he was touched by their concern and predicted a weekend with his daughter would lift his spirits.

"It is pretty lonely here for Mrs. Waring and myself," he wrote. "Instead of getting better, things have gotten worse and are coming to a head by reason of the bitter campaign that is being fought for the Senate. And L. Mendel Rivers, congressman from this district, has injected himself into it. The only reason I can supply for this last is that he is publicity minded to an extreme degree and undoubtedly wants to make use of this campaign of vilification."

Waring told Judge Parker – ostensibly his boss – he would sneak out of Charleston after the primary, and planned to stay away for a long time. He asked the judge to find someone who could cover the fall term of court, scheduled to begin Oct. 11. Waring had every intention of disappearing for more than two months, which he hoped would be long enough for his critics to cool down.

Parker was sympathetic. He called Rivers' remarks "unfortunate" and praised Waring for his reticence and sound judgment. "You are wise, of course, not to enter into this controversy. … The people realize that a judge cannot enter into a name-calling contest, and the very violence of Rivers' attack will discredit what he says." Waring was so grateful he sent Parker another note to thank him for the reply.

Anne and Stanley arrived that evening and, the next morning, Waring took his daughter for a walk downtown. There was a parade she wanted to see, so they stood on the courthouse steps to watch it pass. She soon noticed that no one on the street spoke to them, or even looked their way. Anne didn't recognize this Charleston. In the hometown she remembered, her father was a popular man. Now they were practically invisible, and it unnerved her.

"You and I were utter strangers to the rest of the people," she later told her father. "I never realized before that thousands of people could be scared of two people. And yet they were. They were afraid to look at you. They were afraid to speak to you. They were afraid not to speak to you. They wouldn't see you."

The couple left on Sunday, and the judge kept a low profile until the Tuesday primary. He spent the day in his chambers, ready to act on any trouble from the Democrats. But there were no issues reported. Both sides, he later said, behaved themselves beautifully. In his typical deadpan style, Waring joked to Judge Parker that "the primary election went off smoothly yesterday and they didn't shoot me."

About 35,000 black South Carolina residents voted in the 1948 Democratic primary, which was a good start – but not enough to change any outcome. Maybank claimed Waring had opened the primary to black voters to cause him problems, but that was just self-serving deflection. In the end, he won re-election easily. With the primary over, and the impeachment postponed, Waring felt relieved. But he knew his difficulties weren't over.

"(A)ll of this is a part of the Southern revolt and is thoroughly in line with the Thurmond movement," Waring wrote to Judge Parker. "I am sorry to say that I am afraid the great majority of this State is being led astray as it was in 1860 and before that in the nullification days. And only time will cure it."

Waring met with Marshall and Boulware in his chambers on the day of the primary. The election was going well, and the attorneys credited that to the judge's threat to jail any party officials who misbehaved. They spent nearly two hours with Waring that afternoon, then went outside to speak with waiting reporters. Neither Marshall nor Boulware would say what they discussed with the judge for so long, and reporters never got the chance to ask Waring.

The next evening, the Warings boarded the 6 p.m. train to New York City. After a few days at the St. Regis Hotel, they would depart for Santa Barbara, California, and an open-ended stay on the West Coast. As the Lowcountry disappeared behind them, the judge finally relaxed. Like Elizabeth, Waring no longer felt comfortable in Charleston. It was his hometown, but he had come to feel like an unwelcome stranger in a strange land. He didn't realize it at the time, but those feelings would never pass. Nothing would ever be the same.

And by the time he returned to Charleston, Waties Waring would be famous.

PART III

"SEGREGATION IS PER SE INEQUALITY"

A MATTER OF BUSES

H e hadn't been fired yet, and that surprised him.

The Rev. Joseph A. DeLaine passed the summer expecting to lose his job as principal of Silver Elementary School, but in September 1948 Clarendon County renewed his contract for another year. With his wife returning to teach at Scott's Branch School across the street from their Summerton home, both the DeLaines were miraculously still employed. He had to wonder whether it was an oversight, or if he'd successfully hidden his role in the school district's recent legal troubles.

For more than a year, DeLaine had quietly led efforts to make the county provide buses to black students. There were dozens of tiny schools scattered across the county's 600 square miles of rolling farmland, and the district had 30 buses to shuttle white students between them. But black students had to walk, sometimes as much as nine miles. Buses from the white schools passed by every day, leaving them in the dust of winding country roads. That's just the way it was.

Clarendon County, halfway between Charleston and Columbia, was no different from any other rural school district in South Carolina. No black schools had their own buses; that was never even a consideration. The only thing that set Clarendon apart from other counties was that it had DeLaine, and he was not a man who gave up easily.

He'd adopted this cause after hearing a speech from James Hinton in June 1947. DeLaine was taking summer classes at Allen University in Columbia, on his way to a second degree, when the state director of the NAACP addressed students on campus. Hinton told the audience it was no coincidence black schools were often dilapidated shacks without heat or running water. It was no oversight that black teachers were paid less than white educators. South Carolina, Hinton declared, meant to keep black people down and in their place.

The NAACP had decided to challenge this inequality by focusing on bus service. Hinton said the state's practice of providing buses for white students, but not black children, violated South Carolina's separate-but-equal laws. The NAACP saw this as a relatively non-controversial issue, and an easy legal victory. The problem, Hinton said, was finding people brave enough to demand equal treatment – and put their name on a lawsuit.

"No teacher or preacher in South Carolina has the courage to find a plaintiff to test the legality of the discriminatory bus-transportation practices in this state," Hinton lamented.

DeLaine was a preacher and a teacher, and he was inspired. Under the auspices of the church board at Pine Grove AME, where he was pastor, he approached the local school superintendent about this dilemma. L.B. McCord said no, of course, matter-of-factly explaining that black people did not pay enough taxes and whites shouldn't be forced to subsidize such a luxury. Undaunted, DeLaine took his request to the state Department of Education and even the U.S. attorney general. No one was willing to help.

Finally, DeLaine realized Hinton was right; the only way to get buses was to win them in court. And that was something he could not do on his own, not with his family's entire income dependent on the school district. He asked around for weeks before finding his plaintiff. Eventually, Levi Pearson agreed to let the NAACP use his name for the lawsuit. He was the perfect candidate: an amiable local farmer with good standing to file suit – he had three children at Scott's Branch. DeLaine warned Pearson that suing the school board could be dangerous, but confessed they had to have someone's name on the lawsuit. Pearson said he'd be fine, and Harold Boulware filed the suit.

Then all hell broke loose.

Some Clarendon County parents had bought a bus for black schools even before DeLaine started his campaign.

The rattle-trap bus broke down regularly, which didn't matter as much as it should because there was scarcely enough money to put gas in it anyway. When these parents asked county officials for help, they were turned down – politely, at first. But the school board became openly hostile in February 1948, after Boulware filed a federal lawsuit in Pearson's name at the Florence County courthouse. The suit said Pearson's children, and all the black students of Clarendon County, were suffering irreparable damage from the district's neglect.

The lawsuit made Pearson a local hero, and community leaders soon asked him to lead a new branch office of the NAACP. Flattered, he accepted immediately – Pearson had found his calling as an activist. DeLaine, who signed on as secretary for the branch, secretly ran the office while Pearson was its public face. This protected DeLaine, but left Pearson dangerously exposed to the full wrath of Clarendon County.

That spring, every store in the county cut off Pearson's line of credit. He was forced to spend every dollar he had just to buy seed for cotton and tobacco; there was no money left for fertilizer. Pearson cut down some trees on his property, in hopes of selling the lumber for enough cash to get him through the planting season. But the lumber mill was owned by R.W. Elliott, the Summerton school board chairman, and he refused to buy from Pearson. The trees lay on the side of the road all summer, where they would eventually rot.

Pearson endured months of anonymous threats, escalating to the point that someone shot at his house. And then, his lawsuit was discredited. The school district produced maps that showed the Pearson farm lay in three different school districts, and he didn't pay taxes to the one that included Scott's Branch. He had no legal standing to bring a lawsuit against Clarendon School District 22. Everything he'd been through was for nothing.

The NAACP suspected the tax records had been altered, but couldn't prove it. When the lawsuit came up in Waring's court in June 1948, an embarrassed Thurgood Marshall asked the judge if he could withdraw the case. And since then, there had been nothing. DeLaine couldn't get answers from Boulware, Hinton or anyone with the NAACP. The bus case was in limbo.

Time passed slowly in Clarendon County, and DeLaine was briefly distracted by efforts to register black voters for the August election (after Waring's court order to open the primary). He made a valuable friend in law enforcement when he delivered a bloc of votes that ensured the incumbent sheriff won re-election. The sheriff wasn't particularly beloved in the black community, but the consensus was that his opponent would be far worse.

As the fall days grew shorter, DeLaine passed his time teaching and awaiting news from the NAACP. His optimism was waning, he worried incessantly. The lawsuit stirred hostility in the white community that had yet to subside. Pearson remained upbeat, even after the white farmers who normally lent him equipment to harvest his crops refused to help. There was no mystery behind their motive, but they spelled it out anyway. They said if he dropped the bus case and forgot about the "N-double-A-CP," everything would return to normal. But Pearson refused to give in, and his crops died in the field – much like the rotting lumber he couldn't sell.

DeLaine hadn't been subjected to such public pressure, but still he felt stretched thin. He'd never been blessed with great health and, at 50, was worn down and bone-tired. When he wasn't at the school, he constantly traveled the county roads preaching on the Pine Grove/Sandy Hill circuit for the AME Church. He lived in constant fear that school officials would discover he'd started this matter about the buses. DeLaine knew that would leave him and his wife, Mattie, unemployed and ostracized – just like poor Pearson.

Although he was a man of faith, DeLaine seemed more passionate about justice than simply teaching scripture. It had always been that way. Born into a large family near Manning in 1898, at the dawn of the Jim Crow era, DeLaine had been fighting all his life. When he was 14, a white boy pushed one of his sisters off the sidewalk while they were walking through downtown Manning. DeLaine pushed back, hard enough to hurt the boy's shoulder. The community was outraged, and demanded he take 25 lashes for the offense. His father, a local minister, advised him to accept his punishment. Instead, DeLaine ran away.

He ended up in Atlanta, doing odd jobs to pay for his education. After he earned his teaching certificate, DeLaine enrolled in college, got a degree in theology and followed his father into the ministry. By the 1930s, he'd settled in Orangeburg County and taken work as a school principal. Eventually, he married one of the teachers. The school district didn't like the arrangement and ordered him to fire Mattie. That was more punishment he wasn't willing to take, so DeLaine quit and returned home to Clarendon County.

By 1948, DeLaine and Mattie had three children, a nine-acre plot of land in Summerton and jobs with the local school district. It was a comfortable enough life, assuming no one found out he was the cause of the school district's troubles. But he wouldn't let go of this campaign to get buses for his students and his children, even if he didn't know what to do next.

DeLaine didn't realize that, for the moment, he was on his own. The NAACP had cooled to the idea of using bus service to challenge equal rights. Hinton's idea was sound, but it didn't break new ground. When Marshall first took the case to Waring, the judge had been dismissive. He said the Clarendon lawsuit did nothing of substance; it would be easy enough for the school district to buy a bus or two – and they would gladly do that to maintain the status quo. He was right.

Marshall realized Waring's attitude was quickly evolving. For a few years, the judge had seemed content with the theory that change must come slowly to be accepted – gradualism, the academics called it. But by the spring of 1948, Waring was clearly beginning to discount that idea. No, he told Marshall, the very notion of segregation had to be challenged if the country would ever see meaningful changes. Buses, the judge said, were small potatoes.

Since then, the NAACP had begun to reconsider its entire legal strategy. Some members felt the organization was only chipping away at the edges of civil rights, and Waring was right – they had to think bigger. But most of them understandably had little faith the courts would force meaningful change.

After all, simply opening the South Carolina Democratic primary to black voters had helped inspire a national campaign built entirely around the preservation of segregation. By the fall of 1948, few NAACP officials were optimistic about their chances to win bigger victories, and even fewer were thinking about tiny Clarendon County.

Soon, DeLaine found himself just as distracted. In November, he learned the church was moving him out of Pine Grove and Sandy Hill. The AME Church liked to rotate its pastors, and he had been on the same circuit for eight years. Against his protests, DeLaine was reassigned to the Antioch and Zion Hill churches – where he'd preached years earlier. In his crusade and his career, DeLaine felt like he was going backward.

But he wasn't finished, not by a country mile.

Strom Thurmond crisscrossed the South and Eastern Seaboard through August and into the fall. On Labor Day, he appeared at a rally in Wildwood, Florida, before flying to Fairfield, Alabama, for an evening speech. At both events, he railed against Truman and his civil rights program. Later that week in Augusta, Georgia, his supporters booed when the governor made mention of the president's insincere ploy to court black voters. His message was spreading – the Louisiana Democratic Party even took Truman's name off the ballot in favor of Thurmond's.

To Southerners, it appeared Thurmond was cutting into the president's base. In September, Truman canceled a planned campaign swing through the South and announced he would instead visit targeted markets. When he turned down an invitation from South Carolina Democrats to speak in Columbia, Thurmond used the occasion to again berate the president and his plan for civil rights.

"I had hoped that he would come to our state and explain to our people why he saw fit to betray the principles of Jefferson and abandon the historic position of the Democratic Party on states' rights by sending his so-called civil rights message to Congress," Thurmond said.

Variations of that theme would re-emerge a week later during several campaign stops in Virginia. Thurmond said only communists wanted civil rights, and predicted federal laws against segregation "would usher in an era of lawlessness such as has never been seen before in America." A win for Truman, he warned in Charlottesville, would lead to federal anti-poll-tax and anti-lynching legislation. Neither of those prospects appealed to the growing legion of Dixiecrats.

Thurmond's stump speeches became so incendiary his wife worried he was limiting his political future. Already the national Democratic committee wanted him to resign from the party, which he refused to do. Finally, Jean asked if he'd considered the ramifications of his rhetoric. "You're really sticking your neck out there," she said. But he was caught up in the moment and wouldn't quit. During campaign stops in Roanoke and Lexington, the governor predicted "those who stabbed the South in the back will be stripped of their power."

As the fall campaign wore on, Thurmond publicly predicted the president might be limited to 100 electoral votes. It was a bold claim, but at that point the Republicans seemed to have the election won. Polls said GOP candidate Thomas Dewey had an "almost unbeatable" lead of 44-31 over Truman. Thurmond was in third place, ahead of the progressives, peaking at 4.4 percent support in one poll.

Just before the governor appeared at a states' rights rally in the Francis Marion Hotel, the Charleston newspapers predicted a Southern sweep and at least 45 electoral votes for Thurmond.

Since the Democratic primary, Charleston had been preoccupied with local politics and tropical storms. One hurricane had hit Mississippi already and another made landfall in Miami, subsequently wiping out nearly every building in Everglades City. The South Carolina coast had been spared, but one storm passed by close enough to flood Charleston, paralyzing the city for a day. It could have been worse, and locals knew the storm season wasn't over.

While the city kept a weary watch offshore, health inspectors cleared local schools to open on Sept. 15 – a day earlier than anticipated. The beginning of the new school year would be overshadowed, however, by a special election. Voters had been asked to choose a form of government to handle county operations, stripping the local legislative delegation of considerable power.

The lawmakers who represented Charleston County in the General Assembly ran all of its limited governmental functions outside of the city's corporate limits. Some legislators had decided there should be a separate governing body for such matters, which led to months of bickering among the delegation. The legislation eventually passed and, on Sept. 14, about 25 percent of registered voters turned out and decided county business should be handled by a seven-member council.

The members of this county council – three from the city, two from the north area and one each from west of the Ashley River and east of the Cooper River – would be elected in the Nov. 2 general election. The Democratic Party would hold a primary on Oct. 7 to whittle down the field, and that gave candidates only 10 days to submit their paperwork. Still, 20 people managed to file by Sept. 25. And it appeared Waring's order to open the primary to black voters had led to unforeseen consequences.

The three county council districts that covered the city had drawn the most interest. Ten candidates were competing for those seats, including a young man named Arthur J. Clement Jr. He was the local agent for the North Carolina Mutual Life Insurance Company, a position he'd inherited from his father. Clement was a well-regarded local businessman but, for one simple reason, most people thought he had no place in politics. He was black.

Clement had been a political activist since returning to his hometown after college. He was a member of the South Carolina Progressive Democratic Party and had just taken over as president of the county branch of the NAACP. He was, in short, a troublemaker. And some people worried that his name on the ballot would influence the entire election. The newspapers fretted that black voters – now lawfully recognized as primary electors – would never cast a ballot for a white Democrat, especially with Clement as an option.

That controversy, or at least the novelty of a black man on the ballot, may have helped drive voters to the polls. Turnout on Oct. 7 far exceeded that of the September referendum, but it didn't help Clement. With 1,819 votes, he finished in fifth place among the 10 downtown candidates – 3,300 votes shy of winning a seat on the first county council. Clement was encouraged, however, and immediately began planning to run for Congress against Mendel Rivers in the 1950 election.

Even though Clement lost his county council bid, his campaign disturbed local party officials. Not only did they have to deal with black people voting, now they had to worry about them running for elected office. It was like Reconstruction all over again, and Waties Waring was to blame. No doubt the judge would have heard the rumblings, but he still had not returned to Charleston.

Waring had been missing for two months.

His absence was discovered a few days after he left town. Someone noticed his office was dark and pried the gossip out of courthouse staff. On Aug. 13, The News and Courier reported that Waring had departed on a New York vacation "without making any public announcement." His further plans, the paper noted, were not complete. But the judge's itinerary became clear a couple of weeks later, when dispatches from around the country began appearing on the wire services. Everywhere he went, Waring was talking to journalists – mostly about the South's moral failings and its deplorable treatment of black people.

Waring was still out there somewhere, and still finding ways to infuriate and torment everyone in South Carolina.

HIS WORLD VIEW

The El Encanto Hotel sat on a lush California hillside in the Riviera neighborhood, overlooking Santa Barbara and the vast, blue expanse of the Pacific Ocean.

For years, the luxury retreat had been a winter residence for captains of industry – the founders of Time magazine and Pepsi-Cola among them. Less than 100 miles from Los Angeles, the hotel was also a fashionable getaway for Hollywood stars. Hedy Lamarr stayed there occasionally; Clark Gable used to bring Carole Lombard for the weekend. Even President Franklin D. Roosevelt had passed time in cottage 320. It was a palm-shaded world away from Charleston and all its ills.

J. Waties Waring felt like he belonged there, like he'd arrived. Word of the judge's rulings had spread across the country and he was quickly becoming a civil rights icon. The New York Herald Tribune praised him for "a remarkable recognition of human rights," and other papers soon followed suit. The Santa Barbara Daily Press even tracked him down at the El Encanto for an interview.

It was all so flattering. For the first time in his life, Waring was recognized outside his hometown. Just on this trip, a porter on the train to New York had told him "We sure do appreciate what you've done for us, judge." And when he and Elizabeth arrived in Los Angeles, some kids stopped him to ask for an autograph. He was touched enough to mention it more than once.

One afternoon, Waring sat on the private porch of his El Encanto bungalow recounting his family history, Southern politics and even his messy divorce. His audience was a man who claimed Hollywood connections and recorded their conversation – possibly as the basis for a screenplay. At 68, Waring seemed to enjoy the attention and the chance to expound on his world view. They talked for more than five hours. In the first hour, prompted by his guest, Waring of-

The South Carolina Inter-state and West Indian Exposition opened in December 1901, the month Waties Waring embarked on his legal career. The fair attracted Mark Twain and President Theodore Roosevelt, but led to no trade agreements or improvements in Charleston's moribund economy. It was merely a modestly successful party. (Photos courtesy the estate of Robert A. Nettles)

Waties Waring finally donned the black robe of a U.S. District judge in January 1942, after nearly a decade of missed opportunities. He wasted little time proving himself a capable, competent jurist. (Photo courtesy The Post and Courier archives)

Waring walks down Meeting Street, circa 1950. This photo was the lead image in the Collier's magazine feature story "The Lonesomest Man in Town," an article that chronicled the judge's ostracism from Charleston society. (Photo courtesy the University of Arizona/ Dan Weiner)

STATE OF SOUTH CAROLINA)
COUNTY OF CLARENDON)

PETITION

To: The Board of Trustees for School District Number 22, Clarendon
County, South Carolina, R. W. Elliott, Chairman, J. D. Carson
and George Kennedy, Members; The County Board of Education
for Clarendon County, South Carolina, L. B. McCord, Chairman,
Superintendent of Education for Clarendon County, A. J. Plowden,
W. E. Baker, Member,

Thomas Lee, Katherine
ers, Beatrice, Willie,
heola, Thomas, Euralia
ilton Bennett;

ld Gibson; Robert,
and Joseph Hilton;
ie and Roosevelt
Lee, Betty J.,
Eddie Lee and
liver; Mose,
and Celestine
n; Hazel, Zelia
William and
doon; Rebecca
ng; Lee, Bessie,
es, Annie
cis and Benie
ther F. Singleton
lie M.,
kes; Gabriel
dren of
school
22, Clarendon
next friends

Page 2

1.   That they are citizens of the United States and of the State of South
Carolina and reside in School District #22 in Clarendon County and State
of South Carolina.

2.   That the individual petitioners are Negro children of public school
age who reside in said county and school district and now attend the public
schools in School District #22, in Clarendon County, South Carolina, and
their parents and guardians.

3.   That the public school system in School District #22, Clarendon County,
South Carolina, is maintained on a separate, segregated basis, with white
children attending the Summerton High School and the Summerton Elementary
School, and Negro children forced to attend the Scott Branch High School,
the Liberty Hill Elementary School or Rambay Elementary School solely because of their race and color.

4.   That the Scott's Branch High School is a combination of an elementary
and high school, and the Liberty Hill and Rambay Elementary Schools are
elementary schools solely.

5.   That the facilities, physical condition, sanitation and protection
from the elements in the Scott's Branch High School, the Liberty Hill Elementary School and Rambay Elementary School, the only three schools to which
Negro pupils are permitted to attend, are inadequate and unhealthy, the
buildings and schools are old and overcrowded and in a dilapidated condition; the facilities, physical condition, sanitation and protection from
the elements in the Summerton High in the Summerton Elementary Schools in
school district number twenty-two are modern, safe, sanitary, well equipped,
lighted and healthy and the buildings and schools are new, modern, uncrowded
and maintained in first class condition.

6.   That the said schools attended by Negro pupils have an insufficient
number of teachers and insufficient class room space, whereas the white
schools have an adequate complement of teachers and adequate class room
space for the students.

7.   That the said Scott's Branch High School is wholly deficient and totally
lacking in adequate facilities for teaching courses in General Science,
Physics and Chemistry, Industrial Arts and Trades, and has no adequate library and no adequate accommodations for the comfort and convenience of
the students.

ene M Stukes
ille M Stukes
ilie mood Stukes
aldwine F. Stukes
ys for Stukes
Gabriel Tindal
Annie D Tindal
Mary L Bennett
Lillian Bennett
Petitioners

Albert Johnson
Bessie J Johnson
Morgan Johnson
Samuel Mary Johnson
Petitioners

Attorneys for Petitioners
Harold R Boulware
Thurgood Marshall
Robert L Carter

This is the original petition that the Rev. Joseph A. DeLaine used in November 1949 to sign up parents for the lawsuit that would become *Briggs v. Elliott*. The petition initially only asked for equal schools, but Waring persuaded NAACP attorney Thurgood Marshall to turn the lawsuit into a full assault on the constitutionality of school seg-regation. (Photo courtesy the S.C. Department of Archives and History)

The disparities between black and white schools in Depression-era Clarendon County were stark, as shown in these photos of Liberty Hill "Colored" and Summerton "Graded." (Photos courtesy the S.C. Department of Archives and History)

In the late 1940s, the Rev. Joseph A. DeLaine led efforts to improve schools in his native Clarendon County – surreptitiously at first. He feared he would lose his job at Silver Elementary School if county officials learned of his efforts, which he eventually did. (Photo courtesy USC's South Caroliniana Library)

DeLaine, his wife Mattie, and their three children lived across the street from Scott's Branch School in Summerton. Eventually, Mattie would serve as its principal just before the school became the focus of the *Briggs v. Elliott* lawsuit. (Photo courtesy USC South Caroliniana Library)

Many of South Carolina's most prominent civil rights activists met with DeLaine in a Clarendon County church just days before the order in *Briggs v. Elliott* – and Waring's dissent – was published. From the left, E.E. Richburg, Modjeska Simkins, J.W. Seals, Joseph A. DeLaine, Harry Briggs, John McCray, J.S. (Flutie) Boyd, James Hinton and Eugene Montgomery. (Photo courtesy the S.C. Department of Archives and History)

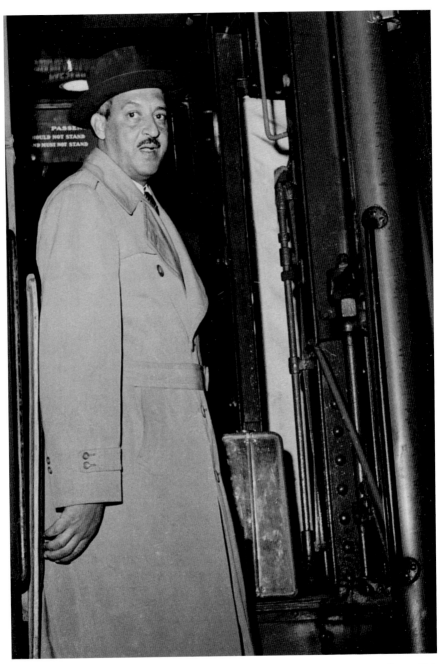

Thurgood Marshall steps off the train in Charleston for the hearing in *Briggs v. Elliott*, 1951. It was the NAACP attorney's sixth case in seven years in Judge Waring's court, where his record was nearly as good as it was in the U.S. Supreme Court. This photo was taken by a young photojournalist named Cecil Williams, who'd go on to chronicle much of the civil rights movement in South Carolina. (Photo courtesy Cecil Williams)

Federal Court Upholds Segregation

Allied Troops Win Seesaw Battle In Central Korea

TOKYO (AP)—The Allies won a savage, seesaw fight with Reds in Central Korea, bumped into a Communist buildup in the West, and scored a new victory in the mounting air battle Saturday.

United Nations troops in the center captured a hill in the old Red "Iron Triangle" after twice being driven off in a bayonet and hand grenade struggle.

In the West, Allied patrols near Parallel 38 north of Seoul contacted two Red regiments, the largest force found there in two weeks. An Allied officer said the regiments appeared to be outposts of a larger Communist force.

Parker   Waring   Timmerman

Waring Is Dissenter As Three Judges Split On School Decision

A three-judge U. S. court today upheld segregation in Clarendon County schools, but ordered the county to provide educational facilities for Negro pupils equal to those for white pupils.

The tribunal split two to one in denying the request of Clarendon Negroes for an injunction forbidding segregation. Judge John J. Parker wrote the majority opinion, concurred in by Judge George Bell Timmerman. Judge J. Waties Waring dissented.

The decree, filed here this morning, orders Clarendon school officials to report within six months their progress in establishing equal education facilities for Negroes.

It is a foregone conclusion that the Negroes will appeal the ruling to a higher court.

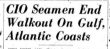

Top Senators Hope To Ease Tax Hike Blow

WASHINGTON (AP)—Senate leaders and today they hope to soften the impact of a whopping $7,500,000,000 tax boost approved yesterday by the House. But they were cautious about predicting any sizeable cuts.

The tax bill, largest single revenue measure ever laid before Congress, would...

CIO Seamen End Walkout On Gulf, Atlantic Coasts

NEW YORK (AP)—Shorter hours and higher wages brought CIO seamen back to their Atlantic and Gulf Coast jobs today, but shipping operators still must settle with radiomen and engineers.

NAACP Plans Appeal Of Judges' Ruling

COLUMBIA (AP)—The National Association for the Advancement of Colored People will appeal today's court decision upholding segregation in South Carolina's public schools, a state NAACP official said.

Negroes May Gain Despite Loss Of Suit

COLUMBIA (AP)—Negroes may have lost their fight against segregation in South Carolina's public school system, but they still may win a lot from a Federal court ruling...

U. S. Urges Normal Flow Of Iran's Oil

WASHINGTON (AP)—The United States hoped today that the British-Iranian oil dispute could be settled...

Governor Has 'No Comment' On School Case

COLUMBIA (AP)—Governor James F. Byrnes today had "no comment" on a federal court decision upholding South Carolina's right to segregate Negro and white public school children.

Truman Urges Stronger Control Bill

WASHINGTON (AP)—President Truman appealed to congress again today for stronger economic controls.

Hungarian Ties U. S. To Spy Plot

BUDAPEST, Hungary (AP)—Communist officials today...

Lost Airliner Is Spotted In African Jungle

MONROVIA, Liberia (AP)—Search planes spotted a missing Pan American World Airways Constellation today in dense jungle about 50 miles...

Macarthur Probers May Call Harriman

By JACK BELL

WASHINGTON (AP)—A move to summon W. Averell Harriman from Europe for testimony on Far Eastern policy threatened today to prolong the Senate's investigation of Gen. Douglas MacArthur's ouster.

ADJOURNMENT FACES DELAY

The Weather

Forecast by U. S. Weather Bureau
For Charleston and vicinity:
Fair and continued hot this afternoon, tonight and Sunday. Light to moderate southerly winds.
Lowest tonight about 70, highest Sunday about 90.
Temperatures up to 7:30 a. m. and the noon reading, taken for city weather service, today were as follows:
7:30 a. m. 75 High noon 88

Charleston native Septima Poinsette Clark began her career in both teaching and activism just after World War I. Her friendship with the judge and Elizabeth Waring began in 1950, just before she became a nationally prominent figure in the civil rights movement. (Photo courtesy Avery Research Center at the College of Charleston)

More than a thousand people tried to crowd into Charleston's federal courthouse to watch the *Briggs v. Elliott* hearing, May 1951. Waring later said they came for "a little breath of freedom." (Photo courtesy The Post and Courier archives)

The Warings hosted a luncheon for civil rights activists at 61 Meeting Street in the spring of 1950, and it was photographed for Collier's "The Lonesomest Man in Town" feature. Some of Septima Clark's friends considered the luncheon a publicity stunt, which she disputed. Clark is far left in this photo, and Ruby Cornwell is seated next to her. The back of Elizabeth's head is in the foreground, and the judge's bailiff, John Fleming, is at the far right. (Photo courtesy the University of Arizona/Dan Weiner)

In November 1950, more than 125 civil rights activists marched from Morris Street Baptist Church to the Warings' home at 61 Meeting Street. Waring was deeply moved by the pilgrimage, as it was called. Note the U.S. marshal standing to the right of the front door, as the Warings were under federal protection at the time. (Photo courtesy The Post and Courier archives)

In November 1954, the Warings arrived by train for their first visit to Charleston in nearly three years. Waring was honored that evening at an NAACP banquet in his honor, which the local newspapers derided for granting the former judge "saintship." (Photo courtesy The Post and Courier archives)

On Oct. 9, 1950, Waring's home at 61 Meeting Street was attacked when unknown assailants pelted the house with bricks and rocks, breaking windows and tearing the screen door. The incident led to a federal investigation, and local controversy, but the culprits were never caught. (Photo courtesy The Post and Courier archives)

Emboldened by the public backlash against Judge Waring, South Carolina Gov. Strom Thurmond mounted his Dixiecrat presidential bid in 1948 and, later, a U.S. Senate campaign. Thurmond promoted an undying devotion to segregation, but his personal feelings may have been more nuanced. (Photo courtesy The Post and Courier archives)

In 1951, the Rev. Joseph A. DeLaine's home in Summerton was destroyed in a fire that was widely considered arson. Firefighters watched the house burn to the ground, later claiming it sat 60 feet outside the department's jurisdiction. (Photo courtesy USC South Caroliniana Library)

Photographers camped out to chronicle the judge's exodus after he retired in February 1952. They were forced to settle for pictures of the Warings' furniture on the sidewalk. The judge and Elizabeth left the city shortly after his 10th anniversary on the bench. (Photo courtesy The Post and Courier archives)

Judge Waring and Elizabeth were honored for their civil rights work at an NAACP banquet in November 1954. The dinner at Buist Elementary School on Calhoun Street marked the last time the Warings visited Charleston. (Photo courtesy The Post and Courier archives)

South Carolina attorneys, led by Charleston lawyer Thomas Tisdale, raised money to erect a statue of Judge J. Waties Waring in the garden behind Charleston's federal courthouse in 2014. A year later, the courthouse was renamed the J. Waties Waring Judicial Center. (Photo courtesy The Post and Courier archives)

fered glimpses of the Waring and Waties families' storied history.

"My great-great-grandfather was a chancellor, and my uncles served all through the Confederacy – one was killed," Waring recalled. "My father was very young, sent in the last year. He was in Columbia when it was evacuated. The results of the Confederacy were devastating. My father came out of it with nothing. He worked for the South Carolina Railroad and we had it pretty hard going. We were quite destitute."

In some ways it was nothing more than standard biography, but Waring was also illustrating that, unlike many Charlestonians, he did not particularly worship ancestral history or romanticize the South's great Lost Cause. He mentioned his brother the newspaper editor, and noted that his siblings were all dead now – the last, Margaret, had passed away recently. He talked briefly about his career and law and politics. When asked about his association with Sen. Burnet Maybank, Waring was typically blunt.

"He did a swell job as mayor," the judge said. "He's done a pretty poor job as governor and senator."

For most of the afternoon, however, Waring talked about the South's racial problems in greater detail than newspaper or radio journalists ever allowed. His revelations were largely academic, and reflected the extensive reading he and Elizabeth had done in recent years – probably not the gripping narrative his interviewer had hoped to mine. Waring finally admitted the injustice he saw from the bench had affected his outlook; the Woodard case, in particular, "gets to your heart."

"Perhaps it sounds a little egotistical to say I feel I have a passion for justice," Waring said. "But the position of a judge is sacred. I always wanted to be a federal judge. I think it is the finest position in the country. You're independent. You are influential and not obligated to anyone and can look in a man's eye and tell him to go to hell. And if he doesn't like it, he can lump it."

Waring said his rulings in the Democratic primary lawsuit were based solely on federal law; he had no designs on reorganizing the country's social order. But he declared it time for people to realize black people had just as much right to work and vote as anyone. Americans, he noted, have a long history of looking down on others – the needy, immigrants, Jews – to make themselves feel better.

"In South Carolina, you can be a bum, a drunkard and a scoundrel, but you're better than that damn nigger," Waring said.

Although he mocked Charleston society and its "phoniness" throughout the interview, he insisted none of his judicial opinions were intended to punish anyone. He pointed out that he'd resigned from most of the city's social clubs after his divorce because he knew there was a stigma attached to it. Waring admitted he'd acted cruelly toward Annie, and his remarks belied his usual feigned indifference. Everything he said indicated he kept some tabs on his former life. He knew that his ex-wife was back in Charleston, and "Among our former social groups, she's been fair and I've said nothing of any kind."

Waring seemed most defensive about the notion that Elizabeth had influenced his progressive views on civil rights. Several candidates had said as much during the primary, which suggested he was little more than a puppet controlled by a domineering, liberal Yankee woman. Eventually, his interviewer delicately brought up the theory. *How much has having a Northern wife influenced your thinking?*

A Southerner to the core, the judge knew any sign of weakness only invited more attack. He tried to mask his irritation at the question, and avoid insulting his wife, by correctly pointing out his rulings in both teacher-pay cases came while he was still married to Annie. In truth, Waring's views had been evolving since he ascended to the bench, although Elizabeth had been at his side when the Woodard case pushed him into outright advocacy. So he carefully and diplomatically allowed that Elizabeth had "enlarged" his view of the world but "did not create it."

As if on cue, Elizabeth joined the conversation at that point. She played the role of dutiful wife and hostess, offering the guest a Scotch or bourbon. But she also praised her husband's bravery and visionary work on the bench, and did little to hide her disdain of Southern society and its backward political views. Finally, the interviewer asked them both: *Do you think there can be civic or social equality in the South?*

"It'll be generations," Waring said.

Nothing had changed in Charleston. Waring finally returned to the city on Oct. 15, just in time to hear new motions in *Brown v. Baskin*. He had to decide if he would make his temporary injunction against the party oath permanent, and shut down Democratic Party officials who wanted him off the case. Based on his comments to newspapers around the country, a state committeeman claimed the judge was "biased in favor of Negroes seeking admission to the state Democratic Party" and should be disqualified from the case.

After leaving California, the Warings had returned to New York City for a luncheon in the judge's honor hosted by the state chapter of the National Lawyers Guild. He used the occasion to again assail the South's prejudice, warning that the region couldn't be trusted to deal with racial problems because of a sentiment among most white Southerners that "the Negro is not an American citizen." He said black citizens wouldn't have the right to vote in South Carolina if not for Thurgood Marshall, who was seated near him.

Marshall had orchestrated the luncheon, a sign of his growing admiration for Waring. In fact, he later complained the guild hadn't done enough to ensure the judge's remarks were distributed around the country. But The New York Times covered Waring's speech, and his most damning comments were published in The Evening Post two days before he got home. The Democrats used the story, and the NAACP's request that the case proceed without a jury, as proof the federal courts were rigged against them.

Waring only seemed to confirm the allegation when he dismissively denied the party's request for a jury trial and refused to recuse himself. "If I had said I was against murder I would have to disqualify myself as being prejudiced under this theory." But nothing he said could quell the pressure building in Charleston.

The day of the *Brown* hearing, Waring received a letter requesting a "favorable decision for the white people" signed by the Knights of the Ku Klux Klan. The letter, postmarked Columbia, outlined the fearful conditions of Reconstruction, when "the court broke down all rules and customs of segregation," and begged the judge to consider the consequences of his actions. The threat of violence was veiled, but clear.

"You must realize the fearful racial hatred that will follow any adverse decision that you may render in the present case under your consideration against the white people of your own State," the letter read.

As far as threatening, anonymous letters went, Waring found it curiously polite. He couldn't dismiss the possibility the note was a fake, perhaps written by some errant party official hoping to scare him. But there was no doubt the Klan had seen a resurgence in recent months. Since August, Klansmen had paraded through a half-dozen South Carolina towns – men in white robes cruising rural communities in cars adorned with crosses made of blinking red lights. Newspapers attributed the parades to increased Klan activity in Georgia, but conceded several had taken place just before the South Carolina Democratic primary.

Although Waring remained suspicious of the letter's surprisingly good grammar and diction, he still had his secretary type up multiple copies for distribution. He sent one to his son-in-law at ABC in New York and gave another to a reporter at The News and Courier who freelanced for The Associated Press. Waring used the letter as evidence to support his claims about the South – and helpfully included his response.

"I believe the people of this country should be made aware of this attempt to threaten and influence a United States judge in his judicial decisions," Waring said.

Some locals claimed Waring was thrilled by the threat, that he relished the idea of being cast as a martyr. Publicly, Waring was defiant and self-righteous. The judge told reporters the Klan's opinion had no bearing on his decision, and he would issue a ruling in *Brown v. Baskin* following a final hearing on Nov. 23 – three weeks after the election.

But privately, Waring was worried. In a letter to a Florida minister, who'd written the judge to praise his brave and progressive stand for civil rights, Waring wrote, "I do not know how far the whole thing is going to go and hope that with the passing of the election there may be some relief. However, the symptoms of public unrest and ill feelings are extremely ominous."

On Nov. 2, Gov. Thurmond cast his ballot at the Edgefield courthouse with all the fanfare of a campaign rally. The town square was filled with hundreds of supporters and politicians, including Charleston congressman Mendel Rivers. When the governor arrived with his wife and mother, he played to the home-town crowd shamelessly. He made a show of planting a victory kiss on Jean and noted that, at 22, this was her first time voting in a presidential election – and she had the chance to elect herself first lady.

Reporters on the scene noted Thurmond's bright red tie was reminiscent of the "Red Shirt" organization that drove the carpetbaggers out of South Carolina in 1876. The Red Shirts were a paramilitary Democratic Party gang that used intimidation – and guns – to dissuade blacks from voting that year. Civil War Gen. Wade Hampton and a young Ben Tillman had been among the group's members. Thurmond didn't say whether the color of his necktie was a coincidence or a not-so-subtle message.

In his final appearance of the election, Thurmond showed the brash confidence expected of a presidential candidate. But he knew the Dixiecrats had no chance of winning. Thomas Dewey's poll numbers had fallen precipitously and, even though the governor still peddled the story that the race could be thrown into the U.S. House of Representatives, he knew that was unlikely. President Truman was enjoying a late surge, although no one was confident enough to predict he'd win. After his appearance in Edgefield, Thurmond retreated to the governor's mansion in Columbia to await the returns.

The turnout in South Carolina was 21 percent higher than it had been for the 1944 presidential election, a clear show of support for Thurmond and his message. The governor won 100,000 votes, dwarfing Truman's 31,000 and Dewey's 5,000. Before the night was over, the Dixiecrats also claimed victory in Alabama, Mississippi and Louisiana. But the predictions of a Southern sweep had been overly optimistic. Nationally, Thurmond got only 1,176,000 votes.

The Democrats had a big night, surprising pundits by retaking both chambers of Congress just two years after losing them. That was no doubt a result of Truman's surprising coattails. The president won 303 electoral votes while Dewey carried only 16 states. By the next morning, Truman was showing off the most presumptuous and erroneous newspaper headline in history, the Chicago Daily

Tribune's banner proclamation "Dewey defeats Truman."

Thurmond finished with 39 electoral voters after a rogue elector in Tennessee cast his ballot for the Dixiecrat ticket. It was a humbling defeat, even more so because the party with civil rights in its platform had prevailed. But the governor claimed his showing across the South was proof that many Americans opposed integration and civil rights, and he promised to continue the fight.

Sen. Olin Johnston, who'd been forced to admit he voted for Truman, said he disagreed with the president's policies and predicted civil rights would be defeated in Congress. After all, as governor he had attempted to protect the Democratic Party and its primary from Judge Waring. It was the senator's attempt to claim a piece of the states' rights mantle, probably because he realized Thurmond – with nowhere else to go – would come for his job next.

The 1948 election may have confirmed Thurmond's belief that South Carolina was vehemently opposed to the Democratic Party's civil rights platform, but he ignored signs that some attitudes in the state were slowly changing. On the same ballot he won 100,000 votes, the people of South Carolina also overwhelmingly approved a state constitutional amendment to legalize divorce.

Waring avoided the election by tending to a busy November docket. His most newsworthy case was a lawsuit filed by the parents of a 10-year-old James Island child. The boy had lost his right leg when a leftover Civil War cannon shell exploded while he and three teenagers were trying to extract gunpowder from it. One of the boys had been killed and another injured. Because the shell was on federal property, the family sued the government for negligence and asked for $125,000 in damages.

The story of the Civil War cannon distracted Charleston for days, and Waring eventually awarded the family $35,000. By then, the injured child had been overshadowed by the showdown between the NAACP and the state Democratic Party – even though most people suspected the outcome was obvious.

Thurgood Marshall had returned to Charleston for the hearing, and asked the judge to make his temporary injunction against the Democratic Party permanent. He argued the party's loyalty oath was meant to force black primary voters into swearing support for segregation. It was little more than an attempt to rig state legislative policy, Marshall said, and prevent black voters from casting ballots. Waring let him talk uninterrupted for nearly half an hour.

"No self-respecting Negro can take that oath," Marshall said. "And I don't believe that there was one member of the convention who believed that a single Negro was prepared to lift his hand and take that oath. The oath is clearly a violation of the constitution of the United States directed against the right of Negroes to vote."

Robert Figg Jr., the Democrats' lawyer, did his best to act indignant. He said South Carolina citizens were the only people in the country denied their "freedom of choice." He said Waring's injunction stripped Democrats of the right to have a political party grounded in their own rules and beliefs. Anyone who didn't like the party's rules, Figg suggested, could start their own. If Marshall's contention was right, he said, "It means we can't have a political party. We have lost the right to determine what we will stand for and what we will stand against."

The Democratic oath had been drafted unskillfully, Figg conceded, but all the party rules had been deemed constitutional prior to the *Elmore* case. Why, he asked, should that change now? Waring quickly dropped all pretense of patience, reminding Figg that *Elmore v. Rice* had been upheld by the appeals court.

"It seems to me that it is as clear as the nose on your face that the Democratic convention … attempted to find a way to get around my decision," Waring said.

The hearing lasted less than two hours, and the judge took only three days to issue a pointedly harsh decision against the Democrats. Waring ruled that black residents had every right to be full members of the South Carolina Democratic Party and vote in its primaries – the state's "true, realistic election." He said the party's claim to be a private club had been debunked in two separate courts, and the oath was a deliberate attempt to continue racial discrimination.

"We cannot escape the conclusion that this was in contravention to the law of the land as enunciated by our courts in prior decisions … and distinctly laid down in the Elmore case," Waring wrote. "Everyone knows that a Negro will not take a solemn oath that he is opposed to legislation that would remove discrimination against him."

The Charleston newspapers reported that, barring the unlikely prospects of a successful appeal, the judge had laid down the law of the land. The editors of The Evening Post called it the end of the Democratic Party – and mocked Waring for remarks he made to New York papers about teaching residents of the South how to behave as Americans.

The editorial suggested that Northern critics should follow the judge's admonition to expose the South's shortcomings tactfully and with "a tolerant patience that should be exercised toward semi-barbarians who just don't know any better. In that way it may be possible to make Americans of us and, in South Carolina's case, to prompt the State to rejoin the Union."

The newspaper's ire reflected a growing discontent with Waring that was spreading across South Carolina. The judge's rulings, and increasingly radical public statements, would inspire the state's Democrats – led by Gov. Thurmond – to look for new ways to thwart his vision of civil rights. They had lost the first round, but from their perspective the battle had just begun. And Waring was their first target.

He had to go.

EXECUTIVE DECISIONS

O n Thursday morning, Dec. 2, 1948, Waties Waring visited the White House for a private meeting with President Truman.

Thirty days after his surprise victory, Truman was relaxed and unhurried. It was Washington's winter lull, and the president's schedule was light – an interview with Collier's magazine at noon, a briefing from the chief of naval operations and a 4 p.m. press conference. Waring had little trouble getting in to see him. On this morning, the president seemed eager to talk.

When Waring was ushered into the Oval Office, he found Truman at his desk, sitting in a black, high-back leather chair. The office was sparse, highlighted by framed photos of Bess and Margaret on a credenza behind the desk. As they shook hands, Waring told Truman he'd voted for him and approved of his civil rights program. He'd not forgotten the president's speech to the NAACP, the remarks he quoted in his *Elmore v. Rice* decision.

Truman was effusive. He thanked Waring for his efforts on the bench and launched into a long dissertation on race relations. It was necessary for the federal government to take a hand in ensuring civil rights for everyone, the president said, but when people thoroughly understood the issue they could be trusted to do the right thing. Waring thought the sentiment was more than slightly naïve, but was too polite to argue. Although he had never been overly impressed with politicians – he knew them too well – the judge seemed star-struck by the president. Or, at the very least, he was intimidated by the Oval Office.

Waring believed Truman was sincere, later calling his comments "heartfelt." But it was clear the president knew little about the judge's record in South Carolina. At one point, Truman started relating the story of a poor World War II veteran, beaten and blinded in the South for the unpardonable crime of being black. Two years later, it seemed the president – like Waring – was still disturbed by the sad plight of Isaac Woodard. When Truman began to recite the details, the judge interrupted him.

"Mr. President, I tried that case," Waring said.

The judge recounted the failings of the U.S. attorney's office in Woodard's trial and recalled how the verdict had upset him and his wife. Truman was astonished to learn of the Justice Department's incompetence, and nearly as surprised to hear such progressive beliefs from a Southern judge. Finally, he suggested Waring contact him anytime he had ideas for improving the White House's civil rights policy. Truman said he needed all the help he could get – particularly in the South.

A few days later, Waring sent Truman a letter to thank him for the meeting. He reiterated his admiration for the administration's brave stand on civil rights and said, "I am more than willing and anxious to answer any call you may wish to furnish information at any time." But the judge tried to disavow the president of any notion that change would come easily.

"The people in this state will <u>not voluntarily</u> do anything along the lines suggested by you," Waring wrote. "It therefore is necessary for the federal government to firmly and constantly keep pressure. There are many, many people here who are ripe and ready for your program, but they do not include any of our so-called political leaders. The whole trouble is <u>fear</u> and it is only when the good people (who, however unfortunately are timid people) see that strength and force is behind your sound program that they will feel it safe to join with you."

A week later, Waring received a reply on White House stationery. The note simply said "I wish we had more Federal Judges like you on the bench."

It was signed, "Harry Truman."

The White House press corps spotted Waring leaving the Oval Office, and pinned him down for an impromptu news conference. The judge mentioned he'd visited U.S. Supreme Court Chief Justice Fred Vinson on Tuesday, but declined to reveal what he'd discussed with the president – other than admitting he told Truman "I voted for him." But Waring could not resist the opportunity to air his views in the national media. He called the poll tax "stupid," but suggested it was up to Congress to figure that out. Every case of lynching, he declared, should be tried in federal court.

The reporters sensed a story ripe for sensationalizing, and asked Waring if he supported the president's civil rights program. The judge acted offended, as if the very premise of the question was ludicrous.

"What do you mean? I believe Negroes should be treated as American citizens," Waring said. "I believe that the federal government should protect all its citizens in their civil rights and should see they are treated as Americans."

Waring's opinion of poll taxes and lynching made national news, circulated across the country by The Associated Press. The New York Times praised the "Charleston-born and Charleston-bred" federal jurist in an editorial the next day, obviously surprised to hear such enlightened views coming from a Southerner.

"When Judge Waring's point of view is generally accepted in the South there will be less need for federal interference," The Times opined. "Indeed, the road to the preservation of states' rights lies through the protection by the states of individual rights within the states."

The Evening Post editorial page unsurprisingly took a different view. The editors suggested Waring was a hypocrite, noting he'd said little about the injustice of poll taxes or the Democrats' un-American activities in all the years he was active in the party. "We can't all be like Congress and judges and rid ourselves of every bit of stupidity within us," the editors wrote. It seemed any time Waring garnered national attention, the local papers showered him with sarcasm.

The Washington trip led to speculation that Waring had been interviewed for a new job – or was at least lobbying for one. When he arrived in Florence a few days later for a short session of court, reporters asked the judge if he was being considered for a seat on the Fourth Circuit Court of Appeals. Waring refused to comment, but tried to dismiss the rumors. He claimed he'd merely "talked shop" with Justice Department officials. For weeks, however, the stories lingered – none of them taking into account the unlikelihood Waring could win Senate confirmation for another job in the federal government.

His true motive for visiting Washington was apparent in a letter Waring sent to Thurgood Marshall two days after he met with the president. The judge recounted his brief chat in the Oval Office as well as a 90-minute conversation with the chief justice. Waring had good news to report. "I may assure you that both interviews were very helpful to many things that you and I agree on."

After five years and four cases together, Waring and Marshall had become friends – or at least kindred spirits. Waring recognized that Marshall was a gifted attorney, and felt he had a small glimpse of the abuse the NAACP counsel endured as a black man fighting injustice. Marshall may have considered Waring a mentor; at the very least he was impressed with the judge's empathy and understanding of civil rights. Had South Carolina officials known how close the two had become, it would have worried them much more than any notion of Waring being appointed to a higher court.

But Marshall wasn't Waring's only confidant in the civil rights group. The judge also had befriended Walter White, the executive secretary of the national NAACP – and Marshall's boss. Waring was encouraging both men to ramp up their efforts to challenge segregation. Progress was not coming fast enough for the judge, and he realized only they could deliver the cases he needed to overturn the country's separate-but-equal doctrine.

The overwhelming resistance to civil rights was driving Waring to become more liberal – and strident – every day. In a letter to a member of the Detroit mayor's Interracial Committee, the judge said he no longer believed the South could work out these problems on its own – or that racial strife was relegated to one part of the country. Only blacks who are subservient and play by the white man's rules get by, he said; those who try to assert their full rights as American citizens don't get very far. To change the country, Waring believed, there must be "constant prodding" and "force."

Soon, Waring would begin to make such controversial statements publicly. The backlash would threaten his job, and his life.

In January 1949, Gov. Strom Thurmond announced plans for sweeping governmental reform, including new laws to protect the rights of political parties "against invasion by those who are not in sympathy with their principles and objectives." Thurmond claimed the state was being run by federal fiat. It was clearly a shot at Waring, and widely seen as the opening salvo of a campaign against U.S. Sen. Olin Johnston.

State law didn't allow anyone to serve successive terms as governor, and Thurmond was coming to the end of his tenure. The U.S. Senate was his most viable political promotion, and he took his showing in the presidential election as a sign that he could win Johnston's job. He saw no reason to change his message, and used his annual address to the legislature to remind everyone of his commitment to states' rights.

Neither Thurmond's political plans nor his legislative agenda was any secret. In December, Columbia Lighthouse & Informer editor John McCray had warned readers that the Democrats might try to skirt Waring's ruling in *Brown v. Baskin* with new legislation. A month after Thurmond's announcement, a Clarendon County senator introduced a bill that would allow political parties to decide who they admitted as members. That legislation stalled, as did most of Thurmond's agenda, after the Fourth Circuit Court of Appeals upheld Waring's ruling. The Democratic Party was informed again that it was in no way a private club.

The Democrats were not only losing at every turn, they were forced to watch the rest of the country heap praise on Waring for orchestrating their misfortune. In late January, the judge received an award of merit for his contribution to the civil rights of American citizens. The Anti-Defamation League, the New York Metropolitan Council of B'nai B'rith, the NAACP, the Freedom House, the Common Council for World Unity, the World Student Service Fund, the Citizen's Housing and Planning Council and the National Citizens Council on Civil Rights jointly honored Waring for "restraining officials who sought to bar Negro voters from participating in primary elections."

Anne accepted the award on her father's behalf in a ceremony at Carnegie Hall. The judge could not attend; he was busy with his winter docket.

A month later, the Negro Newspaper Publishers Association honored Waring again – along with President Truman and Eleanor Roosevelt – for "impressive contributions to the advancement of Negroes." It seemed Waring was wildly popular almost everywhere except South Carolina, where he was wildly reviled.

By late spring, the state newspapers uncovered more of his handiwork and unsuccessfully tried to turn it into another controversy.

South Carolina newspapers reported in May 1949 that federal court juries across the state had been integrated, and jurors allowed to eat together in restaurants. The court's state marshal confirmed Waring and Timmerman had issued the order jointly: restaurants that served one juror must serve them all – and not in separate rooms. The papers conceded this practice wasn't new, and most restaurant managers had heard no complaints. One said a few diners questioned him about the situation, but were satisfied by his explanation. Slowly, it seemed the federal government was attempting to change South Carolina culture.

Of course, the South was not the only region struggling with integration. The same week, Marshall wrote to Waring about his U.S. Supreme Court case against the city of Indianapolis for refusing to seat black grand jurors. Marshall confided that it was a problematic case – he personally didn't like the plaintiff, but was disgusted by the city's whites-only grand jury policy. The NAACP couldn't change the country, he conceded, by focusing solely on a handful of states.

"We are determined that we will not continue to bring such cases in the South and to permit places like Indianapolis to discriminate," Marshall wrote. "At least we will act with equal fairness below and above the 'Smith and Wesson Line.'"

Marshall meant that as a sad joke about violence in the South, but Waring would soon find the sentiment all too accurate.

Rev. DeLaine finally got a letter from the NAACP in March.

Harold Boulware informed him that Thurgood Marshall would be in Columbia on March 12 to map out a legal strategy for schools. Levi Pearson had been invited, Boulware said, and DeLaine should come as well "so that you can help us with all the information regarding Clarendon County." DeLaine asked the Rev. J.W. Seals, who'd become his most trusted supporter, to go with him. Both men would be less than thrilled with the new plan.

Marshall had assembled activists from around South Carolina in the Palmetto State Teachers building to explain that the NAACP was no longer interested in buses. Such lawsuits, he explained, were unlikely to result in significant change and cost too much money – and the group's legal defense fund was tapped out. The organization also had decided not to take on suits with a single plaintiff because "the race haters may liquidate him at any time." The Clarendon case had proven how easy it was to discredit or disqualify one person. From now on, Marshall said, he was interested only in class-action suits that struck at the heart of segregation.

At first, DeLaine argued that it wasn't fair. The people of Clarendon County needed help, and he'd only been asked to produce one plaintiff for the bus lawsuit. Marshall sympathized but said the decision was final. DeLaine finally offered to expand the suit. There had been some trouble at Scott's Branch School, where his wife worked, and that could form the basis of a larger complaint.

The former principal at Scott's Branch had been fired in the fall, and the community suspected it was retaliation for the bus lawsuit. The new principal demanded money from local families to subsidize school supplies and, when they couldn't pay, their children were told they couldn't graduate. This principal had a contentious relationship with the entire faculty and staff. Before long, DeLaine said, they'd probably be asked to buy coal to heat the building – a common requirement in some of Clarendon County's black schools.

DeLaine argued until Marshall finally relented. He promised to consider filing a class-action lawsuit, he said, if the pastor could find at least 20 plaintiffs – and NAACP officials in New York signed off on it. That was a tall order with no guarantees, but it was the best deal DeLaine could get. He and Seals left Columbia with a new mission, and a decidedly more complex problem. They'd had a hard time finding a single person willing to put their name on a lawsuit; now they needed nearly two dozen.

DeLaine hosted the first community meeting at Mount Zion AME on March 30, and another the following day at Union Cypress Church. Both were well-attended, and the people had compiled a long list of grievances. But few were willing to sign a petition. Farmers feared they would suffer Pearson's fate, and teachers worried they'd be fired. By summer, DeLaine had only three names on his petition – and one later asked to remove her name. Her husband, concerned about the potential backlash, insisted she drop out.

Boulware and Marshall's growing list of demands made the task even harder. They said the complaint had to focus on a single Clarendon County school district; it had to be a district in which there was both a white and black high school, so comparisons could be made; and every plaintiff had to have children currently enrolled in that district. DeLaine's job, already a challenge, seemed to grow more insurmountable every day.

The NAACP attorneys had learned from past mistakes, however, and offered DeLaine advice to make his search easier. They suggested he focus on the cities and avoid the rural school districts, some of which had no white schools. That narrowed the prospects to Manning and Summerton. Since both DeLaine and Seals were more familiar with the southern end of the county, and Scott's Branch was in Summerton, they concentrated their efforts there. DeLaine finally recruited some Scott's Branch students, who persuaded their parents to attend a meeting at St. Mark's AME, just a quarter-mile from the high school.

Scott's Branch met all of the NAACP's criteria. It was in Clarendon County School District 22, along with the all-white Summerton High. Both had been built in 1935, but their differences were stark: The district spent $40,000 to build Summerton High, but only $6,000 on Scott's Branch. The students at Scott's Branch were required to pay for equipment that never arrived, and their money was never returned. Seniors were asked for a $27 graduation fee, and anyone who didn't pay got a blank piece of paper instead of a diploma. Summerton students paid no such fees.

The disparities perfectly illustrated the inequality forced on the black community.

It didn't take much to stoke the anger of Scott's Branch parents. The school board had ignored their complaints about the new principal and refused to rescind the student fees. When DeLaine sent out 300 invitations to his June 8 meeting, the church couldn't hold all the people who showed up. They filled the pews at St. Mark's and lined the walls, seething over their treatment and ready to fight for their rights.

One Scott's Branch senior, Reverdy Williams, fired up the crowd so much they decided to organize and approach the school board. If the Committee on Action – as they called themselves – was ignored, they would agree to join an NAACP lawsuit. But no one volunteered to sign a petition, serve as a plaintiff or even lead the committee. Every time a person was nominated, the audience shouted them down. They wanted the man who'd been fighting hardest for their rights, who had proven himself beyond reproach, a leader who could be trusted to not back down. They wanted DeLaine.

At first, he declined. DeLaine said any of the other people nominated would do fine and he would help. But someone shouted, "We don't want nobody who's gonna sell us out. We want action. We want you." DeLaine thought of his children, of Mattie and her job at Scott's Branch. If he led the Committee on Action, there would be consequences. Even if his family wasn't physically harmed, he might end up unemployed and unable to feed them. But ultimately, DeLaine realized this was exactly what he was asking of everyone else.

"Y'all are putting me in this position and I know y'all are gonna fight me when the going gets hard," DeLaine said. "When the whites plot against me and when my life is in jeopardy and even when everything I own might be destroyed, y'all will be ready to turn your backs on me."

Justice does not come easily, DeLaine told the audience. The school board and superintendent would ignore them. The county would dismiss their claims, and they couldn't count on the state Board of Education to help. No one would willingly give them equal facilities, or equal rights. Only the courts would do that.

"We'll have to appeal to the state court and then to the federal court and from there to the Supreme Court before we can get justice," DeLaine said, his preaching voice echoing through the sanctuary. "If I take the leadership, you have to stick with me and fight all the way to the United States Supreme Court."

The sermon hit its mark, and shouts of support echoed through the room. The crowd promised to stick with him, to fight and not give up until their children were treated fairly. Several people volunteered to serve on the committee, enough that DeLaine had his pick. Before they left, the crowd broke into song, a hymn of reassurance for DeLaine. "Together let us sweetly live," they sang. "Together let us die."

A movement began that night, but DeLaine still needed 20 people who lived in District 22 willing to take the same risks he had. It would take him months, but he soon had time to search. Two days after he was named head of the Committee on Action, the District 22 school board informed DeLaine that his services were no longer needed at Silver Elementary School.

He'd been fired.

With no job to protect, DeLaine devoted the summer to his mission. He led a group of parents to a school board meeting, where they outlined myriad complaints about Scott's Branch. The district ignored their requests for months. In October, the school board finally acknowledged its growing problem – in the most underhanded way possible. After the Scott's Branch principal resigned under community pressure, the district offered the position to DeLaine. The school board assumed that would persuade him to abandon all this equal rights nonsense.

It was a calculated, and enticing, offer: a job across the street from his house, a steady paycheck and perhaps a chance to improve conditions at the school. But it also meant betraying the parents he'd promised to lead to the Supreme Court. DeLaine turned down the board; he could not be bribed. But the school district simply devised a new way to pressure DeLaine: Mattie was appointed interim principal at Scott's Branch. If DeLaine wanted to continue his protests, the minister would be forced to lodge complaints against his wife.

DeLaine still would not give in.

On Nov. 11, 1949, DeLaine walked into the Summerton post office and picked up a package from the NAACP's Columbia headquarters. Harold Boulware had drawn up a petition with 14 examples of discrimination in Clarendon County's District 22 schools – insufficient teachers, inadequate facilities, no running water, lack of lighting, janitorial services and bus service among them. The petition said the black schools were in no way the equal of white schools, and county residents demanded relief. It was the first step in filing a class-action lawsuit.

Boulware included detailed instructions for DeLaine to follow, outlining every piece of information he needed to collect from each potential plaintiff. The attorney warned him there could be repercussions, and he should disclose that to everyone who offered to sign. Last of all, he told DeLaine not to allow anyone in his family to put their name on the petition.

For months, DeLaine had been meeting with parents in various churches around the county. But the Klan threatened to visit one pastor if he hosted any more community gatherings, so DeLaine's options had narrowed. No one wanted to contend with the potential of a torched church. The next meeting, he decided, would have to be held in secret.

DeLaine initially considered inviting everyone to his house, but it was too conspicuous and too close to downtown. They needed to gather somewhere far from the prying eyes of Summerton. Finally, he thought to visit a secluded farm just up the road. Perhaps, he thought, Harry Briggs will let us meet at his house.

Briggs not only agreed to host, he joined the cause. His son, Harry Jr., had to walk five miles to school, and Briggs had supported DeLaine's efforts since it was just a simple request for buses. That night, it became apparent the school board's neglect had enraged the entire community. Everyone had finally, collectively, decided enough was enough. DeLaine got his 20 signatures. Briggs and his wife were the first two people to sign the petition that eventually became the lawsuit *Briggs v. Elliott*.

The trouble started almost immediately.

James Brown, who drove the local Esso truck, was fired before the end of the year. His son, a junior at Scott's Branch, lost his job at a local drugstore. Hazel Ragin, the only painter in Summerton, couldn't find work. Mazie Solomon was told to take her name off the petition or she would lose her job at the Windsor Motel. She walked out. Others who signed the petition were served notice of overdue bills they had no memory of incurring, and some teachers were immediately dismissed by the school board.

No one felt the pressure more than Harry and Eliza Briggs. Harry was a World War II veteran who'd served in the South Pacific, returning to Clarendon County the moment he was discharged. For years, he'd pumped gas at the local Sinclair station while Eliza worked as a maid for a local motel. They'd managed to save enough money to build a modest house off the road behind DeLaine's property. By local standards, the family was doing well.

Shortly after signing the petition, Briggs got a court summons that claimed one of his cows had trespassed on a white cemetery. Before long, Harry Jr. was warned off his paper route, which included several white neighborhoods. Then Eliza was fired from the motel. And on Dec. 24, Summerton Mayor H.C. Carrigan – who owned the Sinclair station – wished Harry a Merry Christmas and gave him a carton of cigarettes as a holiday bonus.

Then he fired Briggs.

ELIZABETH TAKES THE STAGE

Septima Clark first met the Warings when she showed up on their doorstep late one night in January 1950. She'd been ordered to rescind their invitation to the YWCA's annual banquet. Instead, she urged them to show up anyway.

It had taken Clark only two years to run afoul of Charleston's power structure – and align herself with the city's most controversial couple.

Clark moved back to her hometown in late 1947. After 18 years in Columbia, teaching school by day and adult literacy at night, she applied to the Charleston County School Sistrict and was offered a job teaching seventh grade at Henry P. Archer Elementary. It was the newest school in the district, and already it was overcrowded. But Clark would just have to get used to large classes; district officials didn't dare ask taxpayers to finance another black school, even though they were at 400 percent capacity.

She'd always considered returning to the Lowcountry, but never gave it serious thought until her mother, Virginia, had a stroke. That was all it took – Clark bought a house behind Emanuel AME Church and moved Virginia and her sister, Lorene, into it. From 17 Henrietta Street, it was only a block to the corner of Calhoun and Meeting streets, where she could catch a bus that carried her to Archer. Soon, her life became almost routine.

The city had grown more prosperous and crowded in her absence, but she quickly realized some things hadn't changed. Charleston society remained cliquish and insular, even in the black community, and not nearly as accepting as Columbia. Still, she volunteered for various charitable organizations, including the local branch of the NAACP and the YWCA.

The Coming Street Y was one of the oldest and most influential institutions in the black community. It had been founded in 1907 by Felicia Goodwin, matriarch of a long line of black civic leaders and business owners. The YWCA offered recreational programs for young girls and a political hub for adults. It remained independent until 1920, when it became an auxiliary of the white YWCA on Society Street. There had been little choice; the Y could no longer pay the mortgage on the Coming Street property.

The women who ran the Society Street Y were progressive for their time. Although initially a tad paternalistic, they had broken from the national organization in the 1940s to take a stand against segregation. It was a bold move for a group of ladies in Charleston. When the two YWCA boards met jointly, Clark was participating in some of the city's first integrated meetings.

Eventually, she was put in charge of the committee that managed the Coming Street Y. Clark handled all the usual administrative headaches, recruited volunteers to refurbish the building and dealt with typical neighborhood problems. The most persistent annoyance was local boys who snuck into the building to cause mischief or harass the girls. This became such a nuisance that the board decided to ask for police protection, and requested an audience with Mayor Edward Wehman Jr. Two women from the Society Street board took the meeting, and invited Clark to join them.

Surprised to see a black woman walk into his office, the mayor opted for the simplest response: he ignored the situation. He seated the two white women and then plopped down with his back to Clark. The Society Street ladies were appalled by his poor manners, but said nothing. They fumbled over their talking points, trying to get out of the room quickly. But they weren't getting through to Wehman. Finally, Clark spoke up.

"Mr. Mayor, we want to see two things done," she said. "The first is to have immediate relief from these boys who are annoying us, and the second is to see a long-range program set up for the boys of the city."

Clark asked that the city post a policeman outside the YWCA to dissuade the teenagers from trespassing, particularly when there were events. She was polite, direct and firm. The mayor picked up his phone, called the chief of police and told him what to do. When he hung up, the mayor promised everything was set.

"All you have to do is let them know down at the police station at one o' clock, when the men go out on their beats," Wehman said, "and they'll have a man stationed there whenever you have anything going on."

The women were amazed by Clark's diplomacy, persuasiveness and poise – and they wouldn't forget it. So when the Society Street board saw a potential disaster looming, they asked Clark to handle it.

The executive secretary of the Coming Street Y had been impressed when she heard Elizabeth Waring speak at a local church. She suggested the judge's wife, a very modern woman, would be a good keynote speaker for their next annual meeting. Clark and the administration board agreed, and the secretary sent Elizabeth an invitation. Mrs. Waring accepted immediately.

But when the Society Street board of directors saw the upcoming speech advertised in the local papers, they called Clark into an emergency meeting. She found the entire experience was unsettling. One minute, the women were talking about religion, how their faith gave them courage; in the next minute, they "professed their desperate fear of having a woman speak to them." Clark was asked to write a letter quietly withdrawing the invitation. They should have expected her to ask why.

Of course, Clark had known about Judge Waring for years – she'd helped search for plaintiffs in the Columbia teacher-pay lawsuit, sparked in part by his decision in the Charleston case. She also saw his name in the newspapers regularly, and knew Waring had been widely criticized for opening the Democratic primary to black voters. But Clark had never met the judge or his wife. And if she knew why Elizabeth was so despised, she didn't let on.

The YWCA board members indelicately described Mrs. Waring as a home-wrecker who'd broken up the judge's 30-year marriage. In the low voices reserved for the most insidious gossip, they told Clark how Waring's first wife now lived in a rented carriage house just around the corner from her old home. Poor Annie Gammell Waring could see the house from her window, a constant reminder that another woman now lived there – and slept in the bed with her former husband.

It was all so scandalous, they said, no proper Charlestonian had anything to do with the couple. The YWCA's reputation would be ruined if that Northern hussy was allowed to speak. They said nothing of the Warings' controversial stand on race relations.

Clark suspected they were piling on, and had no way to discern how much of this hearsay was true. She didn't mention these doubts, of course; Clark simply said black women wouldn't know such stories and she didn't feel comfortable rescinding the invitation. The women suggested her refusal might hurt the chance of getting someone from the Coming Street Y on their board of directors.

"To have Mrs. Waring speak will shatter our dreams," one of them said. "You'll have to write her that letter."

The meeting ended late, without an agreement, and Clark walked home with a friend. She was torn. Clark didn't want to cause the Y any trouble, but even if she'd been inclined to write the letter, which she wasn't, "What sort of reason can we give?" She had no desire to offend the judge. In truth, she admired his court decisions.

Clark fretted about the conundrum for blocks. Finally, she stopped at a pay phone, looked up the number and called Elizabeth. Although she didn't know the Warings, her friend Ruby Cornwell socialized with the couple and spoke highly of them. Clark was bold enough to ask if she and her friend might stop by. Even though it was after 9 p.m., Elizabeth invited the women to come over immediately. They were at 61 Meeting Street.

The Warings had kept a relatively low profile for six months.

In June, a state senator suggested Waring could be run out of South Carolina if "we had enough lawyers with backbone;" a circuit court judge complained that the South had been targeted by "punitive federal laws;" and the Democrats threatened to appeal *Brown v. Baskin* to the U.S. Supreme Court. Waring remained silent until the Charleston papers tried to pull him into a mild controversy.

Vice President Alben Barkley was scheduled to speak at a Columbia banquet in early July, and the newspapers ran front-page stories about influential state leaders – including Strom Thurmond and Sol Blatt – boycotting the event. Waring was included as an unconfirmed attendee, which reporters found noteworthy both because he was a "Trumanite," and no black Democrats had been invited. The papers detailed their efforts to talk to Waring, repeating his secretary's flimsy excuses that the judge didn't give opinions over the phone and had no appointments available.

Waring was livid to be listed alongside a bunch of Dixiecrats, and enraged by the insinuation he was afraid of journalists. The judge finally agreed to talk to an Associated Press reporter in person, but the Charlotte correspondent couldn't get a flight. Finally, Waring issued a blistering statement that he demanded be published in its entirety – or not at all.

"My experience with the lack of fairness and editorial integrity of the Charleston newspaper combination leads me to refuse to furnish any interviews or to authorize any quotation or run the risk of mis-quotation," Waring wrote. "The newspapers are, of course, privileged, and have the right to obtain and publish any authorized opinions or statements or any acts of mine. They also, of course, are entirely free to express their opinions of me and of my judicial views, acts, or doings. But I do not feel it is safe to give my personal opinions to be garbled to suit the propaganda purpose of so biased a newspaper. If I should have any occasion to give any press release at any time, I shall prefer using some newspaper of a higher standard."

Of course, he hadn't answered the initial question. Instead, Waring simply lambasted The Evening Post and The News and Courier, where his nephew worked in the editorial department – and, he assumed, was the author of several pieces critical of his rulings. But after one more editorial, the papers left him alone, and the judge told The Associated Press he considered the Barkley dinner so controversial it wouldn't be appropriate for a federal judge to attend.

Since then, Waring had avoided the headlines. His only significant case in the latter half of 1949 was a lawsuit against the state filed by shrimpers who claimed South Carolina was illegally trying to regulate their business in federal waters. Waring was on a panel of three judges that ultimately ruled in favor of the state.

The Warings traveled frequently throughout the summer and fall. They returned to Santa Barbara and the El Encanto, first stopping in New York, and Waring took every opportunity to sit in for other judges. He stayed away from

Charleston as much as possible, slowly cutting all remaining ties to the city. He quietly resigned from the Charleston Club and the South Carolina Society, although that was merely a formality; he hadn't attended functions for either organization in years.

Waring even sold the Sullivan's Island beach cottage, furniture and all, for $13,750. The cabin had served as a retreat throughout the years, a place where he and Elizabeth could still mingle with their neighbors. But even that had changed. A year earlier, lightning had struck a house on Sullivan's Island, prompting the owner to post a sign in his yard that said: "Dear Lord, he lives next door."

Charleston society may have been offended by Waring's messy personal life, but it seemed everyone was outraged that he'd granted black people the right to vote in the Democratic primary.

By late 1949, the Warings were socializing almost exclusively with black Charlestonians. They entertained their mailman and his family, and made friends with Ruby Cornwell – a civil rights activist, former teacher at the Avery Institute and wife of a respected local dentist. They sometimes hosted YWCA founder Felicia Goodwin, godmother of an entire community. Her grandson, Herbert Fielding, occasionally tagged along for these visits.

Years later, Fielding became the first black man elected to the state legislature since Reconstruction. Throughout his long life in public service, he would always remember how kind the judge had been to his family. Aside from his grandmother, Fielding later recalled, the judge was one of the people who inspired him to pursue a career in politics.

For much of the fall, Waring seemed adrift. He had no major cases on the docket and his name faded from the headlines. The judge spent much of his time contemplating the changing world, and decided it was not evolving quickly enough. But lacking a court case to drive social change, he was relegated to sharing high-minded ideals with like-minded souls. Many days he spent in front of a typewriter.

In October, Waring wrote a gently chastising letter to Eleanor Roosevelt – who he'd met in New York earlier that year – after an editorial in The News and Courier quoted the former first lady saying, "The North is as bad as the South in race relations." He claimed to understand the sentiment, but complained she was "giving our enemies something to harp on." When the author Lillian Smith sent Waring a copy of *Killers of the Dream* – her memoir attacking sin, sex and segregation in the South – it seemed to distill his current mood.

"When the Jim Crow signs on railroads, buses, waiting rooms, and public conveniences generally, are torn down, many of our people, and particularly the younger ones, will begin to forget they were ever there," the judge wrote to Smith. "In my time, I have seen many improvements that are now accepted, but they have been small and gradual, and the time has come when the American government must take the position that all forms of segregation by law are un-American and that all people in this country must have an equal opportunity."

Waring told Smith he'd seen advances that would have been unimaginable when he was a boy – blacks and whites could now share Pullman cars, for example. It was his second reference to trains in one letter, and that was no coincidence. Thurgood Marshall had just sent the judge a brief filed by the solicitor general in the lawsuit *Henderson v. United States*, and it interested him immensely.

The case dated back to 1942, when Elmer Henderson, a federal employee, had been traveling by train from Washington to Atlanta. The porter wouldn't seat him because white people had crowded into the dining car normally reserved for black passengers. By the time they finished, the kitchen was closed. Henderson simply didn't get to eat that night. The resulting lawsuit had dragged on for years.

Henderson was bound for the U.S. Supreme Court and, although it didn't challenge the notion of separate but equal, it could have. The case reminded Waring of *Plessy v. Ferguson*, the 1896 Supreme Court decision that Southern states used to justify Jim Crow laws. *Plessy* was also a lawsuit about segregation on trains.

"The best thing about it is that it boldly goes to the heart of the whole question and advances the sound theory that segregation is un-American and is in conflict with the principles of our form of government," Waring wrote to Marshall. "I am glad that the Department of Justice has, at least, reached the conclusion that we should no longer play with sophistries and illusions to attain basic American rights."

Lawsuits had danced around the issue of segregation for years, yet Waring believed the courts – and Congress – continued to willfully ignore the most basic tenets of the Constitution. In some ways, it seemed society was regressing, "as if the Secession Movement is going to be renewed and the Confederate States revived," Waring told Marshall. He believed the only way to stop that momentum was to reverse *Plessy* – and he desperately wanted a case to test that theory.

As the Charleston days grew shorter and colder, and a new decade dawned, Waring awaited the chance – and the case – that would allow him to challenge *Plessy*. In the meantime, he believed the South should be subjected to constant pressure. Although he felt constricted by what he could say as a federal judge, Elizabeth was under no such restraint. So she welcomed the invitation to speak at the YWCA banquet.

Septima Clark arrived at 61 Meeting Street around 9:30 that night. Mrs. Waring answered the door, ushered Clark and her friend inside and invited them to sit down. Elizabeth was friendly, chatty and seemingly oblivious to both the late hour and awkwardness of the visit. Obviously, she didn't receive many guests.

It was an odd social call by Charleston standards, but Clark never said anything to suggest she was uncomfortable. Most likely, she was too upset by the circumstances to think about the implications of being in a white household at that time of night. On the way there, she'd decided how to handle it. Clark introduced herself as the chairman of the Coming Street YWCA administration committee and said she had two requests.

"If the white people ask you not to speak, will you please speak?" Clark said. "And if the Negroes ask you not to speak, please let me know."

Elizabeth couldn't have been overly surprised, but she asked anyway: "What happened?"

Clark recounted the meeting she'd just had with the Society Street YWCA's chairwoman, leaving out the vitriol and gossip. The board, she explained, had decided it would be "unwise" for her to speak at the banquet. But Clark made it clear she wasn't a party to the decision and refused to rescind the invitation.

In her most diplomatic – if unsubtle – way, she was practically begging Mrs. Waring to not back down.

Elizabeth didn't take the news well. She immediately went to the phone, called the national YWCA headquarters in New York and, despite the hour, somehow got through. By the time Clark got home that night, she had a telegram waiting from the national office asking if Mrs. Waring's account was true. Clark was impressed; it had taken Elizabeth less than an hour to stir up a full-blown controversy.

Clark had to deal with the repercussions the next day. The director of a local charity called and asked her to stop by his office, where he assailed Elizabeth's character for several minutes. She ignored him. Then, Clark was summoned to the Society Street YWCA office, where she was asked to sign a prepared statement that said the organization did not intend for Mrs. Waring to speak. She declined. Soon, the Charleston papers had the story – the controversial judge's wife would speak to the Y on Monday. The Society Street women were right. It was scandalous.

Years later, Clark found it all hilarious. She said the YWCA's annual banquet had never gotten so much publicity. That would turn out to be a monumental understatement.

Elizabeth would not wait until that night to get her revenge. On Monday afternoon, Jan. 16, the ladies were setting up for the banquet when Mrs. Waring walked in wearing a wide hat, elegant dress, high heels and a devilish smirk. Elizabeth told the women – the ones who hadn't ducked into a back room to avoid her – she just wanted to make sure the lectern was the proper height, as she was very tall. Clark believed she was only there to goad her detractors, and Elizabeth soon confirmed her suspicion. Just before she walked out, Mrs. Waring handed one woman a wad of cash.

"I want to leave this donation to help you with the food tonight," she said.

And with that, Elizabeth walked out the door.

They asked for it.

That's what Clark thought afterward, when Elizabeth Waring's speech to the Charleston YWCA became national news. The Society Street ladies and the newspapers had expected her to preach about the evils of segregation, and mostly likely be condescending about it. But they were not prepared for such a hateful attack on the entire South, or to be blamed for all of the country's sins. Clark had no doubt Elizabeth meant every word, but suspected her tone reflected a healthy measure of revenge.

"And because so many mean things had been said about her and the judge, no doubt, she was more vitriolic herself than she would have been had not these assaults been made upon them," Clark later said. "But she talked plainly and she laid it on."

Even before the banquet began, Clark knew the Warings would make a scene. Shortly after Elizabeth strutted out of the building that afternoon, the judge himself called and suggested she station some men near the light switches. "When there is trouble, the first thing the troublemakers do is turn out the lights." It was good advice, and a warning. Waring had practically assured her that Elizabeth was coming to raise hell.

But the judge was worried about more than the lights. He thought Elizabeth's speech was exactly the sort of pressure necessary to further the debate on civil rights, but was concerned it might lead to unexpected retaliation. He wrote a letter to Anne and Stanley, recounting the efforts to cancel Elizabeth's appearance and noting "there is no telling what extent they might go to try and break up this meeting, either by suggestions of financial harm or even eventually by physical violence." The Warings were willing to endure scorn and ridicule for their political beliefs, but feared becoming martyrs.

"Neither Elizabeth nor I are greatly concerned by these matters excepting so far as they may be publicized and it is important, if anything out of the way happens, that the truth should be known," Waring wrote. "For that reason, I thought I would write and advise you of this since, if anything does happen, it will be advisable to see that true publicity is given, and Stanley has access to sources for that."

That night, Waring kept his eyes on the crowd more than his wife – and there were hundreds of people to watch. Although the Warings were widely despised, the room was full. Every chair was taken and people lined the walls. Nobody in Charleston wanted to miss the expected fireworks. The judge spotted a reporter from The News and Courier on the front row, poised to write down every word. He need not have bothered. Waring was carrying copies of the speech to hand out when Elizabeth finished.

"I want every word printed just as she said it," Waring told The News and Courier reporter afterward. "Don't change one word of it."

That night, Victoria Poinsette feared she would be hit by an errant bullet before the judge's wife shut up. Clark's mother, who was sitting beside her on the platform, had no doubt the Klan would descend upon the YWCA and open fire just for allowing Elizabeth Waring to spew such hateful bile about white people. She had never heard such a vicious attack in person, nor had anyone else in the room.

"My very dear friends, it was brave of you to invite me to speak here and brave of all of you to come to hear me, for all the white 'powers that be' have done everything underhanded in their power to keep me from speaking to you Negro people, even to defaming Judge Waring's and my character," Elizabeth began.

"But we only feel sorry for them, for their stupidity, as it will hurt them, and not us, for it is apparent to everyone what their real motive is in not wishing me to speak – fear of the judge and me. We to them are like the atom bomb which they are afraid we will use to destroy their selfish and savage white supremacy way of life. And they are quite correct. That is exactly what the judge and I are doing, and they know it and see the writing on the wall."

She recalled that her husband, in his famous court decision *Elmore v. Rice*, had urged the white supremacists to rejoin the Union. But when they resist, she said, only force will bring about change. Only revolution sparks evolution, Elizabeth said, and it was time to enforce the rights that black people already legally have – the rights that white people were trying to deny them. It sounded very much like a declaration of war.

As Clark said, Elizabeth "laid it on." She accused Southern whites of fearing freedom for all, and the Charleston newspapers of censoring civil rights news.

Segregation is almost dead in Northern colleges, she claimed, and the next generation would see that it was abolished everywhere. She declared the black community way ahead of whites spiritually, and predicted a new day was dawning, one that would mark a glorious time for people of good will.

"You are in the springtime of your growth, when great achievements are attained. You Negro people have already picked up the torch of culture and achievement from the whites down here," Elizabeth said, perhaps pausing for effect. "They are a sick, confused and decadent people. Like all decadent people, they are full of pride and complacency, introverted, morally weak and low. You are building and creating. The white supremacists are destroying and withholding. They are so self-centered that they are drawing the walls around themselves so close and high that they have become completely isolated from the rest of the world and have not considered themselves as a part of the country since the Civil War."

Finally, Elizabeth denounced the myths of Reconstruction, likening the justifications for white supremacy to the propaganda Germany used as to explain Hitler's atrocities. She even compared the Dixiecrats to the Gestapo. Elizabeth interspersed religious imagery with accounts of black people forced to sit in the back of public buses, and promised those times were at an end. And anyone who didn't like it had better get out of the way.

"Freedom is everybody's job," she said.

When she finished, a black woman in the audience walked onto the stage and handed her a bouquet of roses. Elizabeth hugged her.

Somewhere in the crowd, Judge Waring stood proud and smiling. He had just dispatched another soldier in the fight for equal rights – and given South Carolina someone to hate even more than him.

Elizabeth would relish the role.

FALSE GOD

I t only took a day for the threats to begin.

Elizabeth's speech spurred an onslaught of hate mail, anonymous phone calls and political attacks that were far worse than anything the judge endured during the 1948 campaign. Waring had expected a vitriolic reaction, but he never imagined the bitter contempt Elizabeth would inspire with her YWCA appearance. She had managed to offend the entire South.

The reaction might have come even sooner, but deadlines forced The News and Courier to rush its story into print with the innocuous headline "Wife of Judge Waring speaks at annual Negro Y meeting." Few people noticed. But that afternoon The Evening Post summed up the gist of Elizabeth's message in a large, bold headline: "Southern whites 'sick, confused,' U.S. judge's wife says in speech."

The news reached the Statehouse that afternoon. Gov. Thurmond tried to deflect, deeming Elizabeth's remarks "beneath comment," but lawmakers called her "a damn Yankee" on the House floor. They warned that Southerners – including political officials – would respond to her insults soon enough. It was an accurate prediction. Congressman Mendel Rivers publicly questioned the moral standing of a woman who'd grown up in the shadow of Detroit's race riots, and Sen. Burnet Maybank asked the U.S. attorney general's office to investigate her for inciting revolution – and being a communist.

The phone at 61 Meeting Street rang incessantly, often late at night. Most of the anonymous callers demanded the couple leave the South – or else. Some issued direct threats, others simply hurled profanity. The most disturbing calls, however, were the silent ones. The judge picked up the phone and heard nothing but breathing on the other end of the line.

"It rang and you'd pick up the phone and you'd say 'hello' and there was one of two or three groups who was calling," Waring later recalled. "Sometimes it would be vilification and obscenity – disgusting and dirty – directed to me and my wife, a good deal to her as well as to me. Sometimes it would be threatening, 'We're coming to get you.' Of course, one of the pet words is 'nigger-lover.' That's one of the chief defamatory epithets. And 'Get out,' and 'We'll run you out,' and 'Who are you?' and insulting things like that. But then the worst part of it was the silence at the other end."

The calls would continue for more than a year, growing more vicious and more frequent. They were accompanied by a spate of hateful letters – many of which suggested that, since she liked breaking up marriages so much, Mrs. Waring should divorce the judge and marry a black man. Some were perfectly formal, despite their message, while others were shockingly crude. "How would you like to go to bed with a nigger and have a little nigger baby calling you Mama? Did a nigger ever hold you tightly?"

A surprising number of these letters were signed, sent by people unashamed of their views – they often even included return addresses. But the majority were anonymous, the writers claiming to be "Christian" citizens. Their preachy screeds spewed unabashed racism. Some contended that black people were animals, and the Bible forbade relationships "between man and beast." Others tried to argue that, despite their threats, they were not prejudiced. One self-identified Christian outlined the philosophy of white supremacists and segregationists in the bluntest terms: "The nigger is all right in his place, and that is right where we are going to keep them."

Even Septima Clark received threatening calls, apparently for her role in allowing Elizabeth to speak. She asked the Warings if she could take her calls at 61 Meeting Street, simply so her mother wouldn't hear. Victoria Poinsette, a child of the years after Reconstruction, constantly feared the Klan was coming for them. The judge, who already had his secretary sorting through the increased intake of mail, eventually had to get a second, private line installed at his house. The calls came in such quick succession he couldn't get or make business calls.

At night, they simply unplugged the first phone. It rang so much they couldn't sleep.

Elizabeth got some good reviews for the speech, mostly from Northern newspapers and the NAACP. Thurgood Marshall told her she did a good job, and Walter White sent dispatches to newspapers around the country, praising Elizabeth and denouncing the Dixiecrats who threatened her. White argued the animosity stirred up by her speech was an important story, and some editors listened.

Time magazine sent a reporter to chronicle the fallout from Elizabeth's speech. The article noted she and the judge had been blacklisted by Charleston society, and claimed no white person had called socially at their home in two years. That was an exaggeration; the Warings had some white guests, most from out of town. Local residents told the Time reporter their animus toward the couple had nothing to do with race; instead, they claimed, Judge Waring had offended his friends and family by divorcing his first wife after 30 years of marriage.

But no one could explain why it had taken two years – and coincided with his decision in *Brown v. Baskin* – to make their feelings so publicly known.

One night in early February, Elizabeth became violently ill. The judge was so worried he called Dr. Hugh Cathcart out of the St. Cecilia Society ball to treat her, blacklist be damned. Waring feared she was dying.

The doctor rushed to 61 Meeting Street, ultimately pumping Elizabeth's stomach and knocking her out with a heavy sedative. Waring told Cathcart he was afraid someone had tried to poison his wife, but the doctor offered no diagnosis and quickly left. A week later, Elizabeth received a letter that suggested intimate knowledge of her illness. The writer claimed to be a Clemson student from a Charleston family of "better stock than yours."

"It is a known truth that you were sick from alcohol and believed that you were being poisoned by Charleston society," the letter said. "It is a known fact that you received the biggest sedative ever given in Charleston."

The judge insisted only Cathcart could be the source of such information. He sent the doctor a letter from New York requesting he analyze the contents of Elizabeth's stomach – and demanding to know whether he was spreading this gossip. "Of course the statement as to Mrs. Waring being sick from alcohol is a patent lie, but the rest of the statement, and particularly the reference to a sedative, would appear to come from the doctor administering the same."

Waring believed he could no longer trust anyone in Charleston.

Elizabeth recovered in time to keep her appointment with NBC's "Meet the Press." She'd been invited to appear on the Washington-based program shortly after her YWCA speech, and in that time her notoriety had not faded. The show's panel of journalists talked to Elizabeth for half an hour about her "vigorous attack on white supremacy" and the continuing backlash she'd sparked. Elizabeth only gave her detractors more ammunition.

She spent most of the show ridiculing "a very little teeny group in Charleston" that had been offended by the judge's divorce, but maintained they were only ostracized statewide after her husband allowed blacks to vote in the Democratic primary. "Time magazine called the judge 'the man they love to hate' but I call him the man they're afraid not to hate." Elizabeth said white people who continue to oppress the black community were going to "destroy their own souls."

If that had been all, the Warings might have avoided more trouble. But on national television, Elizabeth seemingly endorsed miscegenation – white supremacists' greatest fear.

One panelist recalled a recent newspaper story that mentioned a photograph of Walter White and Poppy Cannon in the Warings' living room. White had scandalously divorced his first wife in 1949 and, a week later, married Cannon – a situation all-too-similar to the Warings' own romance. But White's conduct was even more controversial because Cannon was white. In fact, he'd been forced to temporarily resign from the NAACP as a result of the marriage. A few of his colleagues frowned upon the union nearly as much as some white people.

The Warings, of course, stuck by the couple – and they had become closer through shared experience. They visited each other regularly, and sometimes even traveled together. White and Cannon had tried to join the Warings at the El Encanto shortly after their wedding, but the hotel refused to give them a room. Elizabeth gave the hotel management an earful, outraged that a reputable California establishment should be so provincial.

Mrs. Waring was no more diplomatic in front of the cameras when asked about the photo of White and Cannon: "Does this mean that you favor intermarriage of the races, which is illegal in South Carolina?"

"I certainly do," Elizabeth said. "My husband is a United States judge, and we believe that our state should be part of the United States and not have separate laws. I see no reason why, if two persons choose to do so, they should not marry."

With one remark, Elizabeth fueled months of hostility and continued threats; the phone wouldn't stop ringing until after the summer primary. Strom Thurmond, who was running for the U.S. Senate against Olin Johnston, was more than happy to condemn the Warings this time. He said Elizabeth's statement had revealed the true, ultimate goal of civil rights.

"Thus far, the president and his followers have gone no farther than demanding abrogation of our state laws providing the separation of the races," Thurmond said. "Now they are becoming so bold as to advocate abrogation of our laws against intermarriage of the races."

Even the national Democratic Party was forced to issue a statement clarifying that Mrs. Waring did not speak for them. No one wanted to be associated with the judge or his wife.

Days later, a petition to have the judge impeached began circulating in Colleton and Aiken counties. It declared Waring unfit to serve because he had, "through his wife, advocated both dissension and revolution on the part of Negro citizens against the white citizens of South Carolina." Waring could not fairly adjudicate cases involving white people, it proclaimed, since he and his wife had publicly stated they would protect the interests of black people against whites.

It was signed "WHITE, ADULT, VOTING CITIZENS of SOUTH CAROLINA."

Waring likened the petition to a series of recent cross-burnings in Colleton County, telling The Associated Press he welcomed the comparison "between these views of mine and those of the pro-slavery of white supremacy groups as voiced by their spokesmen of the Ku Klux Klan. The more light shed on this campaign of prejudice, the better."

When the story was published, Waring sent a copy to Samuel Grafton, a reporter from Collier's magazine who was writing a profile of the judge. Waring was most pleased he'd been able to link the petition to cross burnings. "Of course, they all come from the same warped thinking. Most of the people in this locality are really Klan-minded, although the slightly more educated and sensible ones are not actively associated with the Klan and pretend to look down on it."

Waring thought he was merely being clever, but his comments were prescient. Because the Klan *was*, in fact, gunning for him.

A week after Elizabeth appeared on "Meet the Press," the South Carolina House of Representatives formally offered to buy the Warings one-way tickets to leave the state. The resolution – opposed by a single, anonymous "no" vote – promised to spend whatever funds necessary to relocate the couple to another state, or preferably a foreign country, in the hope they "find a social environment that meets with their approval."

South Carolina politicians, accurately gauging public sentiment, spent the next month coming up with increasingly creative ways to harass the Warings. Congressman Mendel Rivers promised to protect federal employees who signed petitions against the judge. State lawmakers offered $10,000 to finance impeachment hearings in the U.S. House of Representatives, and even proposed a legislative committee to investigate Judge Waring's citizenship. After all, he had been divorced in the "foreign state" of Florida.

"It is considered appropriate that the people of South Carolina be informed as to whether or not he relinquished his citizenship in this state and became a citizen of a foreign state," the Senate resolution read, "and, if this be true, whether or not he continued to preside as a judge in this state while a citizen of a foreign state."

One senator finally pointed out such an investigation was useless because, unlike politicians, federal judges were not required to be citizens of any particular state. The resolution was quietly dropped, but the proposal to fund federal impeachment hearings lingered. The bus-ticket offer would stand for the rest of the session.

Weeks later, South Carolina congressman James Hare introduced a federal resolution to remove the judge from office for advocating a "Negro revolution against white supremacy." It was all election-year grandstanding, pandering to the sort of people who continued to circulate impeachment petitions throughout the spring.

Waring's growing legion of critics didn't get the satisfaction of watching his reaction to these attacks. He was in New York, filling in for a vacationing judge, and the Warings were enjoying their sabbatical from the viper's nest. They even had time for Broadway shows. On Feb. 28, the judge and Elizabeth met Anne and Stanley for dinner, then took in a performance of "Gentlemen Prefer Blondes" at the Ziegfeld Theater.

That was a rare night off from their crusade, however. Two days earlier, the judge had addressed the congregation at Convent Avenue Baptist Church in Harlem. He told the audience that segregation was not a black problem, but a white one.

"The white people of my part of the country are sick mentally, obsessed with the false doctrine of white supremacy," he said.

Waring saw more evidence of that sickness every week. His secretary, Persha Singer, forwarded his hate mail to the Essex House Hotel, along with regular updates on court business and Charleston gossip. Singer was disturbed by the "filthy, almost insane ramblings" of his critics, and reported that the impeachment petitions had reached Charleston. One woman came to the courthouse to complain about a gang of boys who'd harassed her to sign one.

"She says they are the same group who is passing the 'petition' around on the bus on which she travels," Singer wrote. "The petition has been going around in her neighborhood and although they have passed it to her on the bus, have not forced her to sign it, but have followed her into town, to the movies, and out where she lives. She has reported it to the police and they say they will make an arrest if one of them tries to molest her or approach her."

Singer told the judge many locals were signing the petition, however. Impeachment proponents claimed to have more than 21,000 signatures.

There seemed to be no end to the strife that spring. In March, the police were called to 61 Meeting Street. Neighbors reported that a four-foot cross had been planted beside the house – and it was on fire. After the blazing cross was extinguished and removed, Herman Berkman, chief detective for the Charleston Police Department, dismissed any suggestion that white supremacists were involved. He called it "the work of pranksters."

That remark prompted Waring to break his media silence. He told The Associated Press he was disgusted by this "exhibition typical of the savagery of Southern white supremacists," and accused Charleston police of being either inept or complicit. Berkman had told The News and Courier there was no evidence linking the cross to the Klan – other than, of course, the "KKK" carved into the wood.

"This was no work of pranksters," the judge said.

It all became too much – the petitions, the bus tickets, the burning cross. The Warings' friends thought it was insane, South Carolina had become a circus of bigotry and lunacy. And they did their best to fight back, even if some of them quietly wished the couple would quit fueling the fires.

James Hinton published a letter in The News and Courier that slyly questioned the patriotism of Waring's critics. The NAACP state director noted that all of the judge's decisions adhered to the U.S. Constitution and had been upheld on numerous appeals. If those decision had been wrong, he wrote, surely they would have been reversed. "Negroes," Hinton wrote, "wonder why all of the unfavorable reaction to the Honorable J. Waties Waring."

The NAACP considered the judge a close ally, but he was not universally popular in the black community. Some believed the Warings' criticism of whites had made race relations worse, and feared black people would ultimately pay the price. The couple was so controversial that some of Charleston's most influential black community leaders refused to socialize with them – and criticized those who did.

Over time, the judge slowly came to realize that not everyone appreciated his efforts. At one point he'd suggested the College of Charleston admit black students, but community leaders didn't embrace the idea; instead, they accepted a quiet compromise – the city offered a few scholarships to S.C. State for local high school graduates. And when S.C. State dedicated its new law school building, Waring wasn't invited to the groundbreaking. He was insulted, and would not forget the slight. But he dismissed most of this as the timid acquiescence of people afraid to rock the boat.

Septima Clark believed the Warings meant well, but conceded they went overboard on occasion. She became fast friends with the couple following the YWCA controversy, often joining Elizabeth and Ruby Cornwell for lunch or afternoon tea. She was at 61 Meeting Street so often, Clark finally told Mrs. Waring she couldn't accept any more invitations until she and the judge visited her home. Elizabeth agreed and dropped by Henrietta Street one afternoon. But it often seemed she was more interested in her ongoing war than tea and cookies.

That spring, Burnet Maybank publicly questioned the Warings' sincerity on racial issues. He said although the couple claimed to be liberals, they didn't really socialize with black people in their home. Clark knew otherwise, and was offended by the senator's remarks – but she was equally taken aback by Elizabeth's retaliation. A few weeks later, she was invited to a luncheon with the judge at 61 Meeting Street. Clark, Ruby Cornwell and some other local activists dined with the Warings that afternoon – while a photographer from Collier's magazine snapped pictures.

Those photos accompanied Samuel Grafton's article about Waring's ostracism from Charleston society. "The Lonesomest Man in Town" cemented the judge's national reputation as a crusader willing to defy the South's social norms. But some of Clark's Columbia friends said the photos proved she was being used by the couple to undercut Maybank's credibility. Clark pointed out that she was smart enough to recognize sincerity, and had no doubt the Warings were her friends.

But that friendship did cause her a measure of grief. At a school faculty meeting, Clark's colleagues complained that she was stirring up trouble by socializing with the controversial white couple. She eventually fought back – "I think that I have a right to select my friends" – but knew her point was lost on the other teachers.

In truth, even Clark worried about the Warings' lack of diplomacy. She feared their sweeping statements about the white community would only alienate people who, while perhaps not progressive, might not be hostile to equal rights.

Although they meant well, they risked setting back race relations by decades. She eventually shared this concern with Elizabeth. Clark told her it was unfair to call all white people decadent and immoral. But Mrs. Waring wouldn't listen.

"They just don't know how to be humanitarian," Elizabeth said. There was no use arguing, Clark knew. The Warings' disdain for white supremacists rivaled South Carolina's hatred for them. And the couple was just as stubborn as all the segregationists and Dixiecrats. For that reason, the feud could only escalate.

Waring believed he and Elizabeth had good reason for their intransigence. All evidence he saw, including the threats against them, suggested the South would never willingly accept civil rights. And that disturbed him.

The resistance to his court decisions – which he considered relatively simple and obvious – convinced him there was no way to ease into equality. White people would never voluntarily recognize black people as their equal. After all, they were burning crosses in his yard and circulating petitions to have him impeached over little more than a speech and a couple of lawsuits. How could he expect them to ever accept integrated restaurants, hotels or classrooms?

Anymore, the couple could barely go out in Charleston without rude confrontations, refusals of service or at least awkward silences. Waring didn't notice it as much, because he rarely shopped. But Elizabeth almost courted confrontation. Sometimes she lectured obscene phone callers until they hung up. She took daily strolls through downtown, daring anyone to say a cross word. When one man threatened her while she was walking with Clark, Elizabeth confided, "I just wish he'd touch me." It would, she reasoned, be good for publicity.

Most famously, Elizabeth one day marched into a hardware store under the pretense of shopping for a mouse trap. Noticing the less-than-pleasant stare from the man behind the counter, she announced, "You know, I'm more afraid of a mouse than I am of the whole Ku Klux Klan."

But that would soon change.

The judge could not help but be surprised by the vitriol and the hostility, and it changed his thinking even further. He'd once agreed with the philosophy that America would accept civil rights if they were enacted slowly. But he'd decided that was a foolishly optimistic notion that gave people too much credit. Waring mostly kept this realization to himself, although he suggested as much to Marshall and a few others.

After months of unending rancor in the spring of 1950, he decided to make his views public. At an American Council for Human Rights banquet in Washington, the judge demanded that Congress and the president immediately enforce civil rights for everyone. The days of chipping away at segregation, he said, were over.

"The only way to meet the issue is to meet it head on," Waring said. "Gradualism is a false god. I once thought the South was working out its own problems in racial relations. Maybe after 500 or 600 years it will arise."

Waring repeated that message in Chicago, Minneapolis and Richmond. He was in great demand as a speaker, and took advantage of his popularity to spread his philosophy. The judge mocked his detractors as insane people in masks, childishly declaring themselves the "master race." He said it was good for the nation to see such displays, because it only illustrated the need to force the issue of civil rights.

But in some news accounts, Waring's message was garbled. By the time these reports reached South Carolina, the headlines said "Warings urge force to obtain rights for Negro."

After Elizabeth compared white supremacy to Russia, coercing people with threats and lynchings, the judge was forced to clarify their statements. He explained that he advocated only court orders – not violence or insurrection. "Every court decree is force," Waring said. "We don't want laws passed to make people live together, but we do want laws to allow them to do it if they want to."

But his equivocation wasn't enough, and the calls for his impeachment only grew.

Waring attempted to clear up these misconceptions in a long interview with The Associated Press. He reiterated that the only force he advocated was court orders – not "soldiers and bayonets" – and denied that he and Elizabeth were promoting social mixing or interracial marriage. He only wanted to abolish laws against such things.

"If a man is entitled to civil rights now, then he shouldn't have to wait forever to get them."

That spring, a California congressman renewed calls for Waring's impeachment in reaction to his "incendiary racial speeches." In South Carolina, both Strom Thurmond and Olin Johnston – warming up for the 1950 primary – promised to remove Waring from office. But by then, the judge had gone silent. After his long interview with The Associated Press was widely misinterpreted, Waring worried things had gotten out of hand. In a "confidential" letter to Ted Poston at The New York Post, the judge admitted he and Elizabeth could be in danger.

"I believe that physical violence is quite possible and perhaps even probable," Waring wrote. "In the event of any trouble arising here, it would be practically impossible to get a true report of the same to the outside world through (the local papers) and any report that was sent would be colored by local prejudice.

"To be more specific, if harm should come to either of us here, it would almost surely be reported out of Charleston as accidental or perhaps even self-inflicted, and so it seems advisable to write you this letter … to say that if any injury or death should come to either Mrs. Waring or myself, it would be more than important for those of you who believe in reporting true events to send unprejudiced investigators immediately into this locality."

Waring's note may have seemed conspiratorial or melodramatic, but his concerns were serious and merited. For months the threatening phone calls had continued nonstop, and more hate mail arrived every day. The pronouncements and condemnation of politicians had grown increasingly outlandish, to the point Waring worried they would incite a riot. A ripple in the status quo had turned to a wave of racism and rancor, and he feared what might come next.

So when the invitation came to sit for a vacationing judge in San Francisco, he welcomed it. The Warings would once again pass their summer in California, as far as they could get from South Carolina.

THE KLAN RIDES AGAIN

On May 17, 1950, Harold Boulware filed a class-action lawsuit against Clarendon County school officials in Judge Waring's court. The suit alleged black schools in Summerton District 22 were inferior in every way to the facilities provided for white students. This, Boulware claimed, was a violation of the black children's rights guaranteed by the 14th Amendment to the United States Constitution. The suit said the disparity was based "solely on account of race and color."

Most of the state was caught up in the drama of the 1950 political campaigns, so the lawsuit attracted only scant attention. But The Evening Post recognized its historic significance. In its short report, the paper noted this lawsuit marked the first time anyone had challenged the legality of South Carolina's segregated public school system.

The Rev. Joseph A. DeLaine was not listed among the plaintiffs, but by that point everyone in the county knew he'd started this trouble. And he'd been dealing with the repercussions for months.

Since he no longer held a job from which he could be fired, the community found other ways to retaliate. The former principal at Scott's Branch filed suit against the pastor, claiming his protests about the fees charged to high school students amounted to slander. Clarendon school officials supported the principal, claiming DeLaine had suggested the man was pocketing those fees.

The principal's lawsuit asked for $20,000 in damages – more than enough to ruin DeLaine. To protect his family and avoid financial devastation, the preacher quietly transferred the title to most of his property to friends. On paper, DeLaine was no longer worth anything. If he lost, the principal wouldn't be able to squeeze a dollar out of him. But the lawsuit was only the first wave in an all-out assault.

In December, a group of men had plotted to rid the county of DeLaine permanently – one way or another. They persuaded another man to attack the preacher in downtown Summerton, the idea being that this plot would work no matter what the outcome. Either he would be maimed or killed, or fight back and be jailed for assault. But when the man confronted DeLaine, one of the *Briggs* plaintiffs stepped in and defused the situation. James Brown saved the pastor just hours before he lost his job driving the gas truck.

None of these schemes dissuaded DeLaine. As a prelude to the lawsuit, he'd presented the District 22 school board with a list of grievances that eventually formed the basis of *Briggs v. Elliott*. When Clarendon officials finally responded in February, they disputed every point. They said Scott's Branch had a better library and newer facilities than any school in District 22; in fact, board members audaciously claimed all three black schools in the district were superior to every one of the white schools.

It was a difficult spring for DeLaine. Weeks passed without a word from the NAACP, and he wondered if the lawsuit would ever come. After the school board dismissed his concerns, he told friends that Boulware and Marshall were probably having a good laugh at his expense – they'd forced him to stick his neck out just to see how much trouble he could get into. And then, when his spirits were at their lowest, the church moved him once again.

In April, AME officials assigned DeLaine to St. James Church in Lake City – a town in neighboring Florence County. It felt like another demotion, and he didn't like it. But church officials believed they were saving his life. If DeLaine kept up this Clarendon County school business, eventually someone would kill him. After all, someone had already tried.

"DeLaine, your work at Summerton is well done," Bishop Frank Reid said. "You have served your purpose. Your life is now at stake."

Most people believed he'd only survived this long because the Clarendon County sheriff had protected him. The sheriff hadn't forgotten that DeLaine delivered the black vote for him during the 1948 election, and he repaid the favor by slapping a restraining order on the man who'd attacked him. But the sheriff could only do so much. In March, the Scott's Branch campus was littered with KKK fliers, and locals claimed DeLaine manufactured the papers to stir controversy. After local police searched his house looking for evidence of this theory, the pastor contacted the FBI.

"Many of the white people honestly think that I am really a disturbance maker and I am unable to defend myself against the propaganda put out," DeLaine wrote.

The FBI investigated briefly, but agents decided it was a local matter and they had no jurisdiction. The feds started a file on DeLaine, but closed the case.

A month before Boulware filed *Briggs v. Elliott*, DeLaine accepted his transfer to Lake City – but he wouldn't give up on Clarendon County. He'd promised those families he would lead them all the way to the United States Supreme Court, and now they were taking the first step. They had a groundbreaking lawsuit that asked the federal court for a permanent injunction against the county's habitual discrimination, and he wouldn't waste the opportunity.

But Clarendon officials ignored the suit for nearly a month and, when they eventually filed a response, DeLaine realized he'd heard it all before. The district argued that segregating children by race was state law, they had no power to change such circumstances and claimed any differences between white and black schools were simply the result of local PTAs. The school district said it did not fund bus service or drinking fountains in any schools; where those amenities existed, the parents paid for them.

DeLaine couldn't help but notice the response mirrored the school board's answers to his original complaint almost verbatim. It seemed Clarendon County had put little effort into defending itself, and the lawsuit was getting nowhere. The wheels of justice were stuck in the mud.

The 1950 election was a weak echo of 1948. Once more, Strom Thurmond was on the campaign trail preaching the gospel of segregation and the evils of Judge Waring. With his term as governor ending in January, Thurmond had surprised no one by announcing his bid to take Olin Johnston's seat in the United States Senate. He dusted off his Dixiecrat propaganda, which had proven popular in South Carolina, and railed on the "turncoat federal judge" who'd tried to inflict civil rights on the state.

At a rally in Lexington, the governor warned that Waring had opened the Democratic primary to blocs of voters who didn't share the party's values. This was a threat to white supremacy, a return to Reconstruction – Thurmond pulled out all his greatest hits. Still, he had a hard time outflanking Johnston. The senator spoke after him at the event, and clearly had studied his opponent's talking points carefully. And he stole them.

"What happened to the petition with thousands of signatures of good and faithful South Carolinians calling for the immediate impeachment of Trumanite federal Judge J. Waties Waring?" Johnston asked.

Just a mention of the impeachment petition prompted thunderous applause, so Johnston tossed the crowd even more to cheer. He accused the judge of ignoring his robe, the traditions of his great office and ultimately his party. Waring, the senator said, had become a "feeble old radical … led asunder by a socially ostracized and hysterical wife."

Johnston promised to meet Waring's impeachment resolution at the Senate door and fight until it was passed. More applause. The senator not only copied Thurmond's message, he insulated himself by swiping the governor's favorite insult: Trumanite. Johnston reminded the crowd of his continued opposition to the president's civil rights program – and slyly suggested Thurmond had abandoned his own party.

"No Truman nor Humphrey is going to run me out of the Democratic Party that my forefathers believed in and formed long before these blabbermouths came along," Johnston said.

Thurmond didn't back down. Two weeks later, at a rally in Walterboro, the governor again reminded voters that in 1948 Johnston voted for Truman – the man behind civil rights. He predicted the end of segregation would lead to lawlessness and riots across the land, and promised to fight such un-American schemes. And Thurmond tried to reclaim the high ground on the Waring impeachment.

"This federal judge has been insulting the people of South Carolina, abusing his office and demonstrating his unfitness to be a judge for several years now,"

Thurmond said, "and I tell you today he is not fit to sit on the bench in South Carolina."

The U.S. Senate race was by far the most entertaining campaign of the 1950 election season; the governor's race, after all, was a foregone conclusion. There were four gubernatorial candidates in the Democratic primary, but the only one who mattered was James F. Byrnes. He'd been in South Carolina politics for 40 years, serving in the U.S. House and Senate going back to 1910. Byrnes had been an associate justice on the U.S. Supreme Court and recently finished a two-year stint as Secretary of State. The Charleston native was political royalty, and the three other candidates combined couldn't match his support. It was more a coronation than an election.

The races for Congress were only slightly more interesting. William Jennings Bryan Dorn was trying to reclaim the U.S. House seat he'd given up for his failed Senate bid two years earlier, and Mendel Rivers faced the promised challenge from Arthur J. Clement Jr. The Charleston insurance agent was the first black man to run a serious South Carolina campaign for Congress in generations, but he couldn't gain any traction. Clement was pushed to the end of the program at most rallies. Often by the time he spoke, two-thirds of the crowd had walked out.

Most of the results in the July 11 primary were predictable. Byrnes won by a landslide, Dorn and Rivers prevailed. Clement took only 7,000 votes, which wasn't even a 20-percent showing. Black voter turnout was higher than it had been two years earlier, but it didn't help Clement. For months, however, some people would swear it improbably helped Johnston.

The incumbent senator defeated Thurmond by an 8-point margin, prompting The Evening Post to make the embarrassing admission that "South Carolina defeats states' rights candidate." The Dixiecrats and complicit editors made various excuses: Johnston benefitted from the governor's opposition to federal money for education, he had strong support in the Upstate. But mostly, pundits and editorial writers believed Johnston won the black vote.

That, of course, was impossible to prove – and it seemed unlikely black voters would cast a ballot for either man. Both spent the campaign championing segregation and decrying the evils of civil rights and Judge Waring. But some people suspected black Democrats decided Johnston was the lesser of two evils – especially compared to the former Dixiecrat presidential candidate. As proof, some noted Thurmond lost by 28,000 votes – and about 40,000 black voters turned out for the primary. Perhaps they hadn't voted for Johnston but against Thurmond.

It was a humiliating defeat, but Strom Thurmond was nowhere near finished. In fact, he would never lose another campaign.

Waring ignored the incessant attacks on his character during the 1950 Senate campaign. Even when Thurmond and Johnston directed their insults at Elizabeth, he refused to respond. Although he rarely turned down the opportunity to insult race-baiting politicians, and was quick to defend his wife, that summer the judge was simply too distracted to engage. In the weeks leading up to his California trip, he was studying.

On June 5, the United States Supreme Court issued three decisions that Waring believed laid the legal foundation to outlaw segregation. The first, *Henderson v. United States*, was the case Marshall had shared with him six months earlier. The court determined the railroad had violated the Interstate Commerce Act when it denied Elmer Henderson the same service extended to white passengers. Even though it carefully sidestepped constitutional questions of separate-but-equal, *Henderson* effectively integrated railway dining cars.

The two other cases – *McLaurin v. Oklahoma State Regents* and *Sweatt v. Painter* – all but abolished segregation on college campuses.

McLaurin and *Sweatt* illustrated the increasingly desperate measures states would take to avoid integration. The University of Oklahoma had forced George McLaurin to sue his way into its doctoral program, then shamed him mercilessly after he won in court. The college set up separate tables for McLaurin in the library and cafeteria, and made him sit just outside the door of all his classes. This treatment prompted him to file another lawsuit.

In an attempt to avoid a similar fate, the University of Texas offered Herman Sweatt an out-of-state scholarship before denying his admission to the School of

Law in Austin. Sweatt made the mistake of filing his first lawsuit in state court, where judges delayed the hearing long enough for the legislature to establish a separate black law school. But it was in Houston, more than 150 miles away. Sweatt's second lawsuit was filed in federal court.

Waring had followed each of these lawsuits through the federal courts, often getting updates from Marshall – who represented Herman Sweatt. Since April, when the Supreme Court heard arguments in all three cases, Waring had optimistically anticipated landmark decisions. He told one Milwaukee attorney "I believe that the court has here an opportunity to strike down and review the erroneous position which it took many years ago in *Plessy v. Ferguson*, which last named case has been the root of much evil."

Ultimately, the Supreme Court didn't go far enough to suit Waring. He spent six weeks poring over the decisions, looking for weaknesses to exploit or any hint that the court might revisit *Plessy*. The judge was mildly disappointed, but told friends he had hopes that the three rulings opened the door to "great progress."

"While they are not as explicit as desired, the implications are inescapable that 'separate but equal' is a futile dream and cannot be realized," Waring wrote.

The judge had some reason for hope. First, none of these controversial cases had generated a single dissent. The United States Supreme Court justices had been unanimous in three consecutive civil rights rulings – which Waring considered an ominous sign for "benighted back-woodsmen." More importantly, the *Sweatt* decision said Texas could never provide separate facilities that would be truly equal. Waring had been making that point privately for years. Now, it appeared the Supreme Court had caught on.

The Warings left town two weeks after the primary. They would remain in San Francisco until the end of August, then spent most of September in New York before – "unfortunately," he told friends – returning to Charleston. In some ways, however, he looked forward to getting back. He had the case out of Clarendon County on his docket, and thought it showed promise. But *Briggs v. Elliott* needed some work if he was going to use it to take down *Plessy*.

The Ku Klux Klan had been on a rampage.

Men in hoods and white robes had paraded through Greenwood, Langley, St. George and even the north area of Charleston that spring, often leaving burned crosses in their wake. In May, a procession of 20 Klan cars drove through the middle of Denmark, most of the men trading their traditional white hoods for dark glasses with fake noses. Four days before the Democratic primary, the Klan hosted a rally in Wagener, where the grand dragon recalled the state's troubles following the Civil War and warned residents of minority groups out to destroy "Americanism."

The newly elected grand dragon, Thomas Hamilton of Leesville, insisted the Klan was not a hate group – the organization was simply trying to educate folks about the evils of communism. But the Klan's idea of education included storming a black pool hall in Anderson County and whipping people on the side of country roads while wearing their hoods. The Klan was out of control, and it led to a deadly showdown in Myrtle Beach.

About 60 Klansmen descended on the resort town Aug. 26 to protest a black night club that allegedly allowed white women to come in and dance. The KKK suggested the women actually frequented the club for "immoral purposes" – and they intended to put a stop to it. Their parade began about 8:30 that night, passing by the club several times. At one point, a Klansman stopped his car in front of the club and warned that it better be closed by midnight.

The club's owner, Charlie Fitzgerald, had heard rumors of the planned demonstration and prepared for the attack as well as he could. Several friends showed up to help defend his business, and some of them had guns. The parade came and went that evening with little more than obscene banter between the two sides, and Fitzgerald thought they were safe.

But the Klan returned shortly after midnight, and dozens of hooded men stormed the club. Fitzgerald and his friends fought back, but couldn't stop the Klansmen from wrecking the dance hall. Then the gunfight started and, before it ended, police estimated 300 shots were fired. One of Fitzgerald's friends was shot in the leg, and Conway policeman James Daniel Johnston was killed. Johnston was wearing his uniform, but he wasn't on duty – he wore it under a long, white robe. He'd been one of the Klansmen.

The incident was particularly embarrassing for the state. Gov. Strom Thurmond ordered an investigation of every police department in South Carolina to make sure no other Klansmen were hiding behind badges. Hamilton and a handful of other KKK members were charged with inciting a riot, and the FBI launched an inquiry. Walter White requested federal intervention because he didn't trust state officials, who arrested Fitzgerald simply for defending his property.

The FBI ultimately charged more than a dozen Klansmen, including the grand dragon, with inciting mob violence. Hamilton remained unapologetic and vowed to shoot any black person who fired on Klansmen – conveniently ignoring the fact that the KKK was responsible for starting the fight. The parades, and the threats, continued into the fall, the Klan growing more defiant after several state grand juries declined to indict them.

The Warings returned to Charleston in the midst of the FBI investigation, and soon became part of it. On Friday, Oct. 6, the Justice Department received a tip from Walter White that the Klan would come for the judge that weekend. The NAACP director was worried enough that he sent identical telegrams to Attorney General J. Howard McGrath and President Truman.

"We have just been informed by a completely reliable person that attempts to molest federal Judge J. Waties Waring and his wife may be made in Charleston, South Carolina, this weekend," White reported. "We are informed that situation is very tense with crowds milling around streets and that additional crowds are expected to come into Charleston from other parts of South Carolina during week end."

White told Truman and McGrath that the Klan was emboldened by the "acquittal" of the grand dragon following the Myrtle Beach riot, and warned that any attack on a federal judge would damage the "prestige of America." White never revealed the source of this tip, but he had contacts inside the Klan.

Years earlier, White – who was so pale he could pass for Caucasian – had infiltrated the Klan as part of an investigation, and no doubt still knew some of the men. Others suspected Waring had alerted White, but that was unlikely. The judge had asked the FBI to investigate some of the threats that followed

Elizabeth's YWCA speech, and he hadn't been impressed with the response. Agents concluded most of the people harassing the couple were just cranks and rednecks, and decided there were no credible threats.

The bureau's nonchalance irritated the Warings, and by the fall of 1950 that feeling was mutual. Many agents, and J. Edgar Hoover, were suspicious of the judge. But McGrath and Truman took White's warning seriously, and dispatched agents to 61 Meeting Street that afternoon. The couple said they'd heard nothing, other than the usual volume of obscene phone calls and hate mail. The FBI left convinced White had gotten bad information.

Waring opened the October court session on Monday, the 9th. The cases had stacked up in his absence, but he dispatched them quickly. More than 70 defendants shuffled through his courtroom that day, most of them conveniently pleading guilty. Half the docket was filled with men accused of violating the Internal Revenue act or shooting federally protected migratory birds. The judge let many defendants go with simple probation, but sent several others to jail – including three car thieves and their two accessories.

The only case on the October docket that intrigued Waring had been unavoidably canceled. Moses Winn, a black man from Summerville, had filed a civil rights complaint against local police after an officer shot him during a 1949 arrest. Waring was scheduled to hear the case during the first week of October, but on Sept. 30 a Summerville policeman went to Winn's house and shot him five times. He was dead.

Lt. James Adams claimed he had orders to arrest Winn on a bad-check charge, and showed up at his house around 3 a.m. only after failing to find him earlier in the evening. Adams said he'd hoped to catch Winn asleep, which he was. Winn's wife answered the door and reluctantly woke her husband, who agreed to follow Adams outside. But when they reached the living room, Winn decided he wasn't going. The two men scuffled and Winn ended up dead on the floor.

Adams told investigators he shot Winn only because he'd heard the click of a gun cocking and was forced to defend himself. Later, officers at the crime scene found a gun underneath Winn's living room couch. It had not been fired. A coroner's inquest ruled Adams justifiably shot Winn in the line of duty. Case closed. The circumstances were suspicious enough that the FBI opened its own investigation.

Waring believed it was obvious Winn had been killed to quash the civil rights lawsuit. He didn't trust Southern law enforcement – after all, they were Southerners first – and his prejudice had only been reinforced by the Conway police officer killed while wearing a Klan robe. The judge was still thinking about Winn when he left the courthouse that afternoon. As he walked the single block to 61 Meeting Street, he didn't notice the crisp, fall air rustling palm fronds and Spanish moss, or anyone who may have been watching him.

They had decided to stay in that night, which wasn't unusual. Short of visiting the Cornwells or Septima Clark, there was rarely anywhere in Charleston the Warings were welcome. They got nasty looks on the streets and in the city's few decent restaurants. Aside from the Riviera, where they could watch a movie anonymously in the dark, the couple seldom ventured out at night.

After dinner, the judge and Elizabeth decided to play canasta in the living room until it was time for bed. It was quiet out – it usually was on the dark streets South of Broad – so when the car pulled up around 9 p.m., they both heard it. But they couldn't see it. The living room windows sat high in the wall, abutting the ceiling – a throwback to the house's past as a horse stable.

Waring liked to say the living room windows admitted light but afforded privacy. Those windows also left them blind to the outdoors, but not deaf. And the next sound they heard very much resembled a short series of gunshots.

"And then a big lump of concrete smashed through the window just above our heads, and some more hit against the front door and side walls," Waring recalled.

They had expected a violent assault for so long the judge and Elizabeth reacted almost instinctively. They both dove to the floor, ignoring the shattered glass scattered around them, and crawled toward the relative safety of the dining room, directly behind the living room. As he pulled himself along the floor, Waring kept one eye on the back door.

The dining room had a door that opened onto a brick patio, which Waring had installed years earlier. It was what passed for a courtyard at 61 Meeting Street. The patio – the garden, he called it – was accessible to the street by a gate that opened onto the sidewalk. That gate wasn't locked, and it was the most clandestine way into the house. If anyone was coming for them, they'd most likely come in that way.

But no one came, and soon the streets South of Broad were silent.

John Fleming, the judge's bailiff, arrived first. Waring had called him from the dining room phone with instructions to summon federal marshals and the FBI. Charleston police arrived just minutes after the bailiff.

The Warings first told their story – the car, the gunshots, the bricks – to Herman Berkman, chief detective for the city police department. He gave the room a cursory look, found a piece of concrete on the floor and suggested that it had shattered the window, not a bullet. Two other detectives and a couple of patrolmen inspected the house's exterior and found no evidence of gunshots. Lacking any physical proof, Berkman said it was probably only vandalism – a prank.

Berkman's conclusion echoed what he'd said about the cross burned at 61 Meeting Street six months earlier, and it infuriated Elizabeth. She ordered the detective out of the house, and told him to take his cops with him.

"We don't need them," she told the judge. "We can call the FBI."

By 9:30, 61 Meeting Street was crawling with federal agents – but they were no more impressed with the crime scene than the city police. Agent Wilmer Thompson told reporters it appeared a brick had been thrown through the living room window, and another had ripped the screen on the front door. But the Warings told reporters an entirely different story. They thought they'd heard gunshots, and blamed the Klan.

"Whatever it was that smashed the window sounded like an explosive," Waring told The Associated Press. "The FBI men are searching the house now to see if they can find one or more bullets. I won't say they were bullets, but something certainly sounded like explosives."

This sort of thing had to be expected in South Carolina, Waring told the reporter, "It's a state dominated by the Klan, a crime-committing Klan that goes unpunished."

The Warings were defiant after the attack, talking tough and putting on a brave front. One agent on the scene later suggested Elizabeth actually seemed to be enjoying herself. After all, this proved her point that Southerners were sick and depraved. She even joked that, if they were killed, at least it would force the federal government to do something about the Klan. But the agents hadn't heard Elizabeth on the phone with Poppy Cannon; then, she was nearly hysterical.

The judge showed little emotion, as usual. He vowed to stay and fight. After he finished his calls to reporters, Waring turned down offers for protection, and a suggestion that guards be placed outside the home. Some of the agents suspected it was just an act, his bravery nothing more than a performance for the press. Because they detected something else in Waring's eyes, and it was fear. Waring was scared.

IN PLAIN SIGHT

The attack on Judge Waring's home would go unsolved.

Neither the FBI nor Charleston police showed much enthusiasm for hunting down the culprits; by the next day, both announced there would be no investigation. If anyone suspected Klan involvement, as the Warings insisted, they wouldn't admit it. When Berkman was asked about the incident, he didn't repeat his claim that vandals were likely to blame – but his dismissive attitude suggested as much.

"I marked the case closed last night," Berkman told The Evening Post.

Although the judge was suspicious of local police, and even the FBI, he had to concede there wasn't a single lead to pursue. He inspected the house at daybreak and could find no bullet holes, although there were scars in the posts bracketing his neighbor's driveway that he believed may have been caused by gunfire. Perhaps, he thought, the shots he heard were simply warnings – someone trying to frighten him, not kill him.

Waring went to work as usual that morning, walking alone from 61 Meeting Street to the courthouse. He plowed through 50 cases that day, clearing the entire criminal docket; after nearly a decade on the bench, he was still efficient. The attack was on his mind, of course, but by then he'd become more concerned with the symbolism than any threat of danger. This was an attack on a federal judge – the very definition of lawlessness.

When he returned to his chambers that afternoon, Waring was annoyed the FBI hadn't called. It reinforced his opinion that no one took the incident seriously. But as soon as he realized someone was, in fact, taking precautions, he was livid. A deputy marshal was waiting in his office with orders from the Justice Department. The judge had been assigned armed, around-the-clock protection.

Waring figured the order had come from McGrath, most likely to placate

Walter White. But he didn't want a security detail in his house, or tailing him every day. As much as he'd become immune to criticism, he worried about how it would look. People would think he had requested protection, that he was a coward.

"I don't want it," Waring told the marshal. "Tell Washington that I don't want it, I don't approve of it."

They argued a few minutes, the marshal explaining that his boss outranked the judge. Finally, Waring admitted he couldn't tell federal agents what to do, stop them from hanging around the courthouse or loitering in the street outside his house. By 2 p.m., there were two armed guards posted at the door to Waring's office. The men followed him home that evening.

Waring wouldn't let the marshals come inside, so they sat in their car, parked on Meeting Street, until a new crew relieved them. The guards rotated in and out on four-hour shifts, watching the house all night, and escorting the judge to the courthouse the next morning. Waring wouldn't let the marshals into his courtroom either, but eventually warmed up enough to chat with them. The judge figured he might as well, since they might be around a while. Their orders had them assigned to Charleston until further notice.

Of course, Waring had accurately predicted the local response. Even though the attorney general's office released a statement clarifying that McGrath had ordered the security detail – and noting that the judge had opposed it – the Charleston newspapers still blamed Waring. For weeks, the editorial pages decried federal occupation of the city and derided the judge's attackers for unwittingly serving as his publicity agents.

Waring worried the guards would make him look bad; the newspapers feared they made Charleston look even worse. News and Courier editors quietly lobbied the New York Post to correct its earlier stories that someone had fired shots at the judge's house. There was no evidence of such a crime, they argued. The Post's editor replied with a polite, but dismissive, letter.

He suggested that if children had attacked the judge, they probably got the idea from all those Charleston adults who spewed incessant vitriol.

The grousing went on for weeks. The Evening Post repeatedly said the attack had been "blown out of proportion" to give Washington an excuse to embed federal agents in the city. It was unfair, one editorial said, to accuse locals of assaulting the judge for racist reasons. But in the same piece, the editors belied their animosity by pointing out that Waring had no problem with the Democratic Party when he benefited from it.

For all Charleston's complaints, the feds actually weren't doing much of anything. J. Edgar Hoover didn't like Waring, saw no reason to investigate and was furious the New York Post kept criticizing the bureau for failing to find the attackers. Finally, Hoover told his men to drop the case, and the director of the Savannah field office drove to Charleston to deliver the bad news. He visited Waring at 61 Meeting Street, where he apologized that "Washington" had called him off the investigation.

"I thought I would come in person and tell you I was doing nothing more about it," he told the judge.

"Well," Waring said, "there's nothing for you to do."

"Excepting that I will say personally I'm ashamed of what I have to tell you," the FBI man said.

The judge formally requested the bureau return all the evidence agents had collected at the scene, forwarding a copy of his letter to President Truman. That was just insurance; he didn't seem particularly upset by the FBI's nonchalance. In a letter to Walter White, he mentioned the bureau only briefly. The purpose of his note was to persuade White to press the Justice Department into investigating Summerville police for killing Moses Winn.

"Of course, the Winn story is completely in pattern with everything here," the judge told White. "I could easily have written the whole story in advance. All of us know the scheme of going to a home in the middle of the night, committing murder, planting a pistol, and being justified at the hands of the community. The local officers work well together. And as long as the Attorney General of the United States twiddles his thumbs, South Carolina and other white supremacy states are going to laugh at the federal government and spit on the American flag."

Almost as an afterthought, Waring mentioned that the FBI's failure to investigate the attack on his home might stir national support for their cause. But White thought it was shameful. He'd heard his wife on the phone with Elizabeth that night, almost whispering, "They've thrown rocks through the window. I've turned out all the lights and we're sitting here in the dark. I had to call you – just to reassure myself that there is a civilized world … outside this jungle." White couldn't believe the FBI would ignore what was essentially terrorism.

White complained to Truman and McGrath the next day. The Justice Department had consistently looked the other way while Waring was abused, he said, simply for ruling in favor of black citizens' constitutional rights. The judge had been threatened by anonymous letters and phone calls, White said, and even the South Carolina legislature. Now, the bureau was violating its oath to not only apprehend criminals but prevent crime before it happened.

"Precious and important as are the lives of Judge and Mrs. Waring, there is even more involved in this case than their safety," White said. "Already the news of the attack upon their home on October 9 is being used by propagandists in other countries as 'proof' of the breakdown of democracy in the United States."

The FBI reopened its inquiry a few days later.

Waring suspected the administration didn't want to investigate for fear of finding evidence the Klan was involved, which would only stir up Southern Democrats. But ultimately it would look even worse if a federal judge was killed for promoting civil rights, so Truman or McGrath leaned on Hoover. That was clear from the FBI's terse announcement that it had been "authorized late this afternoon to make a full investigation of the incident."

Agents still couldn't find any evidence linking the Klan to the attack, but there was ample proof the group was lurking around Charleston. The next day, someone burned a cross on Green Street in front of Hiram Bell's house. Bell's wife told police she believed the KKK was behind the fire because their son – a graduate of Lincoln University, Thurgood Marshall's alma mater – had applied for admission to the local medical college. Police promised an ongoing investigation.

Berkman said it was most likely the work of pranksters.

The FBI interviewed dozens of Charleston residents, including every defendant who'd appeared in Waring's courtroom recently.

When agents asked the judge who might hold a grudge against him, he wasn't very helpful. "Klansmen," he'd said. But then, Waring considered nearly everyone in town a member of the Klan – and conceded most people didn't like him. Recounting the days leading up to the attack, Waring mentioned he'd yelled at some kids in the street who were harassing Elizabeth. Soon, the FBI was rounding up every teenager South of Broad.

The agents knocked around Charleston for more than two weeks without turning up any likely suspects. When The News and Courier learned that local teenagers had been questioned, Assistant Attorney General James McInerney was forced to defend the bureau. He said agents were simply trying to find out what happened and, if children were the culprits, they'd leave that to local police. The Justice Department did not prosecute vandalism.

"If it should turn out to be children who didn't know the character of the official, they probably would be lacking in criminal intent," McInerney said. "Therefore, it wouldn't be a federal offense."

In other words, if Klansmen weren't behind the attack the federal government wasn't interested.

Some parents weren't reassured. They considered the interviews little more than harassment and complained to Mendel Rivers. The congressman, always quick to assess public sentiment, took full political advantage of the situation. He accused the Justice Department of bowing to the demands of the NAACP, then co-opted the local papers' argument that these federal agents were out of their jurisdiction. When Assistant Attorney General Peyton Ford sent the congressman a letter that outlined the Justice Department's specific authority, Rivers backed down.

"I have no quarrel with the FBI investigation, which was perfectly proper," Rivers announced on Halloween, "but I am still quarreling with the department for using deputy marshals to perform ordinary police functions."

Rivers then changed tactics, protesting the cost of the judge's security detail.

He noted it had cost taxpayers $1,103.81 to guard the Warings for one month – an outrageous waste of public money.

"Waties Waring has turned out to be the most expensive luxury on the federal payroll," Rivers said.

One night, marshals were spotted outside Ruby Cornwell's house, where the judge and Elizabeth were visiting – and that prompted more controversy. The newspapers argued taxpayers shouldn't be forced to subsidize the Warings' social life. But mostly, the people of Charleston hated the security detail because it suggested they were prejudiced savages who couldn't be trusted to not assault the judge. Many locals would never concede it was possible the Klan or other racists actually were gunning for the Warings.

The controversy would linger into the winter, drawing a new excuse for criticism nearly every week. When the marshals created a no-parking zone around 61 Meeting Street, residents South of Broad were apoplectic.

On Friday morning, Nov. 17, 1950, Judge Waring held a pretrial conference for the pending Clarendon County schools lawsuit. Beyond a few attorneys and reporters, there was almost no one in the courtroom; it was merely routine business. But it would become one of the most important hearings in American legal history.

The stakes in *Briggs v. Elliott* could be measured by the legal firepower in the room. Thurgood Marshall and Harold Boulware represented the plaintiffs, and the school district had hired Robert Figg – the Democrats' lawyer in *Brown v. Baskin*. Figg had far more experience in federal court than any Clarendon County schools attorney. He'd also faced Marshall before and known Waring for years. Recruiting Figg was a smart move by Clarendon County, possibly a recommendation from state and party officials.

There wasn't going to be any settlement, so both sides simply launched into their lists of issues they wanted resolved before the trial. Figg argued that the lawsuit made false allegations, that the district didn't provide buses to any schools; white parents funded transportation for their children. Marshall complained that inspectors hadn't been allowed into the Summerton schools for a third-party comparison. Waring promised a court order forcing the district to comply.

Just as the hearing appeared to be wrapping up, Marshall mentioned the goal of *Briggs v. Elliott* was to prove that segregation in South Carolina schools was unconstitutional. Waring stopped him immediately. This lawsuit, the judge said, did no such thing.

"You've partially raised the issue," Waring said, "but can and may do what has been done so very, very often heretofore: decide a case on equal facilities – if you can prove what you say you can prove, that the schools aren't at all equal. It's very easy to decide this case on that issue, and not touch the constitutional issue at all, because it is the general policy of American courts not to decide a constitutional issue if it can be decided on some other issue."

Marshall didn't back down right away. He argued the lawsuit did, in fact, raise the question of constitutionality. Again, Waring disagreed. When the judge dismissively shut him down, Figg later said, Marshall looked shocked. But that may have been simple courtroom theatrics for the benefit of the defense – and the press. It's almost impossible the two men hadn't had the exact same conversation before.

The NAACP had been having the same debate privately for months.

Two wildly divergent opinions had taken root inside the civil rights organization. Some believed their cases weren't going far enough to challenge the separate-but-equal doctrine, while others feared overly ambitious lawsuits would lead to horrendous courtroom defeats. And that could set back the cause of civil rights by years. Most people believed Marshall was one of the men tired of dancing around the issue.

NAACP attorney Franklin Williams – one of Isaac Woodard's lawyers – claimed years later that he and Walter White were pushing Marshall to be more aggressive, to target *Plessy v. Ferguson* directly. And that is exactly what Judge Waring, one of White's best friends, was suggesting in open court.

Marshall was the best attorney among them, however, and he understood exactly what was at stake. The Judiciary Act of 1937 mandated that any constitutional challenge of a state law had to be heard by a panel of three judges – and he knew there weren't three judges in the Fourth Circuit willing to dismantle

Plessy. If the *Briggs* case were tried by such a panel, Waring might deliver a favorable vote – but he would be outnumbered. The NAACP would spend much of its dwindling legal fund for a certain loss.

Marshall had no desire to fight a losing battle, so he tried to split the difference by subtly challenging the constitutionality of South Carolina state law in the friendly confines of Waring's courtroom – and without triggering a tribunal. But he was banking on a judicial miracle that Waring knew was pointless. The judge realized if he declared school segregation unconstitutional on his own, the decision would be laughed out of the Fourth Circuit Court of Appeals.

Later, some people speculated that Waring was thinking about his reputation – that his ego couldn't stand the idea of issuing a legally suspect order that would be picked apart by other judges. He'd be accused of judicial overreach, a crusader trying to remake the country to suit his own vision. Which is exactly what people claimed he'd been doing for three years. But in truth, Waring didn't consider any of that. He simply wanted a technically correct decision the U.S. Supreme Court would be forced to uphold.

"I realized that I had gone pretty far in these racial cases," Waring later recalled. "I determined that so far the NAACP and all of the people bringing cases and all of the talk about racial bias in this country had avoided the basic issue, and the basic issue is legal segregation."

The Supreme Court had done the same thing in its three June decisions, chiseling away at separate-but-equal philosophy without once mentioning *Plessy v. Ferguson.* Waring believed the court was on an eventual, unavoidable path to outlaw segregation, but it was moving timidly. The Supreme Court needed a nudge, and he wanted to deliver that push.

"They didn't say segregation is unconstitutional," Waring noted. "But they said, 'segregation such as Herman Sweatt is getting' and 'segregation such as McLaurin is getting' – those forms of segregation are unlawful. Well, it seemed to me very clear that the court when it ran up against a dead wall that had marked on it 'segregation,' they'd have to break it through and there ought to be a case that would make that issue, where the court could no longer speak of 'other things being equal or unequal.'"

Waring's obsession with overturning *Plessy v. Ferguson* had been simmering for more than a year, and Marshall and White – both of whom talked to the judge regularly – knew it. He understood why Marshall was reluctant to make *Briggs* an explicit assault on segregation. Waring was of course familiar with the three-judge rule, he'd sat on several such panels and knew the case would lose 2-to-1. But he also realized any constitutional challenge heard by a panel of three judges was automatically appealed directly to the United States Supreme Court. If *Briggs* was specific enough, it would force the court to make a definitive stand once and for all.

And that's exactly what he was telling Marshall in open court.

Waring never admitted to any collusion with Marshall or White, even in the years after he left the bench. The Fourth Circuit certainly would have questioned the ethics of abandoning judicial neutrality and overtly working with one side in a lawsuit filed in his court. And South Carolina officials most likely would have stormed the federal courthouse. But Waring knew he didn't have much time left, and felt he was answering a higher calling.

The judge wanted a case that would bury legal segregation forever, and believed *Briggs* was that lawsuit. Almost. In order to insulate himself from later questions or criticism that he'd unfairly advised the plaintiffs, he laid out his entire strategy from the bench – and in the court record. If no one complained at the time, and they didn't, they could hardly protest later. It played out beautifully. Waring casually told Marshall he could simply amend his lawsuit to address the constitutionality of segregation.

"Or, better still, what you should do is not to amend, because that'll merely complicate the issue," the judge said. "Dismiss without prejudice, and bring a brand new suit, alleging that the schools of Clarendon County, under the South Carolina constitution and statute, are segregated, and that those statutes are unconstitutional, and that'll raise the issue for all time as to whether a state can segregate by race in its schools."

Marshall questioned Waring about the specifics for a minute, but like any good lawyer he already knew the answers. He'd been arguing cases before the

U.S. Supreme Court for a decade – he didn't need a primer. But it made for great theater leading up to the moment when Marshall asked if *Briggs v. Elliott* could be dismissed without prejudice.

Waring granted the motion.

After the hearing, Marshall and Boulware explained the next steps to reporters outside the courthouse. The NAACP attorneys would rewrite *Briggs* and bring a suit to abolish racial segregation in South Carolina public schools. Marshall said the plaintiffs had yet to be determined, because he couldn't speak for Clarendon County parents, but pledged to file the lawsuit soon.

And with that, Waring finally had the promise of the case he'd always wanted. Segregation was the root of all evil in America, the judge believed, and public schools were the place to challenge separate-but-equal laws. If the schools were integrated, it would strike at the heart of the race problem and ultimately lead to significant change in society.

"Prejudice doesn't start when you're 18 or 21 years old. You've got it then," Waring later explained. "Prejudice starts when you're a little kid and you go to first grade and you're told that people have to go through different doors and use different toilets and there's something wrong with other people."

Even before Marshall and Boulware filed the lawsuit, state officials began to plot new ways to thwart this coming legal challenge. Nearly everyone in South Carolina realized this was the gathering storm they'd long dreaded. And they feared the state was destined to lose. That afternoon, The Evening Post reported that Thurgood Marshall had promised the first lawsuit in history "calling for the integration of races in schools."

In his lifetime, Waring never got widespread credit for starting the legal challenge that, four years later, would change America and accelerate the civil rights movement. But he'd done it in plain sight. The News and Courier story on the *Briggs v. Elliott* pretrial conference ran the next day under the headline "Negroes will seek to enter white schools." The paper's secondary headline even identified the man behind it all.

"Suit is suggested by Judge Waring."

DARKEST SOUTH CAROLINA

An early winter storm devastated Charleston the last weekend of November. That Saturday, three people died of exposure as temperatures dropped into the teens – colder than it had been along the South Carolina coast in seven years. Pipes burst across the city, leaving many residents without water. One woman was found frozen on the waterfront near The Battery and the Fort Sumter Hotel, where the Southern governors were holding their annual convention.

The next day, 125 people set out from Morris Street Baptist Church for a nearly two-mile march to 61 Meeting Street. The walk was not unbearable; the temperature ultimately rose to 48, 10 degrees above the forecast. These people – 100 of them black, 25 white – were led by Modjeska Simkins, the Columbia activist and state chairman for the Southern Conference Education Fund. The "pilgrimage" had been her idea to honor Judge Waring and his wife for their dedication to civil rights.

The group walked uncluttered sidewalks along King and Meeting streets for nearly an hour before arriving at the judge's home. There they found an atypical South of Broad scene: a government car parked beneath a palm tree, an armed marshal casually leaning against the house. It looked like a fortified compound in enemy territory. But the Warings stood outside, near their front door, shaking hands with every one of the pilgrims.

It was a simple ceremony. With the group fanning out on the sidewalk and spilling into Meeting Street, Simkins read a citation that praised Waring for his "wise, just and courageous" work, his understanding of democracy, as well as his dedication to protecting the rights of suffrage and the freedom and equality of men.

"Yet it has been seen that many another, in your place, has found it possible, before obdurate prejudices and customs, to avoid the guidance of the noblest guarantees of our constitution," Simkins said. "Your own faithfulness in this field, despite environmental discouragements others have bowed to, has been exemplary and heartwarming."

The judge was moved by this tribute more than any other he'd ever received. Waring told the crowd he would like nothing better than to be remembered as President Grover Cleveland – loved "for the enemies he has made." His brief remarks were perhaps inspired by his audience, metaphorically equating civil rights and religion. The judge said if he'd done anything to overpower prejudice in a cold and bitter world, it was only because he'd seen the light. And that light was far too rare in 1950 America.

"We do not live in darkest Africa," Waring said, "we live in darkest South Carolina."

The Warings could not remember passing a more enjoyable day in Charleston. They posed for photographs on the sidewalk, then invited their guests inside for coffee. The judge believed this outpouring of support would attract national media attention, and was mildly disappointed more people didn't recognize the grand gesture. From his perspective, South Carolina's climate had been harsh and cold for five years, and this was a welcome ray of sunshine.

Of course, these were Waring's people. They admired him as much for his voice as his actions. Before the march, Aubrey Willis Williams, publisher of the Southern Farmer and president of the Southern Conference Education Fund, had told the Morris Street congregation the Warings' crusade against the false god of gradualism had set the new standard of conduct in the South.

"Southerners have sick minds," Williams said. "You can't educate these things out of people. It is an unmitigated evil which destroys those who exploit as well as those being exploited. The white churches of the South are not making any contributions toward solving these problems. ... Our only progress is being made in the courts, where the evil is met head on. Judge Waring is a true American, living up to the ideals and standards we hold so high and cherish so dearly."

The pilgrimage not only failed to generate public support for the judge, Waring's comments – and Williams' diatribe, with its echoes of Elizabeth's YWCA speech – drew considerable backlash. William Watts Ball, just a month from retirement, noted on The News and Courier editorial page that many of these pilgrims enlightening "darkest South Carolina" had been called communists by the House Un-American Activities Committee. The Charleston papers were staunch supporters of McCarthyism.

"As white men once exploited the 'dark continent,' so now enterprising white men again come into the deep South to exploit the gullible colored people," Ball wrote. "But this time, they are not dealing with primitive tribes. Years of association with Southern white men have taught the Negroes many things, not all of them good and not all of them bad."

Strom Thurmond delivered a nearly identical message to the Southern Governors' Conference the day after the pilgrimage. The outgoing governor warned that President Truman's civil rights program was breeding unrest at a time when the nation desperately needed unity, and blamed the South's problems on outside agitators. But he predicted "most Southern Negroes will not listen to false leaders and realize their best opportunity for progress is a continuation of the harmonious cooperation which brought both races so far along."

The former Dixiecrat nominee for president was little more than a month away from his own involuntary retirement, but he would not remain silent for long. His message resonated throughout South Carolina, and he had little doubt that he'd find another job.

Waring remained reticent to speak out after the assault on his house – the "darkest South Carolina" comment was his only public statement since the incident. The atmosphere in the state was too tense, the judge had decided, and he didn't want to incite more violence. So he said nothing about The News and Courier's or Thurmond's comments, even though he was the target of both. Instead, Waring did something that came most unnatural to him. He kept his mouth shut.

In early December, Elizabeth and the judge drove to Florence – two marshals following behind in a separate car. He welcomed the respite from Charleston, and the busy docket awaiting him, but Waring couldn't escape attention. When he recused himself in the case of a former Myrtle Beach school superintendent accused of mail theft, the newspapers and the politicians smelled judicial impropriety.

Waring had sentenced Ernest Southern to a year in prison two months earlier, but the former superintendent protested. He claimed postal officials had promised him probation, and Waring reneged on the deal out of spite. In some ways, it was Southern's own fault. The former superintendent had represented himself in court, and his bumbling ignorance of the law quickly drew Waring's ire. He criticized Southern's witnesses as "rabble" and questioned the accuracy of their testimony. Southern finally hired an attorney and claimed the judge was biased.

Waring agreed to turn the case over to Judge Timmerman just to get the man out of his courtroom, but Sen. Olin Johnston suggested that somehow this was proof of the judge's "anti-South Carolina bias" and renewed his call for impeachment hearings. When that failed, Mendel Rivers announced his application for a seat on the Un-American Activities Committee – and his plans to investigate the Warings as suspected communists.

Trouble seemed to follow the judge everywhere. On Dec. 15, the Warings visited the Florence home of R.J. Wilson, a black physician. While they were there, the phone rang. Wilson answered, and a voice on the line asked for Waring. Assuming it was simply a business call for the judge, Wilson said "Yes." But the man only said "this is just a warning" and hung up.

It was the third attempt to intimidate Wilson that year. In April and September, men had called the doctor claiming to be members of the Ku Klux Klan. They'd threatened to tar and feather him and burn a cross in his yard. The FBI investigated but failed to turn up any suspects. The Associated Press reported the threatening call, including the judge's now-standard "no comment."

The bureau never proved white supremacists were behind this harassment, but it was obvious someone more inventive than teenage vandals was targeting the couple. The Warings drove a new Cadillac, a car the judge admitted was a bit ostentatious. But he and Elizabeth had splurged, reasoning that if they were going to ride out a few more years in South Carolina, at least they could do it in style.

Waring doted on the Cadillac, but still it suffered a suspicious number of problems. He kept it locked in a garage and had it serviced every week, yet he often found hoses under the hood disconnected and strange puddles of water beneath it. His mechanic could find no leak in the often-empty radiator. And on the drive home from Florence that December, the car broke down on the side of the road.

Frustrated, Waring popped the hood to inspect the engine but could find nothing amiss. He repeatedly tried to restart the car, but it did no good. He and Elizabeth were stuck on the side of the road in rural South Carolina.

Before long, Waring's security detail showed up. They hustled the Warings out of the Cadillac, grabbed their luggage and drove them back to Charleston. One of the marshals stayed behind to guard the car and, bored, decided to inspect it. He discovered the gas tank was full of dirt, which had clogged the fuel filter. "That wasn't accidental," the judge later recalled. "You don't get dirt in the gasoline tank of your car."

But such mysteries had become regular occurrences for Waring.

Rev. DeLaine was upset that the Clarendon County lawsuit had been dismissed yet again. He took little reassurance from Thurgood Marshall's explanation that *Briggs* would be refiled as a suit seeking "equal everything." This had dragged on for years, and all DeLaine knew for certain was that he had to collect another round of signatures from the plaintiffs – and he had to do it quickly.

Moving fast was not an option for DeLaine. His health had suffered throughout the fall, much of his strength sapped by an October court hearing on the slander lawsuit against him. For three days, attorneys for the former Scott's Branch principal laid out their case against DeLaine, and it was devastating to his health and morale. Clarendon County Superintendent L.B. McCord told jurors DeLaine had accused the principal of pocketing all the fees collected from students – which, of course, DeLaine had never said.

But the jury took the word of a white school official over a black preacher. DeLaine was found guilty, although jurors awarded the principal only $5,000 in damages. It didn't matter too much; he wouldn't be able to collect anything because DeLaine had transferred his property to friends. Legally, the pastor had no assets for the court to seize.

DeLaine still hadn't recovered from the grueling days in court, but he had come too far to give up on the schools. He'd made a promise, so he drove over to Summerton from Lake City and got to work re-signing the *Briggs* petitioners – calling on some Clarendon County preachers to help. Harry Briggs was willing to join the new suit, as were most of the original plaintiffs. Only a few refused, mainly because of the reprisals they'd already suffered.

For a while it looked as if the NAACP was going to be a few plaintiffs short of a lawsuit. But DeLaine learned some of the previous signers were out deer hunting, and he drove into the woods to track them down. When he found the group and explained his predicament, DeLaine not only got new commitments from the original plaintiffs, he recruited a few of the other hunters as well. He eventually found 30 names for the lawsuit.

Harold Boulware filed the final version of *Briggs v. Elliott* on Dec. 22, 1950. The suit targeted Clarendon County District 22, and specifically school board Chairman R.W. Elliott, but the scope of the complaint had the potential to affect every black student in the state. *Briggs* asked for a three-judge panel to declare South Carolina's public education system a violation of the 14th Amendment to the United States Constitution. The NAACP and its plaintiffs were asking for nothing less than the abolition of racial segregation in public schools.

The newspapers devoted much more attention to this case, predicting it was only the opening salvo in a much larger court battle. Reporters tried to reach Waring for comment, but courthouse marshals said he was unavailable. He'd made a decision not to break his media silence, but the judge knew what was going on – and he couldn't have been more pleased. The lawsuit was exactly what he'd wanted. Although he knew if they tried and failed, segregation would endure for at least another generation.

More than five years would pass before the judge acknowledged any role in shaping the final version of *Briggs v. Elliott* – and even then he wouldn't admit he orchestrated it. Waring told Columbia University professors, "I take a little credit for myself that I forced that case to be brought on a straight constitutional segregation issue. It could have been decided on the ground of unequal facilities, and there were grave attempts to have it decided on that ground. But we got the pleadings into shape, by constant hammering, where the question was 'Yes or no?' That was really what I wanted to be decided."

For years, he danced around the question. He didn't want to take any credit away from Marshall, Boulware, Walter White or the NAACP, and understandably did not want to reveal any secret machinations on his part. But Columbia University professors, interviewing Waring in 1956 for an oral history, pressed him. *Who had persuaded Marshall to challenge segregation head-on for the first time?* Finally, the judge said, "I had."

It was the most he'd ever say on the subject.

Briggs v. Elliott changed the climate in South Carolina the minute it was filed. State officials were horrified by the prospects of integration, something most of their constituents would undoubtedly find unacceptable. But given recent U.S. Supreme Court decisions, such an outcome was no longer outside the realm of possibility. And state officials knew that, ultimately, they would be blamed. As a result, the Clarendon County suit was clearly on the mind of new Gov. James F. Byrnes.

He spent most of his first address to the General Assembly talking about education – and ways to keep the races in separate classrooms.

On Jan. 24, 1951, the governor endorsed a proposal from Charleston Rep. Ernest F. Hollings to enact a 3 percent state sales tax that would fund more than $70 million in education needs. Byrnes told the legislature it was the only solution to raise the revenue necessary to give South Carolina children the education they deserved. He proposed building new schools, raising teacher salaries and buying a centralized bus fleet.

Byrnes also promised to find a "lawful" way to educate all South Carolina children while providing separate schools for the races.

"The overwhelming majority of colored people in this state do not want to force their children into white schools," Byrnes claimed. "Just as the Negro preachers do not want their congregations to leave them and attend the churches of white people, the Negro teachers do not want their pupils to leave them and attend schools for white children."

The governor suggested these current events echoed Reconstruction, when a carpet-bagging federal government attempted to force the mixing of races, and promised South Carolina would again successfully resist those efforts. He used the threat of integration as an excuse for the sales tax – it would cost money to provide equal, but separate, facilities. Ignoring his long career as a federal official, he subtly had co-opted Thurmond's states' rights argument.

"The politicians in Washington and the Negro agitators in South Carolina who today seek to abolish segregation in all schools will learn that what a carpetbag government could not do in the Reconstruction period, cannot do in this period," Brynes declared. "And the white people of South Carolina will see to it that innocent colored children will not be denied an education because of selfish politicians and misguided agitators."

Basically, Byrnes used white supremacists' fears to build support for a massive tax increase. He suspected the threat of ending segregation was the only way he could persuade many white voters to go along with spending millions on black schools. But the governor argued the best defense against federal government interference was providing equitable schools, which was true. And even though more than half the revenue generated by the sales tax was earmarked for black schools, his ploy worked.

The governor's policies could be interpreted many different ways. He had no desire to see segregation end on his watch, and was probably correct that a good-faith effort by the state was the best argument to avoid that. In some ways, the politics of South Carolina dictated his moves, but some believed he was actually trying to help black children. Clearly, Byrnes wanted to dampen racial unrest. He was quietly pushing legislation to ban adults from wearing masks in public – a proposal aimed at curbing Klan rallies. But his critics could argue that was little more than a reaction to all the negative publicity the KKK had brought South Carolina.

And his later threats certainly didn't support such benevolent theories. As the court date for *Briggs* approached, Byrnes warned that the state would "reluctantly" abandon public education if segregation was outlawed. If South Carolina couldn't keep white and black children apart, it simply wouldn't provide schools for anyone.

However, the governor argued, the need for the sales tax remained because they would still need facilities for the private white schools that would spring up in the place of shuttered public schools. Which certainly didn't qualify as equal treatment.

A few weeks after his speech to the General Assembly, Byrnes ordered the state attorney general to defend Clarendon District 22 in the *Briggs* lawsuit. He said the outcome would affect every school in South Carolina, so it was "therefore proper for the state to defend the case." Byrnes, a former Supreme Court justice, probably worried that poor Clarendon County couldn't afford the legal representation it needed to prevail in a federal courtroom.

There was good reason for such concerns. When Clarendon County finally responded to *Briggs v. Elliott*, it did little more than offer the same arguments it had trotted out in its response to the first equalization case. That was not nearly a strong enough defense in a constitutional challenge. County officials were either inept or oblivious to the national ramifications of the lawsuit.

By the time Byrnes sent reinforcements to Clarendon County, Waring had left the state. He was scheduled to spend most of the winter and early spring filling in for vacationing judges in New York district court. When the marshals escorted the Warings to the Charleston train station on Jan. 31, they said goodbye. Washington had decided to quietly cancel the security detail. The FBI also dropped the investigation into the attack on 61 Meeting Street – and the no-parking zone around it. Waring was on his own.

The judge was happy to be rid of his guards, and for once anticipated his return to Charleston. When he got home, Waring would hear the most important case of his career – the one he'd planned for years.

Briggs v. Elliott was scheduled to begin in his courtroom in late May.

BRIGGS V. ELLIOTT

Rev. DeLaine met the *Briggs* plaintiffs early that morning at St. Mark AME in Summerton. The town was quiet and still, lethargic under a blanket of humidity that promised an uncomfortably sticky day. As such, few people were around to see history unfolding a few blocks off Main Street.

They parked their cars and trucks in a line beside the church, ready for the convoy to Charleston. Many of them had been threatened by their bosses, told they would be fired if they didn't show up for work that day. But that didn't stop them; they'd lost jobs before. They'd had their mortgages called due and their credit declined for joining the lawsuit. Poor Willie Stukes may have been killed over it. Less than a month after signing onto the lawsuit, a car fell on the mechanic in his own back yard. It was ruled an accident, but anymore no one could be sure.

Still, on this morning Harry Briggs and his co-signers – encouraged and reassured by DeLaine – were in good spirits, even happy. They were about to make history; they were going to challenge segregation in federal court. It had been a long, sometimes terrifying journey and now they had only 70 miles to go. The sun was barely up when the convoy pulled out of the church parking lot. It was Monday, May 28, 1951.

There was a lot riding on the case, much more than the fate of a few thousand Clarendon County students. The newspapers portrayed *Briggs v. Elliott* as a test of states' rights and said the entire South Carolina education system was on trial. But it was even more important than that. The entire nation was watching, in part because officials in Georgia and Alabama had said they would follow Gov. Byrnes' lead and abandon public schools if the court abolished legal segregation. This lawsuit could change the nation.

When they reached Charleston, the *Briggs* plaintiffs were first struck by all the noise. They were amazed by the traffic, the busy sidewalks and the sounds of road construction echoing between the buildings. For people who'd scarcely ventured outside their rural county, Charleston seemed like a big city – and a noisy one. Someone had inconveniently picked this week to work on the streets around the city's Four Corners of Law, which compressed the already considerable crowd outside the federal courthouse into a thick sea of people. There was barely room to move. For all the folks from Clarendon knew, the city was always this way.

The door to the courthouse was roped off. The building was already full, and no one else would be admitted. Anticipating the demand for seats, marshals had unlocked the doors at 7 a.m. and, within an hour, Waring's courtroom and the halls were packed. Reporters from New York, Chicago, Baltimore, Toledo, Pittsburgh and Norfolk had been among the first inside. The journalists estimated there were now more than 800 people in the courthouse, most of them black. Local activists, mothers with small children and entire families had turned out in anticipation. It was impossible to count how many people loitered outside, but it must have been more than a thousand.

DeLaine pushed his way to the door and explained to the marshals that he'd brought the Clarendon County parents for the hearing. Finally, he persuaded a guard to usher them into the building and the benches reserved for the plaintiffs. They found the courtroom no quieter than Broad Street, but at least there was some air circulating. The bailiff had left the back door of the room open so people in the hall could watch the proceedings, and relay word to the unlucky souls sweating in the humidity of the late spring morning.

Waring watched the undulating street crowd from a second-floor window in the courthouse, and he found it inspiring. The streets of Charleston had rarely seen so many people since the days of the Ivory City, a half-century past. It was like the pilgrimage to his own home six months earlier, but on a much grander scale. He realized all these people had come for "a little whiff of freedom," and he would never forget it.

"They had never known before that anybody would stand up for them, and they came there because they believed the United States District Court was a free court, and believed in freedom and liberty," Waring recalled. "I really feel that. To me, it was a very heartening thing."

U.S. District Judge John Parker gaveled court into session at 10 a.m. As chief judge of the Fourth Circuit, he would preside over the hearing with Waring and Timmerman serving as the other members of the panel. The audience settled in for a long day with the usual courtroom rustling; they might as well get comfortable. The clerk had predicted it would take three days to hear all the testimony. But the state tried to put a stop to the proceedings in the first hour.

In his opening statement, Robert Figg conceded there was inequity between Clarendon County's black and white schools, and that the state had a responsibility to remedy this disparity. A new statewide sales tax would go into effect on July 1, Figg explained, and South Carolina had committed to spend $75 million on schools. Black schools soon would have bus service and improved facilities, he said, so the lawsuit was really unnecessary.

He was trying to derail the case.

"The differences have been a residue of growth over a period of years," Figg said. "The defendants do not oppose an order finding that inequalities in respect to buildings, equipment, facilities, curricula and other aspects of schools provided for whites and colored children now exist, and enjoining any discrimination in respect thereto."

Figg asked the court to dismiss or delay the lawsuit, or at the very least give the state a reasonable time to formulate its plan for ending this inequality. It was a savvy legal move. If the judges agreed to a continuance or dismissal, that would delay, or stop, any appeal from reaching the U.S. Supreme Court – which would make the ultimate decision on the constitutionality of segregation. South Carolina was willing to pay millions of dollars to delay a federal order that integrated schools.

Thurgood Marshall recognized the strategy immediately, and complained that the state wanted to prevent his witnesses from testifying. He'd planned to put some of the plaintiffs on the stand to describe conditions in their children's school. Now, with the state conceding the inequity issue, their testimony was moot and Marshall had to revise his entire presentation. Harry Briggs and the others had driven to Charleston simply to be spectators.

Waring worried that Parker and Timmerman might accept the state's offer, if for no other reason than to avoid a controversial lawsuit. He had to admit Figg sounded reasonable, his argument plausible. But he also realized the state was attempting to slyly avoid a ruling on the primary issue: segregation. Before Parker could speak, Waring interrupted.

"Judge Parker, this doesn't hit the constitutional issue," Waring said.

"No, it doesn't," Parker agreed. "It has nothing to do with the matter. We know these facilities aren't equal, and that's not what we're after, and we've got to meet the real issue."

The judges denied the motion.

Marshall had planned to put his plaintiffs on the stand first; some of his expert witnesses weren't even at the courthouse. But he had enough on hand to begin his argument, which he'd laid out in an opening statement. Although the Clarendon County schools were unequal, that was only a symptom of the real problem: "Segregation was per se inequality" – the same thing Waring had been saying to him for more than a year.

Figg had disrupted the flow of the entire case, but Marshall soldiered on. He established the particulars of Clarendon County's inequality during his questioning of L.B. McCord, the Manning superintendent, and R.W. Elliott, the District 22 school board chairman. They testified that the district consisted of 10 black and 12 white schools, even though there were nearly three times as many black students. The district spent $305,525 annually on 2,375 white students, and $282,960 on 6,531 black students. The math was stark: The county school system paid $43 to educate each black student, and $128 for every white student – three times as much.

But since Figg had conceded inequality, Judge Parker quickly shut down the school officials' testimony.

"You are asking questions where there is no dispute," Parker said. "Let's get to the disputed matter."

Marshall used his next witness – M.J. Whitehead, assistant registrar at Howard University – to establish the deplorable conditions of the county's black schools. The classrooms had but a few rundown blackboards, broken tables and chairs. Whitehead noted Scott's Branch had only two outhouses for restrooms – one for 394 girls, another for the 309 boys. By contrast, the white schools had indoor restrooms, as well as amenities such as lunchrooms, auditoriums and gymnasiums.

On cross-examination, Figg pointed out that electricity and plumbing wasn't available in some black communities and forced Whitehead to concede drinking fountains recently had been installed at Scott's Branch. But Whitehead said there was no way the black schools of District 22 could be brought up to the same standards as white schools.

Marshall largely relied on the testimony of academics who argued that segregation harmed black students in ways that weren't readily visible – and couldn't be mitigated. Harold McNally, an education professor from Columbia University, was the first of these experts. He said the difference in health facilities had an impact on education, and this disparity led to poor health habits among black children. Robert Carter, one of Marshall's co-counsels, asked the same question all the academics would hear: Can students receive an equal educational experience when segregated?

"No," McNally said. "If one considers the purpose of public school education in a democracy, it is clear that here is the only place where a child encounters others from every economic level; here alone they come together to know one another, and one purpose of education is to develop respect for the historic concept of equality. White children as well as Negro children are being shortchanged where segregation is practiced … segregation itself implies difference, a stigma, and relegates the segregated group more or less to the second class."

Howard University education professor Ellis Knox testified that segregation cannot exist without discrimination, that it is detrimental to the minority group and leaves them unprepared to function in society. Figg asked if mixing the races might not cause unwanted emotional reaction. Knox said perhaps, but that didn't matter – segregation was bad policy.

Marshall's star witness was also his most controversial. Kenneth Clark, a New York psychology professor and founder of a center that treated emotional problems, had created tests to measure the effects of prejudice and discrimination on children. Clark offered his subjects a choice between two dolls – one white, the other black. In segregated communities, black children most often picked the white doll as the more desirable. Clark said he'd tested 16 Clarendon County students the prior week. Most chose the white doll.

"The effects of segregation on the personality of a Negro child are definitely detrimental, producing confusion in the child's concept of his own self-esteem, hostility toward himself and toward life," Clark said.

The professor said 90 percent of psychologists believed segregation was bad for black children and 82 percent said it hurt whites as well. Clark said the isolation created feelings of guilt and confusion about moral ideologies.

"The same people who talk to him about love and brotherhood also teach him to segregate."

Clark's tests found the black children of Clarendon County felt inferior to whites, and he said those perceptions would endure so long as there was segregation in the schools. Waring believed Clark's methods were sound, but on cross-examination Figg criticized him for not testing white students. Integration, he suggested, might harm those children.

"Have you considered the possible psychological effect on white students of forcible mixing?"

After the lunch break, the courtroom almost turned violent. People pushed and shoved their way back into the room, trying to reclaim their seats, while marshals fought to control the surging crowd. One of the marshals rushed to Waring's chambers and said, "These people are not behaving out here. I can't let them in."

Waring told the marshal to make his men stand down. He asked Thurgood Marshall to try to calm the audience. In truth, he couldn't blame the people. They only wanted to hear something that was desperately important to their lives. The judge later recalled that "little breath of freedom" only made them want more. "And they get thirsty for it."

Marshall spent the first half of the afternoon session calling more expert witnesses. He explained that he wanted to present as many academic viewpoints as possible to illustrate the myriad ways segregation affected the black community, beginning with education. James Hupp, a psychology professor at West Virginia Wesleyan, testified that segregation stunted the social development of black children. And Louis Kesselman, a political scientist at the University of Louisville, said segregation breeds suspicion and mistrust. Enforced by the law, it could even result in conflict.

To some people in the audience, Marshall's entire case consisted of nothing more than theories from a bunch of eggheads who wanted only to declare the South backward and uncivilized. When he finished, Figg played to that attitude and offered a stark contrast to the plaintiffs' experts. His chief witness was not a liberal arts social scientist, just a former school superintendent from Sumter with an unfortunate name.

E.R. Crow argued per-pupil spending in many South Carolina school districts was out of proportion because black students didn't attend class as regularly as whites. Figg asked the reason for this disparity, and Crow said it was most likely a result of those children being forced to work on their families' farms – a suggestion that conjured images of field hands during the dark days of slavery.

When Figg proposed such factors should be considered in state education funding formulas, Marshall objected.

"He's testifying about something to be done in the future," Marshall said. "The Supreme Court has often said that human rights are now."

"Yes," Judge Parker said, "but the court in its decree might take into consideration good faith in providing future facilities."

Waring couldn't help but notice the irony: a man whose very name echoed the moniker for the South's Jim Crow laws laid out the crux of the state's defense. He also prompted the most telling exchange of the hearing. Assisted by some leading questions from Figg, the former superintendent said mixing the races in public schools would be unwise, that it would be impossible "to have peaceable association with each other in public schools, impossible to have sufficient acceptance of the idea, and impossible to have public education at all on that basis."

"In my opinion," Crow said, "it would eliminate public schools in most, if not all, of the counties."

"Would there be," Figg asked, "community acceptance or the possibility of violent emotional reaction?"

"There would be violent reaction," Crow said, "I'm sure."

Marshall interjected at that point, and none of the judges stopped him. "Do you mean to say," he asked, "that the white people of South Carolina would deprive their own children of an education because of this?"

"I didn't say that," Crow replied, "but I don't believe the legislature would appropriate money, or that communities would levy taxes, to support mixed schools."

On cross-examination by Marshall, Crow conceded there were no black people on any school board in the state – save for a single man just elected in a Florence County district – but denied that would hurt the chances of black schools getting equitable funding. White people didn't want their kids in school with black children, he said, but had agreed to a sales tax that would provide equal, and separate, facilities.

Marshall steered Crow back to the question of violence. Why, he asked, did Crow believe parents were so hostile to the idea of integration? The superintendent admitted he'd never observed an integrated school system, so he couldn't be sure what would happen, but based his opinion on a life-long observation of South Carolina. His conclusions were informed, Crow said, mostly by the things people had said to him.

"Mostly white people?" Marshall asked.

"Mostly."

"Do you know anything at all about what Negroes believe?"

Crow claimed several black school administrators in South Carolina shared his concerns, and often agreed that mixed-race schools wouldn't work. But when Marshall pressed, and asked him to "please name those Negroes," Crow couldn't – or wouldn't – offer a single name.

"Are the people of South Carolina a law-abiding people?" Marshall asked.

"Is it your testimony that if this court issues an injunction the people of South Carolina would not obey it?"

Figg stood and objected to the question. "No injunction issued by this court will be directed at the people," he said.

Judge Parker didn't like the interruption, or Figg's suggestion. He overruled the objection. "This court is going to assume that any injunction issued will be obeyed."

That was nearly the end of Crow's testimony. Marshall had only a few more questions. First, he asked a hypothetical: Would the state still build separate but allegedly equal schools to keep even one black child out of white classrooms? If Clarendon County were 95 percent white and 5 percent black, Marshall asked, would that change his opinion of segregation?

"No," Crow said. "I believe elimination of segregation would bring undesirable results."

"Isn't it a fact," Marshall asked, "that the only basis of your reasoning is that you have all your life believed in segregation?"

Crow said that played a part, but it wasn't the only reason.

The audience was stunned by Marshall's performance. No doubt few black people in the courtroom had ever heard a man of color speak to a white man in such a strident, yet condescending manner. But then, it was a lopsided match. Marshall was a lawyer who practiced before the United States Supreme Court; the defense's chief witness was a former school superintendent from a small South Carolina town. One of the reporters heard a man in the audience say, "Thurgood is merciless, simply merciless."

Figg's final witness of the day was H.B. Betchman, superintendent of Clarendon County's District 22 schools. He reiterated earlier testimony that black students in the district missed significantly more school than whites, particularly during spring planting and fall harvest. In fact, Betchman said, attendance at the black schools had fallen so precipitously that he might lose a teacher to state funding cuts.

When Marshall got his turn to question Betchman, he asked if the condition of the schools played any role in the high absenteeism.

"No, I think it is a matter of small farmers and work."

"But isn't absenteeism sometimes due to the fact that there is nothing to encourage a child to attend," Marshall asked.

"Perhaps sometimes," Betchman conceded.

The second day of *Briggs v. Elliott* would be the last. When the defense stipulated that black schools were inferior to white facilities, Figg not only avoided damning testimony from Harry Briggs and the other plaintiffs, he effectively cut the length of the hearing in half. But Marshall wasn't finished. He had more witnesses lined up to testify before another standing-room only audience, all of whom said the same thing: Segregation is bad, for both black and white children.

In more than one way, *Briggs* was a landmark case. No other court in U.S. history had heard expert testimony from social psychologists. But the judges had allowed it, and Marshall used these witnesses to his advantage. In fact, he aimed for overkill – he didn't want a doubt left in anyone's mind. The first witness of the day, Harvard social psychologist David Krech, shocked the audience just as Marshall intended. Krech said nothing harmed the mental, emotional and physical development of black children more than legal segregation.

"It gives environmental support to the belief that Negroes are in some way different from white people," Krech said. "Segregation arises from racial prejudice and also causes racial prejudice. Legal segregation starts the process of differentiation at a crucial age and – except in rare cases – if it is continued for 10 or 12 years, the child never recovers."

Segregation, he said, resulted in black children having lower IQs and less ability to cope with life. Krech argued that separating students by race reinforced false notions of white supremacy in children of all colors. But then the Massachusetts professor made everyone in the courtroom gasp.

"Most white people," Krech said, "feel superior to Negroes, and they have a right to feel superior. The fact is that the white is, indeed, superior. The Negro is inferior because the whites have made him so."

If Marshall was going for effect, he got it.

The final witness was Vassar professor Helen Trager, who'd studied the effects of segregation in Philadelphia. Trager had found that, even at the age of 5, white children talked freely about race – but the subject made black children uncomfortable. She said separating the races hurt the self-esteem of black children, frustrating their basic human need to be accepted and feel like they belonged in society.

On cross-examination, Figg attempted to blame segregation on black people. Is it not true, he asked the professor, that black people often choose to segregate themselves? Trager conceded that was sometimes the case, but argued that "learning to live together and to accept one group by another must be made possible by a life situation. Children need experience in meeting and working out difficulties for themselves."

Her point was that black people had no choice; they didn't make segregation laws, white people did.

Thurgood Marshall began his closing statement at 11:30 that morning. With no jury to persuade, he focused solely on the legal arguments the three judges would consider. But first, he had to dispel any notion the court could accept South Carolina's promise to improve black schools. He noted the state had conceded its failure to provide a separate-but-equal education for black children, but had done nothing to remedy this other than offer to borrow money for some new buildings.

"Clarendon County is violating the law every day it operates this school system," Marshall said. "I know of no statute that permits anyone to come into court and ask time to stop doing something which is unlawful."

He cited case law, the testimony of his experts and condemned the "halo of respectability" the South gave legal segregation. There could be no equality with separate schools and there was no chance of that happening in South Carolina. All state officials are white, he pointed out, and all school officials are white. That is not only segregation, Marshall said, it is "exclusion from the group that runs everything. The Negro child is made to go to an inferior school; he is branded in his own mind as inferior. This sets up a roadblock in his mind which prevents his ever feeling he is equal."

Even assuming good faith on the part of state officials, Marshall said, it would be impossible to build new schools or rehabilitate existing facilities within a few weeks or month. Without a court ruling in the plaintiffs' favor, their children would continue to attend substandard schools. And even if better facilities were available, he said, the black children of South Carolina would still suffer from the debilitating stigma of segregation.

"There is no relief for the Negro children of Clarendon County except to be permitted to attend existing and superior white schools," Marshall concluded.

In his closing remarks, Figg focused on the state's plan to equalize schools with sales tax revenue. He said South Carolina had predicted it would raise $75 million for schools, and expected to spend $40 million of that – more than half – on black schools. Figg noted that the courts have recognized "problems of race are not soluble by force, but by the slow processes of community experience." Given that, Figg argued the federal court should allow the state to solve its problems in its own way. At that point, Judge Parker interrupted.

"What sort of decree do you think this court should enter in light of your admissions?" Parker asked.

Figg said the court should give South Carolina a "reasonable time" to formulate a plan for the bond issue it would seek after the sales tax takes effect. The court could maintain jurisdiction, he offered, so it could grant relief in case the state didn't come up with a constitutional plan. Again, he was stopped.

"I'm not much impressed with that suggestion," Judge Parker said. "You're coming into court and admitting that facilities are not equal. It's not up to the court to wet-nurse the schools. … Now what sort of decree do you suggest?"

"I think the court should take into consideration that schools aren't built overnight," Figg said. "The reason we are asking you to keep jurisdiction is so that if the program is derailed, you would have a remedy."

"The court has that power anyway," Judge Parker said. "Through contempt proceedings if the decree isn't obeyed."

Figg cited a Virginia case in which the court had allowed a time limit for compliance. Perhaps, he offered, this court could do the same. Waring was livid.

The state was blatantly trying to twist *Briggs* into a simple equal-facilities case and ignore the larger constitutional question. He could see his one chance to overturn *Plessy v. Ferguson* slipping away. Waring spoke up, interrupting Parker, and noted the Virginia case was a simple "separate but equal" lawsuit.

"This court has got to face the issue of segregation per se," Waring said.

But Figg refused to accept the premise. He continued to argue that South Carolina could build equal – but separate – schools for black children, but would never integrate. Neither Clarendon County, nor South Carolina, was ready for that.

"Nothing would improve racial relations so much as education," Figg said. "There will come a time, I am sure, when this problem we are facing will no longer exist in the United States. But this is not the time to end segregation in South Carolina. It would cause confusion."

Following a lunch recess, Marshall was allowed a final rebuttal – and he used the time to mock Figg's solution. In the 80 years since Reconstruction, he argued, the best South Carolina could do was concede the condition of black schools was $40 million behind white schools. The state had demonstrated an unwillingness to repair the damage it had done to generations of its residents.

"If the white child is permitted to obtain an education without mental road-blocks, the Negro child must be permitted," Marshall said.

He said the plaintiffs might have accepted Figg's promise had it been made 70 years earlier, before South Carolina spent decades discriminating against black people. The state had stolen the rights of its citizens, first with a state constitution written by Ben Tillman and then with the cover of an 1896 Supreme Court decision that set up the false notion that the races could be "separate but equal."

"This phrase has produced nothing but inequality," Marshall said. "The only true word is the word 'separate.' The defense has not justified this segregation statute by a single word of testimony. No one has been put on the stand to testify that race has anything to do with public education, or to give any reason why segregation is necessary."

And that was the point of the case. South Carolina, like the rest of the nation, had no defense.

When Marshall finished, Judge Parker reminded him the Supreme Court had made it clear in three cases the previous summer that it wouldn't revisit *Plessy v. Ferguson*. Surely, Parker said, Marshall wasn't asking them to overturn one of the most monumental Supreme Court cases in history without filing a supporting brief. Marshall sheepishly acknowledged the oversight, and promised to file one within a week.

With that, the hearing concluded.

DeLaine and the *Briggs* plaintiffs left Charleston that afternoon, a convoy driving toward home and an uncertain future. Would their children get better classrooms as a result of all this arguing, or simply be sent to white schools? They were unaccustomed to change, but knew they had to prepare for something.

Most of the African Americans who filed out of the federal courthouse that day were optimistic. Marshall had delivered. He spoke the truth, laid out a strong case with irrefutable facts, and they couldn't imagine the judges saw it any other way.

But Waring knew it had gone exactly as he predicted. Parker was the swing vote, and he'd made it clear he wouldn't cast that vote against *Plessy*. No one else would realize that for a month. For the moment, the hundreds of people scattering into another hot Charleston afternoon only knew their fate was in the hands of three judges, and one of them was the federal government's patron saint of civil rights, Waties Waring.

EXIT STRATEGY

The three judges met in Waring's chambers shortly after *Briggs v. Elliott* adjourned. And before the last stragglers wandered out of the court-house, they had reached the inevitable conclusion.

All three had made up their minds before opening statements, and they weren't budging. "It was a long talk, but hardly much discussion," Waring later recalled.

Judge Timmerman was, in Waring's opinion, a rigid segregationist and staunch advocate of states' rights. He didn't air his views publicly, but his son – the lieutenant governor – was following Strom Thurmond's white supremacy playbook; it would eventually get him elected governor. Timmerman's views weren't so different, and he insisted the 14th Amendment didn't apply to education.

"The Constitution doesn't say anything about education," Timmerman said. "Education is left to the states. They can do as they please."

That was Timmerman.

Judge Parker was the linchpin. On the Fourth Circuit Court of Appeals, he'd proven himself a fair-minded judge. Twenty years earlier, he'd been denied a seat on the United States Supreme Court after losing a narrow Senate confirmation vote – in part because of comments he allegedly made about the evils of black people participating in politics. But if he held such personal views, they hadn't stopped him from affirming Waring's most controversial decisions in favor of the NAACP – the group that had derailed his appointment to the high court.

Waring considered Parker a friend, and a reasonable man with an exceptional understanding of the law. But the judge was completely unwilling to overturn the landmark Supreme Court decision that had justified segregation for more than half a century. Parker told the other judges he simply couldn't give Marshall the victory he wanted.

"We can't overrule *Plessy v. Ferguson*," Parker said.

Waring argued for a while. He said they didn't have to overturn *Plessy*, which actually was nothing more than a Louisiana railroad case that had been co-opted by Southern states to validate their Jim Crow laws. Besides, Waring said, the Supreme Court had already made the argument for *Briggs*. In both the *Sweatt* and *McLaurin* decisions, the court ruled that segregation in education was unconstitutional.

All they had to do, Waring suggested, was take the next logical step and apply that standard to primary education. But neither judge would go along.

Parker said Gov. Byrnes would equalize schools with the new sales tax revenue, and that would lead to improved schools in black communities. That was good enough for him. Waring wasn't convinced. He said Byrnes was worse than Thurmond because he was a hypocrite, and all his talk about equalization was just a ploy to sidestep integration. The three judges argued politics for a while, but never seriously debated the merits of *Briggs*. The decision was set, and Waring had lost.

Parker asked Waring to join him and Timmerman, to show a united front and give the state a unanimous decision. But he refused. Waring had waited years for this case, shaped it into a constitutional challenge and shepherded it into his courtroom. There was no way he'd sign an order he so vehemently opposed. But that wasn't just simple stubbornness; it was part of Waring's calculation. The judge knew a unanimous decision would be easier for the Supreme Court to ignore, and he had to write a dissent that would inspire the justices to overturn Parker and Timmerman's ruling.

Finally, Parker recognized he couldn't change Waring's mind. They were at a stalemate. Before the meeting broke up, Parker said he'd write a majority opinion in favor of the school district, and Timmerman agreed to sign it. Judge Waring could write a dissent.

Waring left the courthouse late that afternoon. At 61 Meeting Street, he found a houseful of waiting company – Elizabeth was entertaining guests who'd come to Charleston for the trial. She could tell he was in a bad mood the moment he walked through the door, but Waring said nothing. He spent the evening chatting amiably with Ruby Cornwell and Ted Poston, who'd covered the hearing for the New York Post. The judge played the gracious host well, but his mind was on the dissent he had to write.

It was the most important thing he'd ever do.

Three weeks passed without an announcement from the court.

"All over Charleston, the issue is the talk of the town," The State newspaper in Columbia reported. "It will be a live topic in South Carolina for many months to come." Most of those conversations were laced with uncertainty. No one doubted where Waring would fall in the case; the concern centered on Judge Parker. He'd upheld several Waring decisions over the years, and if the judge held any sway with Parker, parlor talk held, *Briggs v. Elliott* might spell the end of public education in South Carolina.

The News and Courier editors blamed state officials for that possibility, and accused Figg of bungling the defense. Tom Waring, the judge's nephew, conceded black schools were not as well-funded as white schools, but believed such an admission only fueled the continued slander of Southern white people, furthering the "ridiculous, spiteful and utterly false contention that the Southern colored people have not been well treated." The paper claimed only a small percentage of slaves had been mistreated.

In some ways, those editorials echoed the arguments that white supremacists and Klansman had made for decades – but the newspaper reflected the prevailing public sentiment of the day. The state's segregationists felt they were the victims in this case and, the longer the court withheld its ruling, the more they braced for the worst possible outcome.

Rumors of a decision began to circulate on June 20. Reporters lurking around the courthouse noted that nothing had been filed, but the clerks were busy typing something – and The Associated Press was staffing up as if it had been tipped to a coming story. The vigil continued until Saturday morning, June 23, when the court clerk announced he would have something for them in about an hour.

Parker had sent his order on Monday, again asking Waring to sign it. He was desperate for a unanimous decision, but the judge said he was "not in accord" and would soon forward his own opinion. Waring's dissent would be longer than the decree from Parker and Timmerman, and far more important. By Saturday, Waring had finished, and both the order and the dissent were distributed to the press. The Evening Post allayed Charleston's fears that afternoon with a banner headline that declared "Federal court upholds segregation."

The majority opinion, in which the court found for Clarendon County, was basically a treatise reaffirming states' rights. Although the court ordered South Carolina to provide better schools for black students, Parker said the federal government had no power to order integration – just as South Carolina officials had contended for years.

"Segregation of the races in public schools, so long as equality of rights is preserved, is a matter of legislative policy for the several states, with which the federal courts are powerless to interfere," the decision said.

Instead of ignoring *Plessy*, Parker embraced it. He claimed equal protection wasn't denied when schools were segregated, so long as black and white children had equal facilities and opportunities. Parker dismissed the precedent of *Sweatt* and *McLaurin* with the distinction that higher education was optional, while primary education was compulsory. The court, he wrote, shouldn't use its authority to abolish segregation in a state where it is required by law "if the equality demanded by the Constitution can be attained otherwise."

If South Carolina lived up to its promises of improving black schools, the court said, it could not be forced to integrate.

Gov. Byrnes declined to comment, but the NAACP had plenty to say about the decision. James Hinton disputed the notion – advanced by The Post – that the ruling was a victory for the black community because its schools would be improved. Instead, Hinton predicted the verdict would be overturned on appeal.

"We are on our way to the Supreme Court," he said.

Waring's dissent was a vicious condemnation of segregation, racism and decades of court orders deferring to "the false doctrine and patter called separate but equal." He not only refuted Parker's order, Waring attacked it.

The judge argued that the country's moral awakening did not come until long after the U.S. Constitution was written. The 13th, 14th and 15th Amendments were intended to completely wipe out the institution of slavery, he said, and to declare that "all citizens in this country should be considered as free, equal and entitled to all of the provisions of citizenship."

"If they are entitled to any rights of American citizens, they are entitled to have these rights now and not in the future," he wrote. "If a case of this magnitude can be turned aside and a court refuse to hear these basic issues by the mere device of admission that buildings, blackboards, lighting fixtures and toilet facilities are unequal but that they may be remedied by the spending of a few dollars, then indeed people in the plight in which these plaintiffs are, have no adequate remedy or forum in which to air their wrongs."

Attacking *Plessy* and the Jim Crow laws it enabled, Waring said it was foolish to base civil rights on a 19th-century railway lawsuit while ignoring recent Supreme Court decisions that had considered "education just as we are considering it here." If the states could no longer claim to provide separate-but-equal facilities in colleges, they should not be allowed to do so with primary education.

Much of Waring's argument was a meditation on – and a repudiation of – prejudice. He lampooned the claims that it was dangerous for white children to associate with blacks. If that were the case, he asked, shouldn't the state furnish a series of schools so that black children didn't have to mingle with children of one-half, one-quarter or one-eighth white ancestry? It was a not-so-subtle reference to the hypocrisy of miscegenation in his hometown.

Finally, he said white supremacists' sadistic insistence on segregation was a ridiculous notion with no logical conclusion.

"The courts of this land have stricken down discrimination in higher education and have declared unequivocally that segregation is not equality," Waring wrote. "But those decisions have pruned away only the noxious fruits. Here in this case, we are asked to strike at its very root. Or rather, to change the metaphor, we are asked to strike at the cause of the infection and not merely at the symptoms of disease. And if the courts of this land are to render justice under the laws without fear or favor, justice for all men and all kinds of men, the time to do it is now, and the place is in elementary schools where our future citizens learn their first lesson to respect the dignity of the individual in a democracy."

Long-winded and venomous, Waring had allowed years of frustration to spill out on the page. But the line that made his dissent famous was elegantly succinct: "If segregation is wrong, then the place to stop it is in the first grade and not in graduate colleges. Segregation is per se inequality."

Waring's dissent was an immediate hit in civil rights circles. The clerk's office was inundated with requests for copies, and mailed out dozens in the weeks after its release. Thurgood Marshall handed out even more at the NAACP national convention the next week. Waring had delivered a resounding argument against segregation, Marshall said, and provided the U.S. Supreme Court with a legal road map to overturn *Briggs* – and integrate public schools across the nation.

The press was less than kind in its assessment. The Augusta Chronicle said Waring rambled on like an attorney arguing for the special interests of a client. The Columbia Record said the judge's "anti-white prejudice" should've forced his disqualification from the case. And the Anderson Independent said Waring had done black citizens no favors, as "there are not enough bayonets in the land to enforce the mixing of races in the common schools of South Carolina."

In The News and Courier, Tom Waring claimed the dissent went so far it endangered the welfare of children and denied Americans' their rights. But the paper published the entire document so readers could decide for themselves. On the editorial page, Waring focused less on his uncle's opinion, choosing to praise Parker and Timmerman's ruling as a "victory for American rights."

"Judge Waring's dissent in effect is a sociological treatise on race doctrines," his nephew wrote. "The majority opinion is a legal pronouncement with much wider significance."

It was difficult to see, Tom Waring wrote, how the wise decision of Parker and Timmerman could be overturned.

The Warings left Charleston in July for an extended vacation. The judge had cleared his docket and, with no commitment to hold court in California that year, took the rest of the summer off. The couple stopped briefly in New York before moving on to Rhode Island, where they settled into the Weekapaug Inn near Westerly for six weeks. Waring passed much of his time lobbying NAACP officials to file an aggressive appeal of *Briggs*.

There was no doubt there'd be an appeal; the group had announced as much at its national convention in Atlanta. But internally, NAACP officials weren't sure what form their argument should take. Waring insisted they must be "militant" to force the Supreme Court to take notice, but some suggested they hold off until the final order was issued.

Thurgood Marshall realized an appeal was pointless unless he could provoke the court into ruling on the constitutional question of segregation. Parker side-stepped the issue, just as the Supreme Court had done the prior year. Marshall had little confidence he could prompt a different outcome, and struggled with his argument. From Rhode Island, Waring not only encouraged Marshall – he told him what to write.

On July 26, Waring received a copy of Marshall's appeal. The judge said it made all the necessary points; he didn't see how the Supreme Court could fail to acknowledge that it was a frontal assault on segregation. But the appeal was too long and too rough and, Waring thought, not forceful enough. So he made some suggestions, told Marshall to make the changes and re-file quickly – before the final order in *Briggs* was released.

"The really important matter is to start now in the preparation of a brief that will cover the case adequately and block all efforts by the opposition to induce the Supreme Court to evade this basic question," Waring wrote. "May I suggest the use of the phrase 'segregation is per se inequality.' I have suggested starting work on the brief at this time since in my own work I find it easier to write arguments when the matters are fresh and that they grow stale when delayed. … We do not want this brief to be a rush job."

Waring wasn't finished shepherding this case. Behind Marshall's back, he lobbied Walter White and other NAACP attorneys to ensure the appeal was aggressive. And when he and Elizabeth returned to New York in September, the judge met with Marshall to go over his arguments for more forceful language yet again. At the time, no one knew exactly how much Waring had bet on the success of *Briggs*. They didn't realize it was his final civil rights case.

The couple stayed in New York for weeks. To his friends, it seemed the judge was simply delaying his return to Charleston as long as possible – and they couldn't blame him. But he had another reason to linger in the city, one that he didn't share with many people. He was apartment hunting.

Waring spent much of the summer thinking about his future. He celebrated his 71st birthday in Rhode Island and, more importantly, was only six months away from his 10th anniversary on the bench. That milestone would allow him to retire with full pay, and he didn't see any reason to remain in Charleston after that. He'd gotten the case he always wanted, and it was working its way through the courts. If Waring could get the NAACP to file its appeal, and put the issue of segregation on the U.S. Supreme Court docket, his work would be done.

"So I figured that my usefulness there was about over," Waring recalled. "I had taken a position, a very strong black and white position, in the Clarendon school case. The Supreme Court of the United States hadn't faced that issue, and they had to say whether racial segregation was legal or illegal, constitutional or unconstitutional. If they said it was unconstitutional, then the wall was broken, and it was a matter of implementation and brushing up. I thought that had better be done by someone else who was not as objectionable to the people of the district as I was."

Retirement was a gamble, he knew. If the Supreme Court refused to hear *Briggs*, Waring would no longer have the authority or power to keep promoting civil rights. But he realized that if this court wasn't inclined to overturn segregation, it would be "utterly hopeless" for at least 10 or 20 years. If this case failed, Waring believed the fight for equality and democracy would have to wait another generation.

"I would not have left until I had a chance to decide a flat segregation case," Waring said. "I had decided that case, and I thought this was in the laps of the justices of the Supreme Court and that I couldn't do any more about it, either one way or the other."

As the judge and Elizabeth passed their days on the rocky coast of Rhode Island, they talked about getting out. There wasn't much left for him in Charleston. For four years, they'd suffered nothing but abuse. Waring knew he'd done some good work, but his final play had been set in motion and it was time to go. They decided to retire in a more accommodating, welcoming city.

By fall, friends in New York would be passing along real estate tips.

No one had been more impressed with Waring's dissent than the Rev. Joseph A. DeLaine. As a result of the *Briggs* lawsuit, the pastor had come to know and admire the judge, even spent time at his house. Waring's words spoke to De-Laine, articulated everything that he thought was wrong with the country. Of course, he was deeply disappointed in the court's decision, but still held hope the Supreme Court would intervene. Waring had given him that hope.

DeLaine had started a movement. The NAACP took the Clarendon County model and had applied it to a Kansas case they hoped would further advance the cause. That was the best hope for Harry Briggs and all the other plaintiffs, he knew. Years earlier, he'd simply wanted bus service for black students; now DeLaine knew that wasn't the answer. Waring's dissent was the answer. Integration was the answer.

The preacher had no faith in the state's tax scheme – he'd heard it all before. He was appalled by the duplicity of Clarendon County school officials and their enablers in state government. He couldn't believe the court let them get away with vague promises to improve all those rundown schools.

"To me, granting the county six months to see if they are going to make progress is like granting a maid six months to see if she is going to give a baby milk she hasn't been giving all along," DeLaine said. "Is it right for a judge to give a criminal time to continue his crimes?"

After the lawsuit, most of the *Briggs* plaintiffs went back to their lives. They may have had some hope, like DeLaine, but had seen too much in their time to be truly optimistic. There was no news from the preacher to encourage them; he was in Lake City dealing with his own problems.

The former Scott's Branch principal had gone back to court, asking a judge to declare all of DeLaine's property transfers illegal – which was the only way to get any money out of his slander judgment. Even though the damages had been cut in half on appeal, DeLaine still couldn't pay. The court threw out the principal's request, declaring all of DeLaine's property transfers proper and legal.

But the principal would collect soon enough.

Late on the night of Oct. 10, DeLaine got the call – his home in Summerton was on fire. Although he and his family had moved to Lake City, they hadn't sold their old house across the street from Scott's Branch. The Summerton Fire Department rushed to the scene, where firefighters stood by and watched the house burn to the ground. They later claimed it sat 60 feet outside their jurisdiction, so there was nothing they could do.

Although the house was no longer in DeLaine's name, the insurance was. When he'd transferred the title to his friend, DeLaine tried to reassign the insurance as well, but the company wouldn't allow it. So when the policy paid off DeLaine for the loss of his house, the court seized the money to cover the jury award in the slander lawsuit.

Investigators later declared it arson and, for months, Clarendon County residents tried to guess who'd set the fire. Was it DeLaine's legal foes, or perhaps the Klan retaliating for *Briggs v. Elliott*? Later, some people claimed a town drunk – who the pastor had helped on occasion – burned it out of spite. In the end, it didn't matter which story was true. The outcome was the same. DeLaine was nearly ruined.

And South Carolina was not through with him yet.

Waring opened the October session of Charleston district court the same week DeLaine's house burned down.

His docket was crowded with bootleggers, forgers and men vainly trying to skirt Internal Revenue laws. The most interesting case of the term involved a turf dispute between a railroad and a group of local taxi drivers. The Atlantic Coast Rail Line had contracted with one cab company to serve its station in the north area, but taxis from several different companies kept absconding with fares. Waring listened for a while, then threw the whole lot out of his courtroom.

It was a quiet fall for Waring. He no longer had marshals to guard him, and his phone seldom rang. The most harassment he got was from the newspapers, which ran one-year anniversary stories about the attack on his home and the

FBI's "ongoing investigation." The stories appeared to be little more than efforts to needle the judge, but neither Waring nor the FBI had any comment.

The aftershock of the Clarendon County case still reverberated through the state. In a speech to the South Carolina Association of School Trustees, Gov. Byrnes again threatened to abandon public education if the U.S. Supreme Court overturned *Briggs v. Elliott*. But he said even if integration forces the public schools out of business, the sales tax plan to spend $75 million was still worthwhile. He was still promoting his tax increase.

"Whether we have public or private schools, we are going to need school buildings – we are going to educate our children," Byrnes said.

South Carolina officials were worried about the *Briggs* appeal, and sent mixed signals to the Supreme Court. Not long after the governor's threat to shut down schools, Clarendon County officials reported to the court that the district had dedicated $552,682 to improving black schools. By the beginning of the 1952-53 school year, district officials claimed, all its black students would be in modern buildings "certainly to be equal" of any white schools.

Judges Parker and Timmerman approved the Clarendon County report on Jan. 8, 1952, before forwarding it to Washington. Judge Waring refused to sign the report, instead scribbling a terse note at the bottom to remind the Supreme Court it had two decisions to read.

"In my opinion, the report and this decree have no place in this case and therefore I do not join therein."

Two weeks later, Waring opened the January term of court. He dismissed all the criminal cases – an assault, yet another Internal Revenue violation – in a single day. If the staff noticed he was particularly short, they said nothing of it. Waring promised to open civil court the following week and quickly left the courthouse.

On Monday, Jan. 28, newspaper reporters who showed up to chronicle the civil proceedings were instead handed copies of a letter penned by Judge Waring. It was addressed to President Truman.

"My dear Mr. President, I have decided to retire from regular active service as United States District Judge for the Eastern District of South Carolina to take effect at the close of business on Feb. 15, 1952."

The reporters scrambled out of the courthouse to make the afternoon edition. For Charleston, this was the most significant news in years. The Evening Post rushed a story into print: "Judge Waring to quit bench here Feb. 15."

NEW YORK, NEW YORK

Only the Supreme Court had the temerity to overshadow Waring's resignation.

The same day the judge announced his retirement, the United States Supreme Court vacated the ruling in *Briggs v. Elliott*, sending the case back to district court for another hearing. The news was met with confusion and fear across South Carolina; most often, an order to vacate a previous ruling meant it had been overturned. For a tense few hours, many people were afraid the federal court had just ordered the integration of public schools.

Gov. Byrnes, a former U.S. Supreme Court justice, tried to calm the masses – and newspaper editors – by attempting to translate the convoluted order. "The action of the Supreme Court apparently sustained the position of Clarendon County that the appeal was premature," Byrnes said. But at first, even the governor wasn't quite sure what had happened.

The NAACP had filed its appeal of *Briggs* long before Judge Parker forwarded the state's December progress report to the Supreme Court. South Carolina attorneys immediately asked the court to dismiss the appeal, arguing it was premature – there hadn't been enough time to make improvements to schools. The answer didn't make anyone entirely happy. The justices only said they wouldn't consider an appeal until the district court was satisfied the state had complied with the original order.

The Supreme Court was going to hold South Carolina to its promise to improve black schools.

"Prior to our consideration of the question raised on this appeal, we should have the benefit of the views of the District Court upon the additional facts brought to the attention of that court in the report which it ordered," the Supreme Court opinion read.

The threat of forced integration was not off the table just yet. In fact, Justices Hugo Black and William Douglas had dissented from the decision, arguing the state's report was irrelevant to the "constitutional questions" raised by the NAACP's appeal. It appeared at least two members of the high court were willing to consider Judge Waring's argument. Thurgood Marshall pointed out that *Briggs* was still on the Supreme Court's desk. It was the only victory he could claim.

"The question of the validity of segregation is still the basic issue in the case," Marshall told reporters.

Briggs was only the first salvo in the NAACP's war on segregation. Marshall and his lieutenants had spread out across the country, filing one lawsuit after another to challenge separate-but-equal policy in public schools. On Feb. 28, 1951, two months after the final version of *Briggs* was scheduled for a hearing, Robert Carter – who'd handled much of the work in *Sweatt v. Painter* – filed *Brown v. Board of Education* against the school district in Topeka, Kansas. And on his way to Charleston for the *Briggs* hearing, NAACP attorney Spottswood Robinson stopped in Virginia to deliver the lawsuit *Davis v. School Board of Prince Edward County*.

So far, the civil rights organization had little to show for its efforts. In August, the three-judge panel that heard *Brown* found "no willful, intentional or substantial discrimination" in Topeka schools. *Davis* was set to be heard in late February 1952, and cases in Delaware and the District of Columbia were still percolating through the system. The only progress Marshall could claim was Waring's spirited dissent. And now the NAACP's sole sympathetic ear was stepping down from the bench.

South Carolina officials were overjoyed and relieved by Waring's retirement, but reticent to attack him on the way out the door. Most, including Sen. Olin Johnston, simply declined to comment. The closest thing to a kind remark came from congressman Dorn, who said the judge had made a "wise decision." Sen. Burnet Maybank told The News and Courier he had no comment, but admitted "I am not going to say I regret it."

Mendel Rivers had the most unintentionally hilarious reaction. The Charleston congressman rushed to the White House and asked President Truman to nominate him for the open judgeship. He even delivered letters from various officials endorsing his candidacy. The News and Courier reported that Truman was "most pleasant, surprisingly so" and "showed no resentment" for all the congressman's previous, and numerous, denunciations of the administration – or his support for Thurmond in the 1948 presidential election.

For all those reasons, most people realized the president was only being polite when he promised to consider Rivers. But Walter White wasn't willing to take that chance. He sent Truman a vicious telegram outlining the NAACP's sincere hope that the White House wouldn't nominate a man who "has persistently and blatantly advocated treatment of American Negroes but little different from that of the days of slavery."

"Congressman Rivers has been one of the most vindictive opponents of constitutional rights for minorities and particularly of fifteen million American Negroes," White said. "We could conceive of no person less fit than he to administer even-handed justice and to uphold obedience to the federal constitution."

Unsurprisingly, Rivers did not get the job.

The Charleston newspapers, at least initially, were diplomatic about the judge's retirement. The Evening Post published a wire story in which President Truman called Waring "a great judge" and The News and Courier – at Septima Clark's urging – reprinted a glowing pro-Waring editorial from The New York Times. The Northern paper praised Waring's progressive views and criticized Charleston for his ostracism.

"Or, to put the situation more accurately, many of his old friends ostracized themselves out of his excellent company," The Times opined. "During his session on the bench, Judge Waring once said he 'gradually acquired a passion for justice.' Surely he cannot miss the society of those who regard such a passion as unworthy."

For two weeks, Charleston was abuzz with speculation about the judge's plans. He had said little of his pending departure, and continued to hold court and work a regular schedule. On Feb. 15, reporters roamed the courthouse hoping to cover his retirement party. But they could find no fete for the judge. The clerks simply said, "No comment." Privately, most of Waring's bailiffs and secretaries sent notes wishing the judge well and thanking him for being so kind – and would correspond regularly with him in retirement. But they didn't share that with the newspapers.

Anyone who knew the Warings realized they had no intention of staying in Charleston.

The couple was miserable in the city, which is why they took regular – and often extended – vacations. Their small circle of friends couldn't outweigh the sheer discomfort of icy glares whenever they went out to dinner or took in a movie at the Riviera. It had all become too much, as Elizabeth admitted to Septima Clark. One afternoon, Clark sat in a rocking chair in the couple's bedroom as Elizabeth folded socks and rambled on about their new apartment in New York City.

The Warings' plans wouldn't remain secret for long. The Evening Post announced that the judge and his wife were leaving Charleston after a reporter discovered paperwork that detailed the sale of 61 Meeting Street. An employee of the Atlantic Coast Line Railroad bought the house for $20,000, and it briefly made him a local celebrity.

Samuel Lewis eventually explained how he'd lucked into the deal. The same day Waring announced his retirement, Elizabeth had called the railroad to book their trip to New York City. When she called back later to change their travel dates, Lewis got up the nerve to ask what they planned to do with their house. Elizabeth said it would be sold, and Lewis asked for a price.

"How much will you give?" Elizabeth replied.

Lewis and his wife rushed to 61 Meeting Street that afternoon. The judge refused offers of $16,000 and $18,000 before finally agreeing to take $20,000. Lewis asked for an hour to think it over and, in the meantime, Waring got calls from people offering more than $25,000. But the judge stuck to his verbal agreement, and Lewis got the house.

Waring had no desire to haggle over a few thousand dollars, or do anything that might keep him in South Carolina a day longer. Judge Parker had invited him to sit for the new *Briggs* hearing, and Waring considered it, but politely declined the day before his retirement.

It would be a waste of time, he knew. Nothing Waring could do would make any difference. His dissent had been filed with the Supreme Court, and that had been the plan all along. It was probably better if his name was no longer attached to the case, distracting everyone from the real issue.

On Feb. 18, photographers staked out 61 Meeting Street, but couldn't get a picture of the Warings' exodus. Instead, the papers were forced to settle for photos of errant furniture temporarily abandoned on the sidewalk. Some of the couple's belongings would be shipped to their new home, the rest either sold, donated or discarded. The judge and Elizabeth slipped out unnoticed, and that evening boarded the Florida Special bound for New York City.

In a farewell editorial, The Evening Post denied that discrimination, or his rulings against the Democratic Party, played any role in Waring's widespread unpopularity in Charleston. Rather, the paper argued it all stemmed from his "abuse" of Southern people. "What was indignantly resented, and rightfully so, was the gratuitous insults which Judge Waring voiced in handing down his decision declaring the white Democratic primary unconstitutional."

The paper pilloried Waring for reaping prestigious awards, financial benefits – and a full pension – as a direct result of his lifelong association with a political party he had called "un-American." The Charleston papers would repeat that argument countless times over the next two decades. Waring had profited from his position in the community, and the Democratic Party, and had the audacity to bite the hand that fed him. That, the newspapers opined, was his unforgivable sin.

Of course, those editorials ignored the incessant attacks the judge and his wife endured for five years – and the inherent racism behind the obscene phone calls and threatening letters the couple received only after Waring had affirmed the simple constitutional right of black people to vote in an election.

Waring responded only indirectly, but viciously. Upon his arrival in New York, the retired judge told a waiting UPI reporter that he'd quit the bench in frustration because he'd been unable to do much about all the human injustice he saw. He vowed to continue his efforts to "pierce the iron curtain of prejudice which surrounds the South," and help teach people how to be good Americans. He could not have been more condescending.

"For the little people, I have pity and compassion," Waring said. And for the politicians who stoke prejudice for their own ends, "I have utter contempt."

The Warings sublet apartment 7-C at 952 Fifth Avenue, an unassuming building with a particularly tony Upper East Side address. The apartment overlooked Central Park and sat just five blocks south of the Metropolitan Museum of Art. It was a comfortable and convenient home in a city the judge and Elizabeth loved. They attended Broadway shows, dined out frequently and for once had no shortage of invitations.

At parties, they mingled with Eleanor Roosevelt and Ralph Bunche. When they weren't traveling – the judge gave a speech at Harvard, made an appearance at an NAACP meeting in Philadelphia – they sometimes had dinner with Anne and Stanley. But most often, the Warings passed their time with Walter White and Poppy Cannon. The two couples had common interests and shared experiences binding them.

The Warings occasionally spent the weekend at White's Breakneck Hill home in West Redding, Connecticut – a short train ride outside the city. The judge was more relaxed after leaving the bench, and Charleston, but he could still turn even the most casual conversation to civil rights. At breakfast one morning, the NAACP leader began to cough uncontrollably while smoking a cigarette, eventually excusing himself from the table. When he returned, Waring jokingly admonished White for helping the segregationists' cause.

"Walter, whenever you light a cigarette you ought to say, 'Here's to you, Jimmy Byrnes. Here's to you, Strom Thurmond. Here's to you, Senator (James) Eastland," Waring said. "For let me tell you, that when you die, they're going to declare a national holiday. They'll be so glad to get you off their necks."

White never smoked again, and Cannon credited the judge for that.

Those weekends in the country were rare for the Warings that first year in the city; personal appearances kept the judge traveling. In May he attended the annual conference of the African Methodist Episcopal Church in Chicago, where he received an award for his "most significant contribution to democracy." He urged the church to insist both political parties adopt anti-discrimination planks in their 1952 platform, including the full and equal rights of black citizens in employment, voting, the armed services and government contracts.

Waring did his part for the cause. He wrote letters promoting civil rights to a number of public officials, including Illinois Gov. Adlai Stevenson – a man some Democrats were trying to recruit as a presidential nominee. Rumors had it Truman would not run for re-election. By the time the judge had another chance to meet the president, it was no longer just gossip.

Howard University awarded Waring an honorary doctorate in law that June. The judge and Elizabeth took the train to Washington, stayed in Baldwin Hall on campus and shared the stage with President Truman – who delivered the commencement address. This afforded Waring another opportunity to lobby for his vision of a national civil rights act.

A few days before the commencement, Waring had mailed the president his proposed platform for the Democratic Party's 1952 national convention – and begged him not to compromise with the Dixiecrats. He argued the party shouldn't just adopt Truman's 1948 civil rights program, it should go beyond it. As Waring had demonstrated regularly, he believed diplomacy was overrated.

"I can tell you that no successful compromise or alliance can be made with the Dixiecrat leaders, who, while posing as Russellites, are really led by Byrnes and Talmadge and others of like character where talk of support of our party is merely a desire to retain their own selfish power through the un-American doctrine of White Supremacy," Waring wrote. "I am aware that there are some, even in high places, in our party who are weak-kneed and wish to appease and make terms with the dissident Dixiecrat wing; but I am sure that you will as usual come forward to demand that we adhere to our promises and march forward again to victory as the party which stands for true Americanism by eliminating this cancer of racial persecution which infects parts of our body politic."

The president, who'd made it clear he was retiring, politely ignored the letter. He had no desire to engage the cantankerous former judge. Waring was becoming even more strident in his politics, and he saw the sin of gradualism everywhere. Even the NAACP wasn't safe from his wrath. The group asked the judge to speak at its annual conference that summer in Oklahoma City, and was shocked when he turned down the invitation in a vicious letter to Chairman Louis T. Wright.

"If I were to appear, I would have to be frank in stating my views relative to alliances and commitments of the staff to one political party," Waring said, "and also I would criticize the lack of activities of the legal staff in attacking what I consider the basic evil, namely segregation."

The letter leaked to the press in July, forcing Wright to deny the NAACP was a partisan organization. He praised the judge for his work and asked that they present a united front in the fight for equality. But aside from his friendship with White, Waring was becoming increasingly estranged from the group. The NAACP had planned a banquet in the judge's honor shortly after he moved to New York, but Waring believed it was just a ploy to raise money and refused to cooperate.

Some of the judge's frustration likely stemmed from his growing sense of helplessness. No longer on the bench, he had no power to direct cases and no influence over lawyers. In his first five months in New York, he spoke to Thurgood Marshall only once. Waring was out of the loop and, in truth, his criticism of the NAACP's lackadaisical progress was too harsh. Marshall and his legal staff actually were working overtime on a growing number of civil rights cases.

But the courts were not cooperating.

In March 1952, U.S. District Judge Armistead Mason Dobie of Norfolk joined Parker and Timmerman for the rehearing of *Briggs*. Dobie was a surprising choice to replace Waring on the panel. Along with Parker, Dobie had ruled in favor of *Alston* – the teacher-pay case – on the Fourth Circuit Court of Appeals. That raised concerns with some South Carolina officials, but they were worried for nothing. This time the court delivered a unanimous decision in favor of Clarendon County and the state.

It took little more than a week for the opinion to come out.

That same month, federal judges in Virginia ruled against the *Davis* plaintiffs, declaring the state's "separate but equal" public schools did not run afoul of the constitution. But in April, state courts in Delaware decided that black plaintiffs were entitled to attend white schools. The case was quickly appealed to the U.S. Supreme Court.

There were five school segregation lawsuits in litigation around the country, and all but one of them was gaining steam. The case out of D.C. was still eight months away from a hearing. *Briggs* would reach the Supreme Court before that. In June, the court announced the South Carolina appeal was on the docket for October – around the same time arguments in the Kansas case, *Brown v. Board of Education*, were scheduled to be heard.

On Oct. 8, just days before the *Brown* and *Briggs* hearings, the Supreme Court postponed both cases. It looked like little more than another setback for the Clarendon County plaintiffs, but a few weeks later the court said it would hear all five pending school segregation lawsuits at once, in December, under the title *Brown v. Board of Education*.

Technically, *Briggs* was the first of the five cases and controversy lingered over the naming decision for decades. The court claimed that when the Clarendon case was sent back to South Carolina, *Brown* jumped ahead of it on the docket. But some people suspected politics played a role. The justices considered this a national issue, and didn't want to look as if they were singling out the South. But others believed the court simply wanted to minimize the role of *Briggs* because of Waring's involvement. Later, the judge brushed aside the controversy.

"Now, our case should have been the number one case. As it was, it was number two, because the Kansas case was docketed ahead of this case," Waring said. "The Kansas courts took a rather broad view but said they thought they were bound by *Plessy v. Ferguson*. In effect, they said if they were free they would overrule it."

And that may have been the message the court wanted to convey. Because Waring, Marshall and everyone at the NAACP feared Chief Justice Fred Vinson would never allow *Plessy* to be overturned.

THE VICTORY PARTY

The New Republic explained Waring's mood, and increasingly combative attitude, better than even he could.

In a piece welcoming this "distinguished new resident" to New York City, the magazine argued that Waring had not run away from the South – he'd moved North to wage an even more effective crusade for equality. Now, the New Republic said, he can speak "unhampered by reservations forced on him by cases pending before his court." In other words, this is what a lack of judicial restraint looks like. But it was more than that; Waring was continuing to evolve – and he was worried.

Waring admitted to the magazine he hadn't thought much about race relations growing up. He'd been inclined to adopt the facile attitude of most Charlestonians, and Southerners, that black people only wanted to be liked by white people. No one in his hometown wanted to get mired in questions of legal rights; that was unseemly and, to white people, unnecessary. But the view from the bench changed his perspective.

"There he suddenly came up against a very different figure of the Negro from smiling old Uncle Tom, bowing and scraping to the white folks," The New Republic said. "He found Negroes burning with a sense of injustice, even though they were usually afraid to indicate it. He saw court procedures in which they were systematically excluded from juries, and in which, just as systematically, any Negro presumptuous enough to bring into court a case against a white man was almost sure to lose it. He came to the conviction that there is no difference in principle between treatment of the Negro in the South and treatment of the Jew in Nazi Germany."

As controversial as the comparison was, it summed up the depth of Waring's outrage. Ten years on the bench had exposed him to the litany of ways black citizens were deprived of their rights, and the injustice infuriated him. Now, he was also antsy and powerless. His plan was in motion, but he no longer had any control over it. The Supreme Court showdown he'd set in motion would mean the difference between continued oppression and a dramatic change in the American landscape. And all he could do was wait to see what came of *Brown v. Board of Education.*

The Supreme Court hearing opened on Dec. 9 and, in many ways, played out like a repeat of *Briggs v. Elliott.* Thurgood Marshall again relied on the testimony of social scientists, but this time South Carolina was better prepared. Gov. Byrnes had hired New York attorney John W. Davis to represent the state. A former Democratic presidential candidate, Davis was considered one of the best constitutional lawyers in the country – and he picked apart the NAACP strategy before the session was gaveled to order.

In a brief filed prior to the hearing, Davis argued that since black children were psychologically conditioned to recognize racial issues at an early age, perhaps it was better for them to not attend school with "children whom he regards as superior." He was attempting to use the NAACP's own argument against its case, and the ploy might have worked if Marshall hadn't gotten support from an unlikely ally – the Justice Department.

Philip Elman, an attorney in the solicitor general's office, persuaded his bosses to weigh in on *Brown.* In the book *Simple Justice,* journalist Richard Kluger said Elman's 32-page brief was more influential than any other argument filed in the five desegregation cases. Elman wrote "the proposition that all men are created equal was no mere rhetoric." He reminded the court that justice was colorblind, or it was supposed to be.

For three days, Marshall and his co-counsel debated social science and constitutional law with Davis and an army of attorneys from Kansas, Virginia, Delaware and the District of Columbia. Many of the *Briggs* witnesses made an appearance, and neither their testimony nor their conclusions had changed in 18 months. But when it was over, Davis walked out of the courtroom and declared victory. "I think we've got it won, five-to-four – or maybe six-to-three."

Rev. DeLaine sat through the hearing with a coveted courtroom pass from Marshall. He'd spent that time trying to gauge the justices' reaction to the testimony, and had come to the same conclusion as Davis. Some members of the court were clearly moved by what they heard, but the chief justice seemed unfazed. "I was afraid of Vinson's face," DeLaine said.

The Supreme Court met privately the following weekend to discuss the case, and DeLaine had been correct; Vinson wasn't inclined to overturn segregation. Several justices worried about the backlash to an NAACP victory. South Carolina would almost certainly abolish public education, a few justices fretted, and several Southern states might do the same. But other justices argued that classifying American citizens based on race was unreasonable.

The Supreme Court debated the case on and off throughout the winter, and it appeared the vote could go either way. But soon, it became apparent the court was simply stuck. Finally, the justices announced they would re-hear arguments in *Brown v. Board* the following fall.

Another hearing was only marginally better than an outright loss for the NAACP. A second round of arguments would cost thousands of dollars, and the organization's modest resources were no match for the states fighting to maintain the status quo. Shortly after the court's announcement, Waring allowed the group to put his name on a fundraising letter alongside Thurgood Marshall's. The letter urged donors to contribute up to $15,000 to the NAACP legal defense fund.

A year earlier, Waring had complained the NAACP proposed a banquet in his honor solely to turn a profit; now, he was helping them solicit donations. His change of heart reflected the judge's renewed faith that the plan might work. Marshall had handled the case so well the Supreme Court couldn't dismiss *Brown* outright. Perhaps there was hope, an end to segregation in sight. It invigorated him. Soon, Waring was once again reviewing NAACP legal briefs and offering Marshall advice and encouragement.

"I feel confident that you are going to be successful in this fight which will, in my opinion, be the turning point in our struggle to achieve human equality in America," Waring told Marshall in one letter.

But first, there was another delay. *Brown v. Board* was on the Supreme Court's October 1953 docket, but the case was postponed when Chief Justice Fred Vinson died of a heart attack on Sept. 8. Waring admitted Vinson's death changed the dynamics of the case, but later said he believed the chief justice – a man he admittedly liked – would have ultimately cast his vote for progress, however reluctantly.

President Eisenhower, elected in a landslide less than a year earlier, took only three weeks to find a replacement for Vinson. He chose California Gov. Earl Warren, a former vice presidential candidate and state attorney general. Eisenhower wanted a chief justice with a strong background in law enforcement who could also appeal to the Republican Party's liberal wing. Installed as a recess appointment, Warren immediately pushed the *Brown* hearing back to December – a full year after it had first been heard by the Supreme Court.

On Monday morning, Dec. 7, 1953, Rev. DeLaine stood in line outside One First Street waiting for the doors of the Supreme Court Building to open. Once again, Marshall had secured a courtroom pass for him; after all, he'd started all this. It was below freezing in Washington that day, but DeLaine felt good. When a reporter spotted him in the crowd and asked for a comment, the pastor said he was optimistic.

"There were times when I thought I would go out of my mind because of this case," DeLaine said. "If I had to do it again, I would. I feel that it was worth it. I have a feeling that the Supreme Court is going to end segregation."

The second hearing for *Brown v. Board of Education*, like the first, would take three days. Both sides hauled in the same witnesses and repeated their previous arguments, honed and perfected from a year of practice. The greatest difference this time was the chief justice.

John Davis, who returned to represent South Carolina, modified his argument to undermine the NAACP's case, which rested on the 14th Amendment. He said the question was not whether the amendment granted equal protection to black citizens; he conceded that it did. But Davis questioned whether segregation denied them those rights. And he cautioned the justices that integration would be controversial in Clarendon County's school district, which had significantly more black students than white.

With a maximum of 30 students per class, Davis pointed out, that would throw three white students into a classroom with 27 black children.

"Would white children be prevented from getting a distorted idea of racial relations if they sat with 27 Negro children?" Davis asked the court. "You say that is racism. Well, it is not racism. Recognize that for 60 centuries and more, humanity has been discussing questions of race and race tension, not racism."

Davis was eloquent and slick, but he made the same basic states' rights argument South Carolina had employed from the start. He told the United States Supreme Court, "Your honors do not sit, and cannot sit, as a glorified board of education for the state of South Carolina – or any other state."

Later, even Warren joked about Davis' emotional argument, but his clients were satisfied he had made a sound legal, constitutional case. At the very least, he hadn't faltered once – as the NAACP did initially.

Marshall rambled uncharacteristically during his opening statement, but gained momentum as the hearing went on. By his closing argument, Marshall was brilliant and scathing, displaying his own commanding knowledge of constitutional law. He recounted the injustices suffered by African Americans since Reconstruction, and said the South's only justification for segregation was that "they got together and decided it is best for the races to be separated." His undisguised disdain rivaled even Waring's.

"I got the feeling on hearing the discussion yesterday that when you put a white child in a school with a whole lot of colored children, the child would fall apart or something," Marshall said. "Everybody knows that is not true. Those same kids in Virginia and South Carolina – and I have seen them do it – they play in the streets together, they play on their farms together, they go down the road together, they separate to go to school, then come out of school and play ball together.

"There is some magic to it," Marshall said. "You can have them voting together, you can have them not restricted because of law in the houses they live in. You can have them going to the same state university and the same college, but if they go to elementary and high school, the world will fall apart."

In one of the most important court cases in U.S. history, Marshall finished with an impressive performance – as well as the final word. The *Brown v. Board of Education* hearing concluded on the afternoon of Dec. 9. South Carolina's attorneys left the courtroom reasonably certain they had won, and DeLaine walked out of the building as optimistic as he'd been three days earlier. The pastor would have to wait months to find out if his confidence was warranted, and his prediction correct.

The Supreme Court was quiet throughout the winter, but Waring filled the silence – and raised the ire of South Carolina officials nervously awaiting a verdict. On Feb. 28, 1954, he told a New York City church group about the injustice Rev. DeLaine had suffered in his fight against segregation. Discrimination was an infection, Waring said, but it could be fought. DeLaine had proven as much with his courageous crusade for the rights of black school children in Clarendon County.

"As a result, Mr. DeLaine's house was burned, the county fire department failed to fight the blaze, saying it was outside its area, and an insurance company refused to pay for the damages," Waring said. "An ex-superintendent of schools sued Mr. DeLaine for libel and won a favorable verdict from an all-white jury."

The News and Courier challenged Waring's account, and erroneous depiction of the insurance settlement, and Clarendon County officials helped the newspaper by twisting the facts. A lawyer for the school district told reporters DeLaine wasn't listed as a plaintiff in any of the segregation lawsuits. And Summerton schools Superintendent H.B. Betchman told the paper, "Preacher DeLaine served here until he was transferred – he is a Methodist preacher – to a church in the Lake City area, or so I understand, about two years ago. If he ever had any part in the segregation suits, I never heard about it."

Clarendon County officials had taken his job and his home; now they were trying to deny DeLaine his legacy.

The day after Waring's spirited defense of DeLaine, the United States Senate took a break from its regularly scheduled communist hunting and confirmed Earl Warren as Chief Justice of the United States Supreme Court. With his job secured, Warren went to work on the school case. Waring sent him a congratulatory note, perhaps a bit of lobbying the new chief justice didn't need.

From the start, Warren believed *Brown v. Board of Education* was an easy decision. Of course, he thought, segregation violated the constitutional rights of black citizens. He told the other justices that only someone who believed blacks were inferior to whites could support segregation. So he drafted an order to that effect and shopped it around for weeks. He wanted a unanimous decision, something no one could question.

Warren was a politician, a master at persuasion and diplomacy, and he used those skills to bend the Supreme Court to his will. For two months, Warren listened to his colleagues' perspectives, amended and softened his opinion until, finally, he won over the last "no" vote – Justice Stanley Reed.

One Monday morning in May, Elizabeth Waring got out of bed and found her husband furiously scribbling notes at the table in their apartment. His concentration was so complete that he didn't notice her until she spoke.

"What are you doing?" she asked.

"You know," he said, "I don't believe the Supreme Court's going to decide that school case today, but it might. And it just occurred to me that some newspaper's going to call me up and ask for a comment, and I just thought I'd make a note or two here to remind me as to what I would say, because it has to be brief."

"Well, that's a queer thing," Elizabeth said. "During the night, I happened to think of the thing, that, if there's a decision we ought to ask some people in. I made a note of some people to call up."

Their morning routine continued like that until noon, when a secretary from the NAACP publicity department called. Something was happening. Henry Moon, the association's public relations director, said he'd heard a rumor that the Supreme Court was about to issue its decision. The Warings turned on their radio and listened until there was a break in the programming – a news flash.

After the announcer read the bulletin, Elizabeth went to the phone and began calling the people on her list. "We're going to be home tonight," she told them all, "and any time after 8 o'clock, drop in and let's talk about the decision." The Warings' Fifth Avenue apartment would host the NAACP victory party.

On May 17, 1954, the U.S. Supreme Court issued its decision in *Brown v. Board of Education*. The court ruled that racial segregation in public schools violated the equal protection clause of the 14th Amendment of the United States Constitution. In calm, neutral language, the court overturned *Plessy v. Ferguson* and ordered the integration of public schools. There was no dissent; the decision was unanimous.

Warren's decree was much shorter than Waring's dissent in *Briggs v. Elliott*, but he managed to say almost exactly the same thing with a greater economy of words.

"Segregation of white and colored children in public schools has a detrimental effect upon the colored children. The impact is greater when it has the sanction of the law, for the policy of separating the races is usually interpreted as denoting the inferiority of the Negro group. A sense of inferiority affects the motivation of a child to learn. Segregation with the sanction of law, therefore, has a tendency to [retard] the educational and mental development of Negro children and to deprive them of some of the benefits they would receive in a racial[ly] integrated school system.

"Whatever may have been the extent of psychological knowledge at the time of *Plessy v. Ferguson,* this finding is amply supported by modern authority. Any language in *Plessy v. Ferguson* contrary to this finding is rejected.

"We conclude that, in the field of public education, the doctrine of 'separate but equal' has no place. Separate educational facilities are inherently unequal."

Without referencing Waring in any way, the Supreme Court presented his argument, cited the same cases and reached the exact conclusion the judge made in his *Briggs v. Elliott* dissent. Politically astute, Warren avoided Waring's hyperbole and attacks upon the South – but he said the same thing. "Separate educational facilities are inherently unequal."

In other words, "segregation is per se inequality."

Most people – Waring and Walter White included – assumed the Supreme Court would issue its ruling in early June, as was its custom. In Charleston, The Evening Post rushed to get the story into print for the afternoon edition with the banner headline "Segregation in schools declared unconstitutional." Waring's phone rang constantly for the better part of a week, giving him numerous opportunities to read the statement he'd prepared that morning on nothing more than a hunch.

"This decision will make history and will erase the shame of the Dred Scott and Plessy against Ferguson cases," Waring declared. "The court has affirmed our belief in the Declaration of Independence and the Constitution and has finally killed the hypocrisy of those who practice a vicious form of racial bias under the sophistry of the so-called separate but equal doctrine.

"For a long time we have suffered under the taunts of foreign enemies who have proclaimed that we did not live up to our protestations of true democracy," Waring said. "We are now freed from that charge, and democracy and decency prevail."

Later, Waring praised the court for its measured stance and tacitly acknowledged why his dissent wasn't credited as the basis of the order. He knew the South would never accept a ruling with his name attached, not after the ferocity of his attacks on Southerners. He'd been too strident, too harsh, and recognized the Supreme Court managed to accomplish the same goal without sparking riots. Waring took comfort in knowing that his plan – which he could never admit to orchestrating – had been more successful than he could've imagined.

"With considerable gratification, I sometimes laughingly say that nine Supreme Court justices were just as big damn fools as I was, apparently, because they happened to decide my way," Waring later said.

The menu was simple.

Waring put whiskey and water and ice on the table, and announced that anyone who wanted a drink could go fix it. People drifted in and out of the apartment all evening, multiple conversations overlapping to the soundtrack of laughter and a ringing telephone. There was an election-night vibe in the apartment, and the party would go on for a long time.

Alan Paton was the first to arrive. The South African novelist, author of *Cry, The Beloved Country*, was an anti-apartheid activist who'd met the Warings through mutual friends – probably Poppy Cannon, herself a native of South Africa. Soon, Henry Moon showed up with an entourage from the NAACP's legal defense and publicity offices. There was Elwood Chisolm and June Shagaloff, who had helped Kenneth Clark and his wife, Mamie, with the experiments he testified about in the *Briggs* case. The Clarks eventually showed up, too.

By 9 p.m., the crowd included New York City Council members, pastors, journalists, judges and NAACP board members – including John Hammond, the record producer who discovered Billie Holiday (and would go on to sign Aretha Franklin, Bob Dylan and Bruce Springsteen). A number of prominent African Americans dropped by, including black judges Ellis Rivers and Hubert Delany, along with Dr. May Chinn, the first black woman to graduate from Bellevue Hospital Medical College and the first to intern at Harlem Hospital.

Walter White and Poppy Cannon showed up late. They'd had plans for the evening, but decided this was one party they couldn't miss. When White walked through the door, the crowd applauded. He took it as a cue and began to speak. White said he'd been feeling poorly of late, but had been reinvigorated by the news about the school case – he'd figured it would come in June.

"That's what you told me," Ted Poston said. "You said June seventh."

"Wrong as usual," White joked.

He listed a long string of cases the NAACP had filed over the course of two decades, all of them, White said, leading to this moment. Since the 1930s, they had been chipping away at the notion of separate-but-equal, but he'd always believed *Brown* would be the one that changed everything. "I had a feeling, 'Well, we might not win a complete victory, but it should be a pretty substantial one.'

"And I thought of Waties," White said. "I thought of the pounding he took when he wrote the dissenting opinion in South Carolina and the position he took then. I remembered several conversations with Waties – one in particular when he said to me, 'Eventually the Supreme Court, if not in this generation in some future generation, is going to come to the position I have taken here.' And then he said, 'I'm not saying this out of pride of authorship but because it is the only position which the court can eventually take.'

"Waties, I pay tribute to you that, in so short a time and in spite of all the hell that you and Elizabeth went through, you have been proved right," White said. "I am remembering the night they stoned your house. That night you telephoned. And we talked because there was a bridge between friends. Now in so short a period of time the Supreme Court of the United States has taken a position unanimously in affirmation of the position which you took against the pressures of Jimmy Byrnes and all the rest of the evil system that existed then."

There were more fights to come, White said, including residential segregation and job discrimination. But they had taken the first step. It had taken 58 years to overturn *Plessy v. Ferguson* but, White said, the people in that room – as well as some people in Clarendon County, South Carolina – had the courage to stand up for what was right.

"Without them, neither the NAACP nor Waties Waring nor the Supreme Court of the United States could have taken the stand which they have taken today," White said.

Waring made a short speech, and Paton talked as well, but mostly everyone just drank and laughed and celebrated. It had been a long time since Waring had felt like part of a community, but 700 miles north of Charleston, he was once again a prominent, important and socially connected man. But this wasn't the hollow society life of his youth. Waring was now part of an influential group of people striving to change the entire country.

Brown v. Board of Education would mark a turning point in the civil rights movement. Some of the most momentous events of the 20th century were sparked by a Supreme Court decision that, in a way, Waring prompted through sheer force of will. As a result, new leaders would rise and take the struggle for equal rights to heights the retired judge couldn't have imagined.

In his lifetime, Waties Waring would be praised and feted and honored by his friends and activists, but he never received widespread recognition or credit for his contribution to the cause of civil rights. Still, he was satisfied. He had achieved something far more important to him than fame.

Waring had proven that he was right.

AFTERMATH

DREAMS OF A MOVEMENT

A RETURN TO CHARLESTON

The train pulled into the Charleston station just before 3 p.m. that Saturday. Waring stepped off the car in his old gray hat and wool overcoat, and was immediately overcome by the smell of pluff mud – a scent that permeated his hometown, and his very bones. It was a welcome familiarity but, if nostalgia tugged at him, he said nothing of it.

Nearly 300 people greeted the judge and Elizabeth on the platform, and almost all of them were black. The couple waded into the crowd, occasionally stopping to hug old friends. Elizabeth picked up several children and planted lipstick kisses on their cheeks. Waring was surprised to see a television camera recording their arrival; one of the local radio stations had recently added a television channel. But then, this was big news.

It was Nov. 6, 1954, and the Warings were making their first appearance in Charleston since leaving nearly three years earlier.

The South Carolina NAACP was hosting a banquet for the judge that night at Buist Elementary School on Calhoun Street. The testimonial dinner had been planned for months, announced less than two weeks after the Supreme Court decision. The banquet was billed as an opportunity to honor Waring for championing civil rights, but in truth many of his old friends simply wanted an excuse to see him again. Nothing less could have lured him back to the city.

Arthur Clement, president of the NAACP's local branch office, met the couple outside the station, along with the women's auxiliary. Marion Wright, president of the Southern Regional Council, showed up to say hello. Wright would deliver the banquet's keynote address that night. They all chatted and posed for photographs, Waring first removing his hat. The newspaper photographer snapped pictures of the women's auxiliary presenting Elizabeth with a bouquet of flowers. After a few minutes, the couple was hustled into a motorcade and driven away.

The details of the visit were confidential. Some South Carolina residents still harbored ill feelings toward the couple, particularly in the wake of *Brown v. Board of Education*, and the Warings' friends would take no chances with their safety. The newspapers reported the judge's lodgings and whereabouts had been kept secret, but anyone who knew the Warings realized where they were going. That afternoon, the NAACP motorcade delivered them to 95 Congress Street – Ruby Cornwell's two-story brick home just off King Street.

Of course, there had been some controversy surrounding the banquet. Thurgood Marshall declined an invitation to speak, citing health problems. Although he had been stranded in a Kansas City hospital recently, the excuse struck some people as odd; Marshall had used the claim to beg off an NAACP dinner for Waring in New York months earlier. And then George Elmore, the plaintiff in the judge's first voting-rights case, publicly criticized the banquet in a News and Courier story written by the conservative W.D. Workman.

Elmore claimed his role in the civil rights movement had been overlooked by the NAACP until Workman profiled him as the forgotten man in Judge Waring's long saga. Since then, he'd been invited to the banquet and the NAACP sent him two round-trip train tickets. But Elmore said he wanted nothing to do with the organization, which catered only to "big shots."

To be sure, there were a number of prominent civil rights leaders among the 500 people who crowded into the Buist cafeteria that night. State NAACP director James Hinton spoke briefly, and special counsel Robert Carter took a seat at the head table next to Elizabeth. Mrs. Waring addressed the crowd politely, a tone decidedly different from her infamous YWCA speech five years earlier.

During his address, Wright evoked Biblical parables to describe Waring. He was an unlikely hero, a man born to privilege in a family of slave owners, a man who had defied his heritage to see the light. "Every contact, every exterior influence, every local pressure, every tug upon his heartstrings attached him to a status which had been kind to him and his class. Those were powerful influences, but they were exterior." And, Wright said, Waring overcame the pressures of his station to fight for justice.

"In the heart of the man silent and mysterious forces were at work," Wright said. "There must have been long hours in the dark with his conscience in which a miraculous conversion occurred, a conversion no less miraculous than the blinding flash of light which fell upon Saul as he journeyed down to Damascus. This and other generations will do reverence to his name because this transformation of personality occurred."

Waring was his usual witty, and verbose, self. In his remarks, he lectured the audience on the long history of *Plessy v. Ferguson* – no doubt a crowd-pleaser – and praised the Supreme Court for putting the case "in the garbage pail where it belongs." The judge commended the court for summing up his argument in the *Briggs* dissent much more eloquently and briefly than he had.

"Maybe I should have just said 'it's all nonsense' and signed my name," he deadpanned.

That night, Waring also delivered an important and prescient warning to the civil rights leaders. Although the *Brown* decision was an important historical event – the judge compared it to Moses on Mount Sinai and Christ's Sermon on the Mount, continuing the Biblical references – it was only a first step. The fight, Waring said, was far from over. He lambasted South Carolina officials still resisting the Supreme Court's order and predicted a monumental battle to end segregation. It was a rare instance of understatement from Waring.

The Warings lingered at Buist for an hour after the banquet, posing for more photographs and chatting with old acquaintances. Their closest friends followed them back to the Cornwells' house, and on Sunday the couple hosted a party for the Warings. It was a relaxing weekend, and they were happy to see old friends. But they weren't entirely out of touch. Both the judge and Elizabeth corresponded regularly with Cornwell, Clark and courthouse staff. They knew what was going on in the city. Waring even maintained his subscriptions to the local papers.

Waring's absence had not healed his hostile relationship with the Charleston newspapers. The Evening Post criticized the NAACP banquet for granting "saintship" to the judge, reminding readers that Waring was living off a full pension – the perk of a job he secured through ties to a political party he later betrayed. Old wounds had not healed in the Ivory City.

The judge ignored the papers, had a good time, and on Monday morning boarded a train for New York.

It was the last time he'd ever see Charleston.

South Carolina had changed very little in Waring's absence.

Gov. Byrnes didn't shut down the public schools, but he tried to ignore the *Brown* decision. He continued to promote his plan for equalizing black and white schools as if the Supreme Court ruling was just a suggestion, and the legislature was complicit. The General Assembly vested more authority in local school boards, then vowed to cut off funding to any district that accepted a student as a result of any court order.

South Carolina's reaction was relatively modest compared to some Southern states. Robert Figg, serving again as the state's attorney, asked the Supreme Court to delay implementation of *Brown* to avoid a legislative shutdown of public schools. But Mississippi Sen. James Eastland vowed his state wouldn't follow any ruling from such a "political body" as the United States Supreme Court. Virginia attempted to repeal compulsory attendance laws and offered tuition grants to families that didn't want their children going to school with black students. The backlash the justices had feared was stirring.

In the wake of *Brown*, Citizens' Councils formed across the South to oppose school integration. The councils first appeared in Mississippi, but spread to South Carolina when petitions circulated asking the state to comply with *Brown*. The Citizens' Councils claimed to oppose violence, but distributed pro-segregation propaganda and promoted economic boycotts against black businesses – or any whites sympathetic to civil rights.

The News and Courier claimed the groups represented the best people in the state, including members of local churches and civic organizations. But the Charleston NAACP said the councils were simply "the tuxedo gang of the KKK." They just weren't burning crosses – not yet anyway.

Septima Clark told the Warings the atmosphere in South Carolina had become so vitriolic she feared black people would accept segregation rather than endure more conflict. Her own students fretted about the possibility of attending classes with white kids. "The first one to call me a nigger, I'll bop him on the nose," one told her. The children were scared, and Clark told Elizabeth the Citizens' Councils were doing their jobs well.

In June 1955, the Supreme Court gave the South cover to continue this behavior. The original *Brown* decision ordered schools to be integrated by the beginning of the 1955-56 school year, but the court amended its ruling to say that plans must be carried out with "all deliberate speed" – a much more nebulous timeframe. Waring was livid, but Elizabeth spoke out loudest.

The Washington Afro-American published a letter from her that said the Supreme Court "has not pleased the South or the colored people but has relieved the rest of the country of the fear of the South's carrying out its threats of revolution. They have been terrifying the North with this threat since early slave days and hence always accomplished compromise. This time it may be wolf-wolf once too often."

Elizabeth said the South's refusal to integrate had led to "bitter disappointment of many colored people, and also white," and predicted their obstruction would spark another court battle before a "righteously indignant Supreme Court." Such intolerance, she said, might revive the idea of using force to make Southern states comply with *Brown v. Board of Education*. She was flirting with language that had gotten her – and the judge – into trouble before, but it was a mostly hollow threat. The Warings were simply frustrated by everything Clark told them about conditions in Charleston.

It seemed even the NAACP was discouraged. Later that summer, the Columbia newspapers reported that Thurgood Marshall had backed off his insistence that Clarendon County schools be desegregated. The stories claimed Marshall had decided to focus his efforts elsewhere, and Waring correctly surmised the source of the article was Clarendon school attorneys. Waring urged Marshall to dispute the report, which was "very damaging to our fight to end segregation."

Marshall eventually told reporters the story was entirely inaccurate, that he'd only promised that the NAACP would not "formally present Negro children to the white schools for admission in September because such an action was not necessary in the present posture of the case and would have no legal significance.

I made it clear that we would not give up any of our rights."

His explanation did little to calm Waring. He reminded Marshall that black parents in South Carolina were under tremendous pressure to withdraw their support for integration, and that threatened to impede all the progress they'd made. It didn't help, Waring said, when the NAACP's lead attorney naively believed the "sincerity of Dixiecrat lawyers."

"Perhaps a few more 'legal lynchings' will enlighten you," Waring wrote.

Marshall's only response was a terse note and a "self-explanatory" copy of the letter he sent to the Columbia Record.

The exchange was just further proof of the strained relationship between two men with different styles. Marshall was a tactician and Waring wanted Armageddon. The judge didn't believe in mercy or patience, and he had good reason to doubt the intent of people in South Carolina. Because by then, he knew what had happened to DeLaine.

The Citizens' Councils expanded into most of South Carolina's rural counties over the summer of 1955, but quickly discovered propaganda and boycotts did nothing to stop the petitions demanding state compliance with *Brown*. This was an emotional issue, and sterile tactics did little to quell their frustrated rage or recruit new supporters. The only way to win, these Citizens' Councils decided, was to target the people causing all this trouble – the civil rights activists. Before long, some reverted to Klan-like measures.

The Lake City branch never hesitated. When the group formed in August 1955, their first order of business was clear: The biggest agitator in South Carolina lived amongst them, the man who'd started all this in Clarendon County, the reason their children might have to sit in classrooms with black kids. And he had to go.

"The nigger preacher y'all are feeding is the real backbone of the desegregation movement," one man told the Lake City Citizens' Council at its first meeting. "Y'all got to get rid of him before you'll be able to stop the others."

That night, a car drove past DeLaine's house and one of the passengers threw an orange at the window. The fruit struck with so much force that juice ran down the window. The car returned four nights later, and this time the men hurled a bottle of ketchup and a Pepsi at the house. The soda broke a window and the ketchup bottle shattered on a wall, the red sauce dripping down the siding like blood. Police collected the shards for fingerprints, but nothing ever came of the investigation.

The attacks continued intermittently for months. Once, DeLaine and his son chased the men down a dark dirt road and memorized the car's license plate number before it pulled away. He told the police, but officers said they couldn't trust his memory. So DeLaine began his own investigation, and eventually determined the culprits were a gang that hung around a nearby Esso station. But when he took his evidence to the police, they wouldn't charge the men.

In October, while DeLaine was in Charleston for an AME conference, his church burned down, leaving little more than its skeletal frame. Police refused to call it an arson, suggesting a member of the congregation may have set the fire accidentally. They didn't amend their finding after the pastor received a threatening letter addressed to "J.A. Delane. Collard."

"We have been notified by the best of authority that you are the one that started school segregation mess at Manning, S.C. and that you was run out of manning four dirty work there. so you come to Lake City to continue your dirty work. Maby you dont know Lake City but you are going to find out real soon. Several hundred of us have had a meeting and pleged our selves to put you where you belong, if there is such a place. I wonder if ever heard about the Negro Postmaster that was send to Lake City and was notified to leve. He refused. However he left, but in a coffin. So we have decided to give you 10 days to leave Lake City and if you are not away by then rather than let you spread your dirty filthy poison here any longer. We have made plans to move you if it takes dynamite to do it. This is final"

Lake City police said the illiterate note was proof of nothing; there wasn't even a mention of the church. But the police chief assigned a patrolman to drive by DeLaine's church and house every 15 minutes at night. He also suggested the pastor was free to shoot anyone who came onto his property threatening him or his family. DeLaine was stunned – he was living in the Wild West.

DeLaine awoke to the sound of gunfire just after 11 p.m. on Oct. 10. He jumped up, gathered his family away from the windows and, when the shooting stopped, took his wife and children to a neighbor's house. He returned home, loaded his .38 Winchester rifle and slipped outside to wait. It had escalated, and he suspected his attackers would return.

Around midnight, he heard the car approach – quickly followed by the crack of two gunshots. DeLaine stepped out of the shadows and returned fire, planning to mark the car so there'd be no mistake who was terrorizing him. Before the car sped away, he got off two shots and hit the car both times. Afterward, he walked over to the burned-out shell of his former church and sat down, waiting for the Lake City police officer assigned to watch over him.

As he waited on the charred church stoop, DeLaine began to worry. What if the police were in on this? So far, they had refused to do anything about the attacks on his home, on his family. He feared they would arrest him for shooting at the car, despite the chief's suggestion that he defend himself. Maybe, he thought, he should just run.

DeLaine told friends that God spoke to him that night. The Lord said the time had come to flee Lake City before his family got hurt. In truth, he later admitted that advice came from a black Lake City police officer, who showed up a few minutes after the incident. The patrolman listened to DeLaine's account and quietly warned him not to press this.

"It's time for you to leave here," the officer said.

That was all it took; DeLaine was convinced. He quickly packed a bag, threw it in his car and sped away. His family was safe with the neighbors, he knew, and he'd send for them later. It would be too dangerous to travel with them at night, he believed – a suspicion soon confirmed. On one dark, dirt road, a car appeared in the rear view mirror and tailgated him for several minutes. It peeled away only when DeLaine reached downtown Florence.

Septima Clark was next.

She was still teaching in Charleston, but that increasingly felt like a side job. Her true calling was civil rights, and she had become an important figure in the movement. Clark had been spending her summers at the Highlander Folk School in Monteagle, Tennessee. The school, opened in the 1930s, originally offered job training to adults during the Great Depression – and helped organize labor unions. By the 1950s its mission shifted to adult education, primarily to help people pass the literacy tests required to vote. Clark was the school's best teacher.

Esau Jenkins, Clark's friend from Johns Island, had helped develop the adult education program and recruited her to teach there. Highlander was training young civil rights leaders, and the judge and Elizabeth supported the school financially – but worried about Clark's involvement. Tennessee officials were itching to shut down the school, and the Warings constantly warned her to be careful. They didn't trust officials in any Southern state.

In December 1955, one of Clark's Highlander students was on a Montgomery bus when the driver ordered her to give her seat to a white man. She refused, just as Clark had taught her. Rosa Parks' defiance sparked a national controversy, the Montgomery bus boycott and escalated the fight against racial segregation.

After that, South Carolina officials realized that Clark was dangerous.

The 1956 South Carolina General Assembly passed a law forbidding teachers – or any government employees – from holding membership in the NAACP. State lawmakers said they wouldn't subsidize agitators, and believed the law would cripple the civil rights organization. In some ways it worked; NAACP membership plummeted, as most people couldn't afford to lose their jobs. But Clark was not intimidated. She even joked about it.

"The governor of Oregon has offered the Negroes of South Carolina a home there," Clark told the Warings. "He says that his people want to mix with all people."

Clark refused to resign from the NAACP and, at first, no one said anything. But before she departed for Monteagle that summer, the Charleston school board informed Clark that her contract hadn't been renewed for the coming academic year. She was not only fired, Clark also lost her pension. The board wouldn't even grant her an audience to protest.

"I anticipated this long ago," Clark told the Warings. "I can easily take it on the chin. No shock. No surprise."

Highlander hired Clark as a full-time instructor. There, she developed what came to be called Citizenship Schools – classes that taught black people how to become active in their communities. She helped thousands learn to read, write and understand their constitutional rights. Ultimately, the idea was to create new voters. By the fall, Clark was setting up Citizenship Schools in North Carolina, Florida, Georgia, Alabama and Mississippi. On occasion, the work even took her to New York or New Jersey. When she was there, Clark always visited the Warings.

Eventually, Tennessee shut down Highlander and arrested several employees on trumped-up charges – Clark was accused of having illegal alcohol on the premises. After she was released from jail, Clark received another job offer. She was invited to continue her Citizenship Schools program under the umbrella of a new organization in Atlanta. It was called the Southern Christian Leadership Conference.

The pastor in charge of the SCLC was a man Clark knew well. He'd spent time at Highlander and organized the Montgomery bus boycott. His name was the Rev. Martin Luther King Jr.

ONE GENERATION PASSETH

On Feb. 8, 1957, Waties Waring appeared on the NBC public affairs show "The Open Mind." He was flattered by the invitation – and the attention. Since *Brown v. Board of Education*, the pace of the civil rights movement had increased exponentially, and he'd largely been left in its wake.

Waring tried to remain active and relevant, writing letters to The New York Times, lobbying public officials to support federal civil rights laws and lending his name to various causes, including the American Civil Liberties Union and the Urban League. But there was only so much a retired federal judge could do, particularly when his name was fading from the headlines.

"The Open Mind" was a new but influential program that offered Waring a national television audience in prime time. The talk show was hosted by a Rutgers University professor and protégé of Edward R. Murrow named Richard D. Heffner, and he'd invited the judge on the air to talk about "The New Negro." His reputation remained solid among New York City intellectuals. Still dapper and fit at 76, Waring cut an authoritative and commanding presence when the show aired two nights later, but he may have been overshadowed by the show's other guest.

Heffner's second panelist was the young Baptist preacher who'd led the famous Montgomery bus boycott. In the past year, he'd been arrested, saw his house bombed and sparked a federal court case. He had persevered and triumphed through it all. As a result, Martin Luther King Jr. was quickly becoming the face of the civil rights movement.

If Heffner hoped for lively debate, he was disappointed. Waring and King were in complete accord. The judge praised his efforts in Montgomery as "fine, necessary and effective." The courts had declared the equal rights of African Americans, Waring said, but it is up to them to go out and get them – exactly as King had done.

"Now it's up to them to move out," Waring said. "They haven't got to go out with guns and bombs and gas, but they've got to go out with determination and courage and steadfastness like this man Luther King has done, and say: Here I am, and I stand here on my rights."

King said black citizens had a newfound sense of dignity, destiny and self-respect. After years of hiding their true feelings about conditions in the country, the pastor said African Americans were now willing to say in no uncertain terms that they did not like how they were being treated. Waring's own opinion echoed King's.

"My observation of the Negro ... has been that up to recently he has been a half-man, or part-man, and now he at last is waking up to the fact that he's a whole man, that he's an American citizen, and that he is entitled to rights – no more, no less – than just the ordinary, run of the mill American citizen," Waring said. "He's never had that before; he hasn't been allowed to have it. He's been under public domination; he's been oppressed; he's had economic deprivation; he's been a servant, formerly a slave."

More than 60 years later, the brief meeting between Waring and King seems like a metaphorical passing of the torch from one generation to the next. One man had done his part for civil rights; the other was just getting started. To his credit, the judge recognized King's potential immediately. Professors from Columbia University had been calling on the judge regularly for more than a year, interviewing him as part of their oral history project. The last of their talks took place in Waring's Fifth Avenue apartment on March 6, 1957. Four weeks after his appearance on NBC, Waring was still talking about King.

"This man, Martin Luther King, whom I have met ... is a very fine leader," Waring gushed. "He's highly educated. He's quiet and a thinker, non-violent, not given to emotional outbursts, steadfast, always moving forward in a deliberate way. He might be said to embody the Supreme Court decision of 'with all deliberate speed.' He never steps backwards. He doesn't run, but he walks, and he takes a few steps every day – and it's all in one direction."

Waring had spent a year reminiscing about his life to the Columbia professors, from his days in Charleston society to the behind-the-scenes machinations of *Briggs v. Elliott*. Some weeks, he bored them with the minutiae of bankruptcy cases from 15 years earlier; other times, he talked nostalgically of riding horse carriages to school in the waning years of the 19th century. Often, he complained about the South and the politics of segregationists.

There was little else for him to do. Although he'd joined the ACLU and the National Urban League hoping it would give him a platform to push for more sweeping societal change, in truth he was just another high-status name for letterheads. On occasion, he was invited to speak at Harvard or Yale, but the invitations now trickled in slowly.

Mostly, the judge and Elizabeth spent their days in the apartment. Their social appointments were diminishing, their friends – and even their enemies – were dying out. Burnet Maybank had died in the middle of a campaign; Walter White passed away in 1955, just a year after the *Brown* decision.

The Warings still kept in touch with Ruby Cornwell and Septima Clark, who was now working with King. Cornwell kept the couple updated on Charleston gossip and commiserated about the slow march of progress. They saw much of the movement through Cornwell's letters, particularly the vicious backlash in the South. The lynching of 14-year-old Emmett Till in Mississippi horrified them all, but especially Cornwell.

"My heart is very heavy sometimes," Cornwell wrote to the Warings. "The little murdered boy in Mississippi. I see him every night before I go to sleep. And those beasts – how can those savage fiends hide behind intelligent, civilized looking faces? Can we hope that justice will be done there?"

Despite his perpetually gruff exterior, Waring remained hopeful for the future of civil rights. He watched King rise to prominence with great pride, but knew the South remained a problem. The white supremacists were still in control, a fact he often lamented to his captive audience of Columbia professors, but he predicted their days were numbered.

"I believe that as the border states become more and more Americanized, the people of the few states of the Deep South that are now in dire opposition will begin to get very lonely, and the economic conditions and political conditions and moral conditions and religious conditions and labor conditions will eventually bring them around," Waring said. "Now, a few of the diehards – people like Thurmond and Talmadge – are going to continue to fight down the line. The only remedy for them, I would assume, is the undertaker."

The backlash to *Brown v. Board* – and Burnet Maybank's untimely death – helped Strom Thurmond revive his political career. When Maybank passed away in September 1954, while up for re-election, the Democratic Party replaced him on the November ballot with state Sen. Edgar Brown. Thurmond recognized the opportunity and immediately mounted a write-in campaign. The Supreme Court decision gave him a convenient new target for all the old slogans he'd been peddling since 1948.

Thurmond won the only successful write-in campaign in U.S. Senate history that year, in large part due to his stand against integration. He also promised to resign before the term ended and stand for a Democratic primary in 1956. Thurmond won that race, too, and would hold the Senate seat until his death in the early 21st century. In 1957, he eclipsed his fame as a presidential candidate when he filibustered civil rights legislation for more than 24 hours – chugging orange juice on the Senate floor to keep up his strength. A legend was born.

Thurmond was paradoxically a man both behind and ahead of his times. In 1964, two months after passage of the Civil Rights Act – which ended all public segregation and banned racial discrimination – he resigned from the Democratic Party and declared himself a Republican.

"The Democratic Party has abandoned the people," Thurmond said in a television address. "It has repudiated the Constitution of the United States. It is leading the evolution of our nation to a socialistic dictatorship."

Thurmond blamed all of society's ills on Democrats, including the popular fallacy that communism was on the rise in the country. But his claim that civil rights deprived white people of their own rights resonated, despite the obvious faults behind such logic. As Waring would argue, white people had lost nothing other than the right to discriminate against black people – and prevent them from voting. But once again, Thurmond had an unerring political radar for his constituency.

In 1968, former Vice President Richard Nixon would use a more subtle – and politically palatable – version of Thurmond's politics to win the White House. And within a quarter-century, nearly all of the old-line segregationists in the Democratic Party would follow Thurmond's lead. He had done nothing less than completely reshape the nation's political landscape. Waring wouldn't live long enough to see his optimistic prediction on the shelf life of white supremacy proven wrong.

Rev. DeLaine eventually followed Waring to New York.

The night of the shooting, he'd hid in the Florence home of some NAACP friends and, by the next day, it was clear he couldn't go back to Lake City. The police had a warrant for his arrest. The men harassing DeLaine had filed charges against him for having the audacity to shoot back at them, and local authorities apparently saw nothing hypocritical about their complaint.

DeLaine quietly retrieved his family and drove them to North Carolina, where they caught a plane to New York City. Church officials took them in, and DeLaine reached out to the FBI for help – and to make it clear he was not attempting to evade the law. He wrote J. Edgar Hoover that he "wasn't trying to dodge justice but dodge injustice."

The bureau quietly suggested he stay put. For months, the Justice Department and the New York governor's office denied South Carolina's attempts to extradite DeLaine – even when the Columbia newspapers accused federal officials of harboring a fugitive from justice. Gov. George Bell Timmerman Jr. – son of the federal judge who'd presided alongside Waring in the *Briggs* case – laughably accused the Justice Department of "discrimination" for refusing to arrest DeLaine.

When the governor finally realized the standoff only made the state look foolish and impotent, he tried to turn the situation to his advantage. He declared "South Carolina is well rid of this professional agitator" and dropped the extradition efforts. Finally, DeLaine was free.

"I never would have left South Carolina if I hadn't been forced to leave," the pastor told a newspaper in 1957. "But somehow, I feel my work there was finished, and that I'll never go back. I think of my friends there, and I would like to see them. But I'm satisfied that my work there is done. I won't be going back."

The family lived with Bishop D. Ward Nichols for eight months, until AME officials gave DeLaine his own church in Buffalo. It was a world away from rural South Carolina, and he didn't like the snow, but at least his family was safe. The threatening letters would continue for years, and DeLaine dutifully passed them along to the FBI. In one, the writer mentioned "black apes" and suggested that he and "old man Waring" had better stay in New York.

Not long after he settled in Buffalo, DeLaine grew disenchanted with his new post and asked for permission to establish an entirely new church. Even the Charleston newspapers took note when, in July 1956, western New York's newest church opened as DeLaine-Waring AME.

The accolades for Waring continued intermittently for years. In late 1957, the American Jewish Congress hailed him for his contributions to civil rights, and two years later the National Committee for Rural Schools recognized the judge for his efforts to battle segregation. Waring was honored alongside Jackie Robinson, the first African-American Major League Baseball player.

Even at 80, the judge occasionally emerged to take up a cause. In 1961, he joined Columbia activist Modjeska Simkins, Martin Luther King and Eleanor Roosevelt on a petition drive urging Congress to abolish the House Un-American Activities Committee. The News and Courier noted that all of them had been subjected to investigation by the panel, and most of the 350 signers were "identifiable as political left-wingers and others as race agitators."

For the most part, however, Waring was finished with political activism. In 1960 he donated all his papers to Howard University for use by "anyone who wants to write on the rise of the Negro's status. I think they will have some historical value for anyone doing research in racial studies." The collection filled 70 boxes, and included his robe, personal letters and several early drafts of his dissent in *Briggs v. Elliott.*

Waring would live long enough to see all that followed *Brown v. Board of*

Education, which of course had followed his dissent in *Briggs*. And his predictions about King were prophetic. The young leader of the Southern Christian Leadership Conference was at the center of the civil rights movement. In 1963, King led protests to end segregation in Birmingham, Alabama. He was arrested – prompting his famous "Letter from a Birmingham jail," the tone of which echoed Waring much more than the young King who'd appeared with him on television all those years earlier.

When the police turned the dogs and high-pressure water hoses on the Birmingham protesters, the civil rights movement gained sympathy – but it was only the second most-notable King victory of the year. In August, he led the March on Washington to end segregation in schools and pass meaningful civil rights legislation. King's "I have a dream" speech, delivered in front of the Lincoln Memorial, was one of the most iconic moments of the 20th century.

A year later, Congress passed the Civil Rights Act – the most significant achievement since *Brown* – and King won the Nobel Peace Prize. His small entourage to Oslo to accept the prize included Septima Clark, whose Citizenship Schools did as much to help further the cause of equal rights as anything. She was, as King called her, the Queen Mother of the civil rights movement.

The 1965 Voting Rights Act vindicated Waring for his decisions against the South Carolina Democratic Party. But by then he was too old to say anything about it. The judge and Elizabeth had taken a smaller apartment at the Hyde Park Hotel on East 77th Street, and Mrs. Waring almost never left it – or let anyone see her.

Years earlier, Elizabeth had developed an extremely painful hernia, and it changed her lifestyle. She'd gained a considerable amount of weight and had to sleep upright in a chair. When President Kennedy invited the Warings to the White House to celebrate the centennial of the Emancipation Proclamation in 1963, they politely declined. Elizabeth simply could not travel.

Waring still went out on occasion, usually with Anne. After a decade of chilly relations, father and daughter finally had made up. Their problems began shortly after the judge and Elizabeth moved to New York.

Waring had sent Anne some financial papers – or, as he saw it, a peek at her inheritance – and she didn't respond. Before long, Elizabeth went to see her and made matters worse, the drama finally ending in a vitriolic letter from the judge. He accused Anne of never showing him affection as a child, complained about her "ghastly failures" in school and her refusal to ever come hear him speak publicly, except for those occasions that afforded her the opportunity to meet Jackie Robinson or Eleanor Roosevelt. For a long time, the father and daughter did not speak – a symptom of much larger, and more complicated, familial problems.

Anne Waring Warren had a tough decade. Her mother, Annie Gammell Waring, died in Charleston about a month after the judge's last visit in 1954. The next year, she and Stanley divorced. Anne's only surviving family was a stepmother who irritated her and a father who'd made it clear that, in many ways, he considered her a disappointment. But the years eroded that hostility and, in 1960, Anne made her father proud by taking up the family business.

She wrote a series of articles for The New York Post magazine called, "The South Revisited," which in some ways seemed almost like a response to Collier's "The Lonesomest Man in Town." Anne visited Charleston to chronicle race relations in the city, stopping to interview her cousin, News and Courier editor Tom Waring. She compared him to her father.

"It would be difficult to find two men of keener intelligence, personal integrity and idealism," she wrote. "And yet between these two men and their beliefs on the matter of civil rights lies most of Southern or – for that matter – world opinion."

Anne had taken the family laundry public, and the critics – as well as the judge – loved it.

As the most contentious, inspiring and momentous events of the civil rights movement unfolded, Anne and her father blended into the crowds at baseball games or the occasional Broadway show. She was living in Brooklyn, and visited him regularly in Manhattan. Although Elizabeth wouldn't step outside the apartment, Anne regularly persuaded the judge to get some fresh air. She worried, because clearly the old man was dying.

Waring was going blind and deaf, and in the mid-1960s was diagnosed with intestinal cancer. His doctor suggested an operation to remove the tumor, but he refused. No matter how much Elizabeth, Anne or the doctor needled him, Waring wouldn't listen. On the days he felt good, he took it as confirmation that he didn't need surgery.

This went on for two years or so, and the judge was characteristically stubborn throughout. On Christmas Day 1967, Waring went out to dinner with Anne, and she later recalled he was in good spirits. But he was 87 and sick; she knew he didn't have much time left.

Two weeks later, the pain he'd ignored so long overcame him and Elizabeth called an ambulance. Anne sat with the judge that night at St. Luke's Hospital, and together they called Elizabeth on the phone. Waring talked into the evening and, in the hours before dawn, slipped into a coma. It was mercifully quick.

Julius Waties Waring died shortly after 9 a.m. on Jan. 11, 1968.

VINDICATION

I t would take years for Charleston attitudes on Judge Waring to change, but eventually they did.

The News and Courier and Evening Post were largely respectful in their retrospectives on the judge's life and career. Both ran appropriately significant obituaries on their front pages that didn't skirt his historical relevance. Tom Waring – who Anne had portrayed as her father's philosophical opposite – lauded his uncle's brilliant legal mind.

"He was a man of intelligence and force who had been among the leading citizens of his community when the social and political storm broke about him 20 years ago," The News and Courier's editorial page said. "He was a judge of uncommon ability that was recognized and admired by all regardless of opinion."

The Evening Post went even further, praising the judge's courage and "unusual perception into the future." The paper speculated that historians may decide his ruling in *Elmore v. Rice* was "a first step of what later developed into a social and constitutional revolution. His place in history is assured and, as the years go by, it is destined to become less and less controversial."

But that would come later.

The Charleston papers showed their own foresight in predicting the future rehabilitation of Waring's local reputation. But perhaps they were simply adhering to the great Southern tradition of not speaking ill of the dead. Because in truth, the judge and the Charleston newspapers fought until the bitter end – just as they apparently wanted it.

Waring's last public statements came two days after Martin Luther King Jr.'s March on Washington in 1963. The Associated Press did a profile of the judge, a feature that recalled how the nation had changed in a single decade. In the story, Waring reminisced about the charms of Charleston and his old life, which in the end "got very lonely."

"I never was particularly aware of a racial issue in South Carolina," he said. "We all accepted it. As a lawyer, I didn't have any racial problems. Negroes didn't vote and I was in politics, but I always felt they were citizens and entitled to certain rights, but why should I bother with it. Then I became a judge and a judge's job is to handle justice. I saw injustices in my court."

For nearly a quarter-century, Waring had passed judgment on the entire South – but he was the one who served the sentence. If he harbored any hint of melancholy or nostalgia for his old life, he'd made his peace with it. He always knew there would be consequences, and he'd learned to accept them. Waring had answered a higher calling and, if he suffered, it was a noble fate. He had no regrets.

"It's damn nice to be in a caste system when you're in the top caste. It's damn nice to live down there and run things – and it's not right in America. I belonged to a caste system and enjoyed it and will do everything I can to break it down. It was wrong."

For generations, Waring's "old crowd" in Charleston would dispute the judge's account of his ostracism. They claimed all the local hostility had nothing to do with racism, but stemmed from Waring severing social and family connections after his second marriage. Which was completely true on one level and entirely misleading overall. His friends and family were offended by his behavior, and he did make it worse. But people weren't burning crosses in Waring's yard because he divorced Annie.

It was a cold day in Charleston.

Tuesday, Jan. 16, was the eighth day of the year with temperatures below freezing, an atypical weather pattern for the Lowcountry. Sunny skies would warm the city only into the mid-40s by 2 p.m., when the NAACP memorial service began at St. Matthews Baptist Church on Huger Street. Although many of the people in attendance hadn't known the judge personally, the short service was emotional and reverent.

"Judge Waring was probably held higher in the esteem of South Carolina

Negroes than any other white public figure in the history of the state," the Rev. I. DeQuincey Newman said in his eulogy. "In terms of contribution to the dignity of the Negro, he ranks along with Presidents Lincoln, Kennedy and Lyndon Johnson."

That wasn't hyperbole, but a reflection of the sentiment toward Waring in a community still finding its way in society. Although the newspapers had made their tentative peace with the judge, most of Charleston hadn't. Of the 200 people in St. Matthew's that day, fewer than a dozen of them were white – including five members of the family sitting with Anne. She later said that's how her father would have wanted it, and the city most likely realized that. Waring would have scoffed at any belated, insincere homage.

The television journalist Charles Kuralt was one of the few other white people in the church. He'd come to Charleston to deliver a segment that Walter Cronkite would air nationally that evening, a tribute that both explained Waring's long, tortured history with his hometown and cemented his esteemed role in American history.

Kuralt called the judge's decision to open the South Carolina Democratic primary to black voters "the first of the postwar landmark civil rights decisions," and pointed out it took the Supreme Court three years to catch up to Waring, to agree that segregation is "per se inequality."

Arthur Brown was the only local who would appear on camera for the segment, praising the judge's infinite fairness. Kuralt ended by quoting Waring's famous claim that he'd actually given black people nothing; they already had the right to vote, he was just the judge who'd decided the case according to the law.

"The question has long since been decided, of course," Kuralt said. "You may have forgotten that it was J. Waties Waring who decided it, but Charleston has not forgotten. There are few white mourners here today. Many people have paid a price for their civil rights advocacy, a United States District Court judge among them."

Following the service at St. Matthew's, the hearse led a motorcade through the city to Magnolia Cemetery. They buried him in an out-of-the-way, shaded plot next to the water that the judge and Elizabeth had bought in 1946. If they had waited just one year, they might have made another decision. But in some ways it was perfectly Waring – forcing himself upon his hometown for all eternity. Again, he would have the last word.

As the short line of cars passed through the gate at Magnolia, hundreds of black South Carolina residents followed on foot in homage to the judge's life. They were there, heads bowed and silent, to pay their respects to a man who had shown them an abundance of it. Ruby Cornwell, Waring's longtime friend, summed up their feelings eloquently.

"He was a prophet," Cornwell wrote after the service. "He catapulted his native land, his beloved city into the mainstream of world progress in social consciousness. 'There is no power on earth that can withstand the force of an idea whose time has come.' Judge J. Waties Waring was the instrument. The time had come! The judge comes home. We welcome you, our judge. We love you. We are honored to have you rest here in our midst."

Waring would remain a hero to the city's, and the state's, black citizens who endured the tumultuous years of the mid-20th century. But as one generation passed, and another came, the judge was forgotten in many circles. It would be another half-century before Charleston widely recognized his courage, foresight and historical achievements.

Waties Waring lived long enough, just barely, to see his old friend Thurgood Marshall appointed to the United States Supreme Court in late 1967. Marshall became the first black Supreme Court justice, a monument to his brilliant legal mind and a changing country. He would have a long and storied career on the bench, and left behind scores of opponents relieved they no longer had to face him in a courtroom.

Waring's death marked the beginning to one of the most important and tragic years in the nation's history. The Viet Cong launched the Tet Offensive against U.S. forces in Vietnam just weeks after his death. In April, Martin Luther King Jr. was assassinated in Memphis, followed that summer by Robert Kennedy in California. A bitter, divisive presidential campaign followed. The sole saving grace of 1968 came when Apollo 8, the first manned spacecraft to orbit the moon, broadcast a message of hope back to Earth on Christmas Eve.

South Carolina had not escaped the year unscathed. A month after the judge's death, the Orangeburg Massacre became the most deadly event of the state's civil rights era. Three people were killed and another 27 wounded when police tried to break up protests of a segregated bowling alley near the campus of South Carolina State. The state blamed the incident on local civil rights activist Cleveland Sellers, who'd left his house that night only to see what was going on – and was among those shot. Sellers paid for this with a prison sentence South Carolina had been unable to give the Rev. Joseph A. DeLaine.

Elizabeth Waring died in October 1968 at a Massachusetts nursing home near her children, where she'd been moved following the judge's death. The Charleston papers published only a short story on her death, and the services at Magnolia Cemetery were private. Only nine people – including Elizabeth's son, Anne and Septima Clark – were at her burial. She was not only the judge's confidante, partner and greatest advocate, Elizabeth was a pioneer, a strong woman and an advocate for civil rights at a time when none of that was widely acceptable.

Her passing was not mourned by most people in Charleston, however, many of whom still considered her the Witch of Meeting Street. Within months of her burial, Elizabeth's grave would be vandalized.

The change that Waring had predicted came slowly to South Carolina.

In 1969, workers at Charleston's Medical College organized a strike after they realized the hospital paid them less than the federal minimum wage. Coretta Scott King, widow of the slain civil rights leader, led a march down Calhoun Street shortly after the anniversary of her husband's death. State officials responded much as their predecessors would have; the National Guard occupied the city and imposed curfews. After 100 days of this, Esau Jenkins – an old friend of Waring's – helped negotiate the settlement.

It was considered one of the last major events of the civil rights era.

But really, it wasn't over. In 1970, more than 16 years after *Brown v. Board of Education*, South Carolina still clung to segregation. Eleven black students integrated Charleston schools in 1963, but only because their parents filed a lawsuit; other black children still weren't allowed to attend classes at white schools. One of those 11 pioneers was Millicent Brown, the daughter of NAACP leader and Waring friend J. Arthur Brown.

A decade later, Clarendon County still hadn't integrated its schools. Most of the county's white children had transferred to private schools to maintain self-segregation and sidestep federal law. In Summerton schools, where it all began, there were 3,000 black students enrolled – and one white. DeLaine watched this obfuscation of the law play out from Charlotte, North Carolina, which was as close as he would get. The pastor died in 1975 without ever returning to South Carolina. The state still held a warrant for his arrest.

In 1976, DeLaine and Waring – their stories relegated to obscure historical trivia – were featured as the lead characters in a CBS television dramatization of the *Briggs* lawsuit. Tom Waring said the film was "more drama than history," and did little to foster the progress of black and white citizens once again learning to live in harmony. "Only the good things about the heroes appear in the play, and only the bad things about the villains," he noted.

Anne died in 1979, when she was just 61. She'd worked most of her later years at Blair Academy in Blairstown, New Jersey. The Charleston papers briefly noted the passing of the famous judge's daughter. The school held a memorial service for Anne and donated her body to science. She would not join her father at Magnolia Cemetery.

Finally, Tom Waring passed away in 1993, and The Post and Courier – the paper borne of the merger of The News and Courier and The Evening Post – hailed him as one of the last great newspaper editors. For all his decades in service to Charleston journalism, Waring remained perhaps best-known for clashing with his famous uncle. Editor Arthur Wilcox, who worked alongside the younger Waring for many years, noted that those divisive times had built his legacy.

"I thought, at the time, he was a forceful, honest editor expressing his viewpoint – a viewpoint of much of the community at the time, but by no means all of the community," Wilcox said. "It was a changing time."

And it was an old time that had not been forgotten – even if the Warings largely had been.

On the 60th anniversary of *Briggs v. Elliott*, Waring's legacy was finally resurrected in Charleston. The South Carolina Supreme Court Historical Society and the state Bar's Legal Education division hosted a colloquium titled "J. Waties Waring and the Dissent that Changed America" at the federal courthouse. State Supreme Court Chief Justice Jean Toal and U.S. District Judge Richard Gergel – who often presided in Waring's former courtroom – were among the Waring admirers behind the seminar.

Judge Matthew Perry, who'd been in the courtroom during *Briggs*, and Joe DeLaine, son of the man who'd prompted the lawsuit, mesmerized South Carolina attorneys with their tales from the early days of the civil rights movement. It was a testament to how thoroughly Waring had been erased from local history that most lawyers didn't realize one of the most important Supreme Court decisions of the 20th century began in a Charleston courtroom.

After the colloquium, the state Bar Association decided Waring should be honored in a way that ensured his memory would never again be forgotten. Veteran Charleston attorney Thomas Tisdale was put in charge of efforts to raise money for a statue of the judge.

Like most Charleston natives, Tisdale had his own Waring story; in fact, he was distantly related to the judge. He could still remember the day in 1951 – the year of *Briggs* – when his grandmother conceded that Judge Waring was among the family's cousins. But, she told young Tom, "you should never feel compelled to have to admit it."

Those attitudes were fading by the early 21st century. Through four decades of dedication to civil rights, Mayor Joseph P. Riley Jr. – who put a bust of Waring in City Hall early in his tenure – had reshaped Charleston into one of the most progressive cities in the Southeast. He was able to accomplish this because the times were changing, and because Riley shared Waring's ideals – but not his temperament.

The Waring statue was unveiled in a shaded garden behind the federal courthouse – just a few steps from the sidewalk the judge walked every day – in April

2014. It depicted him standing, taking a step toward the future. His monument stood near a statue of James Byrnes, a geographical predicament Waring would have found ironic, but completely in character for South Carolina. The Waring statue was an extraordinary tribute, but it wasn't enough for retired U.S. Sen. Fritz Hollings.

Charleston's federal courthouse had been named for Hollings in 1988, a recognition of his efforts to renovate and expand the grand old Victorian-era building. Ironically, this honor had been suggested by South Carolina's senior senator, Strom Thurmond.

Since the days of Judge Waring, Hollings had become a South Carolina legend. As governor, he was responsible for the state's technical college system; as a United States senator, he created the Women, Infants and Children nutrition program and wrote landmark environmental law. But he began his career in the state legislature in the waning days of Waring's tenure. Hollings drafted the state sales tax law that Gov. Byrnes co-opted to avoid school integration.

As a young attorney, Hollings occasionally appeared in Waring's courtroom. Unlike many Charleston natives of his generation, he held the judge in high esteem. "He was damned nice to me," Hollings later recalled. "He made sure young lawyers weren't bumfuzzled or run over by senior lawyers."

Hollings had come to admire Waring even more over time, recognizing his courage and his revolutionary, prescient passion for justice. Eventually, Hollings suggested renaming the courthouse in honor of the judge. At first, U.S. District Judges Michael Duffy and Richard Gergel ignored the request. Although they admired the judge – Waring was nothing less than Gergel's hero – both feared renaming the courthouse would look like a slight to Hollings. Frustrated, the ever-blunt and charismatic senator finally went public with his idea in 2015.

"I just got the money for the building," Hollings said. "He made history in it."

Within weeks, congressman Jim Clyburn – who'd co-written a book on the *Briggs* plaintiffs – and Sen. Lindsey Graham agreed to honor Hollings' request. It took only a few weeks for South Carolina's entire congressional delegation to sign off on the plan. Some of them had never heard of Waring, and Clyburn said the federal government had never had anyone request their name be removed from a courthouse or post office in favor of someone else.

In October 2015, the Charleston courthouse was officially renamed the J. Waties Waring Judicial Center. Hundreds turned out for the weekday morning ceremony, even though torrential rain forced the crowd into St. Michael's Church. Across the street from the courthouse, the church sat just a block from Waring's old house at 61 Meeting Street.

"This extraordinary story of courage, integrity and commitment to the rule of law has been told and retold over the years, eventually coming to this remarkable day when Charleston, South Carolina, and America reclaim Judge J. Waties Waring as their own," Gergel said during the ceremony. "For those of us who do the work of justice in this courthouse, it will be an enduring honor to work in the building now known as the J. Waties Waring Judicial Center."

Afterward, the crowd wandered out of the church and into the intersection of Broad and Meeting streets, where decades earlier Waring had watched hundreds making their way into the courthouse for opening arguments in *Briggs v. Elliott*.

There are many heroes of the civil rights movement, as many as any war. Waties Waring was an early, integral soldier in that struggle. He maintained that he'd done nothing; African Americans had fought for their rights, and deserved the credit. As judge, he had simply agreed that their arguments were legally correct. As usual, Waring was right.

But that shouldn't diminish his place in the history of a great and continuing struggle. Thurgood Marshall, one of the early icons of civil rights, succeeded in part because he had a friend on the inside at a time when he desperately needed one. Waring used his judgeship to help the NAACP attorney challenge decades of Jim Crow laws and centuries of oppression. Waring was not only decades ahead of his time on voting rights, he devised the plan that forced the United States Supreme Court to end segregation in public schools.

In 1951, 64 years before Charleston put his name on the federal courthouse, Waring sat in 61 Meeting Street writing out his own personal justifications for breaking with his friends, family, Charleston – and much of the country. His predicament bothered him more than he ever admitted in his lifetime, and that year was perhaps the hardest for him. At the time, he didn't realize *Briggs v. Elliott* was destined to change America – or that he had already set in motion the plan that would abolish segregation. Waring didn't know if he'd done anything worthy of upending his entire life.

He typed lists of "gains" and "losses," weighing his actions and their consequences. One list was promising, but short. The other was long – and it was permanent. Waring once said he felt like the Southerners who'd sided with the Union in the Civil War, a traitor to his class and his state. But he never doubted that abandoning his life as a lord of Broad Street was a worthy sacrifice. His lists turned into a private journal entry that few people would see in his lifetime.

"The result has been a complete abandonment by many of my friends and acquaintances," Waring wrote. "In rabid states' righters like the newspaper here, the governor, congressmen and other politicians, it is evidenced by open vituperation. But in former associates, socially in business, and particularly by members of the Bar, it is evidenced by a curtain of silence and a spirit of evading. By the last named I mean a great number of them actually physically dodging around corners so as to avoid the danger of meeting and have to be either pleasant or unpleasant.

"Now, of course, all of this is very disagreeable, and while the loss of social contact really means very little since what I had before was quite frivolous, still it was sometimes quite pleasant and amusing. The greatest deprivation, however, is, I believe, the opportunity to have contact with some people who, at times, were interesting, and particularly some members of the Bar, with whom one could really exchange some information and opinions.

"The absence of social contacts has necessarily caused my wife and myself to be thrown more closely together and to be in constant communication and dependent upon each other's society," the judge wrote.

But Waring, who often felt alone in the early days of the civil rights movement – and feared no one other than Elizabeth truly supported him – had been vindicated.

It was evident on that day in October 2015, when Charleston gave his name to the courthouse where he'd once presided. As hundreds of admirers spilled out onto the Four Corners of Law, where he spent so much of his life, and within sight of the room where he privately recorded his sacrifices and doubts, one thing was clear: Once again, he belonged in Charleston.

Julius Waties Waring was no longer the lonesomest man in town, no longer in a lonely place, no longer forgotten. He had changed history, and finally his place in it was secure.

NOTES

Between 1955 and 1957, Judge Waring sat for a series of interviews with two Columbia University professors, offering his own oral history account of this story. The manuscript of their conversations, which runs 410 pages, includes his thoughts and comments on most of the major events of his life from childhood through *Brown v. Board of Education*. Even the long stories of seemingly meaningless trials offer insights into the judge's personality and thought process. *The Reminiscences of J. Waties Waring* is fascinating reading, and informs the judge's point of view in this narrative.

Waring made a trial run at his reminiscences in 1948, when he met with an unnamed man at a California hotel and allowed their five-hour conversation to be recorded. Although his perception would change, most of his story to that point wouldn't. The tapes are part of the judge's voluminous papers at Howard University. Waring donated his papers to the college in the early 1960s, in hopes they would be used for this specific purpose. Collectively, the 70 boxes of letters, newspaper clippings, telegrams and rough drafts of his decisions lay out the entire story. The only problem is that his papers include no information prior to 1945. For the first 65 years of his life, I had to rely on other resources – including the Charleston newspapers, which published a surprising amount of information on Waring's movements even before he became a judge. This is a roadmap of the sources used to build this narrative.

October 9, 1950

9 *The sound of*: This account comes from *The Reminiscences of J. Waties Waring* (New York: Columbia University, Oral History Research Office, 1957), 307-309, 312-315; "Two missiles thrown at judge's residence," The News and Courier, Oct. 10, 1950; and "City police close books on stoning of Waring house," The Evening Post, Oct. 10, 1950.

Part I: The Ivory City

Open to the world

21 *They began trickling*: "A Grand Jubilate," The News and Courier, Dec. 2, 1901 and "Open To The World!" The News and Courier, Dec. 3, 1901. Additional information from "Blacks and the South Carolina Interstate and West Indian Exposition" by William D. Smyth, *South Carolina Historical Magazine*, Vol. 88, No. 4, (October 1987), 211-219.

24 *The signal came*: "When the button was pressed," The News and Courier, Dec. 3, 1901.

25 *Oh yes. We*: Ibid.

Rice and Recollections

27 *Waring was scheduled*: "Supreme Court proceedings," The News and Courier, Dec. 14, 1901.

27 *How's the judge*: Reminiscences, 26. Much of this chapter is reconstructed from Waring's rambling memories of his childhood.

28 *The Warings arrived*: Ibid, 26; Robert L. Terry, "J. Waties Waring, Spokesman for Racial Justice in the New South" (unpublished thesis, University of Utah, 1970), 1-20.

29 *In 1885, a*: Walter J. Fraser, Jr. *Charleston! Charleston! The History of a Southern City* (Columbia: University of South Carolina Press, 1991), 314-318.

30 *Waring was close*: Reminiscences, 2, 11-17.

33 *At 12, he*: "The University School," The News and Courier, June 30, 1892; June 27, 1895.

33 *McKenney introduced Waring*: Reminiscences, 4, 22-26, 29-42.

35 *On Thursday, Dec.*: "Supreme Court proceedings," The News and Courier, Dec. 14, 1901.

Sabotage at the Exposition

36 *Just after Christmas*: "The little folk will make merry," The Evening Post, Dec. 27, 1901; "Negro Day at Exposition," The News and Courier, Jan. 2, 1902; "Liberty Bell in Charleston," The Evening Post, Jan. 9, 1902; "Thousands of soldiers march," The Evening Post, Feb. 22, 1902.

37 *President Roosevelt planned*: "Charmed with the President," The Evening Post, March 4, 1902.

37 *On Feb. 28*: "Clear the record," The Evening Post, Feb. 28, 1902; "Tillman and the dinner," The Evening Post, Feb. 25, 1902.

38 *Just five months*: "Tillman's pitchfork," The Evening Post, Oct. 30, 1901.

38 *Of course, in*: "Clear the record," The Evening Post, Feb. 28, 1902.

39 *Tillman wasn't finished*: "Trying to scare the President," The Evening Post, March 3, 1902.

39 *The president saw*: "Charmed with the president," The Evening Post, March 4, 1902.

40 *The Huckleberry Finn*: The account of Mark Twain's visit is taken from "Tom Reed and Mark Twain," The Evening Post, April 5, 1902; "Mark Twain in town," The Sunday News, April 6, 1902; and "Mark Twain with a julep," The Evening Post, April 7, 1902.

41 *When the Roosevelts*: "The Greatest Day of a half century of history" and "The President's address," The News and Courier, April 10, 1902.

His place in Charleston

44 *Bryan gave him*: Reminiscences, 43-49.

45 *In the waning*: "Mistrial was ordered," The Evening Post, May 23, 1902.

45 *His only memory*: Reminiscences, 88.

46 *On the final*: "Cases heard in the police court this morning," The Evening Post, June 2, 1902.

46 *Julia Jenkins said*: "Verdict for the defendant," The Evening Post, July 15, 1902; "In the common pleas," The News and Courier, Nov. 22, 1902.

46 *In the first*: Fraser, 338-343. Additional information from *Year Book City of Charleston, South Carolina 1903* (Charleston: Daggett Printing Company, 1904).

48 *Later, long after*: Tinsley E. Yarbrough, *A Passion for Justice* (New York: Oxford University Press, 1987), 30.

48 *In September 1903*: "Society," The Evening Post, Sept. 23, 1903; "Funeral notice," The Evening Post, Dec. 23, 1903.

49 *In January 1904*: "Appointed commissioner," The Evening Post, Jan. 7, 1904.

49 *For the most part*: "Held as robber of post office," The Evening Post, Oct. 12, 1904.

49 *After a year*: "All around town," The News and Courier, Dec. 10, 1904.

49 *Before long, he*: "Endorse Jervey," The Evening Post, March 28, 1905.

50 *At 24, Waring*: Waring's civic activities were chronicled in The Evening Post and The News and Courier regularly. His work with college students appeared on May 30, 1905; the attempted acquisition

of Hampton Park is from June 15, 1908. Waring wasn't a member of the committee that reported against admitting women, but several of his friends were – including J.P.K. Bryan.

50 *His growing list*: "United States commissioner," The News and Courier, April 7, 1906.

51 *Waring's connections eventually*: "City Council proceedings," The Evening Post, April 30, 1909; "Lower rates likely for lighting here," The Evening Post, April 29, 1909; "Drayton Hastie resigns," The News and Courier, Sept. 1, 1911.

A wedding, a recount, a shooting

52 *He'd known Annie*: Two society notices in The Evening Post – one from April 14, 1898 and another from Jan. 16, 1899 – mention that Marie Gammell visited Waring's mother at their Rutledge Avenue home. It's unclear whether Annie accompanied her either time, or why these visits were newsworthy, but obviously the families were acquainted.

52 *Yesterday the sea*: Annie Gammell letter to Waring, March 15, 1912. From the South Carolina Historical Society file Waring, Annie Gammell, 1879-1954. Letters to J. Waties Waring, 1912-1913. (43/2501).

53 *Her father died*: "Mr. W.A. Gammell," News and Courier, June 12, 1889; "Mrs. W.A. Gammell, death in Toronto yesterday of a Charleston lady," Evening Post, Aug. 1, 1901.

53 *She'd written her*: "A former Charlestonian recalls friendship with Sarah Bernhardt," The News and Courier, Sept. 25, 1946.

54 *In the spring*: Annie Gammell letter to Waties Waring, postmarked April 5, 1913. South Carolina Historical Society. Waring, Annie Gammell, 1879-1954. Letters to J. Waties Waring, 1912-1913. (43/2501).

54 *After two years*: "Marriage Notice," The Evening Post, Nov. 6, 1913.

54 *Waring's friends considered*: Yarbrough, 29-31.

55 *In August 1914*: "J. Waties Waring named to succeed Mr. Young," The News and Courier, Aug. 15, 1914.

55 *Weston worked out*: Reminiscences, 50-52, 53, 55-59.

56 *Just as the*: "German vessel interned here sinks in river," The News and Courier, Feb. 2, 1917.

56 *He and Annie*: The history of 61 Meeting Street was compiled from several sources, including Melissa Bigner, "Past Perfect: The Peters Make a Storied Home on Meeting Street's Mansion Row Their Own," Charleston Magazine, Jan. 2011, 46-50; and Jonathan H. Poston, *The Buildings of Charleston: A Guide to the City's Architecture* (Columbia: University of South Carolina Press, 1997), 263-264. Advertisements from The News and Courier, including one on March 23, 1912, show it was the location of the Hyde Drug Co. The News and Courier reported that the house was sold to Bessie Woolsey – Annie's sister – on May 15, 1913. And a business permit issued to W.W. Woolsey – Bessie's stepson – for work on the house, reported in The Evening Post on July 11, 1913. And on Aug. 27, 1913, the family published a notice in The News and Courier inviting to contractors to bid on remodeling and painting work for the residence.

57 *Charleston was not*: The city's condition and the account of the 1915 mayoral race was taken from various newspaper accounts, as well as Fraser, 357-358.

57 *The recount was*: "Riot and bloodshed at election canvass," The News and Courier, Oct. 16, 1915.

59 *Edward Waring died*: "Mr. E.P. Waring dead," The Evening Post, March 21, 1916.

59 *The war brought*: "Buy bonds, urges Admiral Beatty," The News and Courier, April 7, 1918; "J. Waties Waring will discuss German spy system," The Evening Post, April 13, 1918;

59 *And when Sarah*: "Bernhardt is supers," The Evening Post, Jan. 15. 1917.

60 *He formed a*: "New law firm," The Evening Post, April 6, 1920; The Evening Post and The News and Courier, March 2-3, 1921.

60 *Waring stayed on*: "Resigns after long service," The Evening Post, Sept. 28, 1921.

Two cities

61 *As the city's*: Fraser, 308.

61 *Peter Porcher Poinsette*: Septima Clark with LeGette Blythe, *Echo in My Soul* (New York: Dutton, 1962), 13-18.

63 *The Navy base*: Fraser, 361.

63 *Thomas E. Miller*: Clark, 25, 60-61; "Don't favor the change," The News and Courier, July 6, 1914; "Resolutions passed endorsing policy in changing faculty," The Evening Post, July 18, 1914.

65 *In 1903, when*: Clark, 16-17; 22; 32; 49-59.

66 *One Saturday evening*: "Race riots occur here," The News and Courier, May 11, 1919; "2 dead; 27 wounded in street rioting," The News and Courier, May 12, 1919; "All quiet in town after the rioting," The News and Courier, May 13, 1919; "No shooting by sailors," The Evening Post, May 15, 1919.

68 *That summer the*: Clark, 61.

The livin' is easy

70 *Once again, Charleston*: Fraser, 368-370; Robert Rosen, *A Short History of Charleston* (San Francisco: Lexikos, 1982), 131.

71 *Much of his*: "Hyde trial is far from end," The Evening Post, Dec. 4, 1924; "Mrs. Ingram's case in court," The News and Courier, May 12, 1925.

71 *Waring's sister, Margaret*: "Mrs. Harvey visits governor's mansion," The Evening Post, May 16, 1922; "Wilson G. Harvey succeeds R.A. Cooper as governor of the state of South Carolina," The Evening Post, May 20, 1922.

72 *Like most old*: Reminiscences, 87-90.

72 *Waring finally had*: The first public mention of Waring's beach house came in the Personals column of The Evening Post, July 13, 1923. "Mr. and Mrs. Waties Waring and little daughter, Anne, are occupying their home at Station 26, Sullivan's Island." Similar notices appeared frequently in the local papers throughout the 1920s and 1930s.

73 *By the end*: "Island society names officers," The News and Courier, Aug. 18, 1923.

73 *Many of Waring's*: Stephanie E. Yuhl, *A Golden Haze of Memory: The Making of Historic Charleston* (Chapel Hill: University of North Carolina Press, 2005), 24-26.

74 *DuBose Heyward was*: James M. Hutchisson, *DuBose Heyward: A Charleston Gentleman and the World of Porgy and Bess* (Jackson: University of Mississippi Press, 2000) 7-9.

75 *Heyward hadn't intended*: "Du Bose Heyward's book is remarkable analysis of the Negro's psychology," The Evening Post, Oct. 5, 1925.

79 *In 1926, a*: Fraser, 370; Rosen, 132-133.

76 *After years of*: Reminiscences, 92-94; Fraser, 377-378.

76 *One of Maybank's*: "City to name counsel," The News and Courier, Jan. 26, 1932.

77 *He argued government*: "Pay Warrant Authorized," The Evening Post, Jan. 13, 1932; *Reminiscences*, 91-99; *Reminiscences*, 98, 125.

77 *Year later, when*: Yarbrough, *A Passion for Justice*, 13.

77 *Every New Year's*: "New Year reception given yesterday," The News and Courier, Jan. 2, 1932. The papers often advertised the party in society columns in advance of the drop-in.

78 *The summers at*: "Personal notes of interest," The News and Courier, Aug. 7, 1932; Aug. 8, 1934.

78 *In September 1933*: "Personal notes of interest," The News and Courier, Sept. 2, 1933.

78 *The famed composer*: "George Gershwin arrives to plan opera on 'Porgy,'" The News and Courier, Dec. 4, 1933; "Gershwin, gone native, finds it 'shame to work' at Folly," by Frank B. Gilbreth, The News and Courier, June 29, 1934.

The campaign

80 *Waring had quietly*: Reminiscences, 128a-129a; "Judge Cochran, 68, found dead; services today," The News and Courier, March 5, 1934; "Services for Judge Cochran at residence," The Evening Post, March 5, 1935.

81 *Waring later said*: Reminiscences, 129a-133a; "Myers not given place on Smith's slate for bench," The News and Courier, March 22, 1934.

82 *When Myers' name*: Reminiscences, 132a-133a; "F.K. Myers named judge; Burguson, marshal, and Baker, collector of port," The Evening Post, June 6, 1934.

83 *He prosecuted the*: "Bikle, guilt, gets sentence of five years," The Evening Post, March 14, 1035; "Bikle indictment center of attack," The News and Courier, Feb. 12, 1936; *Reminiscences*, 105, 117-119.

83 *For several weeks*: "Society and club news," The Evening Post, Aug. 8, 1935.

84 *His brother, Thomas*: "Rites today for Thomas R. Waring," The News and Courier, June 2, 1935; "E.P. Waring dies in Jacksonville," The News and Courier, Nov. 23, 1936.

84 *Anne was home*: Anne Waring's various parties were noted in The Evening Post and The News and Courier society pages, including stories on Dec. 11, Dec. 18 and Dec. 29, 1937.

84 *In early 1938*: *Reminiscences*, 107; "Fast convention moves smoothly," The News and Courier, May 3, 1938.

85 *Buoyed by a*: "Smith is re-nominated, Maybank and Manning leading race for governor," The News and Courier, Aug. 31, 1938.

85 *With most of*: "Maybank is nominated governor," The News and Courier, Sept. 14, 1938; "Manning protest dismissal starts celebration here," The News and Courier, Sept. 21, 1938; *Reminiscences*, 107.

86 *The charges by*: "Charlestonians at Columbia to cheer Maybank victory," The News and Courier, Sept. 21, 1938.

87 *That night, thousands*: "Frenzied throngs meet Maybank," The News and Courier, Sept. 21, 1938; *Reminiscences*, 134a.

88 *He resigned as*: "College board vacancy filled," The Evening Post, Nov. 7, 1938.

88 *When Gov. Maybank*: *Reminiscences*, 134a-136a.

90 *Sen. Smith already*: "Waring expected to be appointed as federal judge," The News and Courier, Nov. 28, 1941; *Reminiscences*, 137a-138a; "Waring and Timmerman nominated by president as district judges," The News and Courier, Dec. 19, 1941.

Part II: The Seeds of Justice
A servant of the public

95 *On this day*: "Americans blast 7 enemy vessels in naval battle," The News and Courier, Jan. 26, 1942; Rosen, 144; Fraser, 386-393.

96 *Mayor Lockwood brought*: "J.W. Waring sworn in as federal judge," The Evening Post, Jan. 26, 1942.

97 *This court is*: Transcript of Judge Waring's acceptance speech. Julius Waties Waring Papers, manuscript division of the Moorland Spingarn Research Center at Howard University, Series F, Box 110-34, folder 1012.

97 *When he finished*: "J.W. Waring sworn in as federal judge," The Evening Post, Jan. 26, 1942; "Waring receives oath as judge," The News and Courier, Jan. 27, 1942.

97 *After the White*: "The judges appointed," The News and Courier, Dec. 12, 1941; "Smith unopposed to nominations," The News and Courier, Jan. 13, 1942; "Nominations are confirmed," The Evening Post, Jan. 20, 1942.

98 *Waring found this*: *Reminiscences*, 142a-143a.

99 *The couple wed*: "Miss Waring weds Mr. Warren," The Evening Post, Nov. 5, 1942.

99 *That spring, Waring*: "Orth hearing is concluded," The Evening Post, April 23, 1943; *Reminiscences*, 63-64.

100 *The visiting judge*: "Newark newspaper praises work of Charleston judge," The News and Courier, Oct. 8, 1944; *Reminiscences*, 153a-154a.

Prisoners at the bar

103 *In the fall*: The background of Viola Louise Duvall comes from "Tribute to Viola Duvall Stewart," a resolution by Congressman James E. Clyburn, Congressional Record Vol. 156, No. 83, 2010; and *Civil Rights in South Carolina: From Peaceful Protests to Groundbreaking Rulings* by James L. Felder (Charleston: The History Press, 2012), 27-30.

105 *You know these*: "Teachers' Role in Ending School Segregation," American Educator, Summer 2004.

105 *Charleston officials asked*: "School board contends that Negro teacher cannot sue now," The Evening Post, Dec. 3, 1943; "Court refuses to dismiss Negro teacher suit," The Evening Post, Feb. 10, 1944.

105 *In eight years*: Thurgood Marshall's background and early legal career was culled from many sources, including Juan Williams, *Thurgood Marshall: American Revolutionary* (New York: Times Books, 1998) and Richard Kluger, *Simple Justice* (New York: Knopf, 1976).

107 *On Feb. 10*: Felder, *Civil Rights in South Carolina*, 30-31; "Court refuses to dismiss Negro teacher suit," The Evening Post, Feb. 10, 1944; *Reminiscences*, 225-226; Katherine Mellen Charron, *Freedom's Teacher: The Life of Septima Clark* (Chapel Hill: University of North Carolina Press, 2009), 164-165.

109 *He had pegged*: Patricia Sullivan, *Lift Every Voice: The NAACP and the Making of the Civil Rights Movement* (New York: New Press, 2009).

109 *Waring's order followed*: Judgment in the case of *Duvall v. Seignious*, Feb. 14, 1944. Waring Papers, Series D, Box 110-27, folder 835; "Court orders Negro teacher pay equality," The News and Courier, Feb. 15, 1944; "The Submissive South," The News

and Courier, Feb. 16, 1944; "Viola D. Stewart, 91, civil-rights pioneers, Philadelphia teacher," The Philadelphia Inquirer, Dec. 18, 2010.

The fires of Columbia

112 *The military had*: Fraser, 389; "167,000 people now living in county, bureau reports," The Evening Post, May 1, 1944; "Court orders youth sent to state hospital," The Evening Post, April 8, 1944; "Orangeburg man gets suspended sentence," The Evening Post, April 18, 1944.

113 *Within a month*: "Education system demanded attention in legislature," The News and Courier, March 19, 1944; Charron, 171.

114 *White supremacy will*: "Assembly repeals sections of state code on primaries," The News and Courier, April 16, 1944; "Governor shouts to Assembly that white supremacy must be maintained in primaries," The News and Courier, April 15, 1944.

115 *On its editorial*: "Why look to white primaries?" The News and Courier, April 16, 1944; "Of course they can vote," The News and Courier, April 22, 1944.

115 *At one community*: Clark, 67-83.

117 *Albert Thompson had*: Felder, *Civil Rights in South Carolina*, 33; *Reminiscences*, 226-232; Clark, 81; *Reminiscences*, 226.

118 *Richland County did*: "Distinction in teachers' pay is based on merit, court told," The News and Courier, May 10, 1945; *Reminiscences*, 226-232; "Columbia school board enjoined by court order," The Evening Post, May 26, 1945.

120 *Waring realized the*: *Reminiscences*, 230; Letter from Waring to state Sen. Edgar A. Brown, June 12, 1945. Waring Papers, Series C, Box 110-8, folder 212.

121 *It is fortunate*: Letter from Waring to J. Heyward Gibbes, June 12, 1945, Waring Papers, Series C, Box 110-11, folder 279.

121 *It made me*: *Reminiscences*, 235-236.

Exile on Meeting Street

122 *This commencement, which*: "Men of peace honored at final college exercises," The Evening Post, May 30, 1945; "Class is told education ideal effective here," The News and Courier, May 30, 1945.

123 *Waring acted as*: "Federal court moves swiftly on opening day," The Evening Post, May 28, 1945; Waring's account of his split from Annie is in *Reminiscences*, 402-404.

123 *For years, Charleston*: *Reminiscences*, 236-246; Yabrough, 29-31.

125 *Elizabeth was unlike*: The background information on Elizabeth comes from a number of sources, including *Reminiscences*, but most notably from Jessica Letizia Lancia, "Giving the South the Shock Treatment: Elizabeth Waring and the Civil Rights Movement," (Masters thesis, College of Charleston and The Citadel, 2007) published in book form by UMI.

126 *To get around*: *Reminiscences*, 402-404.

126 *You probably think*: Letter to Rowena Taylor Waring, March 17, 1945, reprinted in Yabrough, 34-35; 1947 taped Waring interview, Waring Papers, Series N, Box 110-78.

128 *The News and*: "Judge J.W. Waring and wife divorced," The News and Courier, June 9, 1945; "Judge Waring to attend judicial conference," The Evening Post, June 2, 1945; "Judge Waring weds Mrs. Hoffman at Greenwich, Conn.," The News and Courier, June 18, 1945.

128 *When they returned*: Biographical interview, Waring Papers, Series N, Box 110-78; "Audience to meet cast at Dock

St.," The News and Courier, Feb. 13, 1946; "Judge Waring leaves for New York court," The Evening Post, Aug. 16, 1945.

Excessive force

130 *He heard cases*: "Warden's assailant given two years; Legette case ends," The News and Courier, Jan. 24, 1946.

131-134 *On Tuesday, Feb.*: Isaac Woodard's story is taken from several sources, including "Resonant Ripples in a Global Pond: The Blinding of Isaac Woodard," a paper by USC Upstate American Studies professor Andrew Myers delivered to the American Humanities Conference in 2002; a memorandum in *United States v. Lynwood Lanier Shull*, Waring Papers, Series D, Box 110-31, folder 938. Although the meaning never changes, there are slight variations in the wording of Woodard's quotes from one account to the next. Any quotes here come from sworn testimony, NAACP depositions and his lawsuit against the Greyhound Bus Co.

134 *Woodard's parents took*: Myers, "Resonant Ripples in a Global Pond" and "NAACP asks removal of chief of Batesburg police," The News and Courier, Aug. 20, 1946.

134 *He was just*: Orson Welles, *Commentaries* ABC radio broadcast, July 28, 1946.

135 *Cornered by a*: "Blinded soldier was hit while resisting arrest," The News and Courier, Aug. 18, 1946.

135 *On Sept. 19*: Myers, "Resonant Ripples in a Global Pond."

136 *The warrant for*: *Reminiscences*, 215-218; Waring memo to U.S. attorney's office, Waring Papers, Series D, Box 110-31, folder 938.

137-139 *The trial of*: "Isaac Woodard testifies against Batesburg chief," The Evening Post, Nov. 5, 1946; "Batesburg chief is acquitted of attack charge," The News and Courier, Nov. 6, 1946; Myers, "Resonant Ripples in a Global Pond;" *Reminiscences*, 219-222.

139 *After he charged*: *Reminiscences*, 222-224.

A calculated call

142 *Two weeks after*: "Address of the Hon. J. Waties Waring, U.S. District judge, to citizens naturalized at Charleston, S.C. on Nov. 22, 1946, Waring Papers, Series F, Box 110-34, folder 102.

142 *When the judge*: "Lonesomest Man in Town," by Samuel Grafton, Collier's, April 29, 1950, 20-21, 49-50.

144 *It was so*: Ibid.

144-145 *In August 1946*: "Injunction asked against white primary," The Evening Post, Feb. 21, 1947. Some of the biographical information on Elmore comes his daughter, Yolande Cole, as reported in "One man's sacrifice ends white voting clubs," The State, March 3, 2003.

146 *In January, the*: "University of S.C. trustees sued by Charleston Negro," The News and Courier, Jan. 9, 1947; "House action boosts deficiency spending to $5,590,000 total," The News and Courier, March 25, 1947; "Law school at State College planned by board," The Evening Post, May 21, 1947.

147-149 *He explained this*: *Reminiscences*, 246-258.

Declaration of War

150 *Gov. Melvin Thompson*: "Thompson vetoes white primary bill in Georgia," The Evening Post, March 28, 1947.

150 *The pending lawsuits*: "Against their own interest," The News and Courier, Jan. 9, 1947; "Know not what they do," The News and Courier, Jan. 11, 1947; "Protect lawful rights," The News and Courier, Feb.

18, 1947; John D. Stark, *Damned Upcountryman: William Watts Ball: A Study in American Conservatism* (Durham: Duke University Press, 1968).

151 *By doing so*: "Law of primary elections," The News and Courier, March 7, 1947; "Answer filed to suit on white primary," The Evening Post, April 15, 1947.

151 *In May, Waring*: "Judge Waring sets June 3 hearing on Democratic primary," The News and Courier, May 16, 1947; "USC exclusion of Negroes, white primary to get tests," The News and Courier, June 1, 1947.

152-155 *The temperature inside*: The account of *Elmore v. Rice* is taken from several sources, including "State functions in primary, lawyer argues," The News and Courier, June 4, 1947; "NAACP lawyer attacks S.C. primary rule," The Evening Post, June 3, 1947; "Early decision promised in primary suit," The Evening Post, June 4, 1947; "Vested interest is charged in primary case," The News and Courier, June 5, 1947; and *Reminiscences*, 262-265.

155 *The white man's*: "Social clubs may nominate," The News and Courier, June 5, 1947; "Might help the situation," The News and Courier, June 9, 1947.

156-158 *The Wrighten lawsuit*: "Negro plan made plain," The News and Courier, July 7, 1947; "Arguments begin in suit against USC," The Evening Post, June 5, 1947; "Court told Negro law school set," The Evening Post, June 6, 1947; *Reminiscences*, 258-259.

159 *He breathlessly wrote*: "Would close state colleges," The News and Courier, June 10, 1947; "Warning, shall warn again," The News and Courier, June 11, 1947.

159 *These were sensitive*: *Reminiscences*, 257-260.

159 *Our immediate task*: President Truman address to the NAACP, June 29, 1947, Public Papers of Harry S. Truman 1945-1953, No. 130, Harry S. Truman Presidential Library and Museum. www.trumanlibrary.org.

160 *Waring felt Truman*: Reminiscences, 256, 266-267.

160 *I cannot see*: Order in *Elmore v. Rice*, July 12, 1947. Waring Papers, Series D, Box 110-29, folder 883.

In the Court of Appeals

162 *John McCray, chairman*: "Negroes comment," The Evening Post, July 12, 1947.

162 *This is the*: "Stoney condemns court's opinion against the party," The Evening Post, July 12, 1947; "Primary decision evokes comment by local leaders," The News and Courier, July 13, 1947. "Maybank believes primary ruling 'clearly wrong'," The Evening Post, July 14, 1947; "Negro leaders flay Maybank's vote statement," The News and Courier, July 15, 1947.

163-164 *In Sunday's News*: "Federal court decisions," The News and Courier, July 13, 1947; "Rights of citizens again invaded," The Evening Post, July 14, 1947; "Rejoining the Union," The Evening Post, July 15, 1947.

164 *One of the*: Letter from Annie B. Gibson to Waring, July 14, 1947, Waring Papers, Series C, Box 110-23, folder 715.

164 *Any white man*: "Negro plan made plain," The News and Courier, July 7, 1947.

165 *The Lighthouse and*: Jack Irby Hayes, Jr. *South Carolina and the New Deal* (Columbia: University of South Carolina Press, 2001), 180.

165 *For the first*: Letter from Walter Manigault to Waring, July 15, 1947. Waring Papers, Series C, Box 110-23, folder 700.

165 *On the day*: "Comparable law school planned for S.C. Negroes," The News and Courier, July 13, 1947.

166 *The state Democratic*: "Primary case appeal voted by S.C. party," The Evening Post, July 17, 1947; "Negro voting in S.C. temporarily banned by judge," The Evening Post, Aug. 19, 1947.

167 *In the spring*: "Defendants would call Judge Waring as witness," The News and Courier, Oct. 8, 1947; "Judge would grant new trials in Richmond bank case," The News and Courier, Oct. 11, 1947.

167 *The evening after*: The Warings are mentioned as banquet attendees in "Strong U.S. must fight communism, Lynch council told," The News and Courier, Oct. 14, 1947.

168-169 *In October, the*: "Motion made to get Negro in law school," The Evening Post, Oct. 4, 1947; "Court dismisses state's appeal in law school case," The Evening Post, Nov. 21, 1947; "Court dismisses law school appeal," The News and Courier, Nov. 22, 1947.

169-171 *John Ellis Wilhelm*: "Hartsville man fined for violation of civil liberties act," The News and Courier, Dec. 3, 1947; "S.C. man fined for violating Civil Liberty Act," The Evening Post, Dec. 3, 1947; *Reminiscences*, 196-203.

171 *While Waring was*: "Court of Appeals to hear white supremacy arguments," The News and Courier, Nov. 15, 1947; "Judge Waring's decision on Negro vote upheld," The News and Courier, Dec. 31, 1947.

Rise of the Dixiecrats

173 *President Truman gave*: Annual Message to the Congress on the State of the Union, Jan. 7, 1948, Public Papers of Harry S. Truman 1945-1953, No. 2, Harry S.

Truman Presidential Library and Museum; "Truman offers $40 individual tax credit cut," The News and Courier, Jan. 8, 1948; "S.C. senators hit reference to civil rights," The News and Courier, Jan. 8, 1948.

174 *When Truman delivered*: "Truman asks U.S. laws on civil rights," The News and Courier, Feb. 3, 1948; "Two attack Truman civil rights message," The News and Courier, Feb. 3, 1948; "Democrats urged to bolt," The News and Courier, Feb. 3, 1948.

175 *He ruled against*: "Insurance firm suit dismissed by judge," The Evening Post, Jan. 17, 1948; "Charges against two Berkeley men dismissed," The News and Courier, Jan. 20, 1948; and "School teachers denied $50,000 in damage suit," The News and Courier, Feb. 5, 1948.

175 *His attorney argued*: "Darlington man must serve full time in peonage case," The Evening Post, Feb. 3, 1948.

175 *On Feb. 7*: "Democrats take fight to high court," The Evening Post, Feb. 7, 1948.

176 *The day after*: "Thurmond will lead white supremacy group to Washington," The News and Courier, Feb. 9, 1948.

176 *Shortly after Thurmond*: "Hurd named trigger man in testimony," The Evening Post, May 14, 1947.

176 *Strom Thurmond was*: Much of the biographical detail of Thurmond's life comes from Jack Bass and Marilyn W. Thompson, *Strom: The Complicated Personal and Political Life of Strom Thurmond* (New York: Public Affairs, 2005).

176 *The South demands*: "Thurmond will lead white supremacy group to Washington," The News and Courier, Feb. 9, 1948.

177 *Essie Mae was*: Bass and Thompson, *Strom*, 33-35, 95, 118-119.

177 *In April, the*: "Primary voting may be limited to registrants," The Evening Post, April 20, 1948; *Reminiscences*, 272.

178 *Those delegates met*: "Convention ended by Dixie Democrats," The News and Courier, May 11, 1948; "Delegates at conference serious and determined," The News and Courier, May 11, 1948.

178 *The delegates called*: "Call 'em Dixiecrats," The News and Courier, May 11, 1948. The Charlotte News came up with the famous moniker, according to this Associated Press story.

178 *When South Carolina*: "Thurmond party's presidential choice," The News and Courier, May 20, 1948.

179 *The four-paragraph*: "Party's new oath backfires" and "Phrase dealing with religion is denounced," The Evening Post, May 26, 1948.

179 *The NAACP had*: "Negro school bus suit is dismissed," The News and Courier, June 9, 1948; "State A&M law school ruled 'equal,'" The News and Courier, June 19, 1948.

180 *David Brown was*: The background on David Brown and his lawsuit comes from Judge Waring's notes on the case, Waring Papers, Series D, Box 110-27, folder 824.

181 *Four days later*: "NAACP officials to seek injunction against party heads," The News and Courier, July 7, 1948; "Negro enrollment ordered by court," The News and Courier, July 9, 1948.

'Campaign of vilification'

182 *The Democratic National*: Some details of the convention come from "1948 Democratic Convention: The South Secedes Again," by Alonzo L. Hamby, Smithsonian magazine, August 2008.

183 *One state delegate*: "Party officials meet today to consider ruling" and "Thurmond puts S.C. delegation behind Laney," The News and Courier, July 13, 1948; "S.C. delegates decline to bolt convention" and "2 Dixie states walk; Truman nominated," The News and Courier, July 15, 1948; "Thurmond will go to Dixiecrat meet," The News and Courier, July 17, 1948.

183 *The Evening Post*: "There is no out," The Evening Post, July 10, 1948.

184-186 *On July 16*: The two-hour hearing in *Brown v. Baskin* is chronicled in "Waring orders books opens" and "Senate candidate ejected from courtroom during enrollment hearing," The Evening Post, July 16, 1948; "Full participation of Negroes in Democratic primary ordered," The News and Courier, July 17, 1948; and *Reminiscences*, 287-288.

186 *They planned a*: "Delegates plan strategy to unite Southern states," The Evening Post, July 17, 1948.

187 *Thurmond got two*: Bass and Thompson, 116-119; "Thurmond to campaign 'many states,'" The News and Courier, July 21, 1948.

188 *Between campaign stops*: Bass and Thompson, 117-119.

188 *The ruling was*: "Court tells party to be 'American'" and "5 men withdraw, others may do so," The News and Courier, July 21, 1948.

189-190 *At a campaign*: "Three candidates for Senate speak at Newberry," The Evening Post, July 27, 1948; "Waring's order is 'deplorable,' says Maybank," The Evening Post, July 21, 1948; "Unfair tactics," The Evening Post, July 23, 1948; "Cotton Ed Smith's son says Maybank nominated Waring," The News and Courier, Aug. 3, 1948.

190 *On July 27*: "Dorn says resolution may lead to impeachment move," The News and Courier, July 28, 1948; "Dorn demands Judge Waring be impeached," The Evening Post, July 29, 1948; "'Unbecoming,' says Dorn of Waring ruling," The News and Courier, July 29, 1948; "Dorn cites judge's divorce, says neighbors snub him," The News and Courier, July 30, 1948.

191 *As the campaign*: "Democrats deny judge's right to open books," The Evening Post, July 29, 1948; "Judge clarifies original order on voter's oath," The Evening Post, July 22, 1948; "The master minds," The Evening Post, July 23, 1948; *Reminiscences*, 296-298.

192 *He predicted that*: "Rivers predicts bloodshed over Waring decision," The News and Courier, Aug. 5, 1948. Rivers outdid himself. This is perhaps the funniest political insult ever.

193 *But Rivers inexplicably*: "Rivers drops plan to remove Judge Waring," The Evening Post, Aug. 7, 1948; "Vinson refuses to investigate Waring's conduct," The Evening Post, Aug. 5 1948.

194 *It is pretty*: Letter from Waring to Judge John Parker, Aug. 5, 1948. Waring Papers, Series C, Box 110-16, folder 450.

194 *You are wise*: Letter from Judge John Parker to Waring, Aug. 6, 1948. Ibid.

194 *You and I*: Reminiscences, 310.

195 *Waring joked to*: Letter from Waring to Judge John Parker, Aug. 11, 1948. Waring Papers, Series C, Box 110-16, folder 450.

195 *All of this*: Letter from Waring to Judge John Parker, Aug. 9, 1948. Ibid.

195 *Waring met with*: "NAACP attorney says primary 'going smoothly,'" The Evening Post, Aug. 10, 1948.

195 *That evening, the*: The Warings' travel itinerary was outlined in the judge's letter to Judge John Parker, Aug. 5, 1948. Waring Papers, Series C, Box 110-16, folder 450.

Part III: 'Segregation is per se inequality'

A matter of buses

199 *The Rev. Joseph*: DeLaine's early life is reconstructed here with the Joseph A. DeLaine Papers in USC's South Caroliniana Library; Richard Kluger, *Simple Justice* (New York: Knopf, 1976); and Ophelia De Laine Gona, *Dawn of Desegregation: J.A. De Laine and Briggs v. Elliott* (Columbia: University of South Carolina Press, 2011).

199 *He'd adopted this*: Essay, n.d., "Prelude to Rev. Joseph A. DeLaine's Opposition," by Joseph A. DeLaine Sr., DeLaine Papers, USC Library; Kluger, 14-16.

200 *The rattle-trap*: Gona, 21-22.

201 *The lawsuit made*: Kluger, 17; "Negro school bus suit is dismissed," The News and Courier, June 9, 1948.

201-203 *Time passed slowly*: Gona, 38-39, 41; Kluger, 10, 13.

204-205 *Strom Thurmond barnstormed*: "Thurmond speaks in Florida today; BRT denies support," The News and Courier, Sept. 6, 1948; "Thurmond sorry Truman to skip S.C. speaking," The Evening Post, Sept. 29, 1948; Bass and Thompson, 119; "Thurmond says reds want civil rights," The Evening Post, Oct. 8, 1948; "States righters gain momentum" and "States rights dinner to be held Sept. 30," The News and Courier, Sept. 12, 1948.

205 *The lawmakers who*: "County adopts Plan A, vote overwhelmingly in home rule favor," The News and Courier, Sept. 15, 1948; "Plan A adopted, 7 will be elected to county council," The Evening Post, Sept. 15, 1948.

206 *Ten candidates were*: "20 candidates file for county council primary," The Evening Post, Sept. 25, 1948. Several details of Clement's biography came from campaign advertisements in both Charleston papers between Sept. 26 and Oct. 7, 1948; "Look sharp, states rights men," The News and Courier, Sept. 26, 1948; "6 men are nominated for posts on county council in first race," The News and Courier, Oct. 8, 1948.

207 *His absence was*: "Judge Waring leaves for vacation in N.Y.," The News and Courier, Aug. 13, 1948.

His world view

208-210 *The El Encanto*: All of the information and quotations from the judge's summer 1948 interview in Santa Barbara were recorded on phonograph and filed at Howard University in Waring Papers, Series N, Box 110-78.

211 *Nothing had changed*: "Negroes would prevent jury trial of case," The News and Courier, Oct. 19, 1948; "Klan letter was threat, Waring says," The Evening Post, Oct. 23, 1948; and "Vote case motions designed to put decision up to Waring," The News and Courier, Oct. 20, 1948; "South's prejudice assailed by Waring in N.Y. speech," The Evening Post, Oct. 13, 1948.

211 *Marshall had orchestrated*: Robert J. Silberstein, executive secretary of the National Lawyers Guild, referenced Marshall's complaints about the lack of publicity for Waring's speech in a letter to Marshall dated March 1, 1949. Waring Papers, Series C, Box 110-15, folder 386.

211 *Waring only seemed*: "Waring refuses to disqualify self in case," The News and Courier, Oct. 23, 1948.

211 *The day of*: Letter signed Knights of the Ku Klux Klan, n.d., Waring Papers, Series C, Box 110-23, folder 725; "'Klan'

letter was threat, Waring says," The Evening Post, Oct. 23, 1948.

212 *But privately, Waring*: Letter from Waring to Rev. T.A. Beckett, Oct. 25, 1948. Waring Papers, Series C, Box 110-8, folder 197.

212-214 *On Nov. 2*: "Thurmond votes at Edgefield," The News and Courier, Nov. 3, 1948; Bass and Thompson, 121; "Divorce amendment still favored on incomplete tally," The News and Courier, Nov. 4, 1948.

214 *Waring avoided the*: "Testimony completed in $125,000 suit," The Evening Post, Nov. 3, 1948.

215 *No self-respecting*: "Judge studies injunction arguments," The Evening Post, Nov. 23, 1948.

215 *We cannot escape*: "Waring rules Negroes entitled to full membership in party," The Evening Post, Nov. 26, 1948.

216 *Their editorial suggested*: "Just be nice about it," The Evening Post, Dec. 2, 1948.

Executive decisions

217 *On Thursday morning*: The meeting between Waring and President Truman is reconstructed from *Reminiscences* and a series of letters he wrote to Marshall and Truman – including an unsent draft of a letter written to the president in 1952 – in Waring Papers, Series C.

217 *Truman was effusive*: Letter from Waring to Truman, Dec. 6, 1948. Waring Papers, Series C, Box 110-19, folder 567.

217 *Waring found Truman*: Waring letter to Thurgood Marshall, Dec. 4, 1948. Waring Papers, Series C, Box 110-15, folder 385.

218 *Mr. President, I*: Reminiscences, 223.

218 *Finally, he suggested*: Draft letter from Waring to Truman, undated 1952. Waring Papers, Series C, Box 110-22, folder 662.

218 *The people in*: Letter from Waring

to Truman, Dec. 6, 1948. Waring Papers, Series C, Box 110-19, folder 567.

218 *A week later*: Letter from President Truman to Waring, Dec. 10, 1948. Waring Papers, Series C, Box 110-19, folder 567.

218-219 *The judge mentioned*: "Waring advocates federal trial of lynching cases," The Evening Post, Dec. 2, 1948; "Judge Waring visits Truman, says poll tax is 'stupid,'" The News and Courier, Dec. 3, 1948; "Advances toward democracy," The New York Times, as reprinted in The News and Courier, Dec. 5, 1948; "Another verdict," The Evening Post, Dec. 6, 1948.

219 *The Washington trip*: "Waring is mum on rumor talk about promotion," The News and Courier, Dec. 8, 1948; Waring letter to Thurgood Marshall, Dec. 4, 1948. Waring Papers, Series C, Box 110-15, folder 385.

220 *The overwhelming resistance*: Letter from Waring to George C. Schermer, Nov. 4, 1948. Waring Papers, Series C, Box 110-18, folder 502.

220 *In January 1949*: "Thurmond asks many changes in S.C. laws," The Evening Post, Jan. 13, 149; "Bill offered on rights of political parties," The News and Courier, Feb. 17, 1949.

221 *The Democrats were*: "Judge Waring wins civil rights award," The Evening Post, Jan. 24. 1949; "Negro publishers group honors Judge J.W. Waring," The News and Courier, March 1, 1949.

222 *South Carolina newspapers*: "U.S. court police in effect on feeding mixed S.C. juries," The News and Courier, May 9, 1949; "U.S. judges ban segregation in mixed juries," The Evening Post, May 19, 1949.

222 *Marshall confided it*: Letter from Thurgood Marshall to Waring, May 4,

1949. Waring Papers, Series C, 110-15, folder 386. Note the "Smith and Wesson Line" quip.

222 *Harold Boulware informed*: Letter from Harold Boulware to Rev. Joseph A. DeLaine, March 8, 1949. Joseph A. De-Laine Papers, USC South Caroliniana Library.

249 *Marshall had assembled*: Gona, *Dawn of Desegregation*, 44-46.

223-226 *DeLaine hosted the*: Ibid, 46-47, 57-58, 76-79; Kluger, 20.

226-228 *With no job*: Kluger, 23-25; Gona, 76-79, 82-112; James Clyburn and Jennifer Revels, *Uncommon Courage: The Story of Briggs v. Elliott, South Carolina's Unsung Civil Rights Battle* (Spartanburg: Palmetto Conservation Foundation Press, 2004), 25-32.

Elizabeth takes the stage

229 *Septima Clark first*: Clark, 97.

229 *Clark moved back*: This account of Septima Clark in the 1940s comes from Clark, 89-93; and Charron, 180-187 and 193-194.

229 *It had been*: Interview with Herbert Fielding, Goodwin's grandson, March 2015.

230 *Mr. Mayor, we*: Clark, 92-93.

231 *The executive secretary*: Charron, 193; Clark, 95-96.

232 *In June, a*: "Rep. (sic) Cantwell criticizes Waring on House floor," The News and Courier, June 5, 1949; "Judge Johnson says South is federal target," The Evening Post, June 14, 1949; "Jurist explains statement made on states' rights," The News and Courier, June 17, 1949; and "S.C. party chiefs to meet tomorrow on court appeal," The Evening Post, June 9, 1949.

232 *Vice president Alben*: "Barkley crowd

to include few S.C. political leaders," The News and Courier, June 29, 1949; "Judge assails newspapers, spurns appeasement dinner," The Evening Post, June 30, 1949; "Judge Waring not to attend Barkley dinner," The News and Courier, July 1, 1949.

233 *His only significant*: "3-judge federal court hears shrimping case," The News and Courier, Dec. 20, 1949.

234 *Waring even sold*: "Warings sell summer home on Sullivan's Island," The News and Courier, June 22, 1949; *Reminiscences*, 374-375.

234 *Years later, Fielding*: Interview with Herbert Fielding, March 2015.

234 *In October, Waring*: Letter from Waring to Eleanor Roosevelt, Oct. 24, 1949. Waring Papers, Series C, Box 110-17, folder 492.

235 *When the Jim*: Letter from Waring to Lillian Smith, Dec. 9, 1949. Waring Papers, Series C, Box 110-18, folder 524.

235 *The best thing*: Letter from Waring to Thurgood Marshall, Nov. 14, 1949. Waring Papers, Series C, Box 110-15, folder 386.

236 *Septima Clark arrived*: Clark, 97-99.

238 *Neither Elizabeth nor*: Letter from Waring to Anne and Stanley Warren, Jan. 13, 1950. Waring papers, Series C, Box 110-20, box 584.

239 *I want every*: Clark, *Echo in My Soul*, 100.

239 *My very dear*: Elizabeth's speech to the YWCA was printed in full, just as the judge asked, in "Wife of Judge Waring speaks at annual Negro 'Y' meeting," The News and Courier, Jan. 17, 1950.

False god

241 *But that afternoon*: "Southern whites 'sick, confused,' U.S. judge's wife says in

speech," The Evening Post, Jan. 17, 1950; "Reaction to talk by wife of federal judge is reported," The News and Courier, Jan. 18, 1950; "Legislator raps Mrs. Waring speech," The Evening Post, Jan. 17, 1950.

241 *It rang and*: Reminiscences, 305-307.

242 *How would you*: Terry, "J. Waties Waring, Spokesman for Racial Justice in the New South," 155; and various anonymous letters in the Waring Papers. Series C, Box 110-23, folder. 725.

242 *Even Septima Clark*: Clark, 100; *Reminiscences*, 306.

243 *Time magazine sent*: "South Carolina: Marching through Charleston," Time, Jan. 30, 1950; "Magazine reports on Negro 'Y' talk by wife of judge," The News and Courier, Jan. 27, 1950.

243 *The judge was*: Letter from Waring to Hugh Cathcart, Feb. 1950. Waring Papers. Series C, Box 110-9, folder. 220.

243 *It is a*: Anonymous letter to Elizabeth (signed "a true Rebel"), Feb. 14, 1950. Waring Papers, Series C, Box 110-23 folder 725.

244 *The show's panel*: "Mrs. Waring plugs intermarriage in broadcast from Washington," The Evening Post, Feb. 13, 1950; Lancia, "Giving the South the Shock Treatment," 53-54; Yarbrough, 135-138; and Poppy Cannon, *A Gentle Knight* (New York: Rinehart, 1956), 165.

244 *White and Cannon*: Letter from Elizabeth Waring to Jack Thompson, Dec. 29, 1949. Waring Papers, Series C, Box 110-7, folder 152.

245 *Thus far, the*: "Thurmond says Mrs. Waring hews to Truman line," The Evening Post, Feb. 13, 1950; "Trumanites say Mrs. Waring not spokesman," The Evening Post, Feb. 14, 1950.

245 *Days later, a*: "Petition asks impeachment of Judge Waring," The Evening Post,

Feb. 7, 1950; a copy of the petition is in the Waring Papers, Series D, Box 110-31, folder 957.

245 *Waring likened the*: "Judge links action to cross burnings," The Evening Post, Feb. 7, 1950; "Waring replies to impeachment petition allegations," The News and Courier, Feb. 8, 1950.

245-246 *Of course, they*: Letter from Waring to Samuel Grafton, Feb. 8, 1950. Waring Papers, Series C, Box110-11, folder 283.

246 *A week after*: "S.C. House agrees to buy Warings one-way tickets," The Evening Post, Feb. 15, 1950; "U.S. employees safe in signing Waring petitions," The Evening Post, March 3, 1950; "Probe of Waring divorce called 'useless thing,'" The Evening Post, Feb. 21, 1950; "Judge Waring says attempt to impeach him is 'silly,'" The News and Courier, March 10, 1950.

247 *Waring's growing legion*: Letter from Waring to Anne and Stanley Warren, Jan. 13, 1950. Waring Papers, Series C, Box 110-20, folder 584; "Judge Waring addresses Harlem church audience," The Evening Post, Feb. 27, 1950.

247 *She says they*: Letter from Persha Singer to Waring, Feb. 13, 1950. Waring Papers, Series C, Box110-17, folder 518.

247 *In March, the*: "Small cross burned in front of home of Judge Waring," The News and Courier, March 12, 1950; "Judge and police disagree on who burned the cross," The Evening Post, March 13, 1950.

248 *James Hinton published*: "Court decisions," letters to the editor, The News and Courier, Feb. 9, 1950; Clark, 101-107.

250 *They just don't*: Clark recalled Elizabeth's remark in Yabrough, 131.

250 *Anymore, the couple*: Reminiscences, 306-311; Clark, 104; and Lancia, "Giving the South the Shock Treatment," 57.

251 *The only way*: "Judge wants 'master's voice' to rule Southerners on race," The News and Courier, March 19, 1950; "Warings urge force to obtain rights for Negro," The Evening Post, April 3, 1950; "Mrs. Waring wants to give the South 'shock treatment,'" The News and Courier, April 3, 1950.

251 *Waring attempted to*: "Judge Waring tells AP writer he has 'passion for justice,'" The News and Courier, April 20, 1950.

252 *That spring, a*: "Calif. Congressman suggests Judge Waring be impeached," The Evening Post, April 7, 1950.

252 *I believe that*: Letter from Waring to Ted Poston, April 4, 1950. Waring Papers, Series C, Box 110-16, folder 472.

The Klan rides again

253 *On May 17*: "Clarendon Negro school suit is filed by NAACP," The Evening Post, May 17, 1950.

253-254 *The former principal*: Kluger, 25; Gona, 99-100, 127.

255 *Many of the*: Letter from DeLaine to the FBI, March 10, 1950. Part of the Rev. Joseph A. De Laine, Sr., File # HQ 44-3077, Federal Bureau of Investigation, Joseph A. DeLaine Papers in USC's South Caroliniana Library.

255 *The district argued*: "Clarendon says Negro pupils get better school facilities," The News and Courier, June 8, 1950; "Answer is filed in case against Clarendon schools," The Evening Post, June 8, 1950.

256 *At a rally*: "Senate seekers defend records in opening talks," The Evening Post, May 23, 1950; "Candidates talk of Waring impeachment," The Evening Post, June 2, 1950.

257 *Byrnes won by*: "Byrnes, Johnston win Democratic nominations," The Evening Post, July 12, 1950.

258 *On June 5*: *Reminiscences*, 338-340; and Waring Papers, Series D, Box 110-29, folders 888-894 and Box 110-31, folder 929.

259 *He told one*: Letter from Waring to Bruno Bitker, May 1, 1950. Waring Papers, Series C, Box 110-8, folder 201.

259 *While they are*: Letter from Waring to Dr. and Mrs. William Pope, July 19, 1950. Waring Papers, Series C, Box 110-16, folder 470.

259 *The Warings left*: "Waring on bench in San Francisco," The Evening Post, Aug. 5, 1950.

260 *In May, a*: "230 Klansmen stage parade at Denmark," The News and Courier, May 21, 1950; "Ku Klux not a 'hate' group, leader says," The News and Courier, May 18, 1950.

260-261 *About 60 Klansmen*: "Policeman killed in bout with Klansmen," The Evening Post, Aug. 28, 1950; "Conway policeman's death still a mystery," The News and Courier, Aug. 29, 1950.

261 *We have just*: Telegram from Walter White to President Truman and Howard McGrath, Oct. 6, 1950. Waring Papers, Series C, Box 110-22, folder 682.

262 *Waring opened the*: "Guilty pleas are taken as U.S. court term opens," The News and Courier, Oct. 10, 1950; "Inquest finds Winn was shot in line of duty," The News and Courier, Oct. 11, 1950.

263 *Waring believed it*: Letter from Waring to Walter White, Oct. 10-11, 1950. Waring Papers, Series C, Box 110-20, folder 602.

263-265 *They had decided*: *Reminiscences*, 307-308; "Two missiles thrown at judge's residence," The News and Courier, Oct. 10, 1950; "City police close books on stoning of Waring house," The Evening Post, Oct.

10, 1950; Cannon, *A Gentle Knight*, 166.

In plain sight

266 *I marked the*: City police close books on stoning of Waring's house," The Evening Post, Oct. 10, 1950.

266 *He inspected the*: Reminiscences, 308.

266 *A deputy marshal*: Ibid, 314-315. "Bodyguards are assigned to Judge Waring," The News and Courier, Oct. 12, 1950.

267 *For weeks, the*: "But why the FBI?" The Evening Post, Oct. 10, 1950; Ted Poston shared correspondence between Charleston and New York newspapermen with Elizabeth, along with a letter, on Oct. 27, 1950. Waring Papers, Series B, Box 110-6, folder 135.

268 *Finally, Hoover told*: Reminiscences, 312-313.

268 *The judge formally*: Letter from Waring to President Truman, Oct. 13, 1950. Waring Papers, Series C, Box 110-19, folder 567.

269 *Of course, the*: Letter from Waring to Walter White, Oct. 10-11, 1950. Waring Papers, Series C, Box 110-20, folder 602.

269 *They've thrown rocks*: Cannon, *A Gentle Knight*, 166.

269 *Precious and important*: Letter from Walter White to Howard McGrath, Oct. 11, 1950. Waring Papers, Series C, Box 110-20, folder 602.

305 *That was clear*: "FBI authorized to probe stoning of Waring's house," The News and Courier, Oct. 14, 1950; "Cross-burning believed work of pranksters," The Evening Post, Oct. 16, 1950.

270 *Soon, the FBI*: "FBI refuses comment on investigation," The Evening Post, Oct. 17, 1950; "No offense likely if children are responsible for 'stoning,' says official," The

News and Courier, Nov. 2, 1950; "Rivers disputes McGrath's stand on Waring guards," The Evening Post, Oct. 31, 1950.

271-275 *On Friday morning*: The account of the Nov. 17 hearing is taken from several sources, including Gona, 134-136; *Reminiscences* 341-345; "Clarendon suit dismissed by Waring," The Evening Post, Nov. 17, 1950; and "Negroes will seek to enter white schools," The News and Courier, Nov. 18, 1950.

272 *NAACP attorney Franklin*: Williams' account of his discussions with Marshall over this hearing are recounted in Kluger, 304-305.

273-275 *I realized that*: Reminiscences, 338, 339-344.

Darkest South Carolina

276 *An early winter*: "Severe cold wave takes the lives of 3 persons here," The Evening Post, Nov. 27, 1950.

276-277 *The pilgrimage had*: "Group of 125 visit Judge Waring in 'pilgrimage,'" The News and Courier, Nov. 27, 1950. All of the quotes included in this passage are from that article.

278 *As white men*: "The torch-bearers," The News and Courier, Nov. 28, 1950.

278 *But he predicted*: "Mutual assistance pacts for civil defense urged by governor of Florida," The Evening Post, Nov. 27, 1950.

279 *Waring had sentenced*: "Waring bars himself from Southern case," The Evening Post, Dec. 5, 1950; "Reasons for Southern asking Waring disqualification cited," The News and Courier, Dec. 7, 1950; "Senator Johnston says Judge Waring should be removed for anti-S.C. bias," The News and Courier, Dec. 7, 1950; "Rivers seeks seat in Un-American activities group," The News and Courier, Jan. 1, 1951.

279 *On Dec. 15*: "Waring visit brings

threat to Negro man," The Evening Post, Dec. 16, 1950; "Florence Negro threatened after visit from Waring," The News and Courier, Dec. 17, 1950.

279 *The Warings drove*: Reminiscences, 315-316.

280 *Rev. DeLaine was*: Gona, 137-142.

281 *Harold Boulware filed*: "Negroes challenge segregation in public schools," The Evening Post, Dec. 22, 1950.

281 *Waring told Columbia*: Reminiscences, 345.

282-283 *On Jan. 24*: "Byrnes backs 3% sales tax proposal," The News and Courier, Jan. 25, 1951; "Address of the Honorable James F. Byrnes, Governor of South Carolina, to the General Assembly, Columbia, S.C., Wednesday, January 24, 1951." Waring Papers, Series D, Box 110-25, folder 742.

283 *And his later*: "Byrnes would close schools if suit on segregation lost," The News and Courier, March 17, 1951; "State enters Clarendon school case," The News and Courier, Feb. 3, 1951.

Briggs v. Elliott

285 *Rev. DeLaine met*: Gona, 144-147.

285 *The newspapers portrayed*: "States' rights face court test here," The Evening Post, May 23, 1951; "S.C. school system goes on trial today," The News and Courier, May 28, 1951.

286 *They had never*: Reminiscences, 358.

287 *In his opening*: "Segregation hearing opens; Clarendon County concedes Negro schools below par," The Evening Post, May 28, 1951; "Segregation 'short-changes' Negro school children, three-judge U.S. court is told," The News and Courier, May 29, 1951.

288 *Judge Parker, this*: Reminiscences, 353.

288-289 *The district spent*: "Segregation hearing opens;" "Segregation 'short-changes' Negro school children, three-judge U.S. court is told."

290 *Marshall's star witness*: Kluger, 353-357; Reminiscences, 353-354.

290 *The effects of*: "Segregation 'short-changes' Negro school children, three-judge U.S. court is told."

290 *After the lunch*: Reminiscences, 357-358; "Seat shortage in courtroom causes outbreak," The News and Courier, May 29, 1951.

291 *He's testifying about*: "Segregation 'short-changes' Negro school children, three-judge U.S. court is told."

294 *It gives environmental*: "School segregation case taken under advisement by U.S. court," The News and Courier, May 30, 1951.

296 *What sort of*: Ibid, and "School lawyers end segregation defense with plea for time," The Evening Post, May 29, 1951.

297 *This phrase has*: "School segregation case taken under advisement by U.S. court."

Exit Strategy

299-300 *The three judges*: This account of the judges' debate over *Briggs v. Elliott* is recounted in *Reminiscences*, 358-359.

301 *The News and*: "'Segregation to civilization," The News and Courier, June 6, 1951.

301 *Rumors of a*: "Reporters stand three-day vigil awaiting 'break' in school case," The Evening Post, June 23, 1951.

301 *Parker had sent*: Letter from Waring to Judge Parker, June 18, 1951. Waring Papers, Series C, Box 110-16, folder 454.

302 *Segregation of the*: *Briggs v. Elliott* decree. Waring Papers, Series D, Box 110-24,

folder 736.

302 *We are on*: "NAACP plans appeal of judges' ruling," The Evening Post, June 23, 1951.

302 *Waring's dissent was*: Dissenting opinion in *Briggs v. Elliott*. Waring Papers, Series D, Box 110-24, folder 737. The collection includes several drafts of the dissent as well.

304 *The clerk's office*: Reminiscences, 362.

304 *The press was*: "Comments on racial suit," The News and Courier, June 27, 1951; "Victory for American rights," The News and Courier, June 24, 1951; "Court decree complicates appeal of segregation case," The Evening Post, June 29, 1951.

305 *On July 26*: Letter from Thurgood Marshall to Waring, July 24, 1951. Waring Papers, Series C, Box 110-15, folder 387.

305 *The really important*: Draft of a letter from Waring to Marshall, July 26, 1951. Waring Papers, Series C, Box 110-22, folder 662. A version of this letter eventually reached Marshall, because it is referenced in a letter to Waring from Judge Hubert Delany, July 30, 1951, also in the Waring Papers. Series C, Box 110-10, folder 249.

306 *Waring spent much*: Reminiscences, 375-378.

307 *To me, granting*: Gona, 148, 152-155.

308 *The Atlantic Coast*: "Judge throws out charges against taxicab drivers," The News and Courier, Oct. 12, 1951.

309 *Whether we have*: "Segregation curb not to end school plan, says Byrnes," The Evening Post, Oct. 16, 1951; "Clarendon tells court it will spend $552,682," The News and Courier, Dec. 12, 1951; "Clarendon school report is approved," The Evening Post, Jan. 8, 1952.

309 *My dear Mr.*: Letter from Waring to

President Truman, Jan. 26. 1952. Waring Papers, Series C, Box110-19, folder 567.

New York, New York

311 *Only the Supreme*: "Supreme Court 'vacates' ruling on Segregation," The News and Courier, Jan. 29, 1952.

312 *Briggs was only*: The NAACP cases and its strategy is explained in Walter White, *How Far the Promised Land* (New York: Viking Press, 1955), 49-50.

312 *South Carolina officials*: "Judge's retirement plans produce no tears within state's congressional delegation," The News and Courier, Jan. 29, 1952; "Rivers asks Truman for judge's post," The News and Courier, March 6, 1952; Telegram from Walter White to President Truman, March 28, 1952. Waring Papers, Series C, Box 110-22, 682.

313 *The Charleston newspapers*: "Truman says Waring is great judge," The Evening Post, Jan. 31, 1952; "A judge worthy of honor," The New York Times as reprinted in the letters to the editor section of The News and Courier, Feb. 6, 1952; "Judge Waring still mum on future plans," The Evening Post, Feb. 15, 1952.

314 *An employee of*: "Lewises move into house bought from Judge Waring," The News and Courier, Feb. 22, 1952.

314 *Judge Parker had*: "Clarendon school segregation rehearing is set," The Evening Post, Feb. 14, 1952.

315-316 *The judge and*: "Warings entrain for New York on Florida Special," The News and Courier, Feb. 19, 1952; "A judge retires," The Evening Post, Feb. 16, 1952;"Judge Waring to try to 'pierce the iron curtain' of the South," The News and Courier, Feb. 20, 1952.

316 *The Warings occasionally*: Cannon, *A Gentle Knight*, 219-220; "Anti-discrimi-

nation planks proposed by J. Waties Waring," The News and Courier, May 13, 1952; "Howard University gives Waties Waring honorary degree," The News and Courier June 14, 1952; Letter from James Nabrit to Waring, May 13, 1952. Waring Papers, Series C, Box 110-16, folder 431.

317 *I can tell*: Letter from Waring to President Truman, June 9, 1952. Waring Papers, Series C, Box 110-19, folder 567.

318 *If I were*: "Judge Waring disagrees with NAACP policy," The Evening Post, July 8, 1952; "Judge Waring breaks with NAACP on policy," The News and Courier, July 8, 1952.

318 *In March 1952*: "Segregation again upheld," The News and Courier, March 14, 1952.

319 *Now, our case*: Reminiscences, 365.

The victory party

320 *There he suddenly*: "Judge Waring Moves North," Bruce Bliven, The New Republic, May 5, 1952.

321 *The Supreme Court*: Kluger, 558-581; "Attorney General files segregation case brief," The News and Courier, Dec. 4, 1952; "S.C. does not offend 14th Amendment, Davis Declares" and "Court crowded as segregation hearing starts," The News and Courier, Dec. 10, 1952.

322 *I feel confident*: Letter from Waring to Marshall, Aug. 22, 1953. Waring Papers, Series C, Box 110-15, folder 383.

323 *Waring admitted Vinson's*: Reminiscences, 364-365.

323 *On Monday morning*: Kluger, 667.

323-325 *The second hearing*: This account is taken from various sources, including Kluger, 667-680; "Equal schools are immaterial, lawyers for Negroes claim" and "Davis argues state's case before the court," The News and Courier, Dec. 8, 1953; "U.S.

Supreme Court school segregation debate ends," The News and Courier, Dec. 10, 1953.

325 *As a result*: "Side issue to segregation case," The News and Courier, March 7, 1954.

326 *From the start*: Kluger, 678-699.

326 *One Monday morning*: Reminiscences, 368-370.

327 *On May 17*: Brown v. Board of Education of Topeka, 347 U.S. 483 (1954).

328 *This decision will*: Statement to the press by Judge Waring. Waring Papers, Series A, Box 110-1, folder 8. Also, "Democracy prevails, says Waring," The News and Courier, May 18, 1954.

328 *With considerable gratification*: Reminiscences, 365.

328-330 *Waring put whiskey*: Reminiscences, 370-371; Cannon, A Gentle Knight, 249-255; and Waring Papers, Series A, Box 110-2, folder 11.

Aftermath: Dreams of a Movement
A return to Charleston

333 *The train pulled*: Waring's return to Charleston is recounted in *Reminiscences*, 401-402; "Judge Waring to be honored by NAACP," The Evening Post, Nov. 6, 1954; "NAACP has dinner for Judge Waring," The News and Courier, Nov. 7, 1954; and "Waring praises high court decision outlawing segregation in schools," The Evening Post, Nov. 8, 1954.

334 *The details of*: "Wright will speak here at dinner for Waring," The Evening Post, Nov. 2, 1954 and "Marion A. Wright to speak at dinner for Judge Waring," The News and Courier, Nov. 3, 1954.

334 *Elmore claimed his*: "'Lawsuit' Negro says NAACP caters first to 'big shots,'" The News and Courier, Nov. 7, 1954.

335 *Waring's absence had*: "Saintship has been conferred on him," The Evening Post, Nov. 9, 1954.

336 *The General Assembly*: "Public school, property tax law changes face Assembly," The News and Courier, Feb. 1, 1955; "Warnings voiced to court," The News and Courier, April 13, 1955; Kluger, 710-718; "South mobilizes civic power," The News and Courier, Sept. 28, 1955; Charron, *Freedom's Teacher*, 236.

337 *The first one*: Letter from Septima Clark to the Warings, June 21, 1954. Waring Papers, Series C, Box 110-9, folder 226.

337 *The Washington Afro-American*: "Mrs. Waties Waring criticizes 'soft' edict," The News and Courier, June 22, 1955.

337 *The stories claimed*: "Negroes may delay Clarendon demand," Columbia Record, Aug. 30, 1955. Letter from Thurgood Marshall to the editor of the Columbia Record, Sept. 9, 1955. Waring Papers, Series C, Box 110-15, folder 389.

338 *He reminded Marshall*: Letter from Waring to Thurgood Marshall, Sept. 17, 1955. Waring Papers, Series C, Box 110-15, folder 389.

338 *The Lake City*: Gona, 167-180.

339 *We have been*: Anonymous letter to DeLaine, Oct. 7, 1955. Joseph A. DeLaine Papers in USC's South Caroliniana Library.

339 *DeLaine awoke to*: Essay, 1955, confidential. Joseph A. DeLaine Papers in USC's South Caroliniana Library.

341 *The governor of*: Letter from Septima Clark to the Warings, March 28, 1956. Waring Papers, Series C, Box 110-9, folder 228.

341 *I anticipated this*: Lettter from Clark to the Warings, June 8, 1956. Ibid.

342 *Eventually, Tennessee shut*: Clark, 7-10.

One generation passeth

343 *On Feb. 8*: The transcript for "The Open Mind" is available online from The Martin Luther King. Jr Research and Education Institute at Stanford University. It is also available to view on YouTube. The program was taped Feb. 8, but broadcast on Feb. 10, 1957.

344 *This man, Martin*: *Reminiscences*, 390-391.

345 *My heart is*: Letter from Ruby Cornwell to Elizabeth Waring, Sept. 20, 1955. Waring Papers, Series B, Box 110-5, folder 68.

345 *I believe that*: *Reminiscences*, 383.

346 *The Democratic Party*: Bass and Thompson, 191.

347 *Rev. DeLaine eventually*: FBI report, 1955-56. Joseph A. DeLaine Papers, South Caroliniana Library.

347 *I never would*: "DeLaine likes life in North," The Evening Post, Oct. 17, 1957.

348 *Not long after*: "Buffalo church is named after minister, judge," The News and Courier, July 19, 1956.

348 *The accolades for*: "Judge Waring gets Jewish Congress prize," The News and Courier, Dec. 18, 1957; "Judge honored by school group," Nov. 22, 1959; "2 from S.C. seeks to abolish Un-American Activity group," The News and Courier, Jan. 31, 1961; "400 ask end to Un-American group's work," Feb. 9, 1961; "Judge Waring donates files to Howard," The News and Courier, June 2, 1960.

349 *The judge and*: Waring's correspondence show the couple had moved to the Hyde Park Hotel at 25 East 77th Street at least by the fall of 1960. Elizabeth's health problems are recounted in Lancia, "Giving the South the Shock Treatment," 73-75.

350 *Waring had sent*: Letter from Waring to Anne, Oct. 3, 1952. Waring Papers, Series C, Box 110-20, folder 585.

350 *Her mother, Annie*: "Mrs. Waring dies in local hospital after long illness," The News and Courier, Dec. 15, 1954; "The South Revisited" By Anne Waring Warren, The New York Post, July 5-10, 1960. Waring Papers, Series H, Box 110-40, folder 1238.

350 *As the most*: The reconciliation of Waring and Anne is a minor subtext in "Judge Waring determined to live out life in exile," The News and Courier, Jan. 30, 1963.

351 *On Christmas Day*: Yarbrough, 239; "Waties Waring, former U.S. judge here, dies," The News and Courier, Jan. 12, 1968.

Vindication

352 *He was a*: "Judge Waties Waring," The News and Courier, Jan. 13, 1968; "Death comes to Judge Waring," The Evening Post, Jan. 13, 1968.

353 *I never was*: "Judge Waring determined to live out life in exile," The News and Courier, Jan. 30, 1963.

353 *Judge Waring was*: "Memorial services for judge urged," The News and Courier, Jan. 14, 1968.

354 *Kuralt called the*: Transcript of the CBS Evening News with Walter Cronkite from Wednesday, Jan. 17, 1968. Waring Papers, Series F, Box 110-26, folder 1168.

354 *Following the services*: "Quiet graveside services are held for Judge Waring," The News and Courier, Jan. 17, 1968; "Graveside services held for retired U.S. judge," The Evening Post, Jan. 17, 1968; "J. Waties Waring," by Ruby Cornwell, Letters to the editor, The News and Courier, Jan. 23, 1968.

356 *Elizabeth Waring died*: "Mrs. J. Waties Waring dies; services Saturday," The Evening Post, Oct. 31, 1968.

357 *In 1976, DeLaine*: "A racial drama," The Evening Post, June 17, 1976; "Anne Waring Warren dies in New Jersey," The News and Courier, Nov. 27, 1979; "Retired editor Thomas R. Waring dies" by Robert Behre, The Post and Courier, March 9, 1993.

358 *Like most Charleston*: "Recognition of Waring way overdue" by Brian Hicks, The Post and Courier, Feb. 21, 2013.

359 *As a young*: "Hollings makes a grand gesture to Charleston – and American – history" by Brian Hicks, The Post and Courier, March 15, 2015. After years of not being taken seriously, the senator asked me to write this column to force the courthouse name change.

360 *This extraordinary story*: "Courthouse renamed for civil rights hero," United States Courts Judiciary News, Oct. 14, 2015.

361 *The result has*: These quotes are from an undated typescript written by Waring sometime between mid-January 1951 and February 1952, like the early spring of '51. Waring Papers, Series A, Box 110-2, folder 9.

BIBLIOGRAPHY

Bass, Jack and Marilyn W. Thompson. *Strom: The Complicated Personal and Political Life of Strom Thurmond.* New York: Public Affairs, 2005.

Cannon, Poppy. *A Gentle Knight: My Husband, Walter White.* New York: Rinehart & Co. 1956.

Charron, Katherine Mellen. *Freedom's Teacher: The Life of Septima Clark.* Chapel Hill: University of North Carolina Press, 2009.

Clark, Septima Poinsette with LeGette Blythe. *Echo in My Soul.* New York: E.P. Dutton & Co., 1962.

Clyburn, James and Jennifer Revels. *Uncommon Courage: The Story of Briggs v. Elliott, South Carolina's Unsung Civil Rights Battle.* Spartanburg: Palmetto Conservation Foundation Press, 2004.

Davis, Michael D. and Hunter R. Clark. *Thurgood Marshall: Warrior at the Bar, Rebel on the Bench.* New York: Birch Lane Press, 1992.

Felder, James L. *Civil Rights in South Carolina: From Peaceful Protests to Groundbreaking Rulings.* Charleston: The History Press, 2012.

Fraser, Jr., Walter J. *Charleston! Charleston! The History of a Southern City.* Columbia: University of South Carolina Press, 1989.

Gona, Ophelia De Laine. *Dawn of Desegregation: J.A. De Laine and Briggs v. Elliott.* Columbia: University of South Carolina Press, 2011.

Hutchisson, James M. *DuBose Heyward: A Charleston Gentleman and the World of Porgy and Bess.* Jackson: University of Mississippi Press, 2000.

Kluger, Richard. *Simple Justice: The History of Brown v. Board of Education and Black America's Struggle for Equality.* New York: Knopf, 1976.

Lancia, Jessica Letizia. *Giving the South the Shock Treatment: Elizabeth Waring and the Civil Rights Movement*. A master's thesis submitted to the Graduate School of the College of Charleston and The Citadel, 2007.

McCullough, David. *Truman*. New York: Simon & Schuster, 1992.

Poston, Jonathan H. *The Buildings of Charleston: A Guide to the City's Architecture*. Columbia: University of South Carolina Press, 1997.

Rosen, Robert. *A Short History of Charleston*. San Francisco: Lexikos, 1982.

Stampp, Kenneth M. *The Era of Reconstruction, 1865-1877*. New York: Knopf, 1978.

Stark, John D. *Damned Upcountryman: William Watts Ball: A Study in American Conservatism*. Durham: Duke University Press, 1968.

Terry, Robert Lewis. *J. Waties Waring, Spokesman for Racial Justice in the New South*. A doctoral dissertation submitted to the University of Utah, 1970.

Truman, Harry. *Memoirs of Harry Truman*. New York: Doubleday & Co., 1955.

White, Walter. *A Man Called White: The Autobiography of Walter White*. New York: The Viking Press, 1948.

– *How Far The Promised Land*. New York: The Viking Press, 1955.

Williams, Juan. *Thurgood Marshall: American Revolutionary*. New York: Times Books, 1998.

Yarbrough, Tinsley E. *A Passion for Justice: J. Waties Waring and Civil Rights*. New York: Oxford University Press, 1987.

Yuhl, Stephanie E. *A Golden Haze of Memory: The Making of Historic Charleston*. Chapel Hill: University of North Carolina Press, 2005.

ACKNOWLEDGMENTS

I first pitched the idea of *In Darkest South Carolina* in 2006. The story of J. Waties Waring was always more than standard biography; it is a historical thriller about the early days of the civil rights movement set in the atmospheric world of 20th-century Charleston. Publishers showed little interest, however, and other books intervened. But it was impossible to forget the judge. A studio portrait of Waring sits on a shelf in my office at The Post and Courier, always staring down at me with a slightly disapproving look. It was, I believe, his default expression.

The book was resurrected, in part, through encouragement from two of Waring's most ardent admirers – U.S. District Judge Richard Gergel and retired U.S. Sen. Fritz Hollings. "You've gotta write that book," the senator told me one day in his trademark Lowcountry drawl. As any South Carolinian knows, The Word of Fritz is practically a mandate.

Judge Gergel, who's written his own book about Waring and the Isaac Woodard case, was extremely generous with his time, knowledge and research. As I pored through Waring's papers at Howard University, the judge and I compared notes regularly. I cannot thank Judge Gergel enough for his wise perspective, infectious enthusiasm and unflagging support.

The Post and Courier has also been extremely supportive. Executive Editor Mitch Pugh repeatedly encouraged me to tackle this story. Editor Rick Nelson, a longtime friend who's already collaborated with me on three other books, believed in this project so much he volunteered the thankless, laborious task of editing Judge Waring's story. And Publisher P.J. Browning recognized the importance of the book and made it happen.

Pierre Manigault, John Barnwell and Tom Waring, who shared his family's history with me early in the process, deserve a lot of credit. With their commitment to quality journalism, it's no surprise The Post and Courier is today one of the best local newspapers in the country. Of course, much of that success stems from the paper's great journalists, many of whom helped me with this. Thanks to Stephanie Harvin, Brad Nettles, Charles Rowe, Laura Bradshaw, Leroy Burnell, Tony Bartelme, Robert Behre, Schuyler Kropf, Allison Nugent-Caruso, Liz Foster, Adam Parker, Matthew Fortner, Jennifer Berry Hawes, Glenn Smith, Doug Pardue, Cleve O'Quinn and Becky Baulch.

My good friend Tom Spain read the first draft to tell me what worked, what didn't – and to add his considerable insight into Charleston history. For 20 years, I've been able to trust Tom to call it like he sees it. Likewise, I've come to depend on the solid craftsmanship of Bob Kinney, Gill Guerry, Kristen Milford and Linda O'Quinn, all of whom helped shape this book.

Many thanks as well to the staffs at Howard University's Moorland-Spingarn Research Center, the Charleston County Public Library, the College of Charleston, The Citadel, The Preservation Society and Historic Charleston Foundation. And for their wise counsel, I am particularly indebted to the fabulous Helen Hill, Tom Tisdale, Jack O'Toole, Laurie Thompson, Kent Murray, Warren Lasch, Pete and Pinky Peters, Cecil Williams and the honorable Joseph P. Riley Jr.

And finally, a nod to my incredible family for their immeasurable support and understanding. Thank you for everything.

Brian Hicks
Charleston, South Carolina
July 28, 2018

INDEX

ABOUT THE AUTHOR

B rian Hicks is a columnist for The Post and Courier in Charleston. *In Darkest South Carolina* is his tenth book.

Hicks' journalism has appeared in national and international publications since 1986, and he has written about Southern history and politics for 30 years. He has been featured on CBS Sunday Morning, National Public Radio, the Discovery Channel, the National Geographic Channel and in Smithsonian magazine. His column has won three Green Eyeshade Awards for best commentary in the Southeast from the Society of Professional Journalists, and Hicks is a former South Carolina Press Association Journalist of the Year.

His previous books include *Ghost Ship, Sea of Darkness, City of Ruin, When the Dancing Stopped* and *The Mayor*. *Toward the Setting Sun*, the story of Chief John Ross and the Cherokee removal, and *Raising the Hunley*, the tale of the Confederate submarine coauthored with Schuyler Kropf, were selections of the Book-of-the-Mouth Club, as well as the History and Military Book Clubs.

A native of Tennessee, Hicks has lived in Charleston for more than 20 years.